water
Science and Issues

water
Science and Issues

Volume 1/Acid–Drought

E. Julius Dasch, Editor in Chief

**MACMILLAN
REFERENCE
USA™**

THOMSON
GALE

New York • Detroit • San Diego • San Francisco • Cleveland • New Haven, Conn. • Waterville, Maine • London • Munich

THOMSON

★

GALE

™

T 42968

Water: Science and Issues

E. Julius Dasch

Cover photographs reproduced by permission
of the following sources: hydropower turbine
photo ©Bob Rowan, Progressive Image/Corbis;
Hindu women praying in Old Brahmaputra
River (Bangladesh) photo by Mufty Munir
©AFP/Corbis; Glen Canyon Dam photo
©George D. Lepp/Corbis; Yellowstone Grand
Prismatic Hot Spring photo ©Raymond
Gehman/Corbis; wave photo ©Digital Vision.

Library of Congress Cataloging-in-Publication Data

Dasch, E. Julius.
    Water : science and issues / E. Julius Dasch.
        p. cm.
Includes bibliographical references and index.
    ISBN 0-02-865611-3 (set hardcover : alk. paper) -- ISBN
0-02-865612-1 (v. 1 : alk. paper) -- ISBN 0-02-865613-X (v. 2 : alk.
paper) -- ISBN 0-02-865614-8 (v. 3 : alk. paper) -- ISBN 0-02-865615-6
(v. 4 : alk. paper)
    1. Water—Encyclopedias. 2. Hydrology—Encyclopedias. 3.
Hydrogeology—Encyclopedias. I. Title.
    GB655.D37 2003
    553.7'03--dc21
                                                                    2003001309

Printed in Canada
10 9 8 7 6 5 4 3 2 1

Table of Contents

Table of Contents

VOLUME 2

VOLUME 3

VOLUME 4

Preface

Reflecting for this Preface, I realized my experiences with water in all its forms undoubtedly parallel those of most earth scientists, and most humans in general, for that matter. I became keenly interested in geology as a Boy Scout, and carried this interest through to my doctorate degree at Yale University. So my training has always been shaped by an appreciation of scenery and the mighty influence of liquid water and ice.

What about my personal adventures with water? Once my geology field partner and I lost a Jeep® in a flash flood in West Texas: a bright blue sky was overhead, but torrential rains upstream had quickly filled the streambed we were trying to cross. Then there was a voyage from Iceland to eastern Greenland on an icebreaker, crunching its way through the sea ice to reach the remote Skaergaard igneous rocks. And a flyover of the then-underwater (currently emerged) Kovachi volcano in the South Pacific's Solomon Islands.

The most spectacular experience with water? That would have to be 5 weeks on the ice of Antarctica, searching for meteorites. In my tent during the sunlit "night," I wondered at the occasional cracking noises of the vast but slowly moving continental glacier on which I slept.

Why Water?

My adventures with water have given me a keen appreciation for this simple molecule. After all, it creates much of the impressive scenery on planet Earth—from clouds, oceans, streams, and glaciers, to erosional and depositional landforms such as steep cliffs and river plains. It is Earth's most ubiquitous and most effective dissolving agent, whether in the cells of plants, animals, and humans; in a stream; or in the deep plumbing system of a hydrothermal vent. Water quenches thirst and enables the growth of food and fiber for Earth's 6.1 billion human inhabitants. Put simply, water offers the medium for the origin, development, and maintenance of life as we know it.

But why should water have an entire encyclopedia devoted to it? Why should students, educators, decisionmakers, scientists, and general readers want to learn more about this critical and multifaceted topic? And why now?

It is precisely the necessity—indeed, the urgency—of water resources that makes this encyclopedia a timely contribution. Daily news reports tell the story: droughts, floods, damaged ecosystems, invasive species, chemical pollution, human health threats, and water shortages, to name a few. In 2002 alone, headlines included the severe drought in Canada; the massive floods in Europe; the "dead zones" of Lake Erie and the Gulf of Mexico; the highly invasive snakehead fish in the United States; natural arsenic contamination of groundwater wells in Bangladesh; the West Nile virus in North America; and inadequate drinking-water supplies in many developing countries.

But headlines can only hint at the importance of this vast topic. Water's key role in human civilization is without dispute. Consider the following:

- The history of civilization cannot be discussed apart from water. Water is interwoven with humanity's physical, social, economic, and cultural spheres. It runs like a thread through each person's life.

- The Earth is undergoing rapid and unprecedented change. Humans are truly changing the face of the planet: degrading fresh-water and marine ecosystems; depleting natural water-supply sources; and influencing global climate.

- Human consumption of water rose by a factor of six in the last century—twice the rate of global population growth. Humans now use more than half of the readily available fresh water, which already is in short supply: less than 1 percent of Earth's water is readily usable for human or agricultural needs. (The rest is in the salty oceans or locked up as ice.)

- Worldwide, more than 1 billion people do not have safe water to drink, and 2 to 3 billion lack access to basic sanitation (sewerage) services. Between 3 and 5 million people, mostly children, die each year from water-related diseases. By the year 2025, one-third of the world's population in approximately 50 countries likely will face severe water scarcity. In fact, water scarcity is the greatest threat to global food production, and has been deemed by some experts as the global security issue of the twenty-first century.

In a nutshell, human societies are challenged with assuring the quantity and quality of our most precious water resource while maintaining or improving its environmental integrity. But we cannot meet the challenge in a vacuum. We need a broad understanding of water in its varied forms, distribution, occurrence, and quality—and all within a human context. The encyclopedia *Water: Science and Issues* offers a vehicle to enhance such understanding.

The World of Water (in Four Volumes)

Because the interdisciplinary topic of water covers a wide range of subjects, our development of encyclopedia material was a challenge. The editors chose a three-way organization: fresh waters (groundwater, lakes, streams, and ice); marine waters; and policy and management. Although the entries appear alphabetically, they reflect this threefold categorization. The Topical Outline following this Preface clusters the entries by major themes.

The complexities of water are made understandable in just over 300 essays written by water scientists, professors, educators, and professional communicators. Entries addressing key concepts, current issues, traditional and emerging research, and major legislation are integrated with historical overviews, biographical sketches, and career information.

The table of contents reflects a breadth of topics not found in any other work at this level: namely, a scientific reference work tailored for nonspecialist readers, yet suitable for people already knowledgeable about water topics. Entries ranging from 500 words to 2,500 words cover hydrology, geology, chemistry, ecology, environmental science, waterways and waterbodies, engineering, earth science, oceanography, economics, policy, planning, management, law, rights, and more.

The table of contents also reveals aspects of water never before addressed in a comprehensive water-related encyclopedia. Topics such as security, globalization, sustainability, global warming, pollution, and water scarcity are not new, but have been thrust to the forefront as the twenty-first century opened. *Water: Science and Issues* addresses subtopics as diverse as pharmaceuticals and personal care products in water supplies; caffeine as a tracer; the search for water on Mars; hydrosolidarity; the ocean's role in human health (good and bad); protecting the water-supply infrastructure; issues in developing countries; survival needs; the search for drinking water; and water's role in war.

Our goal is to tell the interdisciplinary story of water in a format accessible to a wide readership. *Water: Science and Issues* is geared toward high school students and a general audience, but also forays into discussions appropriate for undergraduates and water resource professionals seeking concise overviews of complex subjects. Hence, the audiences include students, educators, communicators, decisionmakers, scientists, and the interested public.

More than 575 color photographs and illustrations help tell this interdisciplinary story. Selected glossary definitions, sidebars, cross-references, and a short bibliography accompany each entry. Reference aids in the frontmatter, a comprehensive glossary in the backmatter, and a high-quality cumulative index provide additional tools.

Acknowledgements

First I thank my wife Pat for her many contributions. And special thanks go to my associate academic editors, who provided tremendous expertise in their respective areas of specialty. The editors and I collectively acknowledge the thoughtful and professional contributions made by members of Macmillan Reference USA and the Gale Group. Hélène Potter and former publisher Elly Dickason (now retired) were instrumental in launching and nurturing the project. Cindy Clendenon has been especially helpful in her editing and managing of the components associated with the 304 articles. Her training, knowledge, and keen interest in the field have resulted in a markedly better product.

E. Julius Dasch

Topical Outline

AGRICULTURE

Agriculture and Water
Aquaculture
Chemicals from Agriculture
Food Security
Irrigation Management
Irrigation Systems, Ancient
Mariculture
Pollution of the Ocean by Sewage, Nutrients,
    and Chemicals

AQUATIC ANIMALS

Aquariums
Birds, Aquatic
Bivalves
Cephalopods
Crustaceans
Fish
Fishes, Cartilaginous
Marine Mammals
Reptiles
Salmon Decline and Recovery

BIOGRAPHIES

Agassiz, Louis
Bretz, J Harlen
Carson, Rachel
Cook, Captain James
Cousteau, Jacques
Darcy, Henry
Davis, William Morris
Douglas, Marjory Stoneman
Earle, Sylvia
Garrels, Robert
Leopold, Luna
Lewis, Meriwether and William Clark

Hem, John D.
Hubbert, Marion King
Nansen, Fridtjof
Powell, John Wesley
Reisner, Marc
Stumm, Werner
Sverdrup, Harald
Theis, Charles Vernon
White, Gilbert

CAREERS

Careers in Environmental Education
Careers in Environmental Science and
    Engineering
Careers in Fresh-Water Chemistry
Careers in Fresh-Water Ecology
Careers in Geospatial Technologies
Careers in Hydrology
Careers in International Water Resources
Careers in Oceanography
Careers in Soil Science
Careers in Water Resources Engineering
Careers in Water Resources Planning and
    Management
Ethics and Professionalism
Minorities in Water Sciences
Women in Water Sciences

CHEMICAL AND PHYSICAL PROPERTIES, PROCESSES, AND APPLICATIONS

Acid Mine Drainage
Acid Rain
Attenuation of Pollutants
Beaches
Brines, Natural
Carbon Dioxide in the Ocean and
    Atmosphere

ICE (ON EARTH)

Glaciers and Ice Sheets
Glaciers, Ice Sheets, and Climate Change
Ice Ages
Ice at Sea
Ice Cores and Ancient Climatic Conditions
Oceans, Polar
Sea Water, Freezing of

INTERESTING WATER FEATURES

Astrobiology: Water and the Potential for
    Extraterrestrial Life
Bays, Gulfs, and Straits
Corals and Coral Reefs
Estuaries
Hot Springs and Geysers
Hot Springs on the Ocean Floor
Ice at Sea
Islands, Capes, and Peninsulas
Karst Hydrology
Life in Extreme Water Environments
Mineral Waters and Spas
Pumps, Traditional
Springs
Stream, Hyporheic Zone of a
Tsunamis
Volcanoes and Water
Volcanoes, Submarine
Waterfalls
Wetlands

ISSUES: NATIONAL AND INTERNATIONAL

Acid Rain
Algal Blooms, Harmful
Amphibian Population Declines
Chemicals: Combined Effect on Public Health
Chemicals from Agriculture
Chemicals from Consumers
Chemicals from Pharmaceuticals and Personal
    Care Products
Conflict and Water
Dams
Developing Countries, Issues in
Drinking Water and Society
Drought Management
Fish and Wildlife Issues
Fisheries, Marine: Management and Policy
Floodplain Management
Food Security

Globalization and Water
Global Warming: Policy-Making
Great Lakes
Human Health and the Ocean
Human Health and Water
Hydropolitics
Hydrosolidarity
Instream Water Issues
International Cooperation
Law, International Water
Law of the Sea
Pollution by Invasive Species
Pollution of Groundwater
Pollution of Lakes and Streams
Pollution of the Ocean by Sewage, Nutrients,
    and Chemicals
Pollution Sources: Point and Nonpoint
Population and Water Resources
Rainwater Harvesting
Rights, Riparian
Rights, Public Water
Salmon Decline and Recovery
Security and Water
Supplies, Protecting Public Drinking-Water
Supplies, Public and Domestic Water
Survival Needs
Sustainable Development
Transboundary Water Treaties
War and Water

LAKES AND STREAMS

Fresh Water, Natural Composition of
Fresh Water, Natural Contaminants in
Great Lakes
Lake Formation
Lake Health, Assessing
Lake Management Issues
Lakes: Biological Processes
Lakes: Chemical Processes
Lakes: Physical Processes
Microbes in Lakes and Streams
Modeling Streamflow
Nutrients in Lakes and Streams
Rivers, Major World
Runoff, Factors Affecting
Stream Channel Development
Stream Ecology: Temperature Impacts on
Stream Erosion and Landscape Development
Stream Health, Assessing
Stream Hydrology

Stream, Hyporheic Zone of a
Streamflow Variability
Waterfalls
Wetlands

LEGISLATION, POLICY, AND LAW

Clean Water Act
Endangered Species Act
Hydropolitics
International Cooperation
Instream Water Issues
Law, International Water
Law of the Sea
Law, Water
Legislation, Federal Water
Legislation, State and Local Water
National Environmental Policy Act
Planning and Management, History of Water
    Resources
Policy-Making Process
Prior Appropriation
Rights, Public Water
Rights, Riparian
Safe Drinking Water Act
Transboundary Water Treaties

MICROBES: ECOSYSTEMS AND HUMAN IMPACTS

Algal Blooms, Harmful
Algal Blooms in Fresh Water
Algal Blooms in the Ocean
Human Health and the Ocean
Human Health and Water
Microbes in Groundwater
Microbes in Lakes and Streams
Microbes in the Ocean
Plankton

OCEAN SCIENCE

Algal Blooms, Harmful
Algal Blooms in the Ocean
Carbon Dioxide in the Ocean and
    Atmosphere
Climate and the Ocean
Ecology, Marine
Estuaries
Ice at Sea
Ocean Basins
Ocean Biogeochemistry

Ocean Chemical Processes
Ocean Currents
Ocean Mixing
Ocean-Floor Bathymetry
Ocean-Floor Sediments
Oceanography, Biological
Oceanography, Chemical
Oceanography from Space
Oceanography, Geological
Oceanography, Physical
Oceans, Polar
Oceans, Tropical
Plankton
Radionuclides in the Ocean
Sea Level
Sea Water, Freezing of
Sea Water, Gases in
Tides
Tracers of Ocean-Water Masses
Waves
Weather and the Ocean

PLANNING AND MANAGEMENT

Balancing Diverse Interests
California, Water Management in
Chesapeake Bay
Coastal Waters Management
Colorado River Basin
Columbia River Basin
Conflict and Water
Conservation, Water
Cost-Benefit Analysis
Data, Databases, and Decision-Support
    Systems
Demand Management
Drought Management
Everglades
Floodplain Management
Florida, Water Management in
Great Lakes
Instream Water Issues
Integrated Water Resources Management
Lake Management Issues
Land Use and Water Quality
Land-Use Planning
Mississippi River Basin
Planning and Management, History of Water
    Resources
Planning and Management, Water Resources
Prior Appropriation
Public Participation

Reclamation and Reuse
Recreation
Reservoirs, Multipurpose
Rights, Public Water
Rights, Riparian
River Basin Planning
Supplies, Protecting Public Drinking-Water
Supply Development
Tourism

POLLUTION AND ENVIRONMENTAL QUALITY

Acid Mine Drainage
Acid Rain
Agriculture and Water
Algal Blooms, Harmful
Amphibian Population Declines
Attenuation of Pollutants
Chemicals: Combined Effect on Public Health
Chemicals from Agriculture
Chemicals from Consumers
Chemicals from Pharmaceuticals and Personal Care Products
Clean Water Act
Erosion and Sedimentation
Lake Health, Assessing
Land Use and Water Quality
Land-Use Planning
Landfills: Impact on Groundwater
Microbes in Groundwater
Microbes in Lakes and Streams
Microbes in the Ocean
National Environmental Policy Act
Nutrients in Lakes and Streams
Ocean Health, Assessing
Oil Spills: Impact on the Ocean
Pollution by Invasive Species
Pollution of Groundwater
Pollution of Groundwater: Vulnerability
Pollution of Lakes and Streams
Pollution of Streams by Garbage and Trash
Pollution of the Ocean by Plastic and Trash
Pollution of the Ocean by Sewage, Nutrients, and Chemicals
Pollution Sources: Point and Nonpoint
Runoff, Factors Affecting
Safe Drinking Water Act
Septic System Impacts
Stream Health, Assessing

Supplies, Protecting Public Drinking-Water
Watershed, Restoration of a
Watershed, Water Quality in a

RESOURCES: LIVING AND NONLIVING

Aquaculture
Energy from the Ocean
Fisheries, Fresh-Water
Fisheries, Marine
Food from the Sea
Geothermal Energy
Hydroelectric Power
Mariculture
Mineral Resources from Fresh Water
Mineral Resources from the Ocean
Petroleum from the Ocean

STRUCTURES AND FACILITIES

Bridges, Causeways, and Underwater Tunnels
Canals
Dams
Hoover Dam
Infrastructure, Water-Supply
Irrigation Systems, Ancient
Land-Use Planning
Moorings and Platforms
Ports and Harbors
Pumps, Modern
Pumps, Traditional
Supplies, Public and Domestic Water
Utility Management
Wastewater Treatment and Management
Waterworks, Ancient
Wells and Well Drilling

TECHNOLOGY

Archaeology, Underwater
Artificial Recharge
Dams
Data, Databases, and Decision-Support Systems
Energy from the Ocean
Geospatial Technologies
Hydroelectric Power
Modeling Groundwater Flow and Transport
Modeling Streamflow
Navigation at Sea, History of
Oceanography from Space
Pumps, Modern

For Your Reference

TABLE 1. SELECTED METRIC CONVERSIONS

WHEN YOU KNOW	MULTIPLY BY	TO FIND
Temperature		
Celsius (°C)	1.8 (°C) +32	Fahrenheit (°F)
Celsius (°C)	°C +273.15	Kelvin (K)
degree change (Celsius)	1.8	degree change (Fahrenheit)
Fahrenheit (°F)	[(°F) −32] / 1.8	Celsius (°C)
Fahrenheit (°F)	[(°F −32) / 1.8] +273.15	Kelvin (K)
Kelvin (K)	K −273.15	Celsius (°C)
Kelvin (K)	1.8(K −273.15) +32	Fahrenheit (°F)

WHEN YOU KNOW	MULTIPLY BY	TO FIND
Distance/Length		
centimeters	0.3937	inches
kilometers	0.6214	miles
meters	3.281	feet
meters	39.37	inches
meters	0.0006214	miles
microns	0.000001	meters
millimeters	0.03937	inches

WHEN YOU KNOW	MULTIPLY BY	TO FIND
Capacity/Volume		
cubic kilometers	0.2399	cubic miles
cubic meters	35.31	cubic feet
cubic meters	1.308	cubic yards
cubic meters	8.107×10^{-4}	acre-feet
liters	0.2642	gallons
liters	33.81	fluid ounces

WHEN YOU KNOW	MULTIPLY BY	TO FIND
Area		
hectares (10,000 square meters)	2.471	acres
hectares (10,000 square meters)	107,600	square feet
square meters	10.76	square feet
square kilometers	247.1	acres
square kilometers	0.3861	square miles

WHEN YOU KNOW	MULTIPLY BY	TO FIND
Weight/Mass		
kilograms	2.205	pounds
metric tons	2205	pounds
micrograms (μg)	10^{-6}	grams
milligrams (mg)	10^{-3}	grams
nanograms (ng)	10^{-9}	grams

TABLE 2. SELECTED SYMBOLS, ABBREVIATIONS, AND ACRONYMS

Ancillary capitalization is used throughout to illustrate how the abbreviations are derived. In appropriate usage, however, most chemical names do not contain mixtures of uppercase and lowercase (e.g., PerChlorEthylene is perchlorethylene).

MEASUREMENTS

μ	"micro" (10^{-6})
m	"milli" (10^{-3})
°C	degrees Celsius
°F	degrees Fahrenheit
μg/L	micrograms per liter
psi	Pounds-force per Square Inch
ppb	Parts Per Billion (or micrograms per liter)
ppbv	Parts Per Billion by Volume
ppm	Parts Per Million (or milligrams per liter)
ppmv	Parts Per Million by Volume
ppt	Parts Per Thousand (or grams per liter)

CHEMISTRY AND POLLUTION

AMD	Acid Mine Drainage
ARD	Acid Rock Drainage
ANS	Aquatic Nuisance Species
ATP	Adenosine TriPhosphate
BOD	Biochemical Oxygen Demand
BTEX	Benzene, Toluene, Ethylbenzene, and Xylene
CFC	ChloroFluoroCarbon
COD	Chemical Oxygen Demand
DDE	DichloroDiphenyldichloroEthylene
DDT	DichloroDiphenylTrichloroethane
DIC	Dissolved Inorganic Carbon
DNA	DeoxyriboNucleic Acid
DO	Dissolved Oxygen
DOC	Dissolved Organic Carbon
MCL	Maximum Contaminant Level
MNA	Monitored Natural Attenuation
MTBE	Methyl *Tert*-Butyl Ether
NPDES	National Pollutant Discharge Elimination System
PAH	Polycyclic Aromatic Hydrocarbon
PCB	PolyChlorinated Biphenyl
PCE	PerChlorEthylene
PPCP	Pharmaceutical and Personal Care Product
PVC	PolyVinyl Chloride
QA	Quality Assurance
QAPP	Quality Assurance Project Plan
RNA	RiboNucleic Acid
RO	Reverse Osmosis
STW	Sewage Treatment Works
TCE	TriChlorEthylene
TDS	Total Dissolved Solids
TMDL	Total Maximum Daily Load
VOC	Volatile Organic Compound

[continued]

OCEAN SCIENCE

DSV	Diving Support Vehicle
ENSO	El Niño Southern Oscillation
HAB	Harmful Algal Bloom
OTEC	Ocean Thermal Energy Conversion
ROV	Remotely Operated Vehicle
SeaWiFS	Sea-viewing Wide Field-of-view Sensor
scuba (or SCUBA)	Self-Contained Underwater Breathing Apparatus
SONAR	SOund Navigation and Ranging
TAO	Tropical Atmosphere Ocean

RESOURCE MANAGEMENT

ADR	Alternative Dispute Resolution
AR	Artificial Recharge
ASR	Aquifer Storage and Recovery
CERP	Comprehensive Everglades Restoration Plan
EAA	Everglades Agricultural Area
EEZ	Exclusive Economic Zone
EIS	Environmental Impact Statement
IQ	Individual Quota
ITQ	Individual Transferable Quota
LOS	Law of the Sea
MSY	Maximum Sustainable Yield
MPA	Marine Protected Area
RDU	Rural Development Unit
TAC	Total Allowable Catch
WUA	Water User Association
WIN	Water Infrastructure Network
WMD	Water Management District

TECHNOLOGY

DSS	Decision-Support System
GIS	Geographic Information Systems
GPS	Global Positioning System
GLIMS	Global Land Ice Measurement from Space
MODIS	MODerate-resolution Imaging Spectroradiometer

TABLE 2 (continued). SELECTED SYMBOLS, ABBREVIATIONS, AND ACRONYMS

Ancillary capitalization is used throughout to illustrate how the abbreviations are derived. In appropriate usage, however, most chemical names do not contain mixtures of uppercase and lowercase (e.g., PerChlorEthylene is perchlorethylene).

MISCELLANEOUS

3D (or 3-D)	Three Dimensional
AC	Alternating Current (also stands for Asbestos-Cement)
B.C.E.	Before the Common Era
AIDS	AutoImmune Deficiency Syndrome
B.P.	Before the Present
B.S.	Bachelor of Science
c.	Circa
C.E.	Common Era
D.C.	District of Columbia
GNP	Gross National Product
M.S.	Master of Science
Ph.D.	Doctor of Philosophy
ULV	Ultra-Low-Volume
UV	UltraViolet

LEGISLATION

CWA	Clean Water Act
CZMA	Coastal Zone Management Act
ESA	Endangered Species Act
NEPA	National Environmental Policy Act
RCRA	Resource Conservation and Recovery Act
SDWA	Safe Drinking Water Act

ORGANIZATIONS

ACE	Army Corps of Engineers
AWRA	American Water Resources Association
CIA	Central Intelligence Agency
EPA	Environmental Protection Agency
FDA	Food and Drug Administration
FEMA	Federal Emergency Management Agency
FWS	Fish and Wildlife Service
IPCC	Intergovernmental Panel on Climate Change
IJC	International Joint Commission
IWA	International Water Association
IWRA	International Water Resources Association
NASA	National Aeronautics and Space Administration
NATO	North Atlantic Treaty Organization
NMFS	National Marine Fisheries Service
NPS	National Park Service
NOAA	National Oceanic and Atmospheric Administration
NRCS	Natural Resource Conservation Service
NSF	National Science Foundation
TVA	Tennessee Valley Authority
UN	United Nations
UNESCO	United Nations Educational, Scientific and Cultural Organization
UNICEF	United Nations International Children's Fund
U.S.	United States
U.S.A.	United States of America
USBR	United States Bureau of Reclamation (also BOR or USBR)
USDA	United States Department of Agriculture
USGS	United States Geological Survey

Era	Period		Epoch	started (millions of years ago)
Cenozoic 66.4 millions of years ago–present time	Quaternary		Holocene	0.01
			Pleistocene	1.6
	Tertiary	Neogene	Pliocene	5.3
			Miocene	23.7
		Paleogene	Oligocene	36.6
			Eocene	57.8
			Paleocene	66.4
Mesozoic 245–66.4 millions of years ago	Cretaceous		Late	97.5
			Early	144
	Jurassic		Late	163
			Middle	187
			Early	208
	Triassic		Late	230
			Middle	240
			Early	245
Paleozoic 570–245 millions of years ago	Permian		Late	258
			Early	286
	Carboniferous	Pennsylvanian		320
		Mississippian		360
	Devonian		Late	374
			Middle	387
			Early	408
	Silurian		Late	421
			Early	438
	Ordovician		Late	458
			Middle	478
			Early	505
	Cambrian		Late	523
			Middle	540
			Early	570
Precambrian time 4560–570 millions of years ago				4560

Contributors

Barbara Johnston Adams
Amagansett, New York

Cain Allen
University of British Columbia
Vancouver, British Columbia,
Canada

Anthony F. Amos
The University of Texas
Port Aransas, Texas

Faye Anderson
University of Maryland
College Park, Maryland

Gail Glick Andrews
Oregon State University
Corvallis, Oregon

William Arthur Atkins
Atkins Research and Consulting
Normal, Illinois

Jeffery A. Ballweber
*Mississippi Water Resources
Research*
Mississippi State University
Starkville, Mississippi

Nadine G. Barlow
Northern Arizona University
Flagstaff, Arizona

Janice A. Beecher
Michigan State University
East Lansing, Michigan

Amy G. Beier
Picton, New Zealand

Paul S. Berger
*U.S. Environmental Protection
Agency*
Washington, D.C.

Christina E. Bernal
Beaumont, Texas

Andrew R. Blaustein
Oregon State University
Corvallis, Oregon

Arthur L. Bloom
Cornell University
Ithaca, New York

Andrew J. Boulton
University of New England
Armidale, Australia

Patrick V. Brady
Sandia National Laboratories
Albuquerque, New Mexico

Amy J. Bratcher
Texas A & M University
College Station, Texas

Arthur S. Brooks
University of Wisconsin-Milwaukee
Milwaukee, Wisconsin

Scott F. Burns
Portland State University
Portland, Oregon

Piers Chapman
Louisiana State University
Baton Rouge, Louisiana

Randall Charbeneau
The University of Texas at Austin
Austin, Texas

Ralph Christensen
EGR & Associates, Inc.
Eugene, Oregon

Timothy A. Chuey
KVAL-13 Television
Eugene, Oregon

Neil Clark
The Writing Company
Watertown, MA

Jeanne Nienaber Clarke
University of Arizona
Tucson, Arizona

Flaxen D. L. Conway
Oregon State University
Corvallis, Oregon

James R. Craig
Emerald Isle, North Carolina

Ron Crouse
Interpretive Solutions
Lincoln City, Oregon

Benjamin Cuker
Hampton University
Hampton, Virginia

Michael Cummings
Portland State University
Portland, Oregon

Mark Cunnane
Western Groundwater Services, LLC
Bozeman, Montana

Scott G. Curry
*Oregon Department of Human
Services*
Medford, Oregon

E. Julius Dasch
RSC International
Washington, D.C.

Pat Dasch
RSC International
Washington, D.C.

Christian G. Daughton
*U.S. Environmental Protection
Agency*
Las Vegas, Nevada

Laura O. Dávalos-Lind
Baylor University
Waco, Texas

Thomas E. Davenport
*U.S. Environmental Protection
Agency*
Chicago, Illinois

Joseph W. Dellapenna
Villanova University
Villanova, Pennsylvania

Andrew P. Diller
University of Florida
Cantonment, Florida

Terry C. Dodge
*Florida Center for Environmental
Studies*
Palm Beach Gardens, Florida

Jane Dougan
Nova Southeastern University
Dania Beach, Florida

Lisa A. Drake
Old Dominion University
Norfolk, Virginia

Laurie Duncan
The University of Texas at Austin
Austin, Texas

Cheryl Lyn Dybas
National Science Foundation
Arlington, Virginia

David A. V. Eckhardt
U.S. Geological Survey
Ithaca, New York

Hillary S. Egna
Oregon State University
Corvallis, Oregon

John F. Elder
U.S. Geological Survey
Middleton, Wisconsin

Audrey Eldridge
*Oregon Department of
Environmental Quality*
Medford, Oregon

Carolyn Embach
University of Tulsa
Tulsa, Oklahoma

Richard A. Engberg
*American Water Resources
Association*
Middleburg, Virginia

Jack D. Farmer
Arizona State University
Tempe, Arizona

Rana A. Fine
University of Miami
Miami, Florida

Denise D. Fort
University of New Mexico
Albuquerque, New Mexico

Doretha B. Foushee
*North Carolina Agricultural &
Technical State University*
Greensboro, North Carolina

Jeffrey Frederick
*Oregon Department of Human
Services*
Springfield, Oregon

Richard Gates
Lake Oswego, Oregon

Bart Geerts
University of Wyoming
Laramie, Wyoming

Deidre M. Gibson
Hampton University
Hampton, Virginia

Larry Gilman
Sharon, Vermont

Meredith A. Giordano
*International Water Management
Institute*
Colombo, Sri Lanka

Michael N. Gooseff
Utah State University
Logan, Utah

Pamela J. W. Gore
Georgia Perimeter College
Clarkston, Georgia

Rick G. Graff
Graff Associates
Portland, Oregon

Neil S. Grigg
Colorado State University
Fort Collins, Colorado

M. Grant Gross
Washington College
Chestertown, Maryland

James R. Groves
Virginia Military Institute
Lexington, Virginia

Steven C. Hackett
Humboldt State University
Arcata, California

Richard Haeuber
Washington, D.C.

Pixie A. Hamilton
U.S. Geological Survey
Richmond, Virginia

Julie K. Harvey
*Oregon Department of
Environmental Quality*
Portland, Oregon

Richard J. Heggen
University of New Mexico
Albuquerque, New Mexico

Stephen R. Hinkle
U.S. Geological Survey
Portland, Oregon

Brian D. Hoyle
Nova Scotia, Canada

Christina Hulbe
Portland State University
Portland, Oregon

Patricia S. Irle
*Washington State Department of
Ecology*
Olympia, Washington

Richard H. Ives
U.S. Bureau of Reclamation
Washington, D.C.

Walter C. Jaap
Lithophyte Research
St. Petersburg, Florida

Jeffrey W. Jacobs
National Research Council
Washington, D.C.

Cindy Johnson
*Suwannee River Water
Management District*
Gainesville, Florida

William W. Jones
Indiana University
Bloomington, Indiana

Jeffrey L. Jordan
University of Georgia at Griffin
Griffin, Georgia

Karen E. Kelley
*Oregon Department of Human
Services*
Springfield, Oregon

Dana R. Kester
University of Rhode Island
Narragansett, Rhode Island

Phillip Z. Kirpich
World Bank (former staff member)
Miami Beach, Florida

Philip Koth
Atkins Research and Consulting
Normal, Illinois

F. Michael Krautkramer
Robinson & Noble, Inc.
Tacoma, Washington

David E. Kromm
Kansas State University
Manhattan, Kansas

Christopher Lant
*Southern Illinois
University–Carbondale*
Carbondale, Illinois

Kelli L. Larson
Oregon State University
Corvallis, Oregon

Brenda Wilmoth Lerner
Lerner & Lerner, LLC
London, U.K.

K. Lee Lerner
Science Research and Policy Institute
London, U.K. and Washington,
D.C.

Judith Li
Oregon State University
Corvallis, Oregon

Roberta J. Lindberg
*Oregon Department of
Environmental Quality*
Eugene, Oregon

Kenneth E. Lite Jr.
Oregon Water Resources Department
Salem, Oregon

Steven E. Lohrenz
University of Southern Mississippi
Stennis Space Center, Mississippi

Daniel P. Loucks
Cornell University
Ithaca, New York

Robert W. Malmsheimer
State University of New York
College of Environmental
Science and Forestry
Syracuse, New York

Michael Manga
University of California, Berkeley
Berkeley, California

William R. Mason
*Oregon Department of
Environmental Quality*
Eugene, Oregon

Olen Paul Matthews
University of New Mexico
Albuquerque, New Mexico

Michael J. Mattick
Oregon Water Resources Department
Springfield, Oregon

Larry W. Mays
Arizona State University
Tempe, Arizona

Sue McClurg
Water Education Foundation
Sacramento, California

Richard H. McCuen
University of Maryland
College Park, Maryland

John D. McEachran
Texas A & M University
College Station, Texas

Vincent G. McGowan
*Southern Illinois
University–Carbondale*
Carbondale, Illinois

Minerva Mercado-Feliciano
Bloomington, Indiana

Grant A. Meyer
University of New Mexico
Albuquerque, New Mexico

Donn Miller
*Oregon Water Resources
Department*
Salem, Oregon

Timothy L. Miller
U.S. Geological Survey
Reston, Virginia

Bruce Mitchell
University of Waterloo
Waterloo, Ontario, Canada

James E. T. Moncur
University of Hawaii at Manoa
Honolulu, Hawaii

Karl A. Morgenstern
Eugene Water & Electric Board
Eugene, Oregon

Earl Finbar Murphy
The Ohio State University
Columbus, Ohio

Richard W. Murray
Boston University
Boston, Massachusetts

Clifford M. Nelson
U.S. Geological Survey
Reston, Virginia

Dennis O. Nelson
*Oregon Department of Human
Services*
Springfield, Oregon

Gary Nelson
Bend, Oregon

John W. Nicklow
*Southern Illinois
University–Carbondale*
Carbondale, Illinois

Vita Pariente
College Station, Texas

Amy B. Parmenter
*Oregon Department of
Environmental Quality*
Eugene, Oregon

Richard J. Pedersen
*Oregon Department of
Environmental Quality*
Portland, Oregon

Howard A. Perlman
U.S. Geological Survey
Atlanta, Georgia

Catherine M. Petroff
University of Washington
Seattle, Washington

Laurel E. Phoenix
University of Wisconsin–Green Bay
Green Bay, Wisconsin

James L. Pinckney
Texas A & M University
College Station, Texas

Ashanti Johnson Pyrtle
University of South Florida
St. Petersburg, Florida

Timothy Randhir
University of Massachusetts
Amherst, Massachusetts

Elliot Richmond
Education Consultants
Austin, Texas

Richard Robinson
Tucson, Arizona

David M. Rohr
Sul Ross State University
Alpine, Texas

Joel S. Rubin
New England Aquarium
Boston, Massachusetts

Christopher L. Sabine
*National Oceanic and
Atmospheric Administration*
Seattle, Washington

Dorothy Sack
Ohio University
Athens, Ohio

Kari Salis
*Oregon Department of Human
Services*
Portland, Oregon

Marie Scheessele
St. Mary's Catholic School
Alexandria, Virginia

Steffen W. Schmidt
Iowa State University
Ames, Iowa

Alison Cridland Schutt
Chevy Chase, Maryland

Martha R. Scott
Texas A & M University
College Station, Texas

Ralph L. Seiler
U.S. Geological Survey
Carson City, Nevada

George H. Shaw
Union College
Schenectady, New York

N. Earl Spangenberg
*University of Wisconsin–
Stevens Point*
Stevens Point, Wisconsin

Sheree L. Stewart
*Oregon Department of
Environmental Quality*
Portland, Oregon

Robert R. Stickney
Texas A & M University
College Station, Texas

Margaret M. Streepey
University of Michigan
Ann Arbor, Michigan

Kimberly J. Swanson
*Oregon Department of Human
Services*
Springfield, Oregon

George H. Taylor
Oregon State University
Corvallis, Oregon

Robert J. Taylor
Texas A & M University
College Station, Texas

Terri A. Thomas
Carbondale, Illinois

David B. Thompson
Texas Tech University
Lubbock, Texas

Eileen Tramontana
*St. Johns River Water
Management District*
Palatka, Florida

Tas D. van Ommen
Australian Antarctic Division
Kingston, Tasmania, Australia

Steve Vandas
U.S. Geological Survey
Denver, Colorado

Joan Vernikos
Thirdage, LLC
Alexandria, Virginia

Warren Viessman Jr.
University of Florida
Gainesville, Florida

Edward F. Vitzthum
University of Nebraska
Lincoln, Nebraska

Noam Weisbrod
*Ben-Gurion University
of the Negev*
Sde-Boqer, Israel

Gilbert F. White
University of Colorado at Boulder
Boulder, Colorado

Donald A. Wilhite
University of Nebraska
Lincoln, Nebraska

Thomas C. Winter
U.S. Geological Survey
Denver, Colorado

Ellen Wohl
Colorado State University
Fort Collins, Colorado

Aaron T. Wolf
Oregon State University
Corvallis, Oregon

Christopher J. Woltemade
Shippensburg University
Shippensburg, Pennsylvania

Jennifer Yeh
*University of California,
San Francisco*
San Francisco, California

Acid Mine Drainage

A high school freshman sits in a grass meadow where two mountain ridges slope down and join. As the young observer gazes across the landscape, he sees a scar on the neighboring ridge. At first it looks like a rockslide or **scree** slope, but on closer examination he sees a hole in the mountainside. It is an abandoned mine with a waste rock pile at its entrance. An orange-red liquid slowly trickles down from the mine into the forest until it reaches the headwaters of a crystal clear mountain creek teeming with small fish and insects. The volume of clear, cold water flowing overwhelms the orange-red liquid and it disappears.

Returning 8 years later as a college graduate, the observer encounters a much different scene. The meadow is now a wasteland without vegetation, and the once healthy creek is flowing red in the headwaters. The observer follows the creek downstream to see it change from red to white to turquoise-blue; no fish or insects appear for several kilometers downstream. What has happened? The answer is acid mine drainage.

Specifically, in the first visit, the high school student saw acid mine drainage from an old mine that had been worked with crude equipment, likely producing no more than a couple tons of ore a day. Acid mine drainage from this old mine was not significant enough to negatively affect the creek.

The following year, however, the mine had been reopened. The newly opened mine operated with high efficiency using modern equipment and produced from 350 to 450 tons of ore per day. Owing to the larger disturbance and production methods, the acid mine drainage from the modern mine had a significant impact on an entire **watershed**.

This scene actually played out in the Siskyou Mountains of southwest Oregon. The Formosa Mine initially operated between 1927 and 1933. The mine re-opened in 1990 and produced from 350 to 400 tons of copper and zinc ore per day. The ore was crushed into powder and processed using ponds to separate the metals.

Upon closure in 1994, the mining company placed the leftover crushed high-grade ore back into the mine workings and filled the former flotation ponds with the **gangue** or low-grade ore. The following winter, the mine workings and former ponds filled up with water from rainfall and began producing acid mine drainage (AMD) as the ore reacted with the water.

scree: weathered and broken rock fragments that have fallen downslope from above, often forming or covering a slope on a mountain

watershed: the land area drained by a river and its tributaries; also called river basin, drainage basin, catchment, and drainage area

gangue: the nonvaluable materials closely associated with the valuable minerals in ore deposits (also referred to as waste rock); common gangue minerals include quartz and calcite; typically must be removed and discarded to extract the valuable high-grade ore

Big Wheeling Creek in Lansing, Ohio is shown here in 1972, when it was polluted with sulfuric acid, iron pyrites, and other mine runoff. Reclamation efforts can slowly return polluted sites to a more acceptable state.

habitat: the environment in which a plant or animal grows or lives; the surroundings include physical factors such as temperature, moisture, and light, together with biological factors such as the presence of food and predators

AMD from the mine flowed into the headwaters of two nearby creeks, which were **habitat** for threatened salmon and steelhead. Studies performed before 1990 documented an abundance of aquatic insects and fish in both creeks. After the mine closed, the creeks flowed red, white, turquoise-blue, and blue-green as the metals in the AMD precipitated out into the streambed. A total of 29 kilometers (18 miles) of stream were contaminated with metals from the AMD. Eighteen kilometers (11 miles) were found to be mostly void of aquatic insects, and fish populations were reduced by over 90 percent.

Acid Rock Drainage and Acid Mine Drainage

sulfide: any compound of sulfur in the reduced state (S^-) and another element; common in igneous rock and some sedimentary rocks such as shale; heavy metal sulfides are generally insoluble

weathering: the decay or breakdown of rocks and minerals through a complex interaction of physical, chemical, and biological processes; water is the most important agent of weathering; soil is formed through weathering processes

hydrothermal alteration zone: a volume of rocks altered by the interaction of hydrothermal water with pre-existing rocks and minerals

Acid rock drainage (ARD) is a natural process in which sulfuric acid is produced when **sulfides** in rocks—for example, pyrite (FeS_2)—are exposed to air and water. This occurs along outcrops or scree slopes where sulfide-bearing rock is naturally **weathered**.

Acid mine drainage (AMD) is essentially the same process as ARD only greatly magnified. In general, rocks that contain valuable metals usually contain sulfides (metals combined with sulfur). The reason for this marriage (metal deposits with sulfide or sulfur) is that thermal waters are typically responsible for depositing many types of metallic ore. These thermal waters travel along fractures or small channels in the host rock. As a result, the thermal waters also change the mineralogy of the host rock along these fractures, creating bodies of rock referred to as **hydrothermal alteration zones**, which may be many times larger than the economically-defined ore zones or veins that fill the fracture.

Mineral Deposits

Gangue minerals are the nonvaluable minerals closely associated with the valuable ore deposits. They generally include minerals like quartz or calcite.

PRODUCING ACID FROM STONE

Acid mine drainage (AMD) is produced by the chemical reaction of sulfide ore and associated minerals with air and water. This reaction (as shown below) illustrates how sulfuric acid (H_2SO_4) and iron sulfate ($FeSO_4$) are produced when the iron sulfide mineral pyrite (FeS_2) reacts with water:

$$FeS_2 + H_2O + 3.5O_2 = H_2SO_4 + FeSO_4$$

The iron sulfate and sulfuric acid continue to react with water and air through several steps to produce iron hydroxide ($Fe[OH]_3$) and additional sulfuric acid.

The sulfuric acid is responsible for leaching metals from mine dumps as well as significantly lowering the pH in streams. The iron hydroxide is responsible for the characteristic reddish color associated with AMD.

Although operating more slowly, the reactions described above do affect natural outcroppings of sulfide ore minerals, resulting in a characteristic reddish stain that is referred to as a gossan. The color of the gossan is so distinctive that it can be seen for miles. Early mineral exploration made use of gossans as an indicator of where potential ore deposits might be found.

During mining activities, the gangue material is commonly discarded as waste rock or low-grade ore in an effort to extract more valuable ore minerals found in the veins. AMD is typically associated with these types of hard rock mines across the world. Another major form of AMD is associated with coal mines in the eastern United States (and elsewhere around the world) where acid is formed by the oxidation of sulfur occurring in the coal and the rock or clay found above and below the coal seams.

When the minerals in the rock were deposited millions of years ago, they were formed at high temperatures and pressures. This makes these mineral deposits (including the gangue material) unstable under surface conditions when exposed to oxygen and water. Most sulfide minerals react with oxygen (oxidation) and water (hydration). Some sulfides, especially those containing iron and copper, generate sulfuric acid in the process. Pyrite (commonly called "fool's gold"), the most common sulfide mineral, reacts with oxygen and water to form ferrous iron and sulfuric acid in solution (see box above).

Laboratory studies have shown that exposing sulfide minerals to oxygen and water produces sulfuric acid, but scientists found that the rate of generation is so slow that it would take decades to oxidize a significant proportion of sulfide. Observations of AMD and other natural systems clearly demonstrate that acid production occurs in a short time period, from months to years. This is because some common strains of bacteria present in almost all environments increase the reaction rate by orders of magnitude.

Once the acid is formed it leaches other metals, such as copper, zinc, cadmium, nickel, arsenic, lead, and mercury, from the mineralized vein. High concentrations of these metals are dissolved by the acid and carried away in solution. As the acid solution flows away from the mine, the **pH** changes and affects the chemistry of the solution such that different metals begin to **precipitate** out of solution.

Color changes typical of creeks affected by AMD start as orange, red, or yellow-brown as the ferrous iron solution is diluted. The pH rises as the AMD mixes with the receiving stream, causing the ferrous iron to precipitate out as ferric iron. Farther downstream, the stream is white as

pH: a measure of the acidity of water; a pH of 7 indicates neutral water, with values between 0 and 7 indicating acidic water (0 is very acidic), and values between 7 and 14 indicating alkaline (basic) water (14 is very alkaline); specifically defined as $-\log_{10}(H^+)$, where (H^+) is the hydrogen ion concentration

precipitate: (verb) in a solution, to separate into a relatively clear liquid and a solid substance by a chemical or physical change

algae: (singular, alga) simple photosynthetic organisms, usually aquatic, containing chlorophyll, and lacking roots, stems, and leaves

aluminum oxide deposits along rocks and the streambed. The iron and aluminum deposits tend to form a sludge-like material, which inhibits **algae**, insect, and fish growth, and damages their habitat. Benthic (bottom-dwelling) organisms are particularly sensitive to this type of pollution. Following the orange iron and white aluminum deposits, the streams can then take on turquoise-blue or green colors as copper and other metals begin to precipitate from solution.

Depressed food supplies, gill clogging, and smothering by iron or aluminum precipitates, along with direct toxicity from ingested metals, contribute to the significant decline of fish, insect, and benthic communities in streams polluted by metal oxides. With their food supply diminished, fish populations can be limited even when degradation is not severe enough to cause direct poisoning of individual fish.

The Problem and the Cleanup

Acid mine drainage is a global problem. In the eastern United States alone, AMD from coal mines has adversely impacted fisheries associated with over 13,000 kilometers (8,000 miles) of streams in Pennsylvania, West Virginia, Ohio, and Maryland. The problem in the western United States is less studied, yet it has become apparent that once-pristine watersheds are suffering from the effects of AMD. Cleanup of abandoned mine sites is difficult because of their remote locations and because these problems will go on for hundreds of years until the mineralized rock is leached free of sulfides and metals.

Typical cleanup strategies for addressing AMD include the following:

- Flooding the acid-producing rock or tailings with water;

organic: pertaining to, or the product of, biological reactions or functions

- Constructing wetlands or treatment ponds containing large quantities of **organic** material, from which sulfide-reducing bacteria react with the metals and cause them to precipitate;

- Using plants to take up the metals from the soil or sediment; and

- Using concrete or cement to solidify the acid-producing material into an inert block.

To be effective in eliminating or significantly reducing AMD, it is necessary to remove one of the three factors that produce it: water, oxygen, or bacteria. SEE ALSO ECOLOGY, MARINE; FRESH WATER, NATURAL COMPOSITION OF; FRESH WATER, PHYSICS AND CHEMISTRY OF; SALMON DECLINE AND RECOVERY; STREAM HEALTH, ASSESSING.

Karl A. Morgenstern

Bibliography

Brodie, Gregory A. "Constructed Wetlands for Treating Acid Drainage at Tennessee Valley Authority Coal Facilities." In *Constructed Wetlands in Water Pollution Control*, eds. P. F. Cooper and B. C. Findlater. New York: Pergamon Press, 1990.

Jambor, J. L., and D. W. Blowes, eds. "Environmental Geochemistry of Sulfide Mine Wastes." Mineralogical Association of Canada, Short Course, 1994.

Morin, Kevin A., and Nora M. Hutt. *Environmental Geochemistry of Mine Site Drainage: Practical Theory and Case Studies.* Vancouver, B.C., Canada: MDAG Publishing, 1997.

Ritcey, Gordon M. *Tailings Management: Problems and Solutions in the Mining Industry.* New York: Elsevier Publishing, 1989.

Smith, Kathleen S., Geoffrey S. Plumlee, and Walter H. Ficklin. "Predicting Water Contamination from Metal Mines and Mining Wastes." U.S. Geological Survey Open-File Report 94-264 (1994).

Sobolewski, Andre. "A Review of Processes Responsible for Metal Removal in Wetlands Treating Contaminated Mine Drainage." *International Journal of Phytoremediation* vol. 1, no. 1 (1999):19–51.

Internet Resources

Koryak, Michael. "Origins and Ecosystem Degradation Impacts of Acid Mine Drainage." U.S. Army Corps of Engineers. <http://www.lrp-wc.usace.army.mil/misc/AMD_Impacts.html>.

Acid Rain

In October 1998, U.S. Senator Daniel Patrick Moynihan testified before Congress on acid rain. A longtime champion of the issue, Moynihan stated that "As far back as the 1960s, fishermen in the Adirondacks began to complain about more than 'the big one that got away.' Fish, once abundant in the pristine, remote Adirondack lakes, were not just getting harder to catch. They were gone."

The issue of acid rain emerged in the United States in the mid-1970s. At the time, little was known about the magnitude and distribution of acid rain or about its impacts on terrestrial (land-based) and aquatic **ecosystems**. However, many believed that acid rain and the air pollutants that caused it posed a threat to forests, aquatic life, crops, structures (e.g., buildings), cultural artifacts (e.g., statues and monuments), and human health.

ecosystem: the community of plants and animals within a water or terrestrial habitat interacting together and with their physical and chemical environment

Since the 1970s, acid rain has been addressed in the United States through hundreds of millions of dollars of research, passage of laws, and implementation of regulatory programs. However, Senator Moynihan's 1998 remark is stark testimony to the fact that acid rain continues to have a negative effect on natural resources, and addressing the problem is an enduring public policy dilemma.

Sources and Forms of Acid Rain

Rain, snow, sleet, and other forms of precipitation are naturally slightly acidic because of chemical reactions with carbon dioxide and other naturally occurring substances in the atmosphere. But this natural acidity can be increased by human-induced air pollution. Acid deposition or "acid rain" occurs when emissions of sulfur dioxide (SO_2) and oxides of nitrogen (NO_x) in the atmosphere react with water, oxygen, and oxidants to form mild solutions of sulfuric acid or nitric acid. Sunlight increases the rate of most of these reactions. These compounds fall to Earth and are deposited in either wet form (e.g., rain, snow, sleet, and hail), known as wet deposition, or dry form (e.g., particles, gases, and vapor), known as dry deposition. Cloud or fog deposition, a form of wet deposition, occurs at high elevations and in coastal areas.

In the United States, nearly two-thirds of annual SO_2 emissions and just over one-fifth of NO_x emissions are produced by electric utility plants that burn **fossil fuels**. Transportation sources (e.g., cars, trucks, and other vehicles) account for more than half of NO_x emissions. Ammonia emissions derive largely from livestock waste and fertilized soil. Industrial combustion

fossil fuel: substance such as coal, oil, or natural gas, found underground in deposits formed from the remains of organisms that lived millions of years ago

A sign in Nova Scotia, Canada proclaims the potential effect of acid rain on a local river and its salmon runs. Acidified waters can be harmful or even deadly to salmon populations.

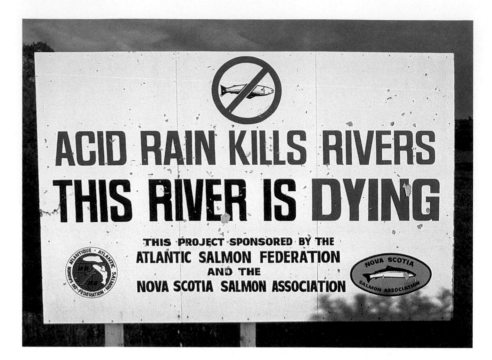

and industrial processes are the other major categories of emission sources. Acid rain is a regional problem because prevailing winds can transport SO_2 and NO_x emissions over hundreds of kilometers, sometimes crossing state, national, and international borders.

Wet Deposition. Wet deposition of sulfur and nitrogen compounds is commonly known as acid rain, although it also takes the form of snow, sleet, clouds, or fog. Wet deposition is intermittent because acids reach the Earth only when precipitation falls. Nevertheless, it can be the primary pathway for acid deposition in areas with heavy precipitation.

The eastern United States receives more acidic precipitation than the rest of the country, with the greatest rates occurring in Ohio, West Virginia, western Pennsylvania, upstate New York, New England, and other northeastern areas. Because nitrogen compounds can remain stored in snow until it melts, **nitrate** concentrations in lakes and streams can increase dramatically during seasonal or episodic acidification, particularly in the Northeast, resulting in **toxic** impacts on aquatic organisms.

Acidic compounds can reach plants, soil, and water from contact with acidic clouds as well. Although cloud deposition affects only a limited number of locations, it can provide a relatively steady source of acids in comparison with wet deposition, particularly at high altitudes. As a result, trees such as the red spruce have declined in areas of significant cloud deposition.

Dry Deposition. Dry deposition occurs when acidic gases and particles in the atmosphere are deposited directly onto surfaces when precipitation is not occurring. Dry-deposited gases and particles can also be washed from trees and other surfaces by rainstorms, making the combination more acidic than the falling rain alone. Dry deposition is the primary acid deposition pathway in **arid** regions of the West, such as Joshua Tree National Park.

nitrate: the highly leachable form of soil nitrogen taken up by most plants through their roots; it is a common groundwater contaminant, especially in agricultural areas and locations with a high density of septic systems, that is regulated by the U.S. Environmental Protection Agency with a drinking water standard of 10 ppm (parts per million) of nitrogen in the nitrate form

toxic: describes chemical substances that are or may become harmful to plants, animals, or humans when the toxicant is present in sufficient concentrations

arid: describes a climate or region where precipitation is exceeded by evaporation; in these regions, agricultural crop production is impractical or impossible without irrigation

Effects on Aquatic Ecosystems

The ecological effects of acid rain are most clearly seen in aquatic environments, particularly streams and lakes. Acid rain mainly affects sensitive bodies of water that are located in **watersheds** whose soils have limited ability to neutralize acidic compounds. The ability of forest soils to neutralize acidity, referred to as buffering capacity, results from chemicals in the soil that neutralize some or all of the acidity in rainwater. Buffering capacity depends on the thickness and composition of the soil as well as the type of bedrock beneath the forest floor.

Lakes and streams become acidic (**pH** decreases) when the water itself and its surrounding soil cannot neutralize the acidity in the rain. Differences in soil buffering capacity are an important reason that some areas receiving acid rain show damage, whereas other areas receiving about the same amount of acid rain do not appear to be harmed.

Several regions in the United States contain many of the surface waters sensitive to acidification. They include the Adirondacks and Catskill Mountains in New York State, the mid-Appalachian highlands, the upper Midwest, and mountainous areas of the western United States. In areas such as the northeastern United States, where soil buffering capacity is low, some lakes have a pH value of less than 5. With a pH of 4.2, Little Echo Pond in Franklin, New York was one of the most acidic lakes reported as of 2002.

Ecosystem Impacts. Acid rain is not the sole cause of low pH in lakes and streams. There are many natural sources of acidity that can drive down pH to low levels (as low as 4) even in the absence of acid rain: for example, organic acid inputs or mineral veins in underlying geologic materials. Similarly, natural sources of buffering capacity such as limestone bedrock can push pH to as high as 8. Notwithstanding these natural influences in specific locations, lakes and streams generally have pH values from 6 to 8. Hence, reductions in pH due to human-induced acid rain create an imbalance in the chemistry and ultimately the entire **ecosystem** of a lake or stream.

Acid rain causes a cascade of effects that harm or kill individual fish, reduce fish populations, completely eliminate fish species from a waterbody, and decrease **biodiversity**. As acid rain flows through soils in a watershed, aluminum and other metals are released from soils into the lakes and streams located in that watershed. Thus, as a lake or stream becomes more acidic (has lower pH), aluminum levels increase. Both low pH and increased aluminum levels are directly toxic to fish. In addition, low pH and increased aluminum levels cause chronic stress that may not kill individual fish but may make fish less able to compete for food and habitat.

The impact of declining pH varies because not all aquatic organisms can tolerate the same amount of acid. For example, frogs are better able than trout to tolerate somewhat acidified water. Generally, the young of most species are more sensitive to environmental conditions than adults.

As pH levels decline, acid-sensitive species may attempt to migrate to better habitat, or, if blocked from migration, will likely die. At pH 5 and below, most fish species disappear, and ecosystem-level processes are affected. Some acid lakes and streams contain no fish.

watershed: the land area drained by a river and its tributaries; also called river basin, drainage basin, catchment, and drainage area

pH: a measure of the acidity of water; a pH of 7 indicates neutral water, with values between 0 and 7 indicating acidic water (0 is very acidic), and values between 7 and 14 indicating alkaline (basic) water (14 is very alkaline); specifically defined as $-\log_{10}(H^+)$, where (H^+) is the hydrogen ion concentration

ecosystem: the community of plants and animals within a water or terrestrial habitat interacting together and with their physical and chemical environment

biodiversity: a measure of the variety of the Earth's species, of the genetic differences within species, and of the ecosystems that support those species

Acidified lakes and streams can be treated with agricultural lime in an attempt to counteract the acidity. Such temporary and localized measures are not as effective as emissions reductions in addressing the long-term and geographically widespread ecological impacts of acid rain.

nutrients: a group of chemical elements or compounds needed for all plant and animal life; nitrogen and phosphorus are the primary nutrients

weathering: the decay or breakdown of rocks and minerals through a complex interaction of physical, chemical, and biological processes; water is the most important agent of weathering; soil is formed through weathering processes

Effects on Forests and Soils

Acid rain has been implicated in forest and soil degradation in many areas of the eastern United States, particularly high elevation forests of the Appalachian Mountains from Maine to Georgia. Acid rain does not usually kill trees directly. Instead, it weakens trees by damaging their foliage, limiting the **nutrients** available to them, or exposing them to toxic substances slowly released from the soil. Quite often, injury or death is a result of acid rain in combination with other environmental stressors, such as insects, disease, drought, or very cold weather.

Chemicals in watershed soils that provide buffering capacity (such as calcium and magnesium) are also important nutrients for many species of trees. As forest soils receive year after year of acid rain, these chemicals are washed away, depriving trees and other plants of essential soil nutrients. At the same time, acid rain causes the release of dissolved aluminum into the soil water, which can be toxic to trees and plants. The chemicals that provide buffering capacity take many decades to replenish through gradual natural processes, such as the **weathering** of limestone bedrock.

Trees also can be damaged by acid rain even if the soil is well buffered. Mountainous forests often are exposed to greater amounts of acidity because they tend to be surrounded by acidic clouds and fog. Essential nutrients in foliage are stripped away when leaves and needles are frequently bathed in acid fog, causing discoloration and increasing the potential for damage by other environmental factors, especially cold weather.

Effects on Human Health and Human Environments

The pollutants that cause acid rain also damage human health. These gases interact in the atmosphere to form fine sulfate and nitrate particles that can be inhaled deep into the lungs. Scientific studies show relationships between elevated levels of fine particles and increased illness and premature death from heart disease and lung disorders, such as bronchitis. In addition, nitrogen oxides react in the atmosphere to form **ozone**, increasing risks associated with lung inflammation, such as asthma.

Sulfates and nitrates in the atmosphere also contribute to reductions in visibility. Sulfate particles account for 50 to 70 percent of decreased visibility in eastern U.S. national parks, such as the Shenandoah and the Great Smoky Mountains. In the western United States, nitrates and carbon also play roles, but sulfates have been implicated as an important source of visibility impairment in some national parks, such as the Grand Canyon.

Wet and dry acid deposition contribute to the corrosion of metals (such as bronze) and the deterioration of paint and stone (such as marble and limestone). These effects seriously reduce the value to society of buildings, bridges, cultural objects (such as statues, monuments, and tombstones), and automobiles.

1990 Clean Air Act Amendments: Title IV

In 1990, the U.S. Congress took action intended to address acid rain issues, passing the Clean Air Act Amendments (CAAA) (42 U.S.C. 7651). The purpose of the Acid Rain Program (Title IV of the 1990 amendments) was to address the adverse effects of acid rain by reducing annual emissions of sulfur dioxide (SO_2) and nitrogen oxides (NO_x)—the main air pollutants that cause the problems—from stationary power generation sources.

Implemented by the U.S. Environmental Protection Agency starting in 1995, the program consists of two major components. The SO_2 emission reduction program employs a two-phase cap-and-trade approach to reduce total annual SO_2 emissions by 10 million tons below 1980 levels by 2010 (roughly a 40-percent reduction in total emissions). When the SO_2 emission reduction is fully implemented in approximately 2010, electric utility emissions will be capped at 8.95 million tons per year (representing approximately a 50-percent reduction in emissions from this sector).

The NO_x emission reduction program aims to reduce annual NO_x emissions from coal-fired electric utility boilers by 2 million tons below what they would have been without Title IV. The NO_x component of the program does not include a cap on NO_x emissions or any emissions trading provisions.

Emissions Trading. In establishing the Acid Rain Program, Congress chose to utilize an innovative environmental management approach known as cap-and-trade, or emissions trading, to reduce SO_2 emissions. Emissions trading is a departure from more traditional "command and control" regulatory approaches in which the government commands industry to install particular control technologies at specific plants in order to reduce pollution. Because emissions trading allows industry the flexibility to reduce pollution from sources that can achieve reductions least expensively, large amounts of emissions are reduced at lower costs, with less administrative burden and fewer lengthy lawsuits, than if sources were regulated individually.

The approach first sets an overall cap (maximum amount of emissions) that policymakers believe will achieve the desired environmental effects. Affected sources are then allocated emission allowances that permit them to emit a certain amount of a pollutant. The total number of allowances given to all sources cannot exceed the cap.

ozone: a chemical compound composed of three oxygen atoms (triatomic oxygen), formed naturally from diatomic oxygen by electric discharge or exposure to ultraviolet radiation

sulfate: a combination of sulfur in the oxidized state (S^{6+}) and oxygen, and a part of naturally occurring minerals in some soil and rock formations; a common constituent in groundwater and surface water; sulfate minerals tend to be highly soluble

ACID RAIN AND THE U.S. CAPITOL BUILDING

The buildings and monuments of Washington, D.C. use many types of stone. Marble and limestone structures are the most likely to show damage caused by acid precipitation and urban pollution. They are vulnerable to accelerated deterioration because they are composed primarily of the mineral calcite (calcium carbonate), which dissolves readily in weak acid.

The United States Capitol building shows evidence of stone deterioration. For example, preferential dissolution of calcite (where the silicate mineral inclusions remain) has caused pockmarks in marble columns and balustrades and their square bases. Although stone deterioration has many causes, both natural and human-induced, it is almost certain that some deterioration can be attributed to acid rain.

Sources are not told how to reach the emissions goal established by the number of allowances they are given. They may reach their goal through various means, including buying allowances from sources that are able to reduce emissions more cost effectively and so have excess allowances to sell. The only requirements are that sources completely and accurately measure and report all emissions and then turn in the same number of allowances as emissions at the end of the yearly compliance period. If emissions exceed allowances, a source faces expensive fines and other penalties.

Cap-and-trade is effective for the following reasons:

- The mandatory cap always protects the environment. Even as the economy grows, or as new sources enter the industry, total emissions cannot exceed the cap.

- Complete and consistent emissions measurement and reporting by all sources guarantee that total emissions do not exceed the cap and that individual sources' emissions are no higher than their allowances.

- The design and operation of the program is simple, which helps keep compliance and administrative costs low.

Effectiveness of the Acid Rain Program

In terms of SO_2 emissions reductions, the results of the Acid Rain Program have been dramatic—and unprecedented. From its 1995 inception to 1999 (completion of Phase I), annual SO_2 emissions from the largest, highest-emitting sources dropped by nearly 5 million tons from 1980 levels. These reductions were an average of 25 percent below required emission levels, resulting in early achievement of human health and environmental benefits. In 2001, SO_2 emissions from power generation were more than 6.7 million tons below 1980 levels.

Emissions of NO_x have been reduced by 1.5 million tons from 1990 levels (about 3 million tons lower than projected growth). Because the NO_x component of the program includes no cap, there is no guarantee that NO_x emissions will stay at these low levels; without a cap, emissions may increase as power generation increases.

Because of the reduction in SO_2 emissions, acidity of rainfall in the eastern United States has dropped by up to 25 percent. As a consequence, some sensitive lakes and streams in New England are showing signs of recovery. Further, sulfate concentrations in the air have decreased, leading to improved air quality and associated benefits to public health, such as fewer irritations or aggravations to respiratory conditions (e.g., asthma and chronic bronchitis). Finally, visibility has improved in some parts of the eastern United States, including areas with scenic vistas, such as Acadia National Park in coastal Maine.

Although the Clean Air Act has had positive effects, emissions and acid deposition remain high compared to background conditions. The rate and extent of ecosystem recovery from acid deposition are directly related to the timing and degree of emissions reductions. Research suggests that deeper emissions cuts will lead to greater and faster recovery from acid deposition in the northeastern United States. SEE ALSO AMPHIBIAN POPULATION DECLINES; CAVERN DEVELOPMENT; CHEMICAL ANALYSIS OF WATER;

ECOLOGY, FRESH-WATER; FRESH WATER, NATURAL COMPOSITION OF; FRESH WATER, PHYSICS AND CHEMISTRY OF; KARST HYDROLOGY; LAKES: CHEMICAL PROCESSES.

Richard Haeuber

Bibliography

Dehayes, Donald et al. "Acid Rain Impacts on Calcium Nutrition and Forest Health." *Bioscience* 49 (October 1999):789–800.

Driscoll, Charles T. et al. *Acid Rain Revisited: Advances in Scientific Understanding Since the Passage of the 1970 and 1990 Clean Air Act Amendments.* Hanover, NH: Hubbard Brook Research Foundation, 2001. Available online at <http://www.hubbardbrook.org/hbfound/report.pdf>.

Driscoll, Charles T. et al. "Acidic Deposition in the Northeastern U.S.: Sources and Inputs, Ecosystem Effects, and Management Strategies." *Bioscience* 51, no. 3 (March 2001):180–198.

Driscoll, Charles T. et al. "The Response of Lake Water in the Adirondack Region of New York State to Changes in Acid Deposition." *Environmental Science and Policy* 1 (1998):185–198.

Ellerman, A. Denny et al. *Markets for Clean Air: The U.S. Acid Rain Program.* New York: Cambridge University Press, 2000.

Kosobud, Richard F., ed. *Emissions Trading: Environmental Policy's New Approach.* New York: John Wiley & Sons, 2000.

Likens, Gene E., Charles T. Driscoll, and D. C. Buso. 1996. "Long-Term Effects of Acid Rain: Response and Recovery of a Forest Ecosystem." *Science* 272 (12 Apr. 1996):244–246.

Lovett, Gary. "Atmospheric Deposition of Nutrients and Pollutants in North America: An Ecological Perspective." *Ecological Applications* 4, no. 4 (1994):629–650.

Stoddard, John L. et al. "Regional Trends in Aquatic Recovery from Acidification in North America and Europe." *Nature* 401 (7 Oct. 1999):575–578.

U.S. Environmental Protection Agency, Clean Air Markets Division. *EPA Acid Rain Program—2001 Progress Report.* EPA-430-R-02-009. Washington, D.C.: U.S. Environmental Protection Agency. Available online at <http://www.cpa.gov/airmarkets/cmprpt/arp01/index.html>.

Internet Resources

Clean Air Markets. U.S. Environmental Protection Agency. <http://www.epa.gov/airmarkets>.

National Acid Precipitation Assessment Program. <http://www.oar.noaa.gov/organization/napap.html>.

National Atmospheric Deposition Program. <http://nadp.sws.uiuc.edu/>.

Nilles, Mark A. *Atmospheric Deposition Program of the U.S. Geological Survey.* U.S. Geological Survey. <http://bqs.usgs.gov/acidrain/Program.pdf>.

Agassiz, Louis

Swiss-American Zoologist and Geologist
1807–1873

Jean Louis Rodolphe Agassiz has been called the "Father of Glaciology" and the "First Naturalist." One of the greatest contributors to the science of water, he discovered evidence of a time when the frozen state of water changed Earth's landscape: the Ice Age.

Born in Switzerland, Agassiz developed his love of nature from exploring the wilderness as a child. Receiving doctorate degrees in medicine and natural history at the University of Munich in Germany, he first distinguished

Louis Agassiz recognized that global climatic conditions in the past had led to ice ages in which glaciers covered a much larger part of the Earth than they do today.

glacier: a huge mass of ice, formed on land by the compaction and recrystallization of snow, which moves slowly downslope or outward owing to its own weight

himself by his work with fossil fish. While teaching and continuing his research at a college in Neuchatel, Switzerland, however, he acquired a new passion: **glaciers**.

Fellow scientist Jean de Charpentier introduced Agassiz to the concept of glaciation on a larger scale. In that time, scientists thought that either the biblical flood or icebergs caused geological features such as misplaced boulders and grooved, polished rock. However, through the careful observational methods for which he was known, Agassiz discovered that they were indeed products of glacial movement. Because these features were found throughout Europe in areas where there were no present glaciers, Agassiz deduced that at one time global climatic changes produced giant sheets of ice that covered the Northern Hemisphere on a **continental** scale.

continental: of or pertaining to the continents

In 1840, Agassiz published his findings as "Etudes sur les Glaciers." Although many scholars at first opposed his ideas, the Ice Age theory was soon accepted around the world. Agassiz continued his teaching and research in the United States, where he became a professor of natural history at Harvard University and founded the Museum of Comparative Zoology, which is still part of the university today. Agassiz also helped create both the National Academy of Sciences and Cornell University, dedicating the rest of his life to expanding knowledge of, and promoting enthusiasm for, natural history. SEE ALSO GLACIERS AND ICE SHEETS; GLACIERS, ICE SHEETS, AND CLIMATE CHANGE; ICE AGES.

Amy B. Parmenter

Bibliography

Gordon, John E. "Early Development of the Glacial Theory: Louis Agassiz and the Scottish Connection." *Geology Today* 11, no. 2 (1995):64–68.

Lurie, Edward. *Louis Agassiz: A Life in Science.* Chicago, IL: The University of Chicago Press, 1960.

Agriculture and Water

Humans depend on water in many ways, well beyond the few liters needed daily for drinking. Water is also essential for the production of food. Various forms of agriculture, practiced on about half of Earth's land surface, provide the vast majority of food that over 6 billion people eat. Agriculture also provides much of the fiber for cotton, wool, and linen clothing.

Rain-fed Agriculture

One of the primary ways in which humans use water is by planting important crops in places where they can capture natural rainfall as rain-fed agriculture. Some forms of agriculture, such as intensive rice and corn production, can be practiced only in rainy climates. Such agricultural forms are much more productive than others, such as cattle and sheep herding, which are usually relegated to **semiarid** climates.

semiarid: a climate or region where moisture is normally greater than under arid conditions but still limits the growth of most crops; either dryland farming methods or irrigation generally are required for crop production

One of the primary reasons rain-dependent forms of agriculture are more productive than dry-land forms is that they have sufficient water to allow plants to grow to their maximum potential. Therefore, the most agriculturally productive regions of the world are all regions where natural rainfall is sufficient to allow rain-fed agriculture to flourish: for example, the

Subsistence agriculture on small farm plots is practiced in the highly elevated Altiplano of Chile and Bolivia (South America). Farmers in the arid highlands must cope with the variable weather conditions and extreme climatic uncertainty.

eastern and central United States; the Pampas of Argentina; central Europe; northern and eastern India and Bangladesh; eastern China; and the valleys and volcanic islands of southeast Asia.

Up to a point, the more rain, the more productive the crops. For example, in the United States, corn is a productive grain that typically yields over 100 bushels per acre, but requires a climate where rainfall is at least 76 centimeters (30 inches) per year. Wheat yields only about 20 bushels per acre under the same conditions, but can still yield nearly this much if rainfall is only 50 centimeters (20 inches). Therefore, farmlands that receive at least 76 centimeters (30 inches) per year, as they do in the Corn Belt states of Ohio, Indiana, Illinois, and Iowa, are much more agriculturally productive than the Wheat Belt lands of the Dakotas, Montana, Nebraska, and Kansas, which receive less than 76 centimeters (30 inches). And the monsoon-blessed rice lands of southeast Asia are more productive yet.

Irrigation

Because agricultural crops are so dependent on water, purposely adding water, beyond what naturally falls as rain, is widely practiced to increase agricultural production. This critical practice is known as irrigation.

Irrigation is an ancient practice that originated along the Tigris and Euphrates Rivers in what is now Iraq, and spread in ancient times to the desert valley of the Nile River in Egypt, the Indus River in Pakistan, and all the way to China. Native Americans also practiced irrigation long ago, especially in the areas now called Mexico and the southwestern United States.

It is estimated that 40 percent of all crops grown in the world today are grown using irrigation. The practice of irrigation can increase the

LEADING IRRIGATION COUNTRIES				
Country	Irrigated Area (1,000 Square Kilometers)	Irrigated Land as a Percentage of Cropland	Water Used in Irrigation (Cubic Kilometers)	Percentage of all Water Withdrawals used for Irrigation
World	2,296	19	2,236	69
China	513	52	400	87
India	490	29	353	93
United States	209	11	196	42
Pakistan	163	80	151	97
Mexico	62	25	67	86
Egypt	33	100	47	86

productivity of crops on what would otherwise be rain-fed agriculture. It can also expand agriculture into areas where it would not otherwise be practiced due to aridity.

Irrigation Worldwide. In the twentieth century, the practice of irrigation was greatly increased to provide food for the world's growing population. Globally, irrigation now accounts for 69 percent of the 3,240 cubic kilometers (772 cubic miles) of water withdrawn for human use, and 87 percent of all water consumed. Proportions in the United States are 42 percent of all withdrawals and 87 percent of all consumption. (A consumptive use of water means that the water is no longer available for another use.)

Asia, with the majority of Earth's population, remains the world's most irrigated region. The three most populous countries—China, India, and the United States—are also the leading countries in irrigated area and in water used in irrigation, as shown in the table. Pakistan and especially Egypt remain the countries most dependent on irrigation, although other countries of dry southwestern and central Asia (e.g., Saudi Arabia, Iran, Iraq, and Uzbekistan) greatly depend on irrigation for their food and fiber supplies.

In the United States, the state of California is by far the most important irrigated region.✳ But irrigation also is critical to the relatively small agricultural outputs of **arid** states such as Utah, Arizona, New Mexico, and Colorado. Irrigation is used extensively in parts of the Great Plains to mirror the Corn Belt style of agriculture farther east, and in Arkansas along the Mississippi River to maximize yields.

Water-Supply Constraints

In every irrigated region, water supplies are a limitation on further expansion of irrigated agriculture. In many regions, renewable supplies have already been exceeded, resulting in falling **groundwater** levels and greatly reduced river flow. In some regions, the depletion of water resources due to irrigation has reached crisis proportions. Today the Colorado River rarely reaches the Sea of Cortez (often called the Gulf of California), and even the Yellow River of China is sometimes drained completely. The Aral Sea in central Asia has lost half its surface area, most of its volume, and all of its once-enormous fishing industry. These are all examples of the depletion of regional water resources by irrigated agriculture.

In the United States, especially in California, attempts have been made to move water away from irrigation and toward urban, industrial, and environmental purposes. Farmers can now "rent" their annual water **allocation**

✳ **See the "Irrigation Management" and "Ogallala Aquifer" entries for photographs of U.S. irrigation.**

arid: describes a climate or region where precipitation is exceeded by evaporation; in these regions, agricultural crop production is impractical or impossible without irrigation

groundwater: generally, all subsurface (underground) water, as distinct from surface water, that supplies natural springs, contributes to permanent streams, and can be tapped by wells; specifically, the water that is in the saturated zone of a defined aquifer

allocate: to distribute resources for a particular purpose

without losing their permanent water rights. Irrigation efficiency is improving with **drip irrigation** systems such as those pioneered in water-short Israel. In the southern Great Plains, some farmers are simply reverting back to dry-land agriculture as groundwater levels fall so low that they cannot afford to pump the water to the surface.

Agriculture and Water Quality

Agriculture uses vast quantities of water and also causes extensive pollution, primarily by introducing **nonpoint-source** contaminants. Runoff from agricultural fields often contains eroded soil, fertilizers, animal manure, or **pesticides** that together form a major source of water pollution.

This form of nonpoint-source pollution remains remarkably unregulated by governments. Yet recent initiatives include **Total Maximum Daily Load** requirements that are imposed on whole **watersheds**. Moreover, the U.S. Department of Agriculture now utilizes two methods to induce farmers to decrease polluted runoff:

- Cross-compliance, in which farmers are required to adopt soil conservation measures to control erosion if they are to remain eligible for public subsidies; and

- Conservation payments to farmers, such as the Conservation Reserve Program, to take highly erodible or streamside land out of crop production.

Despite their good intentions, these policies have succeeded only in chipping away at the growing environmental issue of polluted agricultural runoff.

Hydroponic Production

Hydroponics is a method of gardening without soil. Instead of soil, plants are grown in chemical nutrient solutions and supported by porous materials such as peat moss and sand. The most commonly grown hydroponic produce are tomatoes, lettuce, herbs, cucumbers, and peppers.

A commercial hydroponic operator uses about 5 percent of the water and a fraction of the land needed to produce an equivalent amount of produce in traditional agriculture. For example, with just 650 square meters (7,000 square feet) of greenhouse space, or about one-eighth of an acre, a hydroponic farmer can grow as much as 50,000 pounds of hydroponic tomatoes annually.

In the 1960s, commercial U.S. hydroponics developed in the arid Southwest. Of over 30,000 hydroponic acres in world production as of 2002, about 800 acres were in the United States. Most of these U.S. facilities are family or small business operations that cover less than an acre, with produce sold locally. There are also several larger U.S. facilities that cover over 60 acres, with produce sold nationally. Recently, U.S. production surpassed Canadian production, with the tomato as its leading hydroponic product, followed by the bell pepper and the cucumber.

The U.S. demand for hydroponic produce is growing, and has grown so high that domestic supply in 2002 was inadequate. Consequently, hundreds of thousands of pounds of hydroponic produce are imported daily.

drip irrigation: a system for slowly watering crops at points on or just below the soil surface so that a plant's root zone is thoroughly moistened, with little water being wasted via ponding or runoff

nonpoint source: describes a pollutant release or discharge originating from a land use active over a wide land area (e.g., agriculture) rather than from one specific location (e.g., an outfall pipe from a factory)

pesticides: a broad group of chemicals that kills or controls plants (herbicides), fungus (fungicides), insects and arachnids (insecticides), rodents (rodenticides), bacteria (bactericides), or other creatures that are considered pests

Total Maximum Daily Load: the maximum quantity of a particular water pollutant that can be discharged into a body of water without violating a water quality standard; the amount of pollutant is set by the U.S. Environmental Protection Agency

watershed: the land area drained by a river and its tributaries; also called river basin, drainage basin, catchment, and drainage area

This demonstration of hydroponics in Walt Disney World's Epcot Center (Orlando, Florida) yielded bountiful harvests of lettuce. Lettuce grows easily in a hydroponic system because it is a fast-growing, compact plant with shallow roots.

Although still unable to keep up with increasing demand for hydroponic produce, the United States saw rapid growth of hydroponic farming during the 1990s. SEE ALSO CHEMICALS FROM AGRICULTURE; CONSERVATION, WATER; FOOD SECURITY; IRRIGATION MANAGEMENT; IRRIGATION SYSTEMS, ANCIENT; POLLUTION SOURCES: POINT AND NONPOINT; USES OF WATER.

Christopher Lant

Bibliography

Adler, Robert W., J. C. Landman, and D. M. Cameron. *The Clean Water Act: 20 Years Later.* Washington, D.C.: Island Press, 1993.

Gleick, Peter H. *The World's Water 2000–2001: The Biennial Report on Freshwater Resources–2001.* Washington, D.C.: Island Press, 2000.

Pimentel, David et al. "Water Resources: Agriculture, the Environment and Society." *Bioscience* 47(2):97–106.

Postel, Sandra. *Pillar of Sand: Can the Irrigation Miracle Last?* New York: W.W. Norton & Company, 1999.

Reisner, Marc. *Cadillac Desert: The American West and Its Disappearing Water*, 2nd ed. New York: Penguin Books, 1993.

Internet Resources

Agriculture. Food and Agriculture Organization of the United Nations. <http://www.fao.org/ag/>.

Water Quality and Management Program. U.S. Department of Agriculture, Agricultural Research Service. <http://www.nps.ars.usda.gov/programs/programs.htm?NPNUMBER=201>.

algae: (singular, alga) simple photosynthetic organisms, usually aquatic, containing chlorophyll, and lacking roots, stems, and leaves

dinoflagellates: unicellular algae that move by means of flagella (threadlike or whiplike structures)

Algal Blooms, Harmful

Single-celled **algae** are almost always present in sea water even if the water looks clear. When high concentrations of certain species of **dinoflagellates** are present, patches of water look red because these algae contain red pigments—hence the name "red tide." High concentrations of other algae

The term "red tide" refers to different types of algal blooms, which can be various hues depending on the species and the photosynthetic pigments they contain. Blooms occurring offshore can sometimes float toward the shore, as shown here off the southwestern coast of Molokai, Hawaii. Some blooms have the potential to be harmful to ocean life and humans.

may turn sea water orange, yellow, brown, or purple. Red tides have been witnessed for centuries and have been seen all over the world.

Dense concentrations of algae are referred to as blooms, because the algae have multiplied rapidly to become concentrated in high numbers. In a bloom, there could be tens of millions of cells in a liter of sea water. Most blooms are not harmful, but some have the potential to be harmful, whether by virtue of natural biotoxins (poisons) produced by certain species of algae, or by the oxygen-depleting process initiated upon the death and subsequent decay of large concentrations of algae.

Harmful algal blooms, or HABs, cause millions of dollars in damage when there are massive fish kills to be cleaned up, beaches declared off-limits, fisheries and shellfisheries closed to harvesting, and medical treatment provided for people poisoned by marine biotoxins in the seafood they ate. Many scientists believe that harmful algal blooms are becoming more prevalent, but they point out that increased monitoring efforts are detecting more occurrences.

Mechanisms of Harm

How do certain microscopic algae—that is, types of **phytoplankton**—cause harm to fish, shellfish, marine mammals, seabirds, and people? Basically, there are four ways.

First, the physical presence of so many cells may suffocate fish by clogging or irritating the gills. Second, when the densely concentrated algal cells die off, the decay process, assisted by bacteria, can deplete the water of oxygen, which in turn can lead to the death of oxygen-dependent marine creatures. (Algae, being plants, require nutrients such as nitrogen and phosphorus to grow. When they have used up the nutrients, they tend to die off all at once.) Such oxygen-related impacts are most visible in shallow bays, inlets, or seas.

Third, some algal species produce deadly toxins which directly kill the animals that ingest the poisons. Dinoflagellate toxins have killed mussels,

phytoplankton: microscopic floating plants, mainly algae, that live suspended in bodies of water and that drift about because they cannot move by themselves or because they are too small or too weak to swim effectively against a current

EXAMPLES OF MARINE BIOTOXINS

Human Health Impact	Toxigenic Phytoplankton	Primary Toxin
Unnamed poisoning	*Pfiesteria piscicida* and related species	Unidentified toxins
Amnesic Shellfish Poisoning	Species of the diatom genus *Pseudo-nitzschia*	Domoic acid
Neurotoxic Shellfish Poisoning	*Gymnodinum breve*	Brevetoxin
Paralytic Shellfish Poisoning	*Alexandrium* spp., *Gymnodinium catenatum*, *Pyrodinium* spp.	Saxitoxins
Diarrhetic Shellfish Poisoning	Species of the dinoflagellate genus *Dinophysis;* species of the dinoflagellate genus *Prorocentrum* have also been implicated	Okadaic acid
Ciguatera Fish Poisoning	Primarily *Gambierdiscus toxicus*, a benthic dinoflagellate, but also *Prorocentrum, Ostreopsis* spp., *Coolia monotis, Thecadinium* sp., *Amphidinium carterae*	Ciguatoxin/Maititoxin

diatoms: unicellular algae with a cell wall composed of silica

abalone, and fish. Airborne toxins (i.e., toxins that are aerosolized) have caused respiratory problems and eye and skin irritation to people along beaches where harmful algal blooms were present.

Fourth, shellfish such as mussels, clams, and oysters feed by filtering particles, including phytoplankton, from sea water. Toxins from certain dinoflagellate or **diatom** species accumulate in the tissues of shellfish. When people, sea mammals, or seabirds eat the shellfish, they ingest the toxins as well.

There are different kinds of toxins that cause different kinds of symptoms which, in humans, typically are neurological. Some toxins are deadly. The table above shows the categories of human poisoning; the organism associated with the toxicity; and the causative toxin (sometimes among a suite of toxins).

Types and Examples of Toxicity

food chain: the levels of nutrition in an ecosystem, beginning at the bottom with primary producers, which are principally plants, to a series of consumers—herbivores, carnivores, and decomposers

The algal species that can be toxic in some circumstances are not always toxic. When they are toxic, they cause harm by being eaten by larger organisms. As a toxin is passed up the **food chain**, it becomes concentrated in larger and larger animals such as fish and shellfish, and eventually is ingested by people who eat seafood containing the toxin. In the following overview, only two examples of the various algal species known to cause toxicity are discussed.

Pfiesteria.   An exception to toxin transmission up the food chain is the dinoflagellate *Pfiesteria*. Instead of being eaten, it does the eating—usually small organisms but also fish. It uses its toxins to make the fish lethargic and to injure the fish's skin.

estuary: a tidally influenced coastal area in which fresh water from a river mixes with sea water, generally at the river mouth; the resulting water is brackish, which results in a unique ecosystem

Toxins can also get into the air and cause harm to people, as happened in 1991 when this peculiar organism was first discovered in a laboratory in North Carolina. Later it was found in connection with fish kills in the Albemarle–Pamlico **estuary** and other estuarine environments on the

U.S. Atlantic and Gulf of Mexico coasts. Blooms of the more common dinoflagellate, *Gymnodinium breve*, when present in nearshore waters, can be picked up by surf and wind and carried to the seashore in the air. The microscopic organisms cause skin and eye irritation in people exposed to this toxic **aerosol**.

A red-tide dinoflagellate typically has a vegetative stage, in which it multiplies by cell division, and a cyst stage, in which two cells combine to form **gametes** enclosed in a cyst (a type of covering). The cysts sink to the seafloor until conditions are favorable for a return to the vegetative stage.

The *Pfiesteria* organism has a minimum of twenty-four stages in its life cycle, of which at least four are toxic. The life stages include flagellated cells that swim in the water, amoeboid forms both in the water and in bottom muds, and cysts that rest on the bottom. The different forms vary in size from too small to see with an ordinary microscope, to a speck visible to the naked eye.

Most of the time, the *Pfiesteria* dinoflagellate is a nontoxic predator that feeds on small organisms such as algae, bacteria, and small animals. It becomes toxic when cyst forms detect fish excretions or secretions. Encysted cells emerge and become toxic. They damage the fish with the toxin, then feed on the epidermal tissue, blood, and other substances that leak from sores on the incapacitated fish. When the fish are dead, the cells change to the amoeboid stages and feed on the fish carcass.

Pseudo-nitzschia. Diatoms are single-celled marine or fresh-water algae that have shell-like structures, called frustules, made of silica. Until recently, diatoms were not associated with biotoxin poisonings. But in 1987, an outbreak of domoic acid poisoning was reported in Canada. The domoic acid came from a diatom, *Pseudo-nitzschia*. Domoic acid has caused permanent memory loss and death in humans.

In 1991, examination of the stomach contents of dead seabirds found along the beaches of Monterey Bay, California revealed high levels of domoic acid. The birds had been eating anchovies which had been consuming *Pseudo-nitzschia*. In 1998, sea lion deaths on the California coast also were associated with domoic acid, which entered the food chain via toxigenic diatoms, which were eaten by anchovies that in turn were eaten by the sea lions. To prevent human illness when such toxicity is found, state health departments temporarily close beaches and federal regulatory agencies temporarily close fisheries and shellfisheries along the affected coast.

Human Impacts and Intervention

Although the economic impacts of HAB outbreaks has not been quantified on a national basis, the direct and indirect costs to even a single fishery closure can reach millions of dollars. In addition to loss of revenue to fish and shellfish industries, there are impacts on recreational fishing and tourism and their associated businesses.

Harmful algal blooms also can threaten the **aquaculture** industry. For example, unpredictable and destructive blooms of the small flagellate *Heterosigma* have threatened the commercial farmed salmon industry in Washington state (USA) and British Columbia (Canada). *Heterosigma* blooms also

aerosol: a suspension of colloidal (finely suspended) particles in a gas

gamete: a sex cell; in some of the simplest organisms, the gametes are not differentiated into egg and sperm

aquaculture: the science, art, and business of cultivating marine or fresh-water animals or plants under controlled conditions

net pen: floating cages in coastal waterbodies (e.g., bays) that are used in mariculture (marine aquaculture) operations

have destroyed some captive populations of threatened and endangered salmon being raised in **net pens** before their release to the wild.

All of the U.S. coastal states have developed monitoring programs with regular testing of fish and shellfish from beaches. Officials and volunteers watch the shores for patches of colored water, fish kills, the beaching of marine mammals and other unusual activity, or reports of human illness following consumption of fish or shellfish. When toxins show up in laboratory analyses of samples of edible species, warnings are issued and shellfish harvesting and some kinds of fishing may be halted. Economic losses can be high when commercial fishing and aquaculture operations (including fish and shellfish farms) are affected.

To better manage the human risk associated with HABs, scientists are continuing to research methods of rapid analysis to identify toxic phytoplankton species and to detect marine biotoxins in water, phytoplankton, and animals. Better monitoring can help decrease the incidence of overly conservative fishery closures by delineating the extent of the threat, thus reducing the need for broad-scale closures due to lack of information.

The Harmful Algal Bloom and Hypoxia Research and Control Act was enacted in 1998. The act recognizes that HABs threaten coastal ecosystems and endanger human health. A national assessment, published in early 2001, recognized the threat to human health and coastal economies, but found that management options are limited. HAB impacts can be minimized through monitoring programs that regularly sample shellfish to detect HAB toxins, and issue warnings when toxins are found. Satellite remote sensing can track offshore blooms, alerting coastal communities to potential problems as blooms come inshore. SEE ALSO ALGAL BLOOMS IN THE OCEAN; BIVALVES; COASTAL OCEAN; CRUSTACEANS; ECOLOGY, MARINE; FISHERIES, MARINE; FOOD FROM THE SEA; HUMAN HEALTH AND THE OCEAN; MARINE MAMMALS; OCEANOGRAPHY, BIOLOGICAL; PLANKTON.

Vita Pariente

Bibliography

Falconer, I. R., ed. *Algal Toxins in Seafood and Drinking Water.* London, U.K.: Academic Press, 1993.

Woods Hole Oceanographic Institution. *ECOHAB, The Ecology and Oceanography of Harmful Algal Blooms: A National Research Agenda.* Woods Hole, MA: WHOI, 1995.

Yasumoto, T., Y. Oshima, and Y. Fukuyo, eds. *Harmful and Toxic Algal Blooms.* Paris, France: Intergovernmental Oceanographic Commission of UNESCO, 1996.

Internet Resources

Anderson, Donald M. *The Harmful Algae Page.* Woods Hole Oceanographic Institution, National Office for Marine Biotoxins and Harmful Algal Blooms. <http://www.whoi.edu/redtide>.

Marine Biotoxins and Harmful Algal Blooms. Northwest Fisheries Science Center, National Oceanic and Atmospheric Administration. <http://www.nwfsc.noaa.gov/hab>.

Pfiesteria piscicida and Pfiesteria-like Organisms. The University of Maryland. <http://www.mdsg.umd.edu/pfiesteria>.

The IOC Harmful Algal Bloom Programme. The Intergovernmental Oceanographic Commission of UNESCO. <http://ioc.unesco.org/hab>.

Toxic and Harmful Algal Blooms. Bigelow Laboratory for Ocean Sciences. <http://www.bigelow.org/hab>.

Algal Blooms in Fresh Water

Aquatic ecologists are concerned with blooms (very high cell densities) of **algae** in reservoirs, lakes, and streams because their occurrence can have ecological, aesthetic, and human health impacts. In waterbodies used for water supply, algal blooms can cause physical problems (e.g., clogging screens) or can cause taste and odor problems in waters used for drinking. Blooms involving toxin-producing species can pose serious threats to animals and humans.

Algae in Aquatic Ecosystems

The term "algae" is generally used to refer to a wide variety of different and dissimilar **photosynthetic** organisms, generally microscopic. Depending on the species, algae can inhabit fresh or salt water.

In modern taxonomic systems, algae are usually assigned to one of six divisions (equivalent to phyla; see box on page 22). The misnamed blue-green algae are often grouped with algae because of the **chloroplasts** contained within the cells. However, these organisms are actually photosynthetic bacteria assigned to the group cyanobacteria.

Fresh-water algae, also called phytoplankton, vary in shape and color, and are found in a large range of habitats, such as ponds, lakes, reservoirs, and streams. They are a natural and essential part of the **ecosystem**. In these habitats, the phytoplankton are the base of the aquatic **food chain**. Small fresh-water crustaceans and other small animals consume the phytoplankton and in turn are consumed by larger animals.

Bloom Occurrences and Impact

Under certain conditions, several species of true algae as well as the cyanobacteria are capable of causing various nuisance effects in fresh water, such as excessive accumulations of foams, scums, and discoloration of the water. When the numbers of algae in a lake or a river increase explosively, an algal "bloom" is the result. Lakes, ponds, and slow-moving rivers are most susceptible to blooms.

Algal blooms are natural occurrences, and may occur with regularity (e.g., every summer), depending on weather and water conditions. The likelihood of a bloom depends on local conditions and characteristics of the particular body of water. Blooms generally occur where there are high levels of **nutrients** present, together with the occurrence of warm, sunny, calm conditions. However, human activity often can trigger or accelerate algal blooms. Natural sources of nutrients such as phosphorus or nitrogen compounds can be supplemented by a variety of human activities. For example, in rural areas, agricultural runoff from fields can wash fertilizers into the water. In urban areas, nutrient sources can include treated wastewaters from septic systems and sewage treatment plants, and urban stormwater runoff that carries **nonpoint-source** pollutants such as lawn fertilizers.

An algal bloom contributes to the natural "aging" process of a lake, and in some lakes can provide important benefits by boosting primary productivity. But in other cases, recurrent or severe blooms can cause dissolved oxygen depletion as the large numbers of dead algae decay. In highly eutrophic

algae: (singular, alga) simple photosynthetic organisms, usually aquatic, containing chlorophyll, and lacking roots, stems, and leaves

photosynthesis: the process by which plants manufacture food from sunlight; specifically, the conversion of water and carbon dioxide to complex sugars in plant tissues by the action of chlorophyll driven by solar energy

chloroplast: the protoplasmic body or plastid in the cells of plants that contains chlorophyll and in which photosynthesis takes place

ecosystem: the community of plants and animals within a water or terrestrial habitat interacting together and with their physical and chemical environment

food chain: the levels of nutrition in an ecosystem, beginning at the bottom with primary producers, which are principally plants, to a series of consumers—herbivores, carnivores, and decomposers

nutrients: a group of chemical elements or compounds needed for all plant and animal life; nitrogen and phosphorus are the primary nutrients; excessive or imbalanced nutrients in water may cause problems such as accelerated eutrophication

nonpoint source: describes a pollutant release or discharge originating from a land use active over a wide land area (e.g., agriculture) rather than from one specific location (e.g., an outfall pipe from a factory)

THE FIVE KINGDOMS

Scientists use a system called taxonomy to organize all the biological organisms in the world. Organisms are put into various classification groups according to the distinguishing properties they share. These groups are (from highest to lowest) kingdom, phylum, class, order, family, genus, and species.

Although there are several different kingdom classifications in use, it is now generally accepted that all biological organisms can initially be placed into one of five kingdoms: monera, protists, fungi, plants, and animals.

Prokaryotes (Cells That Have No Distinct Nuclei)

- Monera: Includes aquatic bacteria and blue-green algae, more properly called cyanobacteria. Monerans, though microscopic, are the most dominant organisms on Earth. They have existed for about 3.5 billion years.

Eukaryotes (Cells Have Distinct Nuclei)

- Protista: Includes plant-like and animal-like primitive organisms, such as algae and protozoa. Organisms are generally unicellular.

- Fungi: Includes a large group of parasitic and saprophytic species. Some are parasitic on animals, including humans (ringworm, or athlete's foot). Others are parasitic on plants and include rusts and mildews. Fungi are, along with the bacteria, important decomposers of dead organic matter.

- Plants: Make their food by the process of photosynthesis.

- Animals: Ingest their food and digest it internally in specialized body cavities.

---

anoxia: the state in which water contains less than 0.1 milliliter of oxygen per liter, the threshold below which animal life diminishes significantly

(enriched) lakes, algal blooms may lead to **anoxia** and fish kills during the summer. In terms of human values, the odors and unattractive appearance of algal blooms can detract from the recreational value of reservoirs, lakes, and streams. Repeated blooms may cause property values of lakeside or riverside tracts to decline.

Toxic Blooms

toxic: describes chemical substances that are or may become harmful to plants, animals, or humans when the toxicant is present in sufficient concentrations

Some algae produce **toxic** chemicals that pose a threat to fish, other aquatic organisms, wild and domestic animals, and humans. The toxins are released into the water when the algae die and decay.

The most common and visible nuisance algae in fresh water, and the species that are often toxic, are the cyanobacteria. A cyanobacterial bloom will form on the surface and can accumulate downwind, forming a thick scum that sometimes resembles paint floating on the water. Because these mats are blown close to shore, humans and wild and domestic animals can come into contact with the unsightly material.

Blooms of toxic species of algae and cyanobacteria can flood the water environment with the biotoxin they produce. When toxic, blooms can cause human illnesses such as gastroenteritis (if the toxin is ingested) and lung irritations (if the toxin becomes aerosolized and hence airborne). Other cyanobacterial toxins are less drastic, and cause skin irritation to people who swim through an algal bloom. Toxicity can sometimes cause severe illness and death to animals that consume the biotoxin-containing water.

BIG BLOOMS

Algal blooms can cover a large area. In 1991, a bloom affected an estimated 1,000-kilometer stretch of the Barwon and Darling Rivers in New South Wales, Australia.

Cyanobacterial toxins are known to affect bean photosynthesis when they are present in irrigation water. The toxins also can modify zooplankton communities, reduce growth of trout, and interfere with development of fish and amphibians. In some cases, toxins can be bioconcentrated by fresh-water clams.

Some algal blooms in fresh water may only be a nuisance, but others can deplete dissolved oxygen in the water or generate biotoxins that are harmful to birds, fish, and other animals. This Canada goose swims among a floating layer of heavy, but probably harmless, algal growth.

Microcystins comprise the most common group of about fifty cyanobacterial toxins. Among these toxins are ones that, if ingested in sufficient quantity, can harm the liver (hepatotoxins) or nervous system (neurotoxins). Microcystins can persist in water because they are stable in both hot and cold water. Even boiling the water, which makes the water safe from harmful bacteria, will not destroy microcystins. As a result of this threat, the Canadian government implemented a recommended water-quality guideline of $1.5 \mu g$ per liter of microsystin-LR (the most common hepatotoxin), and other countries will likely follow suit. In Canada as well as the United States, there are few reports of injury and no reports of human deaths resulting from microcystins in drinking water, in large part because surface-water sources of drinking water (e.g., reservoirs, lakes, and rivers) must undergo filtration and chlorination at water utilities prior to being distributed to customers. (Cyanobacterial toxins can be removed from water only by activated charcoal filters and chlorination.)

μg: The abbreviation for microgram, where μ means "micro," or 10^{-6}; hence, a microgram is 0.000001 gram

Control Considerations

Repeated episodes of algal blooms can be an indication that a river or lake is being contaminated, or that other aspects of a lake's ecology are out of balance. While cyanobacterial blooms receive the most public and scientific attention, the excessive growth of other algae and other aquatic plants also can cause significant degradation of a lake or pond, particularly in waters receiving sewage or agricultural runoff. Aquatic biologists and other water-quality specialists often are called to identify the causes and recommend management steps to reduce or control the problem.

However, prevention of a problem is always better than trying to fix the problem after it happens. Controlling agricultural, urban, and stormwater runoff; properly maintaining septic systems; and properly managing residential applications of fertilizers are probably the most effective measures that can be taken to help prevent human-induced fresh-water algal blooms. SEE ALSO ALGAL BLOOMS, HARMFUL ; ALGAL BLOOMS IN THE OCEAN; ECOLOGY, FRESH-WATER; HUMAN HEALTH AND MICROBES; NUTRIENTS IN LAKES AND STREAMS; PLANKTON; POLLUTION SOURCES: POINT AND NONPOINT; WASTEWATER TREATMENT AND MANAGEMENT.

Brian D. Hoyle, K. Lee Lerner, and Elliot Richmond

Bibliography

Carmichael, Wayne W. "The Toxins of Cyanobacteria." *Scientific American*. (January 1994): 78-86.

Elder, G. H., Hunter, P. R., and Codd, G. A. "Hazardous Freshwater Cyanobacteria (Blue-Green Algae)." *Lancet* 341 (1993):1519–1520.

Falconer, Ian R. "An Overview of Problems Caused by Toxic Blue-green Algae (Cyanobacteria) in Drinking and Recreational Water." *Environmental Toxicology*. 14 (1999):5–12.

Oberemm, A. et al. "Effects of Cyanobacterial Toxins and Aqueous Crude Extracts of Cyanobacteria on the Development of Fish and Amphibians." *Environmental Toxicology* 14 (1999):77–88.

Internet Resources

Blue-green Algae (Cyanobacteria) and their Toxins. Health Canada. <http://www.hc-sc .gc.ca/ehp/ehd/catalogue/general/iyh/algea.htm>.

Algal Blooms in the Ocean

The ocean, that vast body of water covering 71 percent of the Earth's surface, is divided into four major basins: the Pacific, Atlantic, Indian, and Arctic Oceans. These large basins are interconnected with various shallow seas, such as the Mediterranean Sea, the Gulf of Mexico, and the South China Sea. Oceans and seas abound with life, ranging from microscopic unicellular (one-celled) organisms to multicellular (many-celled) animals.

Algae is an important life form in the ocean. Life in the ocean is maintained in balance by forces of nature and by predator–prey relationships, unless some external pressures upset the balance. When a balance upset leads to conditions more favorable for the reproduction and growth of algae, an explosive increase in the number of algal cell density occurs. Such rapid increases in the algae population are called algal blooms.

During a bloom, a liter of water may contain millions of algae. The most widely publicized type of algal bloom is associated with species that produce a toxin (chemical substance) harmful to animals that feed on the algae (and hence is known as a harmful algal bloom), and/or algae that cause a tint in the water because of the **photosynthetic** pigments they contain. The latter commonly is known as a "red tide," but different pigments can turn the water red, brown, purple, orange, or yellow. Depending on the circumstances and the species present, a red tide may or may not be harmful. Although not all algal blooms in the ocean produce highly visible effects nor are all blooms harmful, they nonetheless affect life in the ocean and on land in both beneficial and harmful ways.

algae: (singular, alga) simple photosynthetic organisms, usually aquatic, containing chlorophyll, and lacking roots, stems, and leaves

photosynthesis: the process by which plants manufacture food from sunlight; specifically, the conversion of water and carbon dioxide to complex sugars in plant tissues by the action of chlorophyll driven by solar energy

In February 2002, the massive die-off and decay of algae from a nearshore harmful algal bloom (a "red tide") caused a rapid reduction in the water's dissolved oxygen concentration, driving tens of thousands of rock lobsters to "walk out of the sea" near the coastal town of Elands Bay in South Africa's Western Cape province. The lobsters in search of oxygen moved toward the breaking surf, but were stranded when the tide went out. Government and military staff attempted to save some of the lobsters, but others were collected for food. A similar stranding from a massive red-tide event occurred at Elands Bay in 1997.

Requirements for a Bloom

Algae require warmth, sunlight, and nutrients to grow and reproduce, so they live in the upper 60 to 90 meters (200 to 300 feet) of ocean water. The upper layer of water, the epipelagic zone, is rich in oxygen, penetrated by sunlight, and warmer than water at lower levels. As algae and other organisms that live in the ocean die, they fall to the bottom of the ocean, where they decay and release the compounds from which they were made. Under certain conditions, these nutrients can deplete the oxygen in the water.

Temperature and salt concentration determine the density of water and how water moves (currents). Cold water is denser (heavier) and sinks from the surface (downwelling). Other water moves across to replace it. Eventually, water at the surface is replaced by water that has risen, or upwelled, from the bottom to the surface somewhere else in the ocean. These upwellings bring nutrient-rich waters to the top. This increase in nutrients can trigger algae blooms.

An increase in nutrients also may be caused by activities of humans, such as runoff from animal farms or fertilized croplands and lawns, or atmospheric

fossil fuel: substance such as coal, oil, or natural gas, found underground in deposits formed from the remains of organisms that lived millions of years ago

deposition of sulfur and nitrogen compounds or oxides derived from the burning of **fossil fuel**. These nutrients lead to blooms in coastal waters to a greater extent than in the open ocean.

However, some of these nutrients do find their way to the open ocean far from shore, and contribute to the formation of blooms in the open ocean. Their movement is aided by the wind and by ocean currents. Algae blooms in the open ocean are not usually harmful; instead, they provide many benefits, largely deriving from the fact that the open ocean is relatively unproductive (low in nutrients).

Algae and Photosynthesis

organic: pertaining to, or the product of, biological reactions or functions

inorganic: describes an element, molecule or substance that did not form as the direct result of biologic activity

eukaryote: all living organisms other than the eubacteria and archaebacteria; all organisms that contain a cell or cells in which the genetic material is DNA in the form of chromosomes contained within a distinct nucleus

Algae are referred to as plants because, like plants, they produce **organic** compounds from **inorganic** compounds (carbon dioxide and water) by capturing and using the energy from sunlight. Most algae are **eukaryotic**, an exception being the blue-green algae (cyanobacteria).

Photosynthesis takes place in organelles called chloroplasts in eukaryotic cells. Chloroplasts contain an outer and an inner membrane and pancake-shaped structures called thylakoids. Energy is captured from sunlight by pigments (chlorophylls *a* and *b* and carotenoids) stored in the thylakoids.

Photosynthesis occurs in two stages commonly referred to as the light reactions (light is required) and the dark reactions (no light is directly required). During the light reactions, energy captured from sunlight is used to split (dissociate) water molecules. Electrons released from this reaction are passed down a series of electron carrier molecules, leading to the storage of the energy in the form of ATP (adenosine triphosphate). This is the form in which living organisms store energy to be used immediately for carrying out chemical reactions and other activities.

Oxygen is produced as a byproduct of the light reactions. During the dark reactions (Calvin cycle), six molecules of carbon dioxide are used to make sugar (glucose). Because algae use carbon dioxide and release oxygen as a product of the light reactions, these plants play an important role in maintaining the proper concentrations of carbon dioxide and oxygen in the environment, via the carbon cycle and oxygen cycle.

food chain: the levels of nutrition in an ecosystem, beginning at the bottom with primary producers, which are principally plants, to a series of consumers—herbivores, carnivores, and decomposers

Algae, like green plants, produce the first organic compounds in the **food chain** and thus are referred to as primary producers. Other organisms cannot use inorganic molecules to make the organic compounds that they need for life, and therefore depend on algae and other plants as the initial source of organic compounds. These organisms either eat algae to obtain organic compounds, or obtain them from the water when they are released after the algae die.

Types of Algae That May Bloom

Cyanobacteria. Cyanobacteria, also known as blue-green algae, are one of the oldest known types of algae and are believed to have played a major role in the addition of oxygen to the Earth's early atmosphere. Some cyanobacteria carry out nitrogen fixation, which is the conversion of nitrogen gas into nitrogen compounds that can be used by other primary producers.

Diatoms. Diatoms are unicellular and have a cell wall composed of silica, a glass-like material, which comprises a shell-like structure called a frustule.

Coccolithophore blooms are identifiable via space-based remote sensing because their external plates of calcium carbonate, called coccoliths, backscatter light from the water column to create a bright optical effect. This bloom (the cloudy swirl in lower lefthand corner) occurred in summer 2001 in the Celtic Sea off England's southwestern coast.

When diatoms die, the frustules settle to the bottom of the ocean floor and combine with the soil to form diatomaceous earth. Diatomaceous earth is used in products such as filters for swimming pools, as temperature and sound insulators, and as an abrasive in toothpaste.

Dinoflagellates. Dinoflagellates have two unequal **flagella** that help them direct their movement. Many of these organisms contain colored pigments that cause the water to appear colored when these organisms bloom, leading to the terms "red tide" or "brown tide," for example. Some dinoflagellates live in close association with marine animals, such as sponges, sea anemones, giant clams, and corals. The golden-brown photosynthetic cells found in these animals, called zooxanthellae, actually are dinoflagellates.

flagellum: (plural, flagella) any of various elongated, threadlike appendages of plants or animals

Coccolithophores. Coccolithophores are cells covered with button-like structures called coccoliths made of calcium carbonate. The coccoliths give the ocean a milky white or turquoise appearance during intense blooms. The long-term flux of coccoliths to the ocean floor is the main process responsible for the formation of chalk and limestone.

Coccolithophores and some other algae participate in the sulfur cycle and produce the gas dimethyl sulfide. This is the primary way that sulfur is carried between ocean and land.

Dimethyl sulfide leaves the surface of the water and reacts with oxygen in the atmosphere to form tiny sulfuric acid droplets. These droplets are carried over land and fall back to land in the form of precipitation. They also aid in the formation of clouds, which partially block the transmission of harmful ultraviolet light that penetrates the surface water. Cloud formation also is thought to encourage surface winds that promote the movement of surface water, leading to upwellings that bring nutrients to the surface.

Benefits of Algal Blooms

Algal blooms provide large concentrations of algae that produce organic compounds needed by higher organisms, ranging from oysters, clams, and mussels to human beings. For this reason, productivity increases in areas where algal blooms occur. More algae in the water means that more carbon dioxide is used from the atmosphere and that more oxygen is released into the atmosphere. Oxygen is necessary for many living things, including humans. As noted previously, the production of dimethyl sulfide gas helps protect algae from harmful ultraviolet rays so they remain healthy and thus are able to continue the cycle of sustaining life on Earth.

Even in the coldest parts of the ocean, algae provide the primary source of organic material to animals at the bottom of the food chain. Organic materials are moved up the food chain as higher organisms feed on those lower down the chain. For example, algae have been found in Antarctic sea ice. As sea water freezes, algae living in the water are frozen in the ice, where they later can be released during a thaw. These algae are a vital source of food for krill, the shrimp-like organisms eaten by penguins, seals, seabirds, and whales. SEE ALSO ACID RAIN; ALGAL BLOOMS, HARMFUL; ALGAL BLOOMS IN FRESH WATER; CARBON DIOXIDE IN THE OCEAN AND ATMOSPHERE; ECOLOGY, MARINE; FISHERIES, MARINE; MICROBES IN THE OCEAN; OCEAN BIOGEOCHEMISTRY; OCEAN-FLOOR SEDIMENTS; PLANKTON; SEA WATER, GASES IN.

Doretha B. Foushee

Bibliography

Castro, Peter, and Michael E. Huber. *Marine Biology*, 2nd ed. New York: Wm. C. Brown/McGraw-Hill, 1997.

Cousteau, Jacques. *The Ocean World*, 2nd ed. New York: Harry N. Abrams, 1993.

Amphibian Population Declines

An unparalleled diminishment in populations is occurring worldwide in many species of amphibians (frogs, toads, and salamanders). Although there are various causes for declining amphibian populations, the most obvious is habitat destruction. However, introduced **exotic** species, **pathogens**, pollution, and global environmental changes all contribute. Moreover, various factors can act together to produce adverse effects on amphibians.

Because amphibians are important **predators** and **prey** in many **ecosystems**, declines in their populations may affect many other species that live within the same ecological community. For example, populations of aquatic insects and amphibian predators such as snakes, birds, mammals, and fish may be especially affected by a loss in amphibians. Moreover, the populations of animals that amphibians eat, such as mosquitoes, may increase as amphibians disappear.

Water Quality Factors

Amphibians have permeable, exposed skin and eggs that may readily absorb **toxic** substances from the environment. Their eggs are laid in water or in

exotic: describes an organism or species that is not native to the area in which it is found

pathogen: a disease-producing agent, usually a living organism, and commonly a microbe (microorganism)

predator: an animal that hunts and kills other animals for food

prey: an animal that is hunted and killed by another for food

ecosystem: the community of plants and animals within a water or terrestrial habitat interacting together and with their physical and chemical environment

toxic: describes chemical substances that are or may become harmful to plants, animals, or humans when the toxicant is present in sufficient concentrations

moist areas, and their larvae (tadpoles) are aquatic. Because amphibians are intimately tied to an aquatic environment, the quality of the water in which they live can affect their growth, development, and survival. Because pollutants, waterborne pathogens, and global environmental changes can all affect water quality, these factors can in turn affect amphibians. Conversely, amphibians are important indicators of water quality, and are considered a sentinel species, meaning that what affects amphibians presently may affect other animal species in the future.

Acidification. A number of studies have shown that acidification of fresh water (that is, a reduction in pH to acidic levels) via acid rain, acid snowmelt, or other modes of pollution are harmful to amphibian growth and development. Some species are more tolerant of acid conditions than others. Thus, depending on the species, the amount of acidity, and other environmental variables, amphibians may experience developmental deformities and increased **mortality** due to acidification.

Acidification can potentially affect amphibian populations and the communities in which amphibians live. For example, some populations of toads in Britain have probably been reduced by water acidification. Salamander populations in Colorado seem to have declined because of increased acidification during snowmelt. Several studies have shown that acidification of the water can affect competition and predation between amphibians. Thus, the larvae of some frog species may have increased survival rates under acid conditions because their salamander predators show reduced predation at low pH.

Nitrates and Nitrites. Many chemical products used in agriculture and industry pollute aquatic habitats, causing potentially severe damage to ecosystems. For example, the increase in concentration of nitrate in surface water on agricultural land due to numerous sources may be hazardous to many species of fish, wildlife, and even humans. Data suggest that nitrogen-based fertilizers may be contributing to amphibian population declines in agricultural areas. However, some species appear to be more sensitive than others to nitrate and nitrite pollution.

In one experimental study in Oregon, it was shown that some species reduced their feeding activity, swam less vigorously, and showed disequilibrium when nitrate or nitrite **ions** were added to the water. Importantly, all species tested in this study showed high mortality at nitrite levels deemed safe for warm-water fishes by the U.S. Environmental Protection Agency. Furthermore, significant larval mortality occurred at the recommended limits of nitrite concentration for drinking water.

Toxic Substances. Just as amphibian species display variation in sensitivity to nitrate-related compounds, they also show variation in tolerance to other toxic substances that may be found in water. Insecticides such as organophosphates, carbamates, and synthetic pyrethroids, which are used mainly in crop production, have a wide array of effects on amphibians. Depending on the concentrations used and the species involved, some of these substances may be lethal, may affect growth and development, or may affect **metamorphosis**.

Effects of Ultraviolet Radiation

Global environmental changes may also affect amphibians. For example, ambient (natural) but increasing levels of ultraviolet (UV) radiation owing

mortality: for a particular animal population, the number of deaths in a given area or period, or from a particular cause

ion: an atom or molecule that carries a net charge (either positive or negative) because of an imbalance between the number of protons and the number of electrons

metamorphosis: the biological process of transformation from an immature form to an adult form in two or more separate stages

THE CASE OF THE CASCADES FROG

The Cascades frog (*Rana cascadae*) is a species that is threatened throughout its range in the western United States. Populations are disappearing, and eggs are dying as they are laid in lakes and ponds.

Cascades frogs are sensitive to a number of agents associated with water quality. For example, an experimental laboratory study at Oregon State University showed that survival and activity levels of tadpoles of the Cascades frog are greatly affected by ultraviolet radiation, acid water conditions, and nitrate pollution. These stressors, acting together, reduce survival and activity levels in Cascades frog tadpoles.

Scientists believe that certain compounds found in agricultural fertilizers, pesticides, and herbicides are contributing to the decline of many amphibian populations in the United States and other countries with large-scale, chemically enhanced agriculture. Yet synthetic chemicals are only one among several human and environmental factors linked to amphibian impacts. Shown here is a Cascades frog tadpole.

to ozone depletion are harmful to many amphibian species. Recent experimental field studies conducted in the United States, Spain, and Australia have shown that when amphibian eggs of certain species are shielded from UV, they have a greater hatching success than if they are exposed to UV. Several studies have shown that UV may not kill developing amphibian embryos but may cause developmental abnormalities and changes in behavior. The quality of the water can greatly affect how much UV penetration occurs and therefore how exposed amphibians may be to UV. Thus, water that is laden with organic material may effectively block out much of the potentially harmful UV radiation. Furthermore, certain pollutants in the water may interact with UV radiation in a way that increases their toxicity to amphibians.

The adverse effects of UV radiation can be enhanced in the presence of toxic substances and pathogens. For example, different species of amphibians show variation in sensitivity to aquatic pollutants known as polycyclic aromatic hydrocarbons (PAHs), which are found in locations contaminated with petroleum products or urban runoff. PAHs are extremely toxic to amphibians when they are simultaneously exposed to UV radiation. For example, one PAH, known as fluoranthene, causes increased mortality in salamanders and frogs as the amount of UV radiation increases.

UV radiation also increases amphibian mortality when a pathogenic fungus known as *Saprolegnia* is present. One major source of *Saprolegnia* is introduced stocked fish that become infected while being reared in hatcheries. It has recently been shown that when infected fish are released into natural lakes and ponds, *Saprolegnia* can be transmitted to amphibians. Other studies have shown that the adverse effects of UV on amphibians are enhanced when the water is acidic.

Malformations and Deformities

Water quality degradation has been linked to severe physical malformations (including missing, malformed, and extra limbs) reported in dozens of amphibian species from diverse aquatic habitats across North America.

Possible causes for these limb deformities include UV radiation, **pesticides** in water, and **parasitic** infection.

One likely scenario for increased malformations is that trematode parasites that cause limb deformities in developing tadpoles have increased with their intermediate snail hosts. Snail populations may have increased with increased algal growth, their main food. In certain regions, lush algal growth may be occurring because of **eutrophication** of water from nitrogen-based fertilizer use on nearby lands.

Obviously, amphibians are being subjected to a variety of human-induced insults that are related to water quality. Special attention must be given to the presence of pollutants, pathogens, and global environmental changes that may affect amphibian growth and development, increase mortality, and eventually lead to unnatural and accelerated population declines. SEE ALSO ACID RAIN; CHEMICALS FROM AGRICULTURE; ECOLOGY, FRESH-WATER; FOREST HYDROLOGY; FRESH WATER, NATURAL COMPOSITION OF; GLOBAL WARMING: AND THE HYDROLOGIC CYCLE; HYDROLOGIC CYCLE; LAKES: BIOLOGICAL PROCESSES; LAKES: CHEMICAL PROCESSES; POLLUTION OF LAKES AND STREAMS; POLLUTION SOURCES: POINT AND NONPOINT; STREAM HEALTH, ASSESSING.

Andrew R. Blaustein

Bibliography

Blaustein, Andrew R. et al. "Effects of Ultraviolet Radiation on Amphibians: Field Experiments." *American Zoologist* 38 (1998):799–812.

Blaustein, Andrew R., and David B. Wake. "The Puzzle of Declining Amphibian Populations." *Scientific American* 272 (1998):52–57.

Boyer, Robin, and Christian E. Grue. "The Need for Water Quality Criteria for Frogs." *Environmental Health Perspectives* 103 (1995):352–357.

Johnson, Pieter T. et al. "Parasite (*Ribeiroia ondatrae*) Infection Linked to Amphibian Malformations in the Western United States." *Ecological Monographs* 72 (2002): 151–168.

Stebbins, Robert C., and Nathan W. Cohen. *A Natural History of Amphibians.* Princeton, NJ: Princeton University Press, 1995.

Internet Resources

Amphibian Declines and Deformities. U.S. Geological Survey. <http://www.usgs.gov/amphibians.html>.

Ancient Civilizations   *See Irrigation Systems, Ancient; Water Works, Ancient.*

Aquaculture

Aquaculture, a type of agriculture, is the practice of cultivating aquatic animals and plants in managed aquatic environments. Aquaculture in salt-water or marine environments is called mariculture. Fish culture, or pisciculture, refers to the **husbandry** of **finfish**. The most popular aquaculture species are finfish grown in fresh waters, accounting for over 40 percent of total aquaculture production (U.S. Department of Agriculture, 1998).

Ancient and Modern Aquaculture

Aquaculture has a long history, but for much of the world it remains somewhat of a novelty, being practiced less than agriculture or **capture fisheries**.

Deformities in amphibians and other aquatic creatures sometimes can be attributed to chemical contaminants. Other causes may include ultraviolet radiation or biological factors such as parasites or infection.

pesticides: a broad group of chemicals that kills or controls plants (herbicides), fungus (fungicides), insects and arachnids (insecticides), rodents (rodenticides), bacteria (bactericides), or other creatures that are considered pests

parasite: an organism that lives within or on another organism, causing harm to the host organism

eutrophication: the process by which lakes and streams become enriched, to varying degrees, by concentrations of nutrients such as nitrogen and phosphorus; enrichment results in increased plant growth (principally algae) and decay, the latter of which reduces the dissolved oxygen content

husbandry: in aquaculture, the rearing and careful management of captively held fish and other aquatic resources

finfish: an aquatic animal with a backbone and fins, as opposed to a shellfish, an aquatic animal without a backbone and with a shell

capture fishery: the removal of aquatic organisms from natural or enhanced waters

Although carp ponds are rooted in antiquity, they are still popular today, and enthusiasts worldwide maintain associations devoted to these fish. Shown here are colorful koi, originally bred from the common grass carp, swimming in a pond at a Japanese garden and teahouse. Carp have religious and cultural significance in Asia and other parts of the world.

carp: a fresh-water fish, from the Family Cyprinidae (the minnow family), with a single back fin and barbels around the mouth, originally from Asia, but now found worldwide in lakes and slow-moving rivers, and farmed for food in large ponds; it prefers warm waters, feeding near the bottom of waters where it stirs up mud and uproots vegatation, often driving out more desirable fish

tilapia: an African fresh-water perch-like fish that has been introduced to many areas for the purpose of food

rainbow trout: a type of trout highly prized as a game fish; native to cold coastal streams and lakes on both sides of the Pacific Ocean and commonly found around the world

Yet as the world demand for fish increases, recent advances in growing fish in captivity have led to a rapid expansion of the aquaculture industry.

During the last 30 years of the twentieth century, aquaculture grew at an average annual rate of 10 percent, and emerged as the only growth sector of the fisheries industry. At the beginning of the twenty-first century, aquaculture's share of total fish production worldwide was 25 percent, and that proportion is projected to increase. Even though the production of fish from capture fisheries has not substantially increased over the past decade (1990s), capture fisheries nevertheless account for a far greater percentage than aquaculture.

Aquaculture's Beginnings. The roots of aquaculture trace back 4,000 years to China where **carp** were cultured, and before that to Egypt where early pictorial depictions dating to 2500 B.C.E. show **tilapia** being fished out of a tank. The earliest known written record of fish culture techniques is attributed to Fan Li, of China, who in 475 B.C.E. described propagation methods, pond construction, and growth characteristics of common carp.

From those early beginnings to the present, common carp is the best understood of all aquaculture species. Common carp reportedly were grown in Europe 2,000 years ago, and, although the ancient Greeks and Romans held fish in ponds, more advanced techniques for breeding and growing fish in managed environments in Europe were first devised 1,000 years ago.

The Japanese, Polynesian Hawaiians, and Mayans were also early practitioners of fish culture. In the United States, nineteenth-century scientists developed techniques for breeding **rainbow trout** in captivity. Rainbow trout have since been transplanted from their native Western U.S. streams to many countries in Europe, Africa, and South and Central America.

Criteria for Commercially Successful Aquaculture

The twentieth century witnessed the science of fish culture unveiling many new methods for growing aquatic animals and plants. Advances in controlled

Although hatcheries serve a wide range of purposes, many cultivate fish species to supplement recreational fishing. This fresh-water hatchery in Indiana supports the state's stocking strategy, and annually cultivates about 30 million walleye eggs. Eggs change in color from bright yellow to black as the fry develop and hatch inside incubating cylinders.

reproduction of desired species, feed formulation, and water quality management have helped generate the rapid growth of aquaculture. The biological selection of culture species depends on many factors. A few criteria that must be considered in choosing a species to cultivate include the following characteristics of a species:

- Growth rate;
- Place in the food chain;
- Climate and environmental adaptations;
- Disease resistance;
- Breeding characteristics;
- Compatibility with other fish species in cultivation; and
- Conversion efficiency (feed-to-flesh).

For example, aquaculturists prefer fast-growing **planktivores** because of their short food chain.

planktivore: a species that eats plankton, the tiny, often microscopic plants and animals floating or drifting in water

Interestingly, biotechnological selection criteria are not always the most critical; for example, growing fish unsuitable for local or export markets can readily drive a farmer out of business. Thus, consumer preference, market conditions, regulations against nonnative species, and other economic, social, and political criteria play an important role in species selection.

crustacean: arthropods with hard shells, jointed bodies, and appendages that primarily live in water; examples are shrimp and lobsters

Diversity of Aquaculture Species

Hundreds of species of finfish, **crustacean**, **mollusks**, and plants are used in aquaculture. Most are finfish species, and many of these are grown as

mollusk: an invertebrate animal with a soft, unsegmented body and usually a shell and a muscular foot; examples are clams, oysters, mussels, and octopuses

food fishes. The most common fresh-water aquaculture species are carp, tilapia, catfish, and trout. Other species are cultivated as **bait fish**, ornamental fish for water gardens and aquaria, sport (game) fish, laboratory fish for experimentation, industrial and medicinal products, and as native fish to mitigate losses to wild fish populations.

In the United States, catfish and trout, grown as food fishes, are by far the most popular aquaculture species. But other species are also commonly grown for food, including salmon, striped bass, and tilapia. Also, there is a small industry for alligators, frogs, turtles, egg seed stock, and ornamental fishes.

Purposes of Aquaculture

Aquaculture is practiced for a number of reasons, chief among them being food production and income generation. Most fresh-water aquaculture production (over 70 percent) comes from low-income, food-deficit countries. Even in the poorest countries, fish farming is seldom solely a subsistence activity. So while farmers may consume some of their product, typically fish are sold, thereby enabling farmers to earn income to purchase other goods and services.

Additional purposes of aquaculture include:

- Utilizing land unsuitable for agriculture;
- Utilizing inland water bodies such as shallow lakes;
- Reclaiming saline soils;
- Increasing the supply of highly valued species;
- Improving the reliability of fish supplied in the marketplace;
- Offsetting losses in the capture fisheries or in native fish populations;
- Servicing the sport fishing industry;
- Controlling parasites like mosquito and snail larvae that cause diseases such as dengue fever and malaria;
- Storing water; and
- Earning foreign exchange. (Europe and the United States import aquaculture products from Asia, Africa, and Central and South America.)

Types of Aquaculture Operations

Aquaculture operations range from small, backyard water gardens to energy-intensive, large commercial farms encompassing hundreds of **hectares**. Aquaculture is sometimes combined with agriculture as in rice–fish farming, or in duck–fish ponds. It is also practiced as **polyculture**, where a variety of species occupying different ecological niches are cultivated together. Aquaculture involves many levels of intensity and complexity, from gravity-fed ponds with little or no inputs, to intensive systems that use **aeration**, supplemental feeds, antibiotics, and genetically modified species.

Systems for rearing fish depend on the environment and the objective of the aquaculture operation. In the United States and worldwide, the most common rearing unit is the pond, although other types of units are also used: cages, **net pens**, flow-through raceways, and recirculation tanks. Efficient farm management and careful water-quality management are keys to

Small skiffs shuttle 80-meter-circumference salmon rearing pens around the harbor at a commercial fish farm in Dover, Tasmania, Australia. Pens must be moved periodically to reduce negative impacts of fish waste on substrate environments below the pens.

a successful operation, regardless of the culture unit. With poor water quality, for example, fish exhibit higher incidence of disease. In addition, poor water quality often yields effluents (wastewater and byproducts) that can have negative environmental effects.

Potential Adverse Effects

Not too long ago, aquaculture was perceived as a cure for hunger and dwindling wild fish supplies. At the end of the twentieth century, given the rapid growth of the aquaculture industry, critics began questioning the real social and environmental impacts of aquaculture. The social impacts are generally felt more acutely in poorer countries. For example, people have been displaced from their homes and jobs by aquaculture operations, sometimes by operations that pollute land and water previously used by local residents.

Aquaculture, like any farming activity, produces effects on the environment. Aquaculture uses energy and creates wastes. As aquaculture replaces wild **habitat**, changes to the **ecosystem** inevitably occur. Even where aquaculture operations are placed in non-pristine areas, potential exists for exotic (nonnative and genetically altered) aquaculture species to escape and adversely affect native species by competing for food and space, interbreeding and hybridizing native species, and spreading disease. Collecting wild larvae for rearing in aquaculture units can decimate native populations of fish, and can affect biodiversity. Toxic and **bioaccumulative** compounds can be harmful to people, including fish farmers themselves, and to plants and animals. Excessive discharge of organic wastes causes pollution.

The environmental impacts of effluents depend on the type of aquaculture practiced, and on farm management. Aquaculture can, in local situations, improve the environment or be environmentally benign. If ponds are properly managed, nutrient-rich discharges (soil and water) can be dredged for use in crop production, thereby reducing the need for soil amendments such as inorganic fertilizers.

habitat: the environment in which a plant or animal grows or lives; the surroundings include physical factors such as temperature, moisture, and light, together with biological factors such as the presence of food and predators

ecosystem: the community of plants and animals within a water or terrestrial habitat interacting together and with their physical and chemical environment

bioaccumulative: describes the increase in concentration of a chemical in organisms that reside in environments contaminated with low concentrations of various organic compounds

vector: an organism such as a biting insect or tick that transmits a parasite or disease from one plant or animal to another

Fish ponds can increase bird populations, which are pleasing to bird-watchers, but are disdained by fish farmers. While poorly managed fish ponds can serve as breeding grounds for **vectors** of animal and human disease, well-managed fish ponds can be used to control these vectors. Thus, fish farm management geared at minimizing negative environmental effects can be critical for balancing the farm's impact on the environment, and for its own long-term success. SEE ALSO AGRICULTURE AND WATER; FISHERIES, FRESH-WATER; FISHERIES, MARINE; MARICULTURE; POLLUTION BY INVASIVE SPECIES.

Hillary S. Egna

Bibliography

Bardach, John, John Ryther, and William O. McLarney. *Aquaculture: The Farming and Husbandry of Freshwater and Marine Organisms.* New York: Wiley–Interscience, 1972.

Egna, Hillary S., and Claude E. Boyd, eds. *Dynamics of Pond Aquaculture.* Boca Raton, FL: CRC Press, 1997.

Pillay, T. V. R. *Aquaculture and The Environment.* New York: Halsted Press, 1992.

Rath, Rajendra Kumar. *Freshwater Aquaculture.* Jodhpur, India: Scientific Publishers, 1993.

Internet Resources

Review of the State of World Aquaculture. FAO Fisheries Department. FAO Fisheries Circular No. 886 FIRI/C886 (Rev.1), Rome, 1997. <http://www.fao.org/docrep/003/w7499e/w7499e00.htm>.

The State of World Fisheries and Aquaculture 1998. United Nations Food and Agriculture Organization, 2000. <http://www.fao.org/docrep/w9900e/w9900e00.htm>.

U.S. Department of Agriculture. *1998 Census of Aquaculture.* <http://www.nass.usda.gov/census/census97/aquaculture/general.htm>.

Aquariums

The pleasure of viewing and contemplating aquatic species has its roots in antiquity. The ancient Egyptians, Romans, and other peoples kept fish in artificial pools. The Chinese selectively bred goldfish from carp. Yet looking down on fish is very different from seeing them eye-to-eye. It was not until the technology of glassmaking advanced to the point where glass plate and large transparent vessels became relatively common products of industrial commerce that fishkeeping became both a popular hobby and, for some, a profession.

The Foundations of Modern Aquariums

With industrialization, increasing portions of the population, especially in larger cities, possessed enough leisure time to support the rise of the great natural history museums, zoos, and circuses of the mid-to-late nineteenth century. Those three kinds of institutions had very different missions, and the tension between their different ways of presenting animals remains evident in aquariums today. Natural history museums conduct scientific research, because classification of collections was their initial concern. Only secondarily were exhibits developed to educate the public. Circuses strive to entertain and astonish audiences—the more that animals could be trained to mimic human behaviors, the better. In their early years, zoos' focus on exhibiting captive animals by category left only rudimentary thought for animals' needs and the natural habitats from which they had been taken.

$20,000 Aquarium at Venice, Cal.

This postcard from 1909 depicts the aquarium in Venice, California. Originally built in that year for $20,000, the aquarium later became the marine biological station for the University of Southern California.

As for the first aquatic gardens or aquariums, a few were constructed in basements of natural history museums, whereas some were more or less the extension of circuses. For instance, in New York and Boston, P. T. Barnum operated aquarium displays that included trained seals and beluga whales as well as fish in tanks. Other displays occupied a portion of municipal zoos, or were separately administered by the same city agencies. During both the Great Depression (1929–1939) and World War II (1939–1945), many urban areas, along with their zoos and aquariums, went into decline.

Renewal of Public Interest in Aquariums

The mid-twentieth century saw the rise of oceanographic parks emphasizing dolphins and sea lions trained through the behaviorist techniques then dominating psychology. Jacques Cousteau's television series gave the public an entirely new view of underwater life. In response to the public's heightened awareness and new expectations, aquarium managers began to respond with displays that, with increasing sophistication, replicated **coral reefs** and the habitats of fish and other aquatic animals.

coral reef: a resistant marine ridge or mound consisting chiefly of compacted coral together with algal material and biochemically deposited magnesium and calcium carbonates

The New England Aquarium, completed in 1969 in Boston, Massachusetts, was the first aquarium constructed from the ground up to replicate natural habitats. An opportunity for children to touch living sea stars and other hardy local tide-pool invertebrates became a signature exhibit. Its near-immediate success as a tourist attraction helped reverse the decline of the city's waterfront, leading to similar efforts in other cities and the refurbishment of many established aquariums throughout the United States and abroad.

The Modern Aquarium and its Newfound Roles

Today's aquariums are in stark contrast to those of 50 years ago. Scientific research, stewardship, and education are key values supported by both large and small operations.

Study and Management.   Many aquariums include scientific research staff, as do zoos and natural history museums. Early research focused on classification, behavior, and **husbandry** of individual species. Contemporary

husbandry: in aquaculture, the rearing and careful management of captively held fish and other aquatic resources

In New South Wales, Australia, visitors to Sydney Aquarium's open ocean display watch a shark swim overhead. Modern aquariums engage visitors through creative and interactive display designs not possible in early aquariums.

captive breeding: the artificial propagation or maintenance of animals in captivity

stakeholder: an individual or group affected by a potential decision or action; term is usually associated with a limited number of individuals representing the interests of other like-minded individuals or groups

research tends to focus on the holistic management of natural systems. Study and management of water quality is a priority for exhibition of species that both excrete and respire (breathe) in water. Recognition of the need to think systemically about human impacts on aquatic wildlife has led investigators to focus on protection of species that are vanishing from the wild due to overfishing and habitat loss. **Captive breeding** programs are now important to preserve endangered animals. Success reflects increasing skill at meeting the unique needs of diverse aquatic species.

Stewardship.   Vast though they seem, our waters are under relentless, if often unintentional, attack. Major threats include pesticide and fertilizer runoff from lawns and farms, pollutants generated by long-distance automotive commutes, idle littering of cigarette butts, escaped party balloons, spent fishing line, excess packaging, and other nearly indestructible plastic garbage, which is ingested by or entangles thousands of aquatic creatures each year.

At many aquariums, conservation officers work to build **stakeholder** coalitions and prevent destruction of the world's natural heritage, only a small fragment of which can be represented in aquarium displays. Development of the public's sense of stewardship has become a priority as what was once deemed a curiosity—the ability to sustain a slice of ocean in a glass box—threatens to become a last sanctuary for aquatic species.

Education.   Along with research and conservation, education is a third mission today's aquariums strongly support. Most aquariums have a sizable and well-trained corps of volunteer educators eager to interpret exhibits for visitors. Volunteer work is the leading path to careers in the aquarium field.

In an effort to portray aspects of the aquatic world that do not lend themselves to tank displays, aquariums increasingly incorporate multimedia interactive exhibits, including some that do not require actual species on display. For example, Monterey Bay Aquarium (in Monterey Bay, California) and Mystic Marine Life Aquarium (in Mystic, Connecticut) are among aquariums featuring submersibles capable of transmitting data and video imagery from extreme depths.

Interested people who call or write to aquarium personnel are likely to be showered with learning resources. Resources include videotapes, websites, and worksheets for preparing groups coming on school visits. Moreover, aquariums frequently offer curriculum and hands-on science materials through a library or teacher's center, similar to zoos and natural history museums. For a fee, many aquariums come out to schools with traveling exhibits and dramatic programs.

Most aquariums can now be found on the Internet, with live cameras taking people on virtual tours, as well as interactive games and catalogs of gift shop and educational materials. Aquarium personnel frequently lead tours to local and exotic aquatic sites. Events of all kinds are hosted, including camps and overnight programs as well as weddings, corporate meetings, public forums, and other celebrations. Low-income communities often qualify for pass programs, grants, and scholarships. While most visitors come looking for large, fierce, or colorful species and visit during weekends and vacations when the atmosphere is at its most exciting, contemplative individuals choose quiet afternoons during the school year. Such moments can do much to deepen understandings of the aquatic world. SEE ALSO AQUACULTURE; BIVALVES; CAREERS IN ENVIRONMENTAL EDUCATION; CORALS AND CORAL REEFS; COUSTEAU, JACQUES; CRUSTACEANS; ENDANGERED SPECIES ACT; FISH; FISHES, CARTILAGINOUS; MARINE MAMMALS; POLLUTION OF THE OCEAN BY PLASTIC AND TRASH; REPTILES; SUBMARINES AND SUBMERSIBLES.

Joel S. Rubin

Bibliography

Hein, George E. *Learning in the Museum.* New York: Routledge, 1998.

Ryan, Gerald. *Forgotten Aquariums of Boston.* Boston, MA: New England Aquarium, 1997.

Spotte, Stephen H. *Fish and Invertebrate Culture.* New York: John Wiley & Sons, 1970.

Taylor, Leighton. *Aquariums: Windows to Nature.* New York: Prentice Hall, 1993.

Aquifer Characteristics

Groundwater is stored in the open spaces and fractures within geologic materials such as soil, sand, and rock that occur beneath the land surface. Aquifers are the geologic layers that are filled with water and that can transmit enough water to supply a well under normal **hydraulic gradients**.

Aquifer Types

Geologic materials can be classified as consolidated rock or unconsolidated (loose) sediment. Consolidated rock may consist of such materials as sandstone,

hydraulic gradient: the change in hydraulic head between two points (e.g., the difference in water level between two points divided by the distance between the two points)

shale, granite, and basalt. Unconsolidated sediment contains granular material such as sand, gravel, silt, and clay. The four major types of aquifers are:

- Alluvium (sand, gravel, and silt deposited by rivers);
- Sedimentary bedrock (consolidated sediments);
- Glacial sediments (unconsolidated material deposited by **glaciers**); and
- **Igneous** or **metamorphic** bedrock.

Groundwater Movement. Groundwater in gravel, silt, and sand aquifers is found in pore spaces between the particles, whereas groundwater in consolidated aquifers is found in fractures within the rock. The amount of water a given type of rock can hold depends on the rock's porosity, which is the volume of pore space between the grains of the sediment or fractures in the rock.

For water to move through rock, the pore spaces must be connected. Groundwater flows very slowly within the aquifer, and the speed of groundwater movement depends on the size of the spaces within the soil or rock, how well these spaces are connected, and the slope (or pressure gradient) of the **water table**.

Permeability. Coarse-grained sediments like sand and gravel have a higher porosity than small-grained sediments like clay and silt, and the pore spaces are better connected. The coarse-grained materials are permeable because they have large connected spaces or fractures that allow water to flow through.

In some cases, pore spaces can be filled by smaller-grained materials, which makes less room for water to enter and travel through the pore spaces. This decreases the porosity, and the aquifer will be less permeable. It is important to be able to determine aquifer characteristics like permeability in order to predict groundwater behavior in the aquifer.

Well Reports and Pump Tests

Some aquifer characteristics can be estimated from the data found in well reports (drillers' logs). The **static water level**, location of water-bearing zones, geologic materials, and pump test data are examined to obtain information such as aquifer depth, thickness, and nature. The description and location of geologic formations and water-bearing zones within the formations can give clues as to whether an aquifer is shallow (water is located near the land surface) or deep (water is located deeper, perhaps greater than 30 meters, or 100 feet), and whether it is made of consolidated or unconsolidated materials.

The nature of the aquifer refers to whether the aquifer is confined or unconfined. A confined aquifer has a layer of less porous material above the aquifer, resulting in the groundwater being under pressure. When a well is drilled, the water level in the well will rise above the top of the aquifer. An unconfined aquifer does not have a layer of less porous rock above it, and so when a well is drilled, the water level in the well will be at the same level as the top of the aquifer.

Pump Tests. Well drillers conduct pump tests to determine the performance characteristics of a well and to determine the hydraulic properties of

glacier: a huge mass of ice, formed on land by the compaction and recrystallization of snow, which moves slowly downslope or outward owing to its own weight

igneous: rock that solidified from molten (magma) material; the rock is extrusive (or volcanic) if it solidifies on the surface and intrusive (or plutonic) if it solidifies beneath the surface

metamorphic: describes a rock or mineral that formed under the process of metamorphism

water table: the upper surface of the zone of saturation in an unconfined aquifer below which all voids in rock, sediment, and other geologic materials are saturated (completely filled) with water

static water level: the level of water in a well that is not being affected by withdrawal of groundwater

the aquifer such as permeability and transmissivity (aquifer permeability multiplied by aquifer thickness). These properties determine how easily water moves through the aquifer, how much water is stored, and how efficiently the well produces water. Pump tests can allow hydrologists to predict the effect on water levels of different pumping rates, or the addition of one or more pumping wells.

A pump test consists of pumping a well at a certain rate and recording the drawdown (decline) of water level in the pumping well and in nearby observation wells over a certain time period. The responses of the water levels at and near the pumping well reflect the aquifer's ability to transmit water to the well. The response allows hydrogeologists to determine the aquifer's characteristics. Water levels will drop less in more permeable aquifers than in aquifers of lower permeability. Ideally, water levels are measured at predetermined time intervals at the pumping well and nearby observation wells.

When a well is pumped, the water level drops in the vicinity of the well as that water moves from the aquifer toward the well (see the figure below). The lowering of the water level is referred to as drawdown. From a three-dimensional viewpoint, it appears as though a cone pointing down has surrounded the well. This is termed the "cone of depression." The size of the drawdown cone depends on several factors: the pump rate, the length of time the well is pumped, and aquifer characteristics of permeability and transmissivity. Once the well stops pumping, it will take some time before the drawdown cone disappears and the water table returns back to its original state. In the figure below, note that the drawdown at Observation Well 1 (OW1), located away from the pumping well, is less than the drawdown at the pumping well (Q).

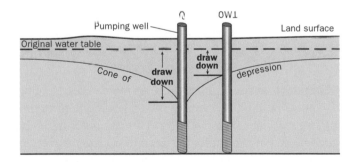

The two most common types of pumping tests are the constant-rate pump test and the multiple-step pump test. In the constant-rate test, the well is pumped over a given time period at one rate, whereas during the step-drawdown test, the well is pumped at successively greater rates over short periods of time. The drawdown of water levels in a well are plotted against the time since pumping began for both constant-rate and step tests. The data from both of these tests can be used to predict the hydraulic characteristics of the aquifer and the well.

During the constant rate pump test (see part (a) on page 42), pumping levels are held constant and the progressive drawdown with time is recorded. The relation between drawdown and time is a function of the aquifer permeability. During the step test (see part (b) on page 42), the pumping level is held constant during any one step, but is increased during each successive step. The step test not only can be used to obtain aquifer characteristics, but also is useful in determining the size of the pump that is to be placed in the well. Note the water-level recovery portion in each graph. The rate at which recovery to the original pre-pumping water occurs depends on aquifer properties.

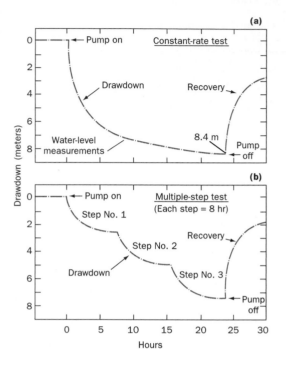

There are several methods for interpreting pump test data, including graphical and computer techniques. Over the past decade, computer techniques have replaced more traditional graphical techniques for data interpretation, but hydrogeologists still rely on graphical analysis to examine trends in groundwater withdrawal and also to predict how an aquifer reacts to pumping over time.

In order to interpret the results of the pump test, hydrogeologists need data such as aquifer thickness, screened interval, pumping rate, static water level before pumping, and static water level during pumping. These data are input into a computer program and the computer generates aquifer parameters such as the specific capacity of the well, hydraulic conductivity, and transmissivity. These results are then available to be used to assist in the management of groundwater quantity in a number of settings (e.g., municipal wells or irrigation). Aquifer and well characteristics also can be measured after pumping ceases as the water table recovers, providing before-and-after datasets that can offer greater reliability. SEE ALSO GROUNDWATER; HYDROGEOLOGIC MAPPING; MODELING GROUNDWATER FLOW AND TRANSPORT; SUPPLIES, EXPLORATION FOR GROUNDWATER; WELLS AND WELL DRILLING.

Kimberly J. Swanson

Bibliography

Driscoll, Fletcher G. *Groundwater and Wells*, 2nd ed. St. Paul, MN: Johnson Division, 1987.

Fetter, Charles Willard. *Applied Hydrogeology*, 3rd ed. Englewood Cliffs, NJ: Prentice Hall, 1988.

Ground Water. U.S. Geological Survey General Interest Publication.

Heath, Ralph C. *Basic Ground-Water Hydrology.* U.S. Geological Survey Water-Supply Paper 2220 (1989).

Waller, Roger M. *Ground Water and the Rural Homeowner.* U.S. Geological Survey General Interest Publication.

Archaeology, Underwater

The development of lightweight sophisticated diving equipment since World War II (from 1939 to 1945) has made underwater archaeology a flourishing branch of archaeology. The science of underwater archaeology involves the recovery and study of submerged archaeological finds and sites, including ancient **springs** and wells, lakeside settlements, and marine sites such as sunken cities, harbors, and shipwrecks.

Time Capsules

Underwater surveys and excavations of, for example, sunken ships and their cargo provide enormous information about ancient societies. Sunken artifacts are often well preserved, protected by layers of **silt** in a stable environment of salt or fresh water. As a result, underwater archaeological finds and sites provide particularly valuable insights into ancient times, since they constitute "time capsules" of brief historical moments.

England.   In the early nineteenth century, English divers made a living by searching the waters around Portsmouth for shipwrecks. These early underwater explorations were accomplished using primitive diving bells, suits, and helmets.

Switzerland.   Some of the earliest scientific underwater investigations occurred during the middle nineteenth century in Switzerland. Recently, wooden house posts were exposed when the water level of Lake Geneva was extremely low. Excavations revealed the remains of a Neolithic (latter part of the Stone Age) lakeside settlement that had been submerged by the rising water level of the lake. The prehistoric remains confirmed the succession of the three archaeological ages: Stone, Bronze, and Iron.

Turkey.   In a comprehensive underwater archaeological project from 1983 to 1994, a team led by American archaeologist George Bass and Turkish archaeologist Cemal Pulak recovered a heavy cargo of a Bronze Age ship at Uluburun, off the southern coast of Turkey. The ship that was wrecked in a storm c. 1310 B.C.E. carried enough tin and copper ingots to forge military weapons for several hundred people.

Mediterranean Breakthroughs

The earliest breakthroughs in underwater archaeology techniques were made in the Mediterranean, where pioneers like George Bass showed the potential of the technique by scientifically excavating ancient and more-recent ships. These breakthroughs are now standard procedures all over the world and in all climates.

Research Team.   A nuclear submarine built for the Cold War (1945–1989) and an underwater remotely operated vehicle (ROV) allowed oceanographers,

spring: location where a concentrated, natural discharge of groundwater emerges from the Earth's subsurface as a definite flow onto the surface of the land or into a body of surface water, such as a lake, river, or ocean

silt: a sediment wherein the individual particles range in size from 0.004 to 0.625 millimeters (0.00015 to 0.02 inches); smaller than a sand particle but larger than a clay particle

Bulky dive suits were used in early explorations of the 1915 wreck of the *Lusitania.* The ocean liner was sunk by a German U-boat off the southern coast of Ireland, killing 1,959 aboard and influencing the course of World War I.

Robert Ballard stands in front of the *DSV Turtle* research submarine (short for Diving Support Vehicle), on display in 1999 at the Mystic Aquarium in Mystic, Connecticut. The *Turtle*, retired in 1991 by the U.S. Navy, was a sister submarine to the *DSV Alvin*, which provided the first glimpses of the *Titanic* wreck site in 1985.

ATLANTIS

The tradition that a lost land of Atlantis once flourished has fascinated popular imagination. Some oceanographers theorize that Atlantis was once located in the Mediterranean Sea. Some predictions are based on archaeological discoveries from the Greek island Thera that experienced a gigantic volcanic eruption around 1640 B.C.E. Other theories are based on archaeological discoveries from the islands of Crete and Malta.

The Ancient Mediterranean Research Association has conducted investigations in Spain and in the Mediterranean since 1972. This research suggests that a part of Atlantis, as described by Plato in the "Timaeus" and "Critias," is submerged under 60 meters (200 feet) of water near the Straits of Gibraltar.

The small, rocky island of Malta has ancient structures that are dated c. 7000 B.C.E., the world's oldest stone ruins. Malta shows evidence of having been destroyed in a cataclysmic Atlantic wave that filled the Mediterranean. The island is too small to be Atlantis, but data show that the Mediterranean was a different place thousands of years ago.

archaeologists, and engineers in the mid-1990s to retrieve 115 artifacts from eight ships sunk to the bottom of the Mediterranean Sea, including five ancient Roman ships.

The expedition leader, oceanographer Robert Ballard of the Institute for Exploration in Mystic, Connecticut, first discovered one of the shipwrecks in 1988. Using the powerful sonar system of the U.S. Navy's *NR-1* nuclear submarine, Ballard and his research team found three more of the wrecks in 1995 and four in 1997. Artifacts on and around the wrecks indicated that one Roman sailing ship dated from the late second or early first century B.C.E., verifying it as one of the oldest Roman ships ever found. The shipwrecks also included four other Roman vessels from the first few centuries C.E., and three ships from the eighteenth and nineteenth centuries.

The wrecks, located west of Sicily in 762 meters (2,500 feet) of water, were the largest grouping of ancient ships ever found in deep water. The explorers believe that the five Roman ships sank in storms while following a high seas trade route between Rome and the ancient North African city of Carthage (located near the modern city of Tunis). This information corrected the previous archaeological belief that Roman ships followed coastal routes, rather than venturing out on the high seas.

The research team recovered artifacts using the *ROV Jason* and a remote-controlled arm on the submarine. Items retrieved from the oldest ship, which was about 30 meters (100 feet) long, included bronze vessels; at least eight types of pottery jars ("amphoras") for carrying and storing olive oil, preserved fruit, and wine; kitchen items; and two pieces of anchors.

Ballard's team focused on mapping all the wrecks and retrieving selected artifacts from each ship. With this method, the researchers could widen their investigation and learn about all the ships, spending about the same amount of time and money as would have been involved in excavating only one wreck completely. Archaeologists say this strategy works well for deep-water wrecks that are likely to remain well preserved. Wrecks in shallow water, however, are subject to damage from looting, from **coral** overgrowth, and from being destroyed on **reefs** by waves and tides.

Methods of Study

Underwater archaeology uses special methods to study underwater archaeological sites, including shipwrecks. Archaeologists who work underwater rely on elaborate diving and excavating equipment and employ special techniques to preserve perishable materials that have been submerged for long periods. For instance, the Tudor warship *Mary Rose* (within Henry VIII's fleet) had to be carefully excavated from the Solent seabed off southern England after scientists discovered that it and its fascinating artifacts had been substantially preserved.

Locals whose fishing nets get caught on underwater obstructions commonly locate sites. Divers searching for sponges have found many sites. Other sites are revealed through the dredging of rivers and harbors. Survey techniques that are used on land can also be applied underwater. Surveying underwater has been revolutionized by the use of GPS (Global Positioning Systems) in which receivers pick up signals from a set of satellites that regularly orbit the Earth; the satellites provide extremely precise location data for the sites.

Poor visibility, large tides, cold weather, and problems associated with increased depths can make underwater excavation difficult. Because of these problems, expensive support ships are often anchored above the site. With the correct equipment, divers can work underwater for relatively long periods of time.

Many excavation techniques used on land are adapted for use underwater. For instance, grids can be laid out to help in mapping the site and marking the location of objects, and to assist the divers as they excavate. Recording, drawing, mapping, and photography are performed with instruments that can be used underwater.

Underwater video cameras are widely used in conjunction with computers for photographic surveying and three-dimensional (3-D) recording. This system is incorporated into GIS (Geographic Information Systems) that builds a static picture of the water landscape under study from a combination of photographs, maps, physical surveys, sites and monuments records, field surveys, and excavations.

Various techniques are used to lift objects and **sediments**: air bags are used to raise baskets of objects, while air pipes suction up debris and sediments. Heavy objects weigh less underwater, and divers can sometimes lift them up to the ship. Post-excavation work begins on research ships and continues at land-based laboratories.

Trained professionals conduct underwater archaeology with the use of lightweight **scuba** gear that provides divers with the maneuverability and independence to properly survey and excavate archaeological sites. Sites are first located using historical documents or local informers. Remote sensing devices, such as a proton magnetometer or an underwater camera, can then focus onto the site.

coral: a marine organism that lives in colonies and excretes an external, calcium carbonate skeleton; groups of these anthozoan coelenterates often form large reefs in tropical seas

reef: a strip or ridge of rocks, sand, or coral that rises to, or near the surface of a body of water

sediment: rock particles and other earth materials that are transported and deposited over time by geologic agents such as running water, wind, glaciers, and gravity; sediments may be exposed on dry land and are common on ocean and lake bottoms and river beds

scuba: an apparatus for breathing underwater consisting of a portable canister of compressed air and a mouthpiece; the acronym for self-contained underwater breathing apparatus

MARINE AND FRESH-WATER SHIPWRECKS

The wrecks of the *Titanic* and the *Empress of Ireland* represent similar tragedies in different water environments. The *Titanic* sank in 1912 about 531 kilometers (350 miles) southeast of Newfoundland in the North Atlantic, killing 1,522. The wreck remained undiscovered until 1985; and in 1998, a large section of its outer hull was raised from a depth of 3,810 meters (nearly 2.4 miles).

In 1914, the Canadian steamship *Empress of Ireland* sank in about 40 meters (130 feet) of water in the St. Lawrence River. The death toll was 1,012. Like the *Titanic*, the *Empress of Ireland* was "rediscovered" in the mid-1980s, but its story and underwater recovery efforts never achieved the *Titanic's* fame.

Today's advanced instrumentation, improved access to data and documentation, and lightweight scuba gear gives underwater researchers the ability to pinpoint their dives and maneuver freely about an archaeological site. These divers, working on an eleventh-century ship that sunk off the coast of Turkey, tag the artifacts before they are brought to the surface for examination and restoration.

EDMUND FITZGERALD

Between 1989 and 1995, the Great Lakes Shipwreck Historical Society conducted three underwater expeditions to the 1975 wreck of the *Edmund Fitzgerald,* an ore carrier that sunk in Lake Superior. The ship's 200-pound bronze bell was recovered in 1995. A special underwater cutting torch was used to separate the bell from the roof of the pilothouse.

Excavation requires as much care in recording and removal as traditional field archaeology. In fact, more care is required with the additional hazards associated while working underwater. During the recovery process all recovered artifacts must be efficiently treated to slow down or stop deterioration as they are exposed to the air.

Knowledge Gained

Underwater excavation is important because of the knowledge that is gained from the investigations. For example, the study of shipwrecks shows how shipbuilding developed from small prehistoric dugout canoes to the large warships of the sixteenth century and later. Excavations of shipwrecks have also greatly increased the knowledge of maritime trade routes during the Bronze Age (the period over 3,500 years ago), and in later Greek, Roman, and medieval times. Organic materials such as leather, food, clothing, and wood, often are better preserved underwater and provide valuable information that is oftentimes lacking on most land sites. SEE ALSO SUBMARINES AND SUBMERSIBLES.

William Arthur Atkins

Bibliography

Ballard, Robert D., with Rick Archbold. *Lost Liners.* New York: Hyperion, 1998.

McIntosh, Jane. *The Practical Archaeologist: How We Know What We Know About the Past,* 2nd ed. New York: Facts on File, Inc., 1999.

Internet Resources

Keiger, John. "The Underwater World of George Bass." *Humanities and the Arts, Johns Hopkins Magazine.* <http://www.jhu.edu/~jhumag/0497web/bass.html>.

Underwater Archaeology. (translated from French to English) Department of Subaqueous and Underwater Archaeological Research of the Subdirectorate of Archaeology. <http://www.culture.fr/culture/archeosm/en/>.

Vikdahl, Anders. *What is Underwater Archaeology?* Nordic Underwater Archaeology. <http://www.abc.se/~m10354/uwa/whatis.htm>.

Army Corps of Engineers, U.S.

The Continental Congress in June 1775 organized what later became the U.S. Army Corps of Engineers (ACE) when it authorized an engineer and two assistants to prepare fortifications for the Battle of Bunker Hill. Engineers were further organized in 1779, but it was not until after the Revolutionary War that the Corps was permanently established, in 1802. Thus, the Army Corps of Engineers, located within the Department of Defense, is the nation's oldest water resource agency, dealing primarily with the construction and maintenance of **navigable** streams and harbors.

Nineteenth Century

The Corps contributed to both civilian and military constructions (e.g., lighthouses, coastal fortifications, and harbors) when national defense and commercial transportation were determined to be interdependent. Many historians claim that the greatest accomplishment of the early Corps was its work on forming a reliable transportation system within the expanding United States, via activities such as mapping navigation channels and building canals and harbors.

The General Survey Act (1824) authorized the Corps to formulate surveys for waterways that were of commercial or military importance, or were used for mail delivery. The Corps was assigned to improve navigation on the Ohio and Mississippi Rivers, and later on the Missouri River. The Corps' work on the interior transportation system of the country was a vital foundation for economic development and westward expansion.

Twentieth Century

The Corps' efforts to improve waterway navigation continued with the deepening of the Chesapeake and Delaware Canal (1926) that eventually became a part of the intercoastal waterway connecting waterbodies from Massachusetts to Florida and westward to the Rio Grande River. Construction and maintenance of canals, locks, and other structures continued, along with important surveys of the Great Lakes and Mississippi Delta. The principal national expenditure up to this time period was directed at **levee** construction.

Dam Regulations. The country's water resources became a concern during the beginning of the century due to neglected waterways, increased **hydropower** demands, and additional western **irrigation** projects. Numerous dams were constructed when studies showed that hydroelectric power was an efficient use of water. However, it was also concluded that dams threatened waterway navigation. As a result, Congress delegated the Corps to regulate dam construction.

navigable: in general usage, describes a waterbody deep and wide enough to afford passage to small and large vessels; also can be used in the context of a specific statutory or regulatory designation

THE GALLATIN REPORT

In 1802, Albert Gallatin delivered a Congressional report outlining his plan to improve the U.S. transportation system. Called the Gallatin Report (1808), it listed improvements to roads and canals connecting northern and southern states, northern states to the Great Lakes, and eastern states with western areas.

levee: a natural or artifically-made earthen obstruction along the edge of a stream, lake, or river; also, a long, low embankment usually built to restrain the flow of water out of a river bank and to protect land from flooding

hydropower: power, typically electrical energy, produced by utilizing falling water

irrigation: the controlled application of water for agricultural or other purposes through human-made systems; generally refers to water application to soil when rainfall is insufficient to maintain desirable soil moisture for plant growth

The U.S. Army Corps of Engineers continues to play a key role in maintaining navigation on the nation's major waterways. Here an ore carrier passes through the locks of Soo Locks, which connect Lake Superior and Lake Huron.

The Rivers and Harbors Acts (1890 and 1899) required that construction plans and specific dam sites be approved by the Corps, while the General Dam Act (1906) forced dam owners to construct, operate, and maintain their facilities in specific ways. During the 1930s, the Corps participated in three major hydroelectric projects: Passamaquoddy Tidal Power (Maine), Bonneville Dam (Columbia River), and Fort Peck Dam (Missouri River).

Flood Control Measures. The failures of an uncoordinated levee system was recognized as early as 1879, when the Mississippi River Commission was created to undertake flood control planning on the lower Mississippi. Despite this Commission, the existing levee-based flood control system was proven to be inadequate when two major floods in 1912–1913 and another one in 1916 flooded the lower Mississippi River valley.

These floods caused significant economic damages and human suffering. Damages to property and commerce were quite costly. And these were recurring events. When over 16 million acres in the lower Mississippi River valley were flooded again in 1928, Congress passed flood control legislation and gave a role to the Corps in its implementation.

Floods continued to cause substantial damage, and, with severe flooding events on the Ohio River, Congress passed the 1936 Flood Control Act. Until this time, Congress had been hesitant to create a strong role for the federal government in floodplain management. This act declared flood control to be acceptable federal government activity and authorized more than two hundred construction projects. Under the act, both the Corps and the Department of Agriculture shared responsibility for these activities.

This legislation was a significant event in Corps history for two reasons. First, it authorized physical structures as the means to control floods, and these construction activities were historically the Corps' expertise. Second, it was the first significant federal use of the cost–benefit ratio as a decision-making criterion. The act includes the famous provision that "the benefits to whomsoever they accrue exceed the costs" and launched the use of **cost–benefit analysis** for water projects. This economically based decision-making criterion spurred the Corps' involvement in water resources planning.

cost–benefit analysis: an analytical technique that is used to guide policymakers by computing the present discounted value of benefits and costs for a set of policy alternatives

The Flood Control Act (1944) allowed the Corps to build multiple-purpose reservoirs, mainly for irrigation, navigation, water supply, hydropower, and recreation.

Electrical Output. After 1945, additional multipurpose hydroelectric projects were built on the Columbia and Snake Rivers in the Pacific Northwest, and the Missouri and the Arkansas Rivers. By 1975, Corps projects were producing 27 percent of the total U.S. hydropower and 4.4 percent of all electrical energy output.

Today

The Corps is an organization that has historically built water infrastructure. The Corps' current regulatory mission is a natural result of its historical mission and society's changing needs. Environmental considerations are becoming increasingly important to the Corps' activities. Public controversies over structural projects have pressured the Corps to account for the environmental impacts of its construction activities and to widen its consideration of nonstructural approaches to solve water problems.

The Corps continues to be involved in ongoing controversies related to its activities, and these conflicts are indicative of the evolution that water planning and management is undergoing. The Corps has historically played an important role in water management, and will continue to do so as its mission and mandates change. SEE ALSO BALANCING DIVERSE INTERESTS; BUREAU OF RECLAMATION, U.S.; CANALS; COST–BENEFIT ANALYSIS; DAMS; FLOODPLAIN MANAGEMENT; HYDROELECTRIC POWER; INFRASTRUCTURE, WATER-SUPPLY; PLANNING AND MANAGEMENT, HISTORY OF WATER RESOURCES; PORTS AND HARBORS; RIVER BASIN PLANNING; TRANSPORTATION; WHITE, GILBERT.

William Arthur Atkins and Faye Anderson

Bibliography

National Research Council. *New Directions in Water Resources Planning for the U.S. Army Corps of Engineers.* Washington, D.C.: National Academy Press, 1999.

Shallat, Todd, and William H. Goetzmann, eds. *Structures in the Stream: Water, Science, and the Rise of the U.S. Army Corps of Engineers.* Austin: University of Texas Press, 1994.

Internet Resources

ACE Institute for Water Resources. <http://www.iwr.usace.army.mil/>.

Brief History. Office of History, U.S. Army Corps of Engineers. <http://www.hq .usace.army.mil/history/brief.htm>.

Artificial Recharge

Water-supply development is challenging. Increasing demands for water joined with concerns for environmental protection require a variety of new water management tools. Such a tool for the **conjunctive use** of surface water and **groundwater** supplies is the artificial recharge (AR) of groundwater. Application and benefits are worldwide.

Artificial recharge of groundwater is the process of adding water to an **aquifer** through human effort. Many different techniques and purposes exist for causing AR, but this discussion focuses on augmentation of a water

conjunctive use: the planned use of water from different sources, usually surface and groundwater sources, to optimize the benefit from available supplies

groundwater: generally, all subsurface (underground) water, as distinct from surface water, that supplies natural springs, contributes to permanent streams, and can be tapped by wells; specifically, the water that is in the saturated zone of a defined aquifer

aquifer: a water-saturated, permeable, underground rock formation that can transmit significant quantities of water under ordinary hydraulic gradients to wells and springs

supply for later use. Projects are varied but usually involve storing surplus surface water in an aquifer for later use. Recovery (withdrawal) of the stored underground water commonly is by wells.

Aquifer storage and recovery is a special type of artificial recharge of groundwater that uses dual-purpose wells for both injecting water into the aquifer and recovering (withdrawing) it later. Although the intent of AR generally is to increase groundwater storage for later use, incidental activities such as excess irrigation, **stormwater** disposal, canal leakage, and leaking water pipes may also result in AR.

Artificial recharge and aquifer storage and recovery are valuable water management tools that effectively help to offset increased demands for water. The variety of techniques, methods, and circumstances for these processes is vast and expanding.

Artificial Recharge

Artificial recharge requires some form of man-made structure. Surface spreading techniques involve keeping water at the surface in areas where the water can percolate down to a shallow, unconfined aquifer. Spreading basins, check dams in stream channels, furrows, trenches, and ditches are common AR examples (see Figure 1).

Surface spreading areas require periodic maintenance since the suspended sediment in the source water will settle out, clog the surface of the recharge area, and reduce the recharge rate. **Microbial** growth in the shallow soils also causes clogging. Many countries and most western states within the United States possess some AR projects that use some form of surface spreading techniques.

Injection techniques use wells to accomplish AR. Injection wells usually place water directly into a deep, confined aquifer where surface spreading would usually not work. Injection wells also require maintenance to remove particles, microbial growth, and chemical precipitates (solid substances).

stormwater: runoff from precipitation events in which precipitation rate exceeds infiltration rate or falls directly on an impermeable surface; stormwater often is discharged directly to streams and may carry pollutants such as bacteria, petroleum products, metals, etc.

microbe: a microscopic organism, or microorganism; the term encompasses viruses, bacteria, yeast, molds, protozoa, and small algae

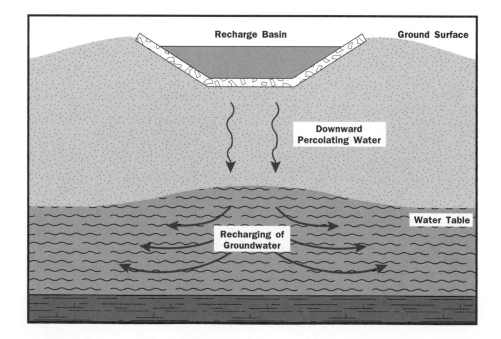

Figure 1. Generalized cross-section of artificial recharge of groundwater using a surface spreading technique.

Injection wells are used in many countries. For example, such wells have been an important part of the water supply system in Israel since 1956. Society generally views the various AR structures as a more environmentally acceptable way to manage water rather than building dams for more surface storage. Yet the use of AR in any location still must overcome a variety of technical, legal, and financial obstacles.

Artificial recharge provides a tool to maintain or increase reliable water supplies. In some areas, agriculture and other uses have resulted in serious groundwater depletion. AR is important in these locations as a means of stabilizing the supply and sustaining withdrawals by wells. A large project in Los Angeles County, California recharges an annual average of 308 billion liters (80 billion gallons, or 250,000 acre-feet).

In some coastal areas, groundwater depletion can reverse the natural movement of groundwater to the sea and cause **saltwater intrusion** of the aquifer inland. In this case, AR provides a valuable hydraulic barrier that will likely prevent water quality degradation.

Site selection for AR is critical. Some aquifers hold little or no potential for successful AR projects, whereas others have great potential. Ideally, an aquifer will hold, store, and transmit desired amounts of recharge water without significant migration and chemical degradation of that water. In addition, the **permeability** of shallow earth materials should not limit the **infiltration** by surface spreading. Site investigation for AR should include **hydrogeologic** mapping of the aquifer to identify aquifer characteristics. Advanced techniques would use computer simulations for modeling groundwater flow and transport.

Water availability is often the most important consideration for the timing of AR. This occurs when the supply from the source is abundant and exceeds other demands. In most cases this involves strong seasonal weather-related influences, but it can also result during peak flow events or unusually wet years. Typically, AR by spreading techniques uses untreated surface water as its source. Injection techniques have used untreated water, treated drinking water, or reclaimed water, as appropriate for the site-specific conditions. The injection of reclaimed wastewater is a more constant supply and less dependent on seasonal availability.

Aquifer Storage and Recovery

Aquifer storage and recovery (ASR) may be defined as the storage of water in an aquifer through a well during times when water is available, and later recovery of the water from the same well (see Figure 2). ASR is a specific type of AR that involves **potable** water. The technique provides for specific placement of water in the aquifer and recovery of essentially the same water. Ideally, the recovered water will remain potable and not require additional treatment. ASR is generally pursued by cities.

ASR can occur in saline (salty) or **brackish** aquifers. This is possible when the potable injection water displaces, rather than mixes with, the natural water. Some mixing on the fringes of the stored water does take place and reduces the quality of some of the recovered water. ASR pilot testing is important to identify the chemical changes associated with any aquifer.

BENEFIT OF ARTIFICIAL RECHARGE TO STREAMS

Water availability from streams varies seasonally due to climate differences. During low-flow periods, many streams may not possess enough water to sustain the aquatic ecosystem. Diverting water during high-flow periods for artificial recharge reduces the impact on aquatic stream life if the stored water later seeps back into the stream via a natural hydraulic connection.

---

saltwater intrusion: the invasion of sea water into coastal aquifers, generally the result of overpumping fresh water from those aquifers; the sea water occupies a portion of the aquifer formerly occupied by fresh water and prevents the fresh water from returning, thereby permanently reducing the long-term capacity of the aquifer

permeability: the capacity of a porous medium to transmit a fluid; highly depends on the size and shape of the pores and their interconnections

infiltration: the process by which water enters the soil and that is controlled by the character of the soil and surface conditions, such as slope and amount of vegetation

hydrogeology: a branch of geology that deals with the occurrence and movement of groundwater in relation to Earth structures; also refers to the hydrogeologic characteristics of a given region

potable: drinkable; specifically, fresh water that generally meets the standards in quality as established in the U.S. Environmental Protection Agency

brackish: describes water having a salinity from 0.05 to 17 parts per thousand; typically a mixture of sea water and fresh water (e.g., as found in an estuary)

Figure 2. Generalized cross-section of aquifer storage and recovery.

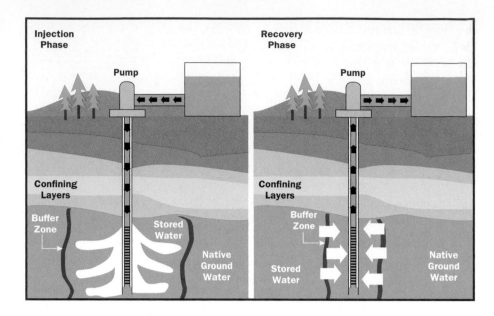

There are now ASR facilities in many countries and several U.S. states. Most of the facilities in the United States are in Florida, Arizona, and California, but the oldest ASR facility in the country is at Wildwood, New Jersey. Starting in 1968, the Wildwood community began the development of a system that now has four ASR wells. Each year the system stores about 380 million liters (99 million gallons) during off-peak months and recovers about 300 million liters (79 million gallons) during the summer months.

ASR has valuable application potential in numerous locations. Many cities are already using ASR to provide a source of water for daily use, peak demands, and emergency supply. The popularity of ASR is likely to expand as a component of total municipal water supply. SEE ALSO AQUIFER CHARACTERISTICS; GROUNDWATER; HYDROGEOLOGIC MAPPING; HYDROLOGIC CYCLE; MODELING GROUNDWATER FLOW AND TRANSPORT; RECLAMATION AND REUSE; SUPPLIES, PROTECTING PUBLIC DRINKING-WATER; WELLS AND WELL DRILLING.

Donn Miller

Bibliography

Bouwer, Herman, *Ground Water Hydrology*. New York: McGraw-Hill, 1978.

O'Hare, Margaret P. et al. *Artificial Recharge of Ground Water: Status and Potential in the Contiguous United States*. Chelsea, MI: Lewis Publishers, 1986.

Pyne, R. David G. *Groundwater Recharge and Wells: A Guide to Aquifer Storage Recovery*. Boca Raton, FL: CRC Press, 1994.

Stiles, Eric, ed. *High Plains States Groundwater Demonstration Program, Program Summary Report*. Denver, CO: U.S. Bureau of Reclamation, 2000.

Internet Resources

Pyne, R. David G. *Aquifer Storage and Recovery*. <http://www.asrforum.com>.

Arts, Water in the

From ancient times, in Western culture and worldwide, water has been an enduring theme in the arts. Water themes (including snow and ice) flow throughout literature, poetry, fine art, theater, music, and film. The images may be enduring, aesthetically appealing, or threatening in themselves; alternately, water (e.g., the sea) may be a metaphor for birth and rebirth, violence and death, self-discovery, spiritual journey, metamorphosis, change, inspiration, and renewal. The following discussion briefly highlights some components of water primarily within the Western arts, from ancient times to the present day.

Literature

Western literature was launched upon the waters. *The Odyssey* (together with *The Iliad,* epic Greek poems attributed to Homer, c. seventh century B.C.E.) details the hero Odysseus's perilous 10-year return across the sea from Troy. Centuries later, arguably the first English novel, Daniel Defoe's *Life and Strange Surprising Adventures of Robinson Crusoe* (1719), vividly relates the life of a man marooned on a desert island, and thus the spectre of the ever-present ocean. Other notable English-language literary works with a water focus include Samuel Taylor Coleridge's (1772–1834) apprehensive ballad, "The Rime of the Ancient Mariner." The English translation of the French writer Jules Verne's (1828–1905) *Twenty Thousand Leagues Under the Sea* had enormous popular appeal and anticipated many twentieth-century underwater technological and scientific achievements.

In North America, the tradition of writing about mankind's adventures in the natural environment dates back to colonial times. James Fenimore Cooper (1789–1851) wove his experiences as a midshipman into stories of adventure on the high seas. Herman Melville (1819–1891) wrote several popular romances of life at sea before creating his symbolic and philosophical masterpiece *Moby-Dick* (1851) about an obsessive whaler's hunt for a great white whale. Mark Twain's (1835–1910) boyhood on the Mississippi River laid the groundwork for what has been called the first modern American novel, *The Adventures of Huckleberry Finn* (1884). This classic work centered on the adventures of a boy and a runaway slave who rafted down the Mississippi.

Contemporary Writers. Henry David Thoreau's (1817–1862) journal of close observation of life at Walden Pond, *Walden, or a Life in the Woods* (1854), which has achieved iconic status, anticipated many major themes in contemporary American environmental writing. Henry Beston's *The Outermost House* (1928) mused upon a year spent living alone off Cape Cod. Marjory Stoneman Douglas's *The Everglades: River of Grass* (1947) became a classic exposé on environmental destruction in fragile swamps. Aldo Leopold's poetic *Sand County Almanac* (1949) strengthened the early environmental case. Before publishing *Silent Spring* in 1962 (a book that went on to factor heavily in the launch of the modern American environmental movement), marine biologist Rachel Carson wrote evocatively in *Under the Sea Wind* (1941) and *The Edge of the Sea* (1955).

Other major works and modern classics of American nature writing that explore and challenge our relationship with the water environment include John Graves's *Goodbye to a River* (1960), Wallace Stegner's *The Sound of Mountain Water* (1969), Annie Dillard's *Pilgrim at Tinker Creek* (1974), and Ann Zwinger's *Run, River, Run: A Naturalist's Journey Down One of the Great Rivers of the West* (1975).

Sea monsters in literature often are exaggerations of naturally occurring creatures. An enormous and "hostile" giant squid became a menacing foe in Jules Verne's 1873 classic *Twenty Thousand Leagues Under the Sea.*

Ice and Explorers. The human imagination and the arts have been inspired by water in both liquid and solid form. A rich body of literature exists based on high adventure to the far-distant frozen Antarctic. In 1816, Thomas Erskine's novel *Armata* envisaged a utopian world in which a sister planet was attached to Earth by two navigable sea channels flowing in opposite directions from the South Pole. Many nineteenth-century works supported the "hollow Earth" theory, most notably and influentially Edgar Allan Poe's *The Narrative of Arthur Gordon Pym of Nantucket* (1837). After Captain Robert Falcon Scott's (1868–1912) ill-fated second expedition to the Antarctic, stories appeared based on whaling adventures, historic expeditions, science fiction, and murder–mysteries (e.g., Hammond Innes' 1949 *The Survivors*, loosely based on Sir Ernest Shackleton's 1914 expedition in which his ship, *The Endurance*, was crushed by ice). Since the 1970s, most Antarctic fiction deals with themes of worldwide catastrophe and survival, from war to under-ice volcanic eruptions and breaking ice caps.

Environmental Literature. Since the first Earth Day (April 22, 1970), environmental literature, as it often is called, has become a major genre around the world. Today's environmental literature denotes a written work that investigates the relationship between people and nature. This may include oral readings, poetry, fiction, nonfiction, and drama.

Contemporary environmental writers such as Rick Bass, Wendell Berry, Alison Hawthorne Deming, Barry Lopez, Peter Matthiessen, Richard Nelson, Robert Michael Pyle, Scott Russell Sanders, Gary Snyder, and Terry Tempest Williams fundamentally link the literary arts with environmental awareness and responsibility, often rooted strongly in a sense of place and community. "A Call to Action: An Ecological Bill of Rights and Responsibilities" (Enviroarts, 1995) challenges the American arts community to forge a creative, national response to "erosion, poisoned water and air," among other social and environmental threats.

Fine Art and Popular Art

In ancient art, water was often represented by stylized curvilinear forms, such as the spiral (as evidenced by the Minoans of Crete) or a horizontal zigzag (as found in the art of ancient Egypt). In the famed eleventh-century Bayeux Tapestry, the English Channel is represented by embroidered wavy black lines. Distinctive indigenous art components include "Oceanic Arts," that is, the visual arts of the southern and northwestern Pacific Islands.

Rivers, lakes, and seas were once the great highways of the world, and much art shows water as a backdrop to everyday life. Royal barges are painted on the walls of Egyptian tombs dating to 1360 B.C.E. Ships and ports appear on medieval manuscripts and Renaissance frescoes. The brilliant Renaissance painter, sculptor, and inventor Leonardo da Vinci (1452–1519) was fascinated by water, which he described as "vetturale di natura" (the vehicle of nature). He drew it in detail, studied it closely, was in awe of its power (he had witnessed terrible floods and storms), and designed complex canal systems and locks.

A tradition of Dutch marine artists dates back to the seventeenth century, and led to the proliferation of professional marine artists in Britain. Of the French seascape painters, arguably the most significant was Claude Monet (1840-1926), whose oil-sketch *Impression: Sunrise* (1874), portraying

the harbor at Le Havre, gave its name to the Impressionist movement he founded. Monet went on to paint beach and river scenes in France and England.

The nineteenth-century Romantic tradition emphasized bold, dramatic paintings of nature—for example, seascapes by the English painter J. M. W. Turner (1775–1851), or dramatic events such as Théodore Géricault's *The Raft of the Medusa* (1819) and its portrayal of despairing shipwrecked sailors. The Hudson River School (1835–1870) housed the first great school of American landscape painters, who produced romantic and naturalistic renderings of the landscape of the Hudson River Valley and beyond.

"Earthworks" or "land arts," dating from the late 1960s and early 1970s, are works in which natural elements are directly employed or the landscape rearranged and the resulting artwork tempered by exposure to the elements. Robert Smithson's *Spiral Jetty* (1970), a huge rock and salt crystal spiral created in the midst of Utah's Great Salt Lake, is no longer visible beneath the rising waters.

Folk Art. The water world provides inspiration for folk art—art produced by mostly self-trained artists or for the preservation of traditional ethnic cultures—including functional and decorative hand-carved wildfowl and fish decoys, decorated sea chests, **scrimshaws**, ship's figureheads, and nautical ornaments. In America, the zenith of traditional folk art flourished in the nineteenth century prior to the rise of industrialization, but a rich contemporary tradition continues of naive, "outsider," and "memory" artists. Traditional Vietnamese water-puppet performances continue a rich and ancient folk art theatre tradition, in which the puppeteers stand behind a screen in water up to their waists, with the floating bamboo water-puppet theatre occupying the middle of a pond.

scrimshaw: any of various carved or engraved articles made by whalers, usually from either baleen or whale ivory

Music and Song

The arts encompass the environment of sight, word, and sound. The aesthetics of sight and sound come together architecturally in decorative water fountains and in Frank Lloyd Wright's famous house Fallingwater.

Popular "everyday" art involving water can find expression in unlikely places, such as elevated water towers. Even a fire hydrant can become a painter's palette, as evidenced during a community-sponsored event in Oldenberg, Indiana.

✳ See "Marine Mammals" for a photograph of Keiko, the real-life whale depicted in *Free Willy.*

Water-inspired classic compositions include works such as Debussy's *La Mer*, Ravel's *Jeux d'eau*, Mendelssohn's *Calm Sea and Prosperous Voyage* and *Hebrides Overture*, Wagner's *Tristan und Isolde*, and Handel's *Water Music*. Traditional folk music often addresses water-related themes, whether the storytelling vehicle is a sea shanty, minstrel tune, or ballad.

Just as the arts recognize a visual landscape, the modern "soundscape" is the creative concern of AcousticEcology.org. This networking and resource information project focuses in part on human-induced environmental impacts on the oceans, and emphasizes "the art of soundscape production and . . . creative interpretations of the sounding world." Ecological concern is also the driving force behind Musicians United to Save the Environment.

Film

Numerous academic studies investigate the linkages between mass media, popular culture, and societal attitudes and behavior towards the environment. In the movies, water has been a threatening environment, including one that shelters "hostile" creatures. Examples include the shark attacks in *Jaws*, the river itself in *Deliverance*, and the ocean in the fact-based *The Perfect Storm*. Water has been the setting for a post-apocalyptic world (*Waterworld*) or an otherworldly encounter (*The Abyss*).

Conversely, particularly in family films, the welfare of a marine animal may be the central focus, as in *Free Willy*,✳ *Orca*, and *Tarka the Otter*. Conservation of the water environment also may be a central theme, as in *Turtle Diary* and *When the Whales Came*.

Increasingly, a diverse assortment of films and videos explicitly address socioecological issues and perspectives. These are promoted and celebrated at annual environmental film festivals throughout the world: within the United States (e.g., the Hazel Wolf Environmental Film Festival, the Washington D.C. Environmental Film Festival, and the Cornell Environmental Film Festival); Canada (e.g., Planet in Focus); Africa (e.g., the African Environmental Film Foundation and Pretoria's International Environmental Film Festival); Australia (e.g., Wild Spaces); and Europe (e.g., London's Green Screen). Fine art and film may come together, such as with the acclaimed 2000 documentary, *Rivers and Tides*, which celebrates the art of Andy Goldsworthy.

Environmental Art

Just as there has been a shift in the role and spread of modern environmental literature since the early 1970s, so too is there a worldwide contemporary movement in environmental art, concerned with human relationship with the natural world. This may also be called eco-art, Art+Nature, or restoration art, and may extend to socially and politically oriented efforts known as "eco-activist art" and "environmental justice eco-art." Examples include Soul Salmon, an "art action" movement of Northwest American artists, businesses, institutions and tribes to protect native salmon, and artist Deborah Small's painted porcelain brick art statement to preserve Mono Lake in California that led to a landmark public trust law case. Eco-Art was represented at the 2002 World Summit on Sustainable Development in Johannesburg, South Africa, with a call for artists around the world to devote their next artwork to an environmental issue.

In the 1975 Steven Spielberg movie version of Peter Benchley's novel *Jaws,* human characters battled a ferocious and malevolent shark. Real-life shark attacks are fairly uncommon, despite sensationalized media coverage.

Numerous illustrations and examples of environmental art abound within North America and internationally, and may be found by reference to organizations and websites such as Enviroarts: Orion Online; Greenmuseum.org, a collaborative online museum of environmental art; and Eikon, an online resource created by Artecology. Art Culture Nature, an association for the study of the arts and the environment, is an interdisciplinary organization founded in 1997, whose mission "brings together artists and teachers in the fine and performing arts as well as environmentalists and educators in the humanities, sciences and social sciences who are interested in the study of the connections between the arts and environmental studies." The Association for the Study of Literature and the Environment provides links to many related environmental arts organization and electronic archives.

Conclusion

Like water itself, the arts are not fixed, but fluid and constantly evolving and responding to change. The arts are also an ideal means by which humans explore, understand, communicate and challenge their culture, values, and ethics. The response to art may have philosophical, ecological, social, or political implications upon how societies and individuals live as an integral part of this water planet. SEE ALSO BIRDS, AQUATIC; CARSON, RACHEL; CEPHALOPODS; CRUSTACEANS; DOUGLAS, MARJORY STONEMAN; ENVIRONMENTAL MOVEMENT, ROLE OF WATER IN THE; FISHES, CARTILAGINOUS; LEONARDO DA VINCI; MARINE MAMMALS; RELIGIONS, WATER IN; REPTILES; SUSTAINABLE DEVELOPMENT.

Jane Dougan

Bibliography

Baldwin, Robert. "A Bibliography of the Sea, Shipwreck, and Water in Western Literature and Art." *Bulletin of Biography* 48(3):153–170.

Slovic, Scott. "Giving Expression to Nature: Voices of Environmental Literature." *Environment* 42 (March 1999):6–11.

ENVIRONMENTAL ART RESOURCES

Art Culture Nature
<http://faculty.ssu.edu/~acn/>

Artecology
<http://artecology.org/>

The Association for the Study of Literature and Environment
<http://www.asle.umn.edu>

Enviroarts: Orion Online
<http://arts.envirolink.org>

Greenmuseum.org (online museum of environmental art)
<http://www.greenmuseum.org>

Musicians United to Sustain the Environment
<http://www.musemusic.org>

The World Forum for Acoustic Ecology
<http://www.AcousticEcology.org>

Wurst, Gayle, and Christine Raguet-Bouvard, eds. *Sounding the Depths: Water as Metaphor in North American Literature.* Liège, Belgium: Université de Liège, 1998.

Zakai, Shai. "Art and Politics at the Earth Summit and Beyond" and "Cultivating an Interdisciplinary Approach to Environmental Awareness." Sections of a document presented as part of a Shadow Report to the Government of Israel's Assessment of Progress in Implementing Agenda 21 at the World Summit on Sustainable Development, Johannesburg, South Africa, September 2002. Available online at <http://www.greenmuseum.org>.

Astrobiology: Water and the Potential for Extraterrestrial Life

Astrobiology is a new interdisciplinary science that seeks to understand the origin, evolution, distribution, and future of life in the universe. As a fundamental requirement of living systems, water holds a special place in the conceptual framework of astrobiology. All of life's processes are carried out in the presence of liquid water, and on this basis it may be regarded as a key indicator for potential habitability. The importance of liquid water as an organizing principle in the exploration for **extraterrestrial** life often is articulated in the simple expression "follow the water."

Water and Planetary Habitability

What is it about water that justifies its central role in the search for extraterrestrial life? Most of water's unique properties (e.g., its excellent **solvent** properties, broad temperature range over which it remains liquid, high heat capacity, and surface tension) are rooted in the ability of water molecules to form **hydrogen bonds** with each other. In addition, on freezing, there is a slight expansion of hydrogen bond angles that produces a solid phase (ice) of lower density than the liquid phase. This uncommon property results in waterbodies that freeze from the top downward, an important factor for sustaining habitability in polar and other cold climates.

Clearly, a knowledge of the past and present distribution of water in the solar system is regarded as crucial for evaluating the potential of other planets (or their moons) to develop and sustain life. Water also holds central importance in the human exploration of the solar system, being essential for the colonization of other planets, such as Mars.

Global Cycles. Throughout Earth's history, water has played a central role in the global cycles that link the solid Earth and the atmosphere. Interactions between crustal rocks and water sustain a broad range of processes that collectively meet most of the important energy and resource requirements of living systems. Such interactions ultimately determine the overall habitability of a planet, thus setting the stage for life's origin and ensuring its persistence over geologic timescales.

The hydrologic cycle (the cycling of water between the atmosphere and oceans) drives a vast transport system that constantly redistributes materials and energy within the Earth's crust. Flowing water and ice transport rock fragments and associated **weathering** products from source areas to basins of deposition. Streams and **groundwater** (inclusive of hydrothermal systems) dissolve, transport, and concentrate chemical compounds required by organisms.

extraterrestrial: from beyond the Earth and its atmosphere

solvent: a substance capable of dissolving other substances; in a solution, it is the liquid that has dissolved the solids (solutes)

hydrogen bond: in water, the type of chemical bond between two water molecules; caused by electromagnetic forces, and occurring when the positive (hydrogen) side of one water molecule is attracted to and forms a bond with the negative (oxygen) side of another water molecule

weathering: the decay or breakdown of rocks and minerals through a complex interaction of physical, chemical, and biological processes; water is the most important agent of weathering; soil is formed through weathering processes

groundwater: generally, all subsurface (underground) water, as distinct from surface water, that supplies natural springs, contributes to permanent streams, and can be tapped by wells; specifically, the water that is in the saturated zone of a defined aquifer

Giant meteorite impacts billions of years ago would have caused setbacks in early Earth's ability to develop a stable biosphere. Yet once these impacts lessened, water and organic materials needed for living systems could have been retained. Most of the important materials for life on Earth (e.g., chemical nutrients) could have been brought in by comets and other icy objects.

Sediments and the dissolved materials formed during weathering processes ultimately reach the **ocean basins**, where they accumulate as dissolved salts or seafloor sediments. Over the long term, even the dissolved load of streams eventually **precipitate** out of solution as secondary minerals (such as sedimentary cements) and chemical sediments (such as **evaporites**). The deposits so formed often preserve signals for environmental change on Earth along with a fossil record of life's evolution.

Over longer spans of time, cycling of the crust by the **subduction** of lithospheric plates and melting of sediment-covered seafloor and entrapped sea water produce magmas (molten rock materials). The water dissolved in these magmas actually lowers their density and crystallization temperature, thus promoting their buoyant rise back to the surface, where they drive volcanic activity.

Outgassing. Over geologic timescales, volcanic outgassing of the Earth's interior regulates atmospheric composition and evolution.

The Earth's close orbital distance from the Sun ensures a vast supply of solar energy that is utilized by photosynthetically based surface ecosystems. However, the energy output of the Sun was probably much lower (30 percent less than present luminosity) at the beginning of solar system history.

Under these relatively faint young-Sun conditions, an atmospheric greenhouse, sustained by carbon dioxide (CO_2) and/or methane (CH_4), was required to maintain habitable surface conditions. An active **plate tectonic** cycle over the entire history of Earth has allowed for the constant renewal of the atmosphere by volcanic outgassing. This atmospheric renewal is essential for long-term sustainability. (By contrast, see the discussion of Mars farther ahead in this entry and elsewhere in the encyclopedia.)

By approximately 2.5 billion years ago, interactions between the global hydrologic system and geologic cycles of the solid Earth (via processes such as plate tectonics, weathering and erosion, and volcanism) had produced a

sediment: rock particles and other earth materials that are transported and deposited over time by geologic agents such as running water, wind, glaciers, and gravity

basin (ocean): the topographic low area occupied by oceans; the floor of ocean basins consists of basaltic crust that is more dense than typical continental rocks

precipitate: (verb) in a solution, to separate into a relatively clear liquid and a solid substance by a chemical or physical change

evaporites: sediments that form as the result of the precipitation of minerals during the evaporation of water, primarily sea water, and that may form sedimentary rock; principle minerals are gypsum and halite

subduction: the process by which one lithospheric plate is forced to move under another plate, moving in the opposing direction

plate tectonics: the theory that the Earth's lithosphere can be divided into a few large plates that are slowly moving relative to one another; plate sizes change and intense geologic activities occur at plate boundaries (e.g., earthquakes, volcanism, mountain building); continents drift on the plates and therefore their position with respect to latitude and longitude and with respect to one another have changed over geologic time

Surface features of Mars suggest ancient activity of liquid water, and groundwater may currently exist deep in the subsurface. Scientists plan further explorations for evidence of past and present water, and perhaps Martian life.

continental: of or pertaining to the continents

photosynthesis: the process by which plants manufacture food from sunlight; specifically, the conversion of water and carbon dioxide to complex sugars in plant tissues by the action of chlorophyll driven by solar energy

biodiversity: a measure of the variety of the Earth's species, of the genetic differences within species, and of the ecosystems that support those species

clear compositional differentiation of the Earth's habitable surface environments into two broad habitats: the **continental** land masses and the ocean basins. Around the same time, oxygenic **photosynthesis** emerged as a major biological innovation, taking advantage of the abundant energy available from the Sun. Oxygen production through photosynthesis eventually outstripped volcanic and weathering controls on atmospheric composition, producing an oxidizing surface environment.

By approximately 600 million years ago, the buildup of oxygen in the atmosphere culminated in the appearance of large, multicellular life forms. This new level of organization in the biosphere enhanced global **biodiversity**, leading in stepwise fashion to the emergence of terrestrial (land-based) faunas and eventually to intelligent life characterized by self-awareness and advanced cultural, social, and technological civilizations.

Exploring for Martian Life

Given the terrestrial experience of humans, it is easy to understand why the search for water in all its forms, past or present, has emerged as the primary theme for exploration of the solar system. For example, over the next decade, scientific efforts to explore for water on Mars will create a context for assessing planetary habitability and the potential for Mars having developed life at some time in its history.

Presently, the surface of Mars is properly regarded as a radiation-rich frozen desert that is hostile to life. Within about 1 billion years of its origin,

Mars appears to have lost most of its atmosphere and, with that, the potential for sustaining liquid water environments at the surface. Interestingly, this early loss of the atmosphere appears to have been the result of the absence of a plate tectonic cycle on Mars.

Yet Mars has not always been a dry, hostile place. Exploration efforts in the late twentieth century revealed that prior to the loss of its atmosphere, Mars probably was much more Earth-like. The ancient southern highlands of Mars harbor a wide variety of water-carved landforms and layered sedimentary deposits of likely aqueous origin. The broad temporal distribution of these features suggests that even though the surface of Mars has been dry for most of the planet's history, liquid water has been present from time to time, providing brief intervals of surface habitability.

Loss of the Martian atmosphere would have spelled doom for any surface life existing at the time. However, if Martian life forms colonized surface environments during earlier wet periods, they are quite likely to have left behind a **fossil** record. The search for this fossil record is in many ways the focus of the current Mars exploration program.

fossil: a preserved plant or animal imprint or remains

Recent Discoveries.

The possibility of living Martian life-forms is one facet of ongoing research. On Earth, scientists have discovered that life occupies an incredible range of environmental extremes, including the deep subsurface, where it utilizes chemical energy instead of sunlight. Models suggest that liquid water (perhaps saline) environments could still exist today in the deep subsurface of Mars, along with energy-containing compounds such as methane, which could sustain chemically based life. The argument for subsurface habitability is strengthened by the existence of ancient out-flood channels, believed to have been formed by catastrophic releases of subsurface water in the past. These landforms provide direct evidence that a groundwater system once existed.

But what about today? Scientists recently discovered what appear to be water-carved gullies on the steep slopes and high latitudes of Mars. Despite the constant subfreezing temperatures at those latitudes, water, in the form of subsurface hydrothermal **brines**, may have risen from deep crustal sources along **faults**, flowing briefly over the surface and carving the channels.

brine: water containing a higher concentration of dissolved salts than normal sea water (which contains approximately 35 parts per thousand); produced in oceans through the evaporation or freezing of sea water, or in groundwater through extensive reaction with bedrock minerals

fault: a fracture in a body of rock along which the mass of rock on one side of the fault moves against the mass on the other side; faults generate earthquakes

The origin of these seep features remains controversial, but the hydrologic interpretation is consistent with a variety of other types of evidence that suggest the presence of a subsurface groundwater system. Further investigation of these features is warranted. If a subsurface groundwater system does exist on Mars, such environments may have provided stable habitats for life over the entire history of the planet. In 2002, the gamma-ray spectrometer onboard NASA's Odyssey orbiter discovered extensive water present as ground ice in surface soils over extensive regions of Mars at high latitudes. This has strengthened the case for an abundance of subsurface crustal water on Mars.

Research Challenges.

In exploring for Martian groundwater, the practical problem faced by NASA (National Aeronautics and Space Administration) is accessibility. Accessing and sampling sources of subsurface Martian water (and potentially life) will require the development of precision landing systems capable of safely landing on steep slopes where potential seep sites are located, and/or long-ranging rovers capable of traveling to prospective

---

LIFE IN A MARTIAN METEORITE?

About 20 percent of the magnetites found in a 4.6-million-year-old Martian meteorite named ALH84001 resemble intracellular magnetites formed by some species of terrestrial bacteria. (Magnetite is a naturally magnetic mineral common in basalt.) Whether the meteoritic magnetites are a reliable indicator of life was under scientific scrutiny as of 2002.

groundwater sites (such as seeps) from safe landing sites located at a distance of perhaps tens of kilometers. Next, scientists will need to drill to depths of tens to hundreds of meters from small robotic platforms, a capability they presently lack.

Although the previously mentioned technological capabilities have all been identified as long-term goals of NASA's Mars exploration program, scientists presently lack the technologies needed to access subsurface water on Mars with robotic platforms. As a result, some have suggested that drilling for Martian groundwater may require a human presence, something that is beyond the scope of the present Mars program. The earliest human missions to Mars, if they can be safely carried out, are unlikely to occur prior to 2025. SEE ALSO COMETS AND METEORITES, WATER IN; EARTH: THE WATER PLANET; FRESH WATER, PHYSICS AND CHEMISTRY OF; LIFE IN EXTREME WATER ENVIRONMENTS; MARS, WATER ON; SOLAR SYSTEM, WATER IN THE; VOLCANOES AND WATER.

Jack D. Farmer

Bibliography

Carr, M. H. *Water on Mars*. London, U.K.: Oxford University Press, 1996.

Chang, S. "The Planetary Setting of Prebiotic Evolution." In *Early Life on Earth*, ed. S. Bengston. New York: Columbia University Press, 1994.

Klein, H. P. "The Search for Life on Mars: What We Learned from Viking." *Journal of Geophysical Research*. 103 (1998):28463–28466.

Lemonick, M. D. *Other Worlds: the Search for Life in the Universe*. New York: Simon and Schuster, 1998.

Malin, M. C., and K. S. Edgett. "Evidence for Recent Groundwater Seepage and Surface Runoff on Mars." *Science* 288 (2000):2330–2335.

Pace, N. R. "A Molecular View of Microbial Diversity and the Biosphere." *Science* 276 (1997):734–740.

Attenuation of Pollutants

The moment that **pollutants** in soils become dissolved in natural waters, their potential for transport is greatly magnified, as is the likelihood that people will ingest them. The primary health risk from many **hazardous waste** sites, dumps, septic tanks, factory outflows, and other pollution sources is the possibility that pollutants will be dissolved into **groundwaters** or surface waters, then ultimately reach drinking water.

Pollutants of concern include industrial solvents such as perchlorethlyene (PCE); trichlorethylene (TCE); motor fuel components such as benzene, toluene, ethylbenzene, and xylene, (collectively termed BTEX); and **inorganic** contaminants such as lead, chromate, arsenic, and nitrate. Just as each contaminant tends to affect specific organs in the human body depending on its chemistry, the behavior of contaminants in groundwaters and surface waters likewise varies from contaminant to contaminant.

Contaminant Behavior and Attenuation

Rarely do chemicals behave identically in natural waters; typically there is at least one natural reaction that causes the bioavailability of a given contaminant to decrease, or attenuate, over time. These attenuation reactions include the following.

pollutant: something that pollutes, especially a waste material that contaminates air, soil, or water

hazardous waste: any solid, liquid or gas that, when disposed, exhibits the characteristics of ignitability, corrosivity, reactivity, or toxicity, as well as any industrial waste that has been specifically listed in the federal regulations as having hazardous properties

groundwater: generally, all subsurface (underground) water, as distinct from surface water, that supplies natural springs, contributes to permanent streams, and can be tapped by wells; specifically, the water that is in the saturated zone of a defined aquifer

inorganic: an element, molecule or substance that did not form as the direct result of biologic activity

- Biodegradation: the breakdown of contaminants by soil **microorganisms** to less toxic or nontoxic compounds.

- Sorption: the "sticking" of contaminant molecules to solid surfaces such as minerals and soil **organic** material. Contaminants that sorb to soil solids are typically unavailable for human uptake unless the soil particle itself is ingested.

- Chemical transformation: the formation of contaminant-containing solids, which causes a decrease in the concentration of the contaminant in water that ultimately may be ingested. Chemical transformation also includes radioactive decay of unstable **isotopes**.

Contaminant attenuation can be split into two components.

- Physical attenuation: the dilution and dispersion of contaminant concentrations in surface waters or groundwaters. Over time, dilution and dispersion tend to "smear out" contaminant **plumes**, causing a net decrease in contaminant levels at any one location. Physical attenuation tends to depend upon the velocity of the particular water (e.g., a fast-moving stream versus a slow-moving river) and its rate of mixing.

- Chemical attenuation: the collective assemblage of reactions that causes contaminant concentrations to decrease in surface waters or groundwaters. Chemical attenuation is rather complicated, and specific to the particular contaminant class.

Chemical Attenuation

Organic contaminants are made up of electron-rich molecules containing linked carbon atoms. Soil microorganisms can derive energy by using oxygen, sulfate, nitrate, or ferrous iron to **oxidize** and break these chains down into carbon dioxide plus water. Often this breakdown is more rapid than engineered remediation. Rapid microbial attenuation is often observed for fuel hydrocarbons such as are found beneath leaking underground fuel tanks. Attenuation tends to be most rapid under oxidizing (**aerobic**) conditions that often prevail in loose soils. In oxygen-poor (**anaerobic**) waters, attenuation tends to be slower.

PCE and TCE are two of the most common contaminants at hazardous waste sites. They are quite toxic and also tend to resist chemical attenuation. Microorganisms are only able to rapidly attenuate them by first reducing them under anaerobic conditions, and then oxidizing them under aerobic conditions. Obviously the potential for PCE or TCE attenuation hinges upon the chemical condition of the **aquifer** or soil.

Chemical attenuation of inorganic contaminants such as lead, chromate, nitrate, and arsenic often involves sorption onto mineral surfaces. Microorganisms generally cannot break down such contaminants into less toxic compounds except in a few cases. Most notably, microorganisms are able to reduce oxidized (and toxic) chromate to insoluble and less toxic trivalent chromium. Likewise, microorganisms can convert nitrate to ammonia and/or nitrogen gas. Most other inorganic contaminants must be sorbed to mineral surfaces to be attenuated.

Soil and aquifer solids tend to be negatively charged because of broken or unsatisfied bonds that exist at their surfaces. This negative charge that exists at mineral surfaces pulls oppositely charged **cations** from solution. Many dissolved metals exist as positively charged cations in natural waters and are hence attracted to, and attenuated at, mineral surfaces. This is

microorganism: a microscopic organism

organic: pertaining to, or the product of, biological reactions or functions

isotope: the one of two or more forms or varieties of a specific element that differ in their atomic mass; the proton number is the same for a given set of related isotopes, but the number of neutrons in the nucleus varies; for example, the common isotopes of oxygen, O-18, O-17, and O-16, all have 8 protons, but have 10, 9, and 8 neutrons, respectively

plume: a concentrated area or mass of a substance that is emitted from a natural or human-made point source and that spreads in the environment; a plume can be thermal, chemical, or biological in nature

oxidation: a chemical reaction involving the loss of one or more electrons from a specific element; results in an increase in the charge of the element; for example, iron (II) (Fe^{2+}) is oxidized to iron (III) (Fe^{3+}) through the loss of an electron; such reactions often take place in the presence of free oxygen

aerobic: describes organisms able to live only in the presence of air or free oxygen, and conditions that exist only in the presence of air or free oxygen

anaerobic: describes organisms able to live and grow only where there is no air or free oxygen, and conditions that exist only in the absence of air or free oxygen

aquifer: a water-saturated, permeable, underground rock formation that can transmit significant quantities of water under ordinary hydraulic gradients to wells and springs

cation: an ion that has a positive charge

Hazardous waste sites require remediation to contain and prevent the further spread of toxic chemicals into the environment. Following removal of the contaminant source, natural attenuation and bioremediation are two components of cleanup strategies.

radionuclide: a type of atom that exhibits radioactivity; radioactive chemicals may be artificial or naturally occurring and may be found in drinking water

sequester: to remove or render inactive a specific chemical or chemical group from a solution

particularly true for such industrial metals as lead, cadmium, zinc, and nickel. It is also true for such important **radionuclides** that are present in radioactive waste as ^{90}Sr, ^{137}Cs, and isotopes of Pu (plutonium) and U (uranium). Chromate and arsenate sorb appreciably to many soil minerals despite the overall negative charge of both partners.

Inorganic contaminants that initially sorb onto mineral surfaces from a contaminant-rich solution might in theory "desorb" back into contaminant-poor waters recharging a contaminated aquifer after the contaminant source has been removed. In fact, numerous field observations suggest that many sorbed contaminants become permanently **sequestered** after prolonged interaction with mineral surfaces. In other words, sorbed contaminants are taken up into mineral lattices (structures) where they are no longer bioavailable. Mineral uptake also makes the complete engineered removal of contaminants from soils and aquifers nearly impossible. In effect, the crystal lattices must be destroyed to remove the bound contaminants.

Applications of Attenuation

Pollutant attenuation is most commonly taken advantage of in the treatment of sewage; that is, oxidation of organic matter is hastened by mixing on-site or by discharging into surface waters that have sufficient capacity to rapidly attenuate the imposed pollutant load.

Increasingly, pollutant attenuation, or equivalently "monitored natural attenuation" or MNA, is being used as a component of hazardous waste site cleanups. Specifically, MNA is relied upon to remove contaminants from groundwaters, in parallel to and, after active remediation has ceased.

Bioremediation of contaminated sites typically involves the engineered acceleration of natural organic activity that leads to the breakdown of organic contaminants—most commonly spilled fuels and solvents—ultimately to carbon dioxide. Less common is the introduction of new organisms, themselves, to contaminated sites. Natural soil organic activity tends to be sufficiently pervasive that, given the appropriate nutrients, breakdown of contaminants can be achieved by native populations of microorganisms. Nutrient additions may include oxygen, a carbon substrate such as molasses, and/or hydrogen.

It must be noted that not all contaminants attenuate rapidly enough to prevent potential impacts on human health. Instead, knowledge of attenuation rates and capacities is critical to the successful implementation of pollutant attenuation in either realm. Each area remains the subject of intense investigation by chemists, biologists, geochemists, engineers, and other scientists. SEE ALSO FRESH WATER, NATURAL COMPOSITION OF; FRESH WATER, PHYSICS AND CHEMISTRY OF; GROUNDWATER; MODELING GROUNDWATER FLOW AND TRANSPORT; MODELING STREAM FLOW AND QUALITY; POLLUTION OF GROUNDWATER; POLLUTION OF LAKES AND STREAMS; RADIOACTIVE CHEMICALS; SEPTIC SYSTEM IMPACTS; WASTEWATER TREATMENT AND MANAGEMENT.

Patrick V. Brady

Bibliography

Brady, Patrick V., Michael V. Brady, and David J. Borns. *Natural Attenuation: CERCLA, RBCAs, and the Future of Environmental Remediation.* Boca Raton, FL: Lewis Publishers, 1997.

Rice, David W. et al. "Recommendations to Improve the Cleanup Process for California's Leaking Underground Fuel Tanks." In *Lawrence Livermore National Laboratory Report.* Lawrence Livermore National Laboratory, CA: 1995.

Balancing Diverse Interests

Water is a natural resource critical to the **environment**. Water also is an economic resource critical to society. Unfortunately, people who champion water as an economic resource essential to society commonly see themselves in direct opposition to those who champion water as a critical component of the environment that must be conserved and protected. This creates a difficult situation for those who must manage the available water resources to best satisfy all of the diverse interests that depend on water.

It is, of course, impossible to successfully manage water resources solely from either of the two extremes. If public policy exclusively protected **ecological** interests at the expense of economic interests, then it could threaten society's ability to meet the basic need all people have for water. From an ecological perspective, this could weaken government and diminish the ability to protect the environment, whereas from an economic standpoint, jobs and essential services such as housing and communications could be lost. Likewise, if water management policies focus entirely on the economy, then the environment often is harmed. A diminished environment affects the public health, the quality of life, and ultimately the ability to survive on planet Earth. Clearly, society is as dependent on a healthy environment as it is on a healthy economy.

Legislation

In many Western Hemisphere countries, water resources are managed through legislation and regulations. In the United States, elected officials in Congress and the state legislatures set the policies that prioritize where water can or cannot be used and how much water must remain to function in the natural environment. These laws are then implemented through regulatory agencies at the federal, state, and local levels of government. One example of this legislation is the federal Clean Water Act, which requires that the quality of surface-water bodies, such as rivers and lakes, be kept at a level that will assure the maintenance of both environmental and economic functions.

Public Opinion. The effectiveness of these policies to meet both environmental and economic interests is dependent, in part, on how well the laws are written, and how effectively they are enforced. However, public opinion strongly affects the type of policies that get enacted. For example, in the 1930s, the United States was emerging from a severe economic depression, so the growth and protection of the economy were paramount in the minds of the public and policymakers alike. As a result, the national policy from roughly 1930 to 1970 was to use the water of major rivers to provide jobs and to allow cities to grow in order to expand the economy. This was often accomplished through the federal government's dam-building projects for **hydroelectric** power and water supply, particularly for **irrigation**.

Shifting Sentiment. The dam-building policy was beneficial to the economy, but by 1970 national policy and public sentiment had shifted towards the environmental health of rivers and lakes, many of which had been harmed by the dam projects. One outgrowth of this environmental pendulum shift was the Endangered Species Act (ESA) passed by the U.S. Congress in 1973. The ESA is an example of legislation that fundamentally changed water

environment: all of the external factors, conditions, and influences that affect the growth, development, and survival of organisms or a community; commonly refers to Earth and its support systems

ecology: the scientific study of the interrelationships of living things to one another and to the environment; also refers to the ecology of a given region

hydroelectric: often used synonymously with "hydropower," describes electricity generated by utilizing the power of falling water, as with water flowing through and turning turbines at a dam

irrigation: the controlled application of water for agricultural or other purposes through human-made systems; generally refers to water application to soil when rainfall is insufficient to maintain desirable soil moisture for plant growth

Conflicts can arise over water management when interests of various stakeholder and user groups differ. Dam-building is one controversial water-related issue that can draw the ire of local, regional, and national environmental groups, as represented here by a symbolically gagged protestor in Bombay, India.

species: the narrowest classification or grouping of organisms according to their characteristics; members of a species can reproduce only with others of that group

arid: describes a climate or region where precipitation is exceeded by evaporation; in these regions, agricultural crop production is impractical or impossible without irrigation

policy without directly addressing water issues. On its face, the law would not seem to be about water policy. When applied to fish **species**, however, it places requirements on water resource management to meet certain stream flow levels in order to protect a given species. Though this is clearly a good policy, it often requires extraordinary efforts in the regional management of water to ensure that the water demands of the society are met without further endangering the listed species. These efforts can be very costly. A balance must be found whereby the environment is protected to maintain the function of the rivers and lakes while still meeting the water demands of the community.

Water Management

Even without the demands of environmental laws, minimizing impacts on streams and rivers while maintaining water supplies for cities and industry is a complex task because of natural constraints on water availability. Areas of the United States like the **arid** Southwest have limited amounts of available water such that any additional use has the potential to significantly harm natural systems. However, water resource management is difficult even in areas with substantial annual rainfall. Here the problem is often one of timing because water may be abundant only in the winter months when water demand is typically low. Conversely, satisfying water demands for irrigation, meeting minimum-streamflow regulations, and providing water to cities is typically far greater in the summer months.

All of this complicates the job of the water resource manager. As with any problem where the timing of supply is not well matched with the timing of demand, the best solution is effective storage. For example, if the annual floods of rivers like the Mississippi River could be captured and stored for use later in the year, drought would be less of a problem. In this way, sufficient water is often available to meet both ecological and economic needs provided the problem is considered regionally and over a long enough period of time.

Conserving natural habitats must be balanced with human needs for water and the economic benefits their use and management can afford. Once considered of little value, wetlands today are the focus of extensive preservation efforts, yet remain at the center of complex debates.

The world is now in an era where neither the economy nor the environment can absorb much negative impact from the mismanagement of water resources. Regional **watershed** management may help shape policy to store water from the high-flow periods of watersheds and use that water to maintain flows for fish and wildlife requirements and meet the demands of the community during low-flow periods. Everyone should continue to strive for balanced policies that allow for the use of water without inordinate harm to either the environment or the economy. The need to balance the various and diverse interests that depend on water is more essential and more complex than ever. SEE ALSO CLEAN WATER ACT; CONFLICT AND WATER; ECONOMIC DEVELOPMENT; ENDANGERED SPECIES ACT; ENVIRONMENTAL MOVEMENT, ROLE OF WATER IN THE; INSTREAM WATER ISSUES; INTEGRATED WATER RESOURCES MANAGEMENT; LEGISLATION, FEDERAL WATER; PLANNING AND MANAGEMENT, HISTORY OF WATER RESOURCES; PLANNING AND MANAGEMENT, WATER RESOURCES; PRIOR APPROPRIATION; RIGHTS, PUBLIC WATER; RIGHTS, RIPARIAN; SAFE DRINKING WATER ACT; SALMON DECLINE AND RECOVERY; WETLANDS.

watershed: the land area drained by a river and its tributaries; also called river basin, drainage basin, catchment, and drainage area

F. Michael Krautkramer

Bibliography

Dunne, Thomas, and Luna B. Leopold. *Water in Environmental Planning.* New York: W. H. Freeman and Company, 1978.

Leopold, Luna B. *Water: A Primer.* San Francisco, CA: W. H. Freeman and Company, 1974.

Leopold, Luna B. *Water, Rivers and Creeks.* Sausalito, CA: University Science Books, 1997.

Winpenny, James. *Managing Water as an Economic Resource.* New York: Routledge, 1994.

Bays, Gulfs, and Straits

Bays, gulfs, and straits are types of waterbodies that are contained within a larger body of water near land. These three waterbodies are usually located at important points of human activities; thus, conflicts with nature and neighbors can result.

An infrared photograph of the San Francisco Bay area, taken from the space shuttle *Discovery,* shows the bay's shape and the heavy development in the region.

Bays

A bay is a small body of water or a broad inlet that is set off from a larger body of water generally where the land curves inward. The San Francisco Bay, off the coast in northern California, is a well-known bay in the United States. Examples of other bays include the Bay of Pigs (Cuba), Hudson Bay (Canada), Chesapeake Bay (Maryland and Virginia), and Bay of Bengal (near India).

Bays usually occur on oceans, lakes, and gulfs, and generally not on rivers except when there is an artificially enlarged river mouth. An example of a bay at a river's mouth is New York Bay, at the mouth of the Hudson River.

GUANTÁNAMO BAY

Guantánamo Bay is a sheltered inlet within the Caribbean Sea, located in southeastern Cuba near the city of Guantánamo. During the Spanish–American War in 1898, the United States gained access to the outer harbor of Guantánamo Bay. Through an agreement signed with Cuba in 1903, the United States obtained the right to maintain a naval base at Guantánamo Bay. In 1934, a treaty reaffirmed the U.S. right to lease the site. The treaty gave the United States a perpetual lease on Guantánamo Bay, and may only be rescinded if the United States should abandon the area or by the mutual consent of Cuba and the United States.

About 18,390 hectares (45,440 acres) of water (32 percent), solid ground (49 percent), and swampland (18 percent) comprise Guantánamo Bay U.S. Naval Base, a complex of airfields and repair, supply, and training facilities. The base is strategically important because of the maritime route between the United States and Central and South America, and its close proximity to the Panama Canal.

Health of Bays.   All bays are important to the continued health of the surrounding **environment**. However, these bays can be degraded when the water's natural state is changed by the introduction of foreign materials into water flowing into the bay, or into the bay itself. For instance, the San Francisco Bay is connected to the Sacramento–San Joaquin Delta **estuary**, which is the largest estuary on the west coast of the United States. This aquatic system supports more than 120 species of fish and is a waterfowl migration and wintering area.

Although known for its natural beauty and importance to the health of its surrounding area, the San Francisco Bay has been degraded by many human activities such as commerce and recreation. For example, more than 95 percent of the tidal marshes along the shore have been filled. Large reductions (and in some cases losses) in fish and wildlife **habitat** have resulted. The flow of fresh water into the estuary and the delta also has been reduced due to diversion of the water by pumps within the delta, thereby increasing the estuary's salinity.

Gulfs

A gulf is a large body of water, sometimes with a narrow mouth, that is almost completely surrounded by land. It can be considered a large bay. The world's largest gulf is the Gulf of Mexico, with a total surface area of about 1,554,000 square kilometers (600,000 square miles). It is surrounded by Mexico, the southern coast of the United States, and Cuba, and contains many bays, such as Matagorda Bay (Texas) and Mobile Bay (Alabama). Examples of other gulfs include the Gulf of California, Gulf of Aden (between the Red Sea and the Arabian Sea), and the Persian Gulf (between Saudi Arabia and Iran). The Persian Gulf is important with respect to world energy because **petroleum** is transported through its waters in oil tankers.

Hypoxia.   Scientific investigations of the Gulf of Mexico have documented a large area off the coast of Louisiana with depleted oxygen levels, a condition known as hypoxia. Most aquatic species cannot survive at such low oxygen levels, and a so-called "dead zone" results. After the 1993 flood of the Mississippi River, this area of hypoxia more than doubled in size, to over 18,000 square

environment: all of the external factors, conditions, and influences that affect the growth, development, and survival of organisms or a community; commonly refers to Earth and its support systems

estuary: a tidally influenced coastal area in which fresh water from a river mixes with sea water, generally at the river mouth; the resulting water is brackish, which results in a unique ecosystem

habitat: the environment in which a plant or animal grows or lives; the surroundings include physical factors such as temperature, moisture, and light, together with biological factors such as the presence of food and predators

petroleum: naturally occurring hydrocarbon compounds, derived from organic matter (e.g., plankton) that has been buried and broken down into simpler organic molecules over geologic time

This satellite view of the Arabian Peninsula illustrates gulfs, a strait, and marginal seas. The narrow Strait of Hormuz (center right) connects the Persian Gulf (interior) and the Gulf of Oman (far right), which joins the Arabian Sea (bottom right). The Red Sea (and the Gulf of Aden) is at the bottom left.

algae: (singular, alga) simple photosynthetic organisms, usually aquatic, containing chlorophyll, and lacking roots, stems, and leaves

ecosystem: the community of plants and animals within a water or terrestrial habitat interacting together and with their physical and chemical environment

kilometers (6,950 square miles). Generally, hypoxia can be traced back to excessive nutrients and excessive growth of **algae**, which ultimately dies and whose massive decay reduces the concentration of oxygen needed for aquatic species.

Because of its enlarged size and continuing existence, the hypoxic zone could threaten the economy of the U.S. Gulf of Mexico region, including its highly valued commercial and recreational fisheries. Like bays, gulfs are important measures of the health of aquatic **ecosystems** because so many waterbodies drain into them. Whatever has been deposited into these waterbodies eventually can reach gulfs.

Straits

A strait is a narrow passageway of water, usually between continents or islands, or between two larger bodies of water. The Strait of Gibraltar is probably the world's most famous strait. It connects the Atlantic Ocean on its west with the Mediterranean Sea on its east. It also separates northern Africa from the Rock of Gibraltar on the southernmost point of the Iberian Peninsula. Historically, almost all commerce between the Mediterranean Sea and Atlantic Ocean was routed through the Strait of Gibraltar. It is still an important route of international trade.

Two other well-known straits are the Strait of Bosporus and the Strait of Hormuz. The Strait of Bosporus is located in southwestern Asia and southeastern Europe. It connects the Black Sea (from the north) and the Sea of Marmara (from the south), and splits northwestern Turkey. The Strait of Hormuz is located at the southeastern end of the Persian Gulf (see photograph on page 70). It is a narrow waterway that can be (and has been) controlled to prevent ships from sailing through the gulf.

Choke Point. When a body of water such as a strait is capable of being blocked or even closed in order to control transportation routes, the body is called a "choke point." Historically, the Strait of Gibraltar has been one of the world's most important choke points. However, the Strait of Hormuz has become an important choke point in recent years because of increasing Middle East tensions. The Strait is surrounded by the United Arab Emirates and Oman (on one side) and Iran (on the other side). Hormuz connects the Persian Gulf to the Arabian Sea and ultimately to the Indian Ocean. SEE ALSO CHESAPEAKE BAY; ESTUARIES; ISLANDS, CAPES, AND PENINSULAS; MARGINAL SEAS; TRANSPORTATION.

William Arthur Atkins

> **STRAIT CLOSURES**
>
> Scientists believe that during its past, the Strait of Gibraltar has closed periodically, stopping the flow of water between the Mediterranean Sea and Atlantic Ocean. Water that today flows into the Mediterranean Sea from the Atlantic Ocean usually remains in the Mediterranean for between 80 to 100 years before returning to the Atlantic.

Bibliography

March, William M. *Environmental Geography: Science, Land Use, and Earth Systems,* 2nd ed. New York: John Wiley & Sons, 2002.

Strahler, Alan H. *Introducing Physical Geography,* 3rd ed. New York. John Wiley & Sons, 2003.

Internet Resources

Guantanamo Bay Naval Base and Ecological Crises. Trade and Environmental Database (TED). <http://www.american.edu/TED/GUANTAN.HTM>.

Access USGS—San Francisco Bay and Delta. United States Geological Survey. <http://sfbay.wr.usgs.gov/>.

Hypoxia in the Gulf Of Mexico. Gulf of Mexico Hypoxia Assessment, National Ocean Service, National Oceanic and Atmospheric Administration. <http://www.nos.noaa.gov/products/pubs_hypox.html#Intro>.

Rabalais, Nancy N. *Hypoxia in the Gulf Of Mexico.* NOAA Coastal Services Center, National Oceanic and Atmospheric Administration. <http://www.csc.noaa.gov/products/gulfmex/html/rabalais.htm/>.

Beach Pollution *See "Pollution of the Ocean" entries.*

Beaches

A beach is a dynamic environment located where land, sea, and air meet. It may be defined as a zone of unconsolidated sediment (i.e., loose materials) deposited by water, wind, or glaciers along the coast, between the low **tideline** and the next important landward change in **topography** or composition.

tideline: an artificial indicator marking the high-water or low-water limit of the tides

topography: the shape and contour of a surface, especially the land surface or ocean-floor surface

Beach materials can be made of sand, pebbles, cobbles, or boulders. The rocky cobble beaches of Acadia National Park, Maine are the result of the progressive erosion and weathering of coastal bedrock under strong wave action.

carbonate: carbonates are common minerals and are the principal constituents of sedimentary rocks such as limestone and dolostones; the most widespread carbonate minerals are calcite, aragonite, and dolomite

intertidal: coastal land that is covered by water at high tide and uncovered at low tide

longshore transport: the transport of sedimentary material parallel to the shore

This change can be a natural feature such as dunes or a cliff, or a human-made structure such as a seawall.

Although most beaches are composed of quartz sand, the fragments may be as large as boulders, or composed of some other material such as **carbonate** skeletal or shell fragments. Sources of beach material include sediment carried by rivers or eroded from cliffs or the seafloor, or biological material such as coral.

Parts of a Beach

A beach is comprised of two major parts: the foreshore and the backshore. The foreshore, also called the beach face, is the **intertidal** seaward portion. The backshore, or berm, is above the high tideline and is covered by water only during storms or unusually high spring tides. The foreshore's slope is steeper, whereas the backshore is nearly flat.

Zones. There are several zones seaward of the foreshore. Farthest out is the breaker zone, where waves coming in from the ocean become steeper and higher and begin to break. Nearer to shore is the surf zone, where waves actually break, and **longshore transport** occurs.

The swash zone is considered part of the foreshore, and is the area exposed to wave uprush and backwash (the forward and backward movements of waves). Beach material is constantly moved in the swash zone,

Large logs that originated from inland watersheds are carried into coastal waters and then can wash ashore. These recently deposited beach logs delineate a high-water mark, probably from a storm.

usually upward at an angle in the process called **beachdrift**. The surf zone and swash zone together make up the zone of **littoral transport**.

Beach Currents

The momentum of the waves, which break at an angle to the shoreline rather than running into it head-on, creates a flow parallel to the beach, known as the longshore or littoral current. This current picks up and carries sediment along with it, in the process called longshore transport or drift. The sediment is later deposited either on the beach, or as longshore **bars** of sediment just above the high tideline that are built up parallel to the coast and may eventually become barrier islands.

In contrast to longshore currents, rip currents or rip tides move sediment offshore. These currents form perpendicular to the shoreline when water brought to shore by breakers returns seaward via depressions in the seafloor or through breaks in offshore bars. Rip currents are narrow and localized and can move with speed and force. They are the source of undertow, about which swimmers are often warned.

Barrier Island Migration. A barrier island is an enlarged longshore bar that may be up to 30 meters (98 feet) high and contain dunes and vegetation.✳ It is slightly offset seaward from the mainland, parallel to the shore due to its formation by longshore transport. The end of the island that faces into the longshore current is constantly being eroded. The sediment, though, is picked up by the current and deposited at the other end of the island. Thus, barrier islands migrate continually in the direction of longshore transport.

Storms and Beaches

Beaches can have different shapes according to the season. Waves tend to be long and low in the summer and wash sand onto the beach, increasing the size of the backshore. During the winter, waves become higher and more closely spaced. They possess greater energy that erodes the backshore and carries sand away temporarily. Winter storms magnify the effect, as do tropical storms and hurricanes in the summer.

beachdrift: the net movement by longshore current of sand up or down and along the beach, depending on the direction of incoming waves

littoral transport: the movement of sedimentary material in the zone extending seaward from the shoreline to just beyond the breaker zone by waves and currents; it includes movement parallel (long-shore drift) and sometimes also perpendicular (cross-shore transport) to the shore

bar: a ridge built up in a river or ocean by deposits of sand, rock particles, and other materials

✳ **See "Coastal Ocean" for a photograph of a newly formed barrier island.**

Despite the inevitability of beach migration and erosion, people choose to live on unstable ground. The sandy foundations of these houses on North Carolina's Outer Banks, a series of barrier islands, are being undercut by the slow progression of wave action and occasional storm surges.

LAKE VERSUS OCEAN BEACHES

The beaches of large lakes, such as North America's Great Lakes, are similar to ocean beaches in terms of form and dynamic processes. There are some differences, however, for smaller lakes.

Ocean coasts receive simultaneous energy and freshwater-sediment input from multiple sources, so no one factor influences changes to any great extent. Yet lakes may have no more than one input source. Lakes are also more highly responsive to any energy input change, which is made more difficult by the smaller distance wind blows across open water, and the need to balance the energy over a much smaller area.

Lake beaches tend to be dominated by unstable waves that keep finer-grained particles in constant suspension. In addition, wind stress may alter the water level in a lake by causing the water surface to "pile up" at the downwind end of the lake, a phenomenon called a seiche.

The primary danger to a beach during a hurricane is the storm surge, which occurs when the low atmospheric pressure associated with a hurricane creates a "hill" of water in the ocean. The mounded water moves with the hurricane toward land. Upon approaching shallow water, the part of the mound over which wind is blowing produces a surge of elevated water pushed by the wind that inundates the beach.

The intense energy from a storm surge can badly erode a beach. Storm surges also can be very destructive to any structures in low-lying areas. Even worse are tidal floods, which are storm surges that form at high tide.

Another danger to beaches—particularly in the Pacific Ocean—is the tsunami, a seismic sea wave created by an earthquake that occurs on the ocean floor. These rare occurrences are commonly but incorrectly referred to as "tidal waves." Ocean water is displaced during the violent movements of major earthquakes and may move at speeds of up to 800 kilometers per hour (nearly 500 miles per hour). As the wave approaches the shore, it slows to less than 60 kilometers per hour (about 37 miles per hour), but increases in height to more than 15 meters (49 feet), causing extreme beach destruction and occasionally causing human deaths.

Erosion-Control Structures

Barrier islands and all beaches are highly fluid and nonpermanent in terms of location. They move all the time. Shorelines are the most dynamic, most changeable real estate in the world. However, many humans choose to live close to or even on beaches. They build homes and businesses on unstable ground.

Migration and erosion of beaches is a natural, expected process that would not ordinarily cause any problems except for these human structures and human presence. Because people desire to continue living in this hazardous area, a variety of measures have been designed to prevent or minimize beach erosion in order to protect such property.

Longshore processes, rather than seasonal onshore and offshore sediment movement, are the primary problems associated with living and working on beaches. Therefore, humans often employ so-called "hard structures" intended to improve navigation and reduce longshore beach erosion.

Groins. One type of structure for erosion control is the groin. Groins are walls placed perpendicular to the shoreline for the purpose of catching sediment to build up a beach. They often are constructed in groups, with the intention that each will trap some of the material being transported by the longshore current. However, while deposition may occur in the **updrift** direction, even more erosion will occur in the **downdrift** direction.

Jetties. Like groins, jetties are placed at a right angle (perpendicular) to shore, but at harbor or inlet mouths in pairs. Their purpose is to prevent the mouths from filling up with sediment or eroding away due to waves and currents. This helps to stabilize channels, but jetties block the longshore transport of sediment, causing updrift beaches to widen, and downdrift beaches to erode. Eventually deposition at jetties may fill the channel anyway, and dredging or scooping out the material is only a temporary solution.

Breakwaters. Breakwaters are walls constructed at some distance from and parallel to the coastline in an effort to break waves and reduce the effects of their force on the beach. Because the waves are not reaching the shore, the longshore current is halted and material accumulates, widening the beach. **Dredging** is sometimes necessary when too much sediment piles up behind a breakwater at the mouth of a harbor, and as with groins and jetties, erosion often takes place downdrift of the structure.

Seawalls. Seawalls are breakwaters constructed up against and parallel to the shore, again as a way to break the force of waves. While seawalls can protect the backshore, they, as well as breakwaters, are subject to failure due to scour, or undercutting by waves.

Drawbacks of Structures. Although all hard structures have relatively modest maintenance costs under optimum conditions, they are complex and expensive to build, and they rarely function as intended. They interfere with the natural, active littoral transport system and more often than not cause unintended, undesirable erosion and deposition. Hard structures protect the property of only a few people at the expense of many, for such projects are normally funded at least partially with tax money. Costs and concerns must be factored in before building begins.

Nonstructural Alternatives

Aside from structures such as groins, jetties, and seawalls, alternate methods of dealing with erosion can be employed. In a method known as beach nourishment or replenishment, sediment is dredged from offshore or brought in from another location and placed on a beach reduced by erosion. The additional measures of burying dead trees within dunes or planting other vegetation to hold sand in place help in constructing a positive beach budget; that is, so more material is gained or held in place rather than eroded and carried away. This helps to provide protection against erosion and has the added benefit of creating a larger recreational beach.

Certainly beach nourishment is aesthetically preferable to inefficient and potentially harmful engineered structures. However, it can cost millions of

updrift: the direction to which the predominant long-shore movement of beach material approaches

downdrift: the direction of predominant movement of littoral (shore-related) materials in seas or lakes

dredging: the process of excavating sediments and other materials, usually from underwater locations, for the purpose of mining aggregate (sand and gravel), constructing new waterways, or maintaining existing waterway cross-sections

LIGHTHOUSE ON THE MOVE

Following the National Park Service's 1989 decision to move the Cape Hatteras Lighthouse, controversy continued. Some groups thought that the lighthouse must be moved to prevent it from being enveloped by the Atlantic Ocean. Other groups felt that any relocation would destroy the lighthouse's structure and its historical significance, consequently reducing tourism that the famous structure generates. An exhaustive study by the National Research Council (a part of the National Academy of Sciences) concluded that the lighthouse could be moved safely. Even with that decision, various injunctions were generated to stop the move, which ultimately was completed in 2000.

The public's affinity for beaches ensures efforts to protect them from erosion and pollution. Here a beach has been newly "nourished" by the artificial addition of many tons of sand. Beach nourishment is a common yet temporary nonstructural measure for erosion control.

dollars to replenish a beach, usually with taxpayers footing the bill. Because beaches are going to move regardless of human intervention, beach nourishment is a temporary solution, and its cost and frequency must be weighed.

Relocating Inland. The most permanent and best solution to minimize the dangers of beach erosion is to move existing structures away from the shoreline. This has been done in the past in the case of irreplaceable historic buildings such as lighthouses. The cost, however, is prohibitive to many owners, and special skills, equipment, and organization are needed.

Beaches are attractive for their commercial and recreational value, so it is not probable humans will ever stop living close to the ocean. They will have to find ways to live with the natural system and deal with its hazards in a manner that will not irreparably damage it. SEE ALSO COASTAL OCEAN; COASTAL WATERS MANAGEMENT; HUMAN HEALTH AND THE OCEAN; POLLUTION OF THE OCEAN BY SEWAGE; SEA LEVEL; TIDES; TSUNAMIS; WAVES; WEATHER AND THE OCEAN.

Christina E. Bernal

Bibliography

Carter, R. W. G. *Coastal Environments: An Introduction to the Physical, Ecological, and Cultural Systems of Coastlines.* New York: Academic Press, 1988.

Davis, Richard A., Jr. *Oceanography: An Introduction to the Marine Environment,* 2nd ed. Dubuque, IA: Wm. C. Brown Publishers, 1991.

Gross, M. Grant. *Oceanography: A View of the Earth,* 3rd ed. Englewood Cliffs, NJ: Prentice Hall, 1982.

Keller, Edward A. *Environmental Geology,* 6th ed. New York: Macmillan Publishing Company, 1992.

Lerman, Abraham, ed. *Lakes: Chemistry, Geology, Physics.* New York: Springer-Verlag, 1978.

Levin, Harold L. *Contemporary Physical Geology,* 3rd ed. Philadelphia, PA: Saunders College Publishing, 1990.

Moore, J. Robert, ed. *Oceanography: Readings from Scientific American.* San Francisco, CA: W. H. Freeman and Company, 1971.

Thurman, Harold V. *Introductory Oceanography*, 8th ed. Upper Saddle River, NJ: Prentice Hall, 1997.

Internet Resources

Cape Hatteras Lighthouse Relocation Article and Images. U.S. Department of Interior, National Park Service. <http://www.nps.gov/caha/lrp.htm>.

Biodiversity

Biodiversity describes the variety of biological organisms in a given **habitat**, area, or **ecosystem**. It includes several components involving variation in species, ecosystems, and genetics.

Species diversity is perhaps what most people think of when they think of biodiversity. Species biodiversity describes the number of different species of plants, animals, fungi, protists, or bacteria within an area of interest. Although there are approximately 1.5 million named species globally, the large majority of species have yet to be studied or named, and there are likely to be as many as 10 million species on Earth.

Ecosystem diversity describes the variety of habitat types found within a given area. For example, there are numerous types of terrestrial (land-based) ecosystems in the United States, including forests, grasslands, **wetlands**, and deserts. There also are many types of aquatic (water-based) ecosystems, including lakes, rivers, **estuaries**, coral reefs, and **intertidal** habitats.

Genetic diversity describes genetic variation within species and represents a third component of biodiversity. Genetic variation allows species to adapt to changes in their environment. Species that are reduced to very small populations lose much of the gene pool and hence can lose much of this adaptability.

Aquatic Biodiversity

Aquatic biodiversity describes the diversity of species and ecosystems found in and around aquatic habitats such as rivers, lakes, and oceans. As with terrestrial ecosystems, aquatic biodiversity varies from region to region. Aquatic biodiversity is greatest in tropical latitudes. For example, an estimated 3,000 species of fish are found in the Amazon River alone. Coral reef habitats also have extremely high biodiversity; nearly a quarter of all known marine species are found in coral reefs. The Great Barrier Reef, off the coast of Australia, is the largest coral reef system in the world. It supports over 700 species of coral, in addition to 1,600 fish species and 4,000 species of **mollusks**.

In the Antarctic Ocean, on the other hand, only 120 fish species are found. These species possess special molecular, biochemical "antifreeze" properties to deal with the cold water temperatures. However, Antarctic habitats nonetheless support many unique aquatic groups, such as the albatross, penguin, and large numbers of marine mammals such as the whale and seal.✳

Many fresh-water habitats also harbor a high proportion of unique species. This is due to the fact that, unlike oceans, fresh-water habitats often are isolated from one another, with natural barriers between them that are

habitat: the environment in which a plant or animal grows or lives; the surroundings include physical factors such as temperature, moisture, and light, together with biological factors such as the presence of food and predators

ecosystem: the community of plants and animals within a water or terrestrial habitat interacting together and with their physical and chemical environment

wetland: an area that is periodically or permanently saturated or covered by surface water or groundwater, that displays hydric soils, and that typically supports or is capable of supporting hydrophytic vegetation

estuary: a tidally influenced coastal area in which fresh water from a river mixes with sea water, generally at the river mouth; the resulting water is brackish, which results in a unique ecosystem

intertidal: coastal land that is covered by water at high tide and uncovered at low tide

mollusk: an invertebrate animal with a soft, unsegmented body and usually a shell and a muscular foot; examples are clams, oysters, mussels, and octopuses

✳ **See "Marine Mammals" for photographs of a killer whale, manatee, elephant seal, and dolphin.**

The concept of biodiversity can be embodied in this colorful reef fish: a genetically distinct species is found in a specific habitat within a larger ecosystem. This particular fish could not survive, for example, in a polar sea or a tidal river.

food web: a complex food chain, with several species at each level, so that there is more than one producer and more than one consumer of each type

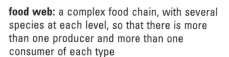

PHOTOGRAPHS OF ECOSYSTEMS

This encyclopedia contains photographs of several types of ecosystems. Entries with notable images include:

Entry	Photograph
"Corals and Coral Reefs"	coral reef
"Desert Hydrology"	desert
"Estuaries"	estuary
"Forest Hydrology"	forest
"Glaciers and Ice Sheets"	snow and ice
"Oceans, Polar"	ocean
"Tides"	intertidal
"Wetlands"	wetland

---

difficult to cross. This results in the evolution of distinct species in different fresh-water habitats. The preservation of fresh-water habitats therefore is particularly critical to conserving aquatic biodiversity.

The Value of Biodiversity

The value of biodiversity is an issue that has caused considerable debate, given that the preservation of habitats often conflicts with the desires of developers. Yet there are several reasons for valuing biodiversity.

First, biodiversity is essential to the functioning of ecosystems. Each species plays a unique role within an ecosystem, and every species is dependent on others for food, shelter, or other resources. The loss of a single species therefore can have profound effects for the ecosystem as a whole. Second, all species are potential sources of genetic variation for the development of new types of agricultural crops, as well as of medical drugs for treatment of human diseases. Third, biota (living organisms) have scientific and educational value. Finally, species have aesthetic and recreational value—consider, for example, the popularity of activities such as snorkeling, scuba diving, and hiking.

Scientists have shown that habitats with greater biodiversity are more resilient—that is, they are better able to adjust to and recover from various disturbances. Because different species may perform overlapping functions in a biologically diverse ecosystem, a disturbance that affects one species may have lesser impact on the ecosystem as a whole. Habitats with little diversity are more vulnerable, because a disturbance affecting one species may cause the entire network of interactions to collapse.

Ecosystems approaches to natural resource management address interactions among species and among **food webs**, as well as the cycling of resources such as carbon, water, and nitrogen. These ecosystems approaches focus not on single species, but on the preservation of complex sets of interactions among species. Preservation of large, intact areas of habitat is necessary for the continued functioning of ecosystems.

Coral reefs are known for their biodiversity as well as their scientific, educational, and recreational value. This brain coral gets its name from its resemblance to the human brain.

Even a few centimeters of water can create a small habitat: in this case, a shallow coastal splash-zone pool on a rocky shore. Like tidal pools, such coastal environments support diverse communities of plants and animals.

amphibian: a cold-blooded, smooth-skinned vertebrate of the class Amphibia, such as a frog or salamander, that characteristically hatches as an aquatic larva with gills and then transforms into an adult having air-breathing lungs

crustacean: arthropods with hard shells, jointed bodies, and appendages that primarily live in water

pollution: any alteration in the character or quality of the environment, including water in waterbodies or geologic formations, which renders the environmental resource unfit or less suited for certain uses

pesticides: a broad group of chemicals that kills or controls plants (herbicides), fungus (fungicides), insects and arachnids (insecticides), rodents (rodenticides), bacteria (bactericides), or other creatures that are considered pests

Threats to Biodiversity

Aquatic biodiversity is threatened on many fronts. Fresh-water habitats support many of the most highly threatened animal groups. These include fish, mussels, **amphibians**, and **crustaceans**.

Fresh-water habitats are threatened by many factors, including **pollution** from industry, increased acidification, and agricultural runoff containing residues of fertilizers or **pesticides**. In addition, the building of dams destroys many river ecosystems. Development can harm aquatic habitats or remove them altogether, as when marshy areas are filled.

Aquatic ecosystems also are particularly fragile because the disturbance of a watershed can affect multiple components downstream, including rivers, lakes, estuaries, and oceans. Perhaps the largest threat to ocean biodiversity is overfishing. In addition to depleting commercial species of fish, bivalves, and crustaceans, many fishing methods cause the needless deaths of non-commercial fish species as well as numerous reptiles, birds, and marine mammals. SEE ALSO AMPHIBIAN POPULATION DECLINES; BALANCING DIVERSE INTERESTS; BIRDS, AQUATIC; BIVALVES; CEPHALOPODS; CORALS AND CORAL REEFS; CRUSTACEANS; ECOLOGY, FRESH-WATER; ECOLOGY, MARINE; ENDANGERED SPECIES ACT; ESTUARIES; FISH; FISH AND WILDLIFE ISSUES; FISHERIES, FRESH-WATER; FISHERIES, MARINE; FISHES, CARTILAGINOUS; INSTREAM WATER ISSUES; LIFE IN EXTREME WATER ENVIRONMENTS; LIFE IN WATER; MARINE MAMMALS; OCEANS, POLAR; OCEANS, TROPICAL; REPTILES.

Jennifer Yeh

Bibliography

Byatt, Andrew, Alastair Fothergill, and Martha Holmes. *The Blue Planet: A Natural History of the Oceans.* New York: DK Publishers, 2001.

Gould, James L., and William T. Keeton, with Carol Grant Gould. *Biological Science,* 6th ed. New York: W. W. Norton & Co., 1996.

Birds, Aquatic

environment: all of the external factors, conditions, and influences that affect the growth, development, and survival of organisms or a community; commonly refers to Earth and its support systems

species: the narrowest classification or grouping of organisms according to their characteristics; members of a species can reproduce only with others of that group

habitat: the environment in which a plant or animal grows or lives; the surroundings include physical factors such as temperature, moisture, and light, together with biological factors such as the presence of food and predators

Aquatic **environments** provide critical habitat to a wide variety of bird **species**. Some aquatic birds divide their time between aquatic and terrestrial environments, while others spend most of their lives in water, returning to land only to breed. Many familiar bird groups are aquatic, including gulls and penguins as well as recreationally important species such as ducks and geese.

Wading and Diving Birds

Wading birds occupy shallow-water **habitats** in both fresh-water and salt-water environments. They have long, thin legs that allow them to walk through water easily while keeping the rest of their bodies dry. Some wading species find food by stirring the water with their feet; others use their beaks to filter food. Larger species with long legs and great height also possess long flexible necks that allow them to reach food below the water surface. Well-known wading species include flamingos, cranes, herons, storks, and egrets. Smaller birds include sandpipers and plovers.

Diving birds describe a broad group of species that occupy waters deeper than wading species. These birds dive, plunge, or swim after fish

The American widgeon is a common marsh duck which spends much of its time in deep water. It is nicknamed "bald pate" because the male has a white stripe on its head.

and other underwater prey. Well-known diving birds include ducks, geese, swans, pelicans, and penguins. These highly aquatic birds have evolved special adaptations to their habitat, such as webbed feet for swimming and waterproof feathers. Salt-water species also possess special salt glands that help excrete the excess salt that results from drinking sea water.

Diving birds associated with marine habitats also are called seabirds. Many seabirds spend large portions of time far from land, and all obtain food from the sea. However, all species return to land to lay eggs. In some places, seabirds can occur in staggering numbers—off the coast of Newfoundland, for example, some 35 to 40 million seabirds are documented yearly. Large breeding colonies of colorful puffins, as well as murres, storm-petrels, and other species attract numerous tourists in the spring.

Penguins. Penguins are perhaps the most aquatic of all diving birds. ✳ In some species, individuals return to land only to breed and molt. Like marine mammals, penguins that dive underwater must return to the water surface to breathe. Many penguins feed on krill (a small, shrimp-like crustacean), though some species hunt larger prey such as squid and fish.

✳ **See "Oceans, Polar" for a photograph of an adelie penguin.**

Penguins possess a streamlined body and are well-adapted to underwater swimming, achieving speeds as great as 15 kilometers (9 miles) per hour. A specialized fat layer and dense, waterproof feathers help them maintain appropriate body temperatures in frigid Antarctic waters. Penguin wings have been modified through evolution to form paddle-like flippers. Penguins are often described as "flying through water" because their wing motions during swimming resemble those of flying birds.

Conservation and Endangered Species

Aquatic bird species are at risk on many fronts. Many have declined due to the large-scale loss of **wetland** habitats. One example is the whooping crane, which was reduced to fewer than twenty individuals in the 1930s due to habitat loss and hunting. Though still highly **endangered**, whooping cranes have recovered somewhat as a result of massive conservation

wetland: an area that is periodically or permanently saturated or covered by surface water or groundwater, that displays hydric soils, and that typically supports or is capable of supporting hydrophytic vegetation

endangered: describes a plant or animal species threatened with extinction by human-made or natural changes throughout all or a significant area of its range; designated in accordance with the 1973 Endangered Species Act

NUISANCE WATERBIRDS

Some aquatic birds have been so successful at coexisting with humans that they occur in high densities and become nuisance species. For example, gulls thrive in many urban areas by feeding on garbage. The Canada goose is another aggressive nuisance species that outcompetes other aquatic birds for nesting space. Mute swans are an invasive species that compete with native waterbirds for nesting sites and food.

Nuisance species can degrade human habitats through their large numbers and excessive droppings in public areas. They may also eat crops or overgraze pastures. In some cases, nuisance species create significant public health problems. Control measures include limiting food supplies or destroying eggs before they can hatch.

efforts involving habitat protection, captive breeding, and the release of captively bred populations into the wild.

Other aquatic bird species are directly put at risk by human activity. Albatrosses, oceanic seabirds known for their large size and ability to fly long distances, have greatly declined in recent years due to the practice of longline fishing. Longlines (fishing lines with a single main line attached to secondary lines with baited hooks) kill over 40,000 albatrosses yearly. Nearly every albatross species is now critically imperiled.

Global warming appears to have impacted many species of Arctic and Antarctic aquatic birds. The loss of tundra breeding grounds in the Arctic has resulted in the decline of geese and sandpiper species. Several species of penguins also appear to be in decline, possibly due to krill shortages, some occurrences of which may be linked to global warming.

Oil spills represent a major threat to aquatic birds. One of the most infamous spills occurred in 1989, when the *Exxon Valdez* released 11 million tons of crude oil into Prince William Sound in Alaska. Thousands of seabirds died immediately upon contacting the oil, which destroys the insulating capacity of feathers. Others died from ingesting lethal amounts of oil when they tried to clean themselves. U.S. Fish and Wildlife Service biologists estimated that between 250,000 and 400,000 seabirds died as a result of the spill.

Aquatic birds are good indicators of the health of the habitats they occupy, and conservation efforts on their behalf have benefited ecosystems as well as other species. The first National Wildlife Refuge was established in Florida by President Theodore Roosevelt for an aquatic bird, the brown pelican, in 1903. SEE ALSO ENDANGERED SPECIES ACT; FISH AND WILDLIFE SERVICE, U.S.; OIL SPILLS: IMPACT ON THE OCEAN; POLLUTION BY INVASIVE SPECIES.

Jennifer Yeh

Bibliography

Enticott, Jim, and David Tipling. *Photographic Handbook of the Seabirds of the World.* London, U.K.: New Holland, 1998.

Gill, Frank B. *Ornithology.* New York: W. H. Freeman, 1995.

Haley, Delphine. *Seabirds of Eastern North Pacific and Arctic Waters.* Seattle, WA: Pacific Search Press, 1984.

Harrison, Craig S. *Seabirds of Hawaii: Natural History and Conservation.* Ithaca, NY: Comstock Publishing Associates, 1990.

Nelson, Bryan *Seabirds: Their Biology and Ecology.* New York: A & W Publishers Inc., 1979.

Terres, John K. *The Audubon Society Encyclopedia of North American Birds.* New York: Knopf, 1980.

Bivalves

species: the narrowest classification or grouping of organisms according to their characteristics; members of a species can reproduce only with others of that group

Bivalves belong to the invertebrate phylum Mollusca, which also includes snails, squids, and octopuses. Some well-known bivalves include clams, scallops, mussels, and oysters. More than 15,000 **species** of bivalves exist. All bivalves are aquatic, encompassing both marine and fresh-water species.

Giant clams can weigh more than 227 kilograms (500 pounds), and are the largest bivalve mollusk in the world. These giant clams are at a fisheries research center on Micronesia's Koror Island.

Characteristics of Bivalves

The name "bivalve" refers to the two-part shell that characterizes these mollusk species. The two halves of the shell are joined by a ligamentous hinge and held shut by a pair of strong adductor muscles. The shell is made of calcium carbonate and is secreted by the mantle (soft body wall). Shells grow with the organisms, extending out from the hinge area. Most bivalve species go through a free swimming larval stage before taking on their characteristic adult form and lifestyle.

Most species of bivalves are filter feeders. Currents of water are drawn into the body and through the gills, where tiny food particles are caught in the gill mucus. This flow of water also functions in respiration, allowing organisms to obtain fresh oxygen. A few bivalve species are predatory, including some deep-sea scallops.

Bivalves make use of a variety of lifestyles. Sedentary species (e.g., mussels and oysters) spend their lives attached to a **substrate**, whereas others burrow underground (e.g., clams) or live on the water bottom and swim (e.g., scallops). Bivalves have highly reduced heads and simple nervous and sensory systems. Most species have some chemosensory cells at the edge of the mantle that are used to detect chemical signals in the water. Some also have simple eyes. Bivalves have an open circulatory system.

substrate: the bottom or underlying materials; in ecology, the bottom sediments in lakes, rivers, and oceans that may contain living organisms

A number of bivalve species have some commercial value, including representatives of all the groups discussed here. Bivalves are valued as food sources, and throughout history their shells have been used for many purposes. Most buttons were made from shells before the advent of plastic. In addition, shell fragments have been used for everything from roads to fertilizer. Finally, the beautiful pearls found in oysters have always been treasured.

In the late 1800s and early 1900s, making buttons out of fresh-water mussel shells was a multi-million-dollar industry. This was common practice until the growth of the plastics industry in the 1940s and 1950s.

At certain times, some mollusks can become toxic to animals and humans who consume them. Toxins produced by certain algae during a bloom (rapid population growth) bioaccumulate in the tissue of mollusks, and then may be ingested by higher-level consumers who eat the mollusks.

Clams

Clams live underground, using a muscular foot to dig down into sand or mud. They take in water for filter feeding and gas exchange through an extended part of the body called the siphon, or neck. The siphon is also used to disperse eggs or sperm. In some species, such as the geoduck clam, the siphon is extremely long, allowing the clam to remain safe deep underground. The geoduck is the world's largest burrowing clam, and can live up to 145 years.

Common predators of clams include starfish and eels. Defensive behavior involves retracting the body and closing the shell as tightly as possible.

algae: (singular, alga) simple photosynthetic organisms, usually aquatic, containing chlorophyll, and lacking roots, stems, and leaves

photosynthesis: the process by which plants manufacture food from sunlight; specifically, the conversion of water and carbon dioxide to complex sugars in plant tissues by the action of chlorophyll driven by solar energy

The giant clam can grow to lengths of 1.2 meters (4 feet) and is unusual in that it harbors **algae** (e.g., dinoflagellates) within its tissues. The algae obtain shelter and protection from their host, while the clam obtains important nutrients that are products of algal **photosynthesis**.

Scallops

Scallops are unusual among bivalves in that they are capable of jet-propelled swimming. Sudden contraction of the adductor muscles quickly closes the shell, causing water to be ejected on either side of the hinge. Scallops thus swim in short spurts.

Scallops generally live on sand bottoms. They may attach themselves to rocks but are able to detach and swim to a new location. Jet propulsion also is used as an escape response to avoid potential predators, such as starfish, snails, and fish. The large, well-developed adductor muscles represent the edible part of the scallop.

Scallops are also unusual among bivalves in that their eyes are well developed. They have a series of eyes around the edge of the shell that are critical in helping to detect predators. The importance of eyes is likely related to scallops' unique locomotor capabilities among bivalves.

Scallops often occur in dense congregations known as scallop beds. These are sometimes temporary, but permanent beds do occur in areas with optimal temperature conditions and food availability. Commercial fishing of scallops has diminished many natural populations, and the use of scallop farms has helped meet consumer demand.

Mussels

Mussels are sedentary bivalves. They attach themselves to a firm substrate using secreted threads known as byssal threads, which are produced by the byssal organ of the muscular foot. Mussels frequently occur in large colonies, forming mussel beds. Like other bivalves, they are filter feeders.

Fresh-water species of mussels occur in streams and rivers. Unlike marine bivalve larvae, which are free-swimming, the larvae of fresh-water mussels are **parasitic**, most often on fish. Numerous species of fresh-water mussels are endangered, including roughly half the species that occur in North America.

parasite: an organism that lives within or on another organism, causing harm to the host organism

The zebra mussel is an invasive fresh-water species that was accidentally introduced into North America in the 1980s from its original European habitat. It spread quickly through eastern North America. The zebra mussel continues to have a detrimental impact on water supplies by clogging intake pipes and other structures, and much effort continues to go into controlling its spread. Zebra mussels can be spread to new waterbodies by fishing activities and by boats, to which they often attach.

Oysters

Oysters are sessile (nonmotile) bivalves that live attached to substrates such as rocks. Like many other bivalves, they occur in beds and are filter feeders. Oyster shells tend to be rough on the outside but smooth on the inside.

Oysters are sequential hermaphrodites: that is, they are sperm-producing males when young and then become female egg producers when older. The largest oysters reach sizes of up to about 38 centimeters (15 inches). Oysters grows continually throughout life and may live as long as 100 years.

Several species of oysters are valued as delicacies, and some are cultivated for food. However, oysters are perhaps best known for their pearls. (All bivalves make pearls, but those of oysters are particularly valued.) When small irritants become lodged within the shell, the oyster deposits layers of pearly material around the irritant. This material is identical to that used to line the inside of the oyster's shell. SEE ALSO ALGAL BLOOMS, HARMFUL; CEPHALOPODS; GREAT LAKES; MARICULTURE; POLLUTION BY INVASIVE SPECIES.

Jennifer Yeh

Bibliography

Brusca, Richard C., and Gary J. Brusca. *Invertebrates.* Sunderland, MA: Sinauer Associates, 1990.

Gould, James L., and William T. Keeton, with Carol Grant Gould. *Biological Science*, 6th ed. New York: W. W. Norton & Co., 1996.

Hickman, Cleveland P., Larry S. Roberts, and Allan Larson. *Animal Diversity*. Dubuque, IA: Wm. C. Brown, 1994.

Bottled Water

Sales of bottled water in the United States have increased dramatically since the 1980s. This increase is largely due to an effective advertising campaign that directly appeals to fitness-conscious Americans looking for healthy alternatives to tap water. These campaigns emphasize the purity of bottled water through advertisements and packaging labels featuring impressive glaciers and flowing mountain **springs**.

However, a significant portion of bottled water is merely bottled public-water-supply water, perhaps polished by a carbon filter or other devices prior to bottling. In other words, the water in the bottle may actually come from a municipal well in an urban area.

Depending on the situation, bottled water may not be safer than tap water, but Americans are still drinking record amounts of it. According to the Beverage Marketing Corporation, Americans spent approximately $6.5 billion on bottled water in 2002, with each U.S. citizen drinking an average of 74 liters (19.5 gallons). Sales of bottled water increased by 225 percent in the 1990s.

Types of Bottled Water

There are several different categories of bottled water, based on the nature of the water and its source. Nonsparkling water includes artesian, spring, purified (including distilled), and mineral. Artesian water is drawn from a well in a **confined aquifer**, and often refers to a naturally flowing well. Spring water is taken directly from the spring or from a well adjacent to the spring that draws water from the **aquifer** feeding the spring. Purified water can be produced through distillation, filtration, or some other water treatment process. Mineral water naturally contains more than 250 parts per million of total dissolved solids. (No minerals can be artificially added to this water nor can it be drawn from a municipal source.) A new type of bottled water comes from icebergs, which are chunks of glaciers at sea.

Sparkling water can be any type of naturally carbonated water. (Soda water, seltzer water, and tonic water are not considered bottled waters.) Some natural waters can be both naturally carbonated and highly mineralized; moreover, they may be delivered to the surface via flowing artesian wells.

Domestic nonsparkling water accounts for over 94 percent of all bottled water sold in the United States, whereas sparkling water and imports each have an approximate 3 percent share of the market.

In the past, consumers sometimes misunderstood the actual source of the bottled water they purchased. Labels such as "pure mountain spring water" were not necessarily accurate: this water may have come from a public water supply, or even from multiple sources. Today, stricter labeling requirements in the United States for both imported water and water

spring: location where a concentrated, natural discharge of groundwater emerges from the Earth's subsurface as a definite flow onto the surface of the land or into a body of surface water, such as a lake, river, or ocean

confined aquifer: describes an aquifer in which groundwater is isolated from the atmosphere by impermeable formations; confined groundwater generally is subject to pressure greater than atmospheric pressure and is often artesian in character

aquifer: a water-saturated, permeable, underground rock formation that can transmit significant quantities of water under ordinary hydraulic gradients to wells and springs

Americans collectively drink more than 20 billion liters of bottled water each year. Wholesale value of the bottled water market has risen steadily since 1990.

shipped in interstate commerce specify that independent of the product name, the source of the water bottled must be identified.

Is Bottled Water Better?

Many individuals purchase bottled water as a matter of convenience, for hiking, sporting events, and other activities. Others purchase bottled water because they believe that it is safer than either public water supplies or private self-supply (usually from wells). Bottled water may taste or look better than public-water-supply water, but it is not necessarily safer. The U.S. Environmental Protection Agency regulates public-water-supply water through the federal Safe Drinking Water Act. Bottled water, however, is regulated through the federal Food and Drug Administration (FDA).

The FDA is required to adopt the same standards as those required by the Safe Drinking Water Act. Moreover, the FDA regulates bottled water as a food product, and bottled water companies must comply with the FDA's Quality Standards, labeling regulations, and Good Manufacturing Practices. In addition, the International Bottled Water Association has prepared a model program for their members that includes adherence to all state and federal regulations as well as random, unannounced inspection visits.

Although bottled water must generally meet the same safety standards as public-water-supply water, the EPA requires frequent, often daily, monitoring of public drinking water, whereas the FDA requires testing only once a year for bottled water. In addition, the FDA regulations only apply to water that is sold in interstate commerce. According to the Natural Resources Defense Council, approximately 60 percent of all bottled waters are sold in the same state where they are bottled; hence, FDA regulations do not apply.

At the state level, bottled water is covered by state regulations and industry standards. Many states have even more stringent standards than the FDA, while others either refer to or duplicate the FDA standards. However, roughly one in five states do not regulate bottled water, or have lax regulations or no enforcement powers. Fewer than half of the states require artificially carbonated waters such as seltzer water, soda water, or tonic water to meet bottled water standards.

Despite these considerations, American consumers continue to drink huge quantities of bottled water. Understanding the nature of public drinking-water supplies, privately bottled water, and the regulations governing each will help consumers make informed decisions about the safety of the water they drink, and the advantages—if any—of purchasing bottled water. SEE ALSO AQUIFER CHARACTERISTICS; DRINKING-WATER TREATMENT; FRESH WATER, NATURAL COMPOSITION OF; FRESH WATER, NATURAL CONTAMINANTS IN; FRESH WATER, PHYSICS AND CHEMISTRY OF; GROUNDWATER; ICE AT SEA; MINERAL WATERS AND SPAS; PRIVATIZATION OF WATER MANAGEMENT; SENSES, FRESH WATER AND THE; SPRINGS; SUPPLIES, PROTECTING DRINKING-WATER; SUPPLIES, PUBLIC AND DOMESTIC WATER; WELLS AND WELL DRILLING.

Elliot Richmond

Bibliography

Bottled Water: Pure Drink or Pure Hype? Natural Resources Defense Council, 1999.

Lamoreaux, Philip E., and J. T. Tanner, eds. *Springs and Bottled Waters of the World: Ancient History, Source, Occurrence, Quality and Use.* New York: Springer Verlag, 2001.

Siskos, Catherine. "Bottled Water Everywhere." *Kiplinger's Personal Finance Magazine.* vol. 52, no. 9 (Sept. 1998): 47.

Internet Resources

Groundwater and Drinking Water. U.S. Environmental Protection Agency. <http://www.epa.gov/safewater/index.html>.

International Bottled Water Association. <http://www.bottledwater.org/>.

Bretz, J Harlen

American Field Geologist
1882–1981

J Harlen Bretz is best known for his hypothesis that floods of enormous volumes once swept across southeastern Washington and on out the Columbia

River Gorge to the Pacific Ocean. Bretz was widely criticized by his contemporaries for his "outrageous hypothesis" while continuing to use his own observations, not popular opinion, to develop his ideas. Like a detective, Bretz gathered as many clues as he could and reached what he believed to be the best solution to the geologic puzzle of the Missoula Floods.

A Pioneering Theorist

Born in Michigan in 1882, Bretz showed an early interest in science, and in college obtained a biology degree. While teaching high school biology in Seattle, Washington, he became interested in **glacial** landforms in the Puget Sound area that were formed during the most recent glacial period (ending about 10,000 years ago). He spent many of his weekends in the field taking careful notes about the **landforms** that he saw. Many of his observations were published in scientific journals.

In 1913, Bretz earned a Ph.D. in geology at the University of Chicago and began studying landforms in eastern Washington state that seemed to defy explanation by traditional geologic theories. These landforms included incredibly high dry falls perched well above the current river level; huge potholes, some 50 to 100 meters (150 to 330 feet) across; huge 200-ton boulders, that because they differed markedly in mineralogy from the surrounding bedrock must somehow have been transported to their current locations; and gigantic gravel bars that were the size of hills, hundreds of meters long and tens of meters high. Bretz's experience in the glacial terrain of the Puget Sound offered him an important perspective. He recognized many of these features were simply gigantic replicas of the same smaller-scale features that he had seen time and time again in glacial streams and **outwash** areas: the depositional and erosional products of meltwater-fed streams during the last **ice age**. Clearly, however, the volume of floodwater required to produce these gigantic landforms would have had to have been prodigious.

The prevailing theory regarding the origin of Earth's landscape was Uniformitarianism, which stated that all landforms on Earth's surface were produced by ordinary geologic processes—for example, stream erosion and deposition—acting over immense geologic time. These processes were deemed capable of producing deep canyons such as the Grand Canyon of the southwestern United States. The contrasting theory, Catastrophism, held that landforms on the Earth resulted from catastrophic events, such as huge earthquakes and biblical floods. To many geologists in 1920, Bretz's flood hypothesis was too close to a biblical interpretation.

Bretz endured nearly four decades of doubt and ridicule by other geologists of the time, in part because Bretz was unable to offer a reasonable explanation for the source of the huge amounts of water that would have had to have been suddenly and catastrophically released across eastern Oregon. Bretz's work was finally vindicated, however, when another geologist, Joseph Pardee, found evidence of a former huge lake (Lake Missoula) in western Montana that was formed when the Clark Fork River had been dammed by a glacier. The lake had rapidly drained when the dam failed, allowing enormous amounts of water to flood eastern Washington (see discussion below).

Only in the 1950s and 1960s was Bretz's hypothesis regarding the Missoula Floods accepted and his contributions recognized. In 1979, the

glacier: a huge mass of ice, formed on land by the compaction and recrystallization of snow, which moves slowly downslope or outward owing to its own weight

landform: a discernible natural landscape that exists as a result of wind, water, ice, or other geological activity, such as a plateau, plain, basin, or mountain

outwash: sand and gravel deposited by meltwater streams in front of or beyond a glacier

ice age: a cold period marked by episodes of extensive glaciation alternating with episodes of relative warmth; the formally designated "Ice Age" refers to the most recent glacial period, which occurred during the Pleistocene epoch

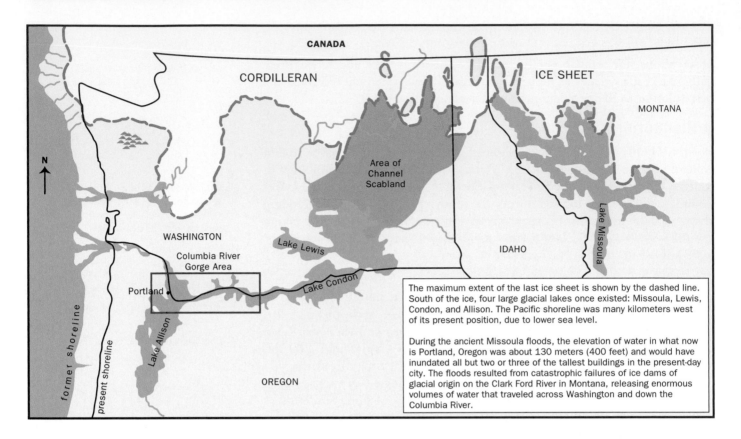

The maximum extent of the last ice sheet is shown by the dashed line. South of the ice, four large glacial lakes once existed: Missoula, Lewis, Condon, and Allison. The Pacific shoreline was many kilometers west of its present position, due to lower sea level.

During the ancient Missoula floods, the elevation of water in what now is Portland, Oregon was about 130 meters (400 feet) and would have inundated all but two or three of the tallest buildings in the present-day city. The floods resulted from catastrophic failures of ice dams of glacial origin on the Clark Ford River in Montana, releasing enormous volumes of water that traveled across Washington and down the Columbia River.

J Harlen Bretz was the first to piece together the geological history of the Missoula Floods. This figure shows the maximum extent of the last ice sheet in what is today the U.S. Northwest, as well as the four ancient glacial lakes: Missoula, Lewis, Condon, and Allison. Scabland is an area of basalt flows that was flooded. Note that the Pacific shoreline was many miles west of its present position, due to lowered sea level.

Geological Society of America awarded J Harlen Bretz, then 96 years old, the Penrose Medal, the highest national geological award for his contributions to geological knowledge.

The Modern View of the Missoula Floods

It is now widely accepted that the Missoula Floods occurred when vast amounts of water rushed across approximately 7,800 square kilometers (3,000 square miles) of southeastern Washington, scouring soil from the surface, gouging out blocks of bedrock, and turning river valleys into river channels. Water levels were so high that the water overflowed the top of the Columbia River Gorge in several places, and reached a depth of approximately 100 meters (328 feet) where present-day Portland, Oregon is located (see the figure). The evidence for the Missoula Floods was compiled by Bretz, who recognized the following characteristic features:

- Dry falls, 180 meters (600 feet) above the present Columbia River level, over which water once cascaded;

- Huge potholes, requiring enormously turbulent water;

- Gigantic boulders, up to 200 tons, transported from eastern Washington to Oregon; and

- Enormous gravel bars, 90 to 120 meters (300 to 400 feet) high.

Lake Missoula was formed by the glacial damming of the Clark Fork River at the end of the last ice age (approximately 10,000 years ago). Ancient lake beaches perched on mountains 640 meters (2,100 feet) above the present-day valley floor indicate the lake's size. When the dam failed, Lake

Missoula waters roared out at the phenomenal rate of approximately 40 cubic kilometers (9.5 cubic miles) *per hour*, almost 200 times the Mississippi River's flow rate at flood stage. The rapid draining is indicated by huge ripple marks, 15 meters (50 feet) high and 150 meters (500 feet) apart, on today's valley floor. The damming and flooding cycle repeated itself as many as 40 times during the last ice age. SEE ALSO GLACIERS AND ICE SHEETS; ICE AGES; STREAM EROSION AND LANDSCAPE DEVELOPMENT.

Dennis O. Nelson

Bibliography

Allen, John Elliot, Marjorie Burns, and Samuel C. Sargent. *Cataclysms on the Columbia*. Portland, OR: Timber Press, 1986.

Mueller, Marge, and Ted Mueller. *Fire, Faults & Floods*. Moscow, ID: University of Idaho Press, 1997.

Bridges, Causeways, and Underwater Tunnels

Bridges, causeways, and underwater tunnels are all passageways that allow travel above, across, and beneath bodies of water such as rivers, bayous, and bays. On the other hand, these artificial structures can create barriers or obstacles to wildlife that live underneath and above these waters. For instance, fish may be hindered or prevented from moving either upstream or downstream.

Bridges

A bridge is a structure designed to provide passage over an obstacle, oftentimes water. Bridges carry such transportation elements as roadways, railroad tracks, and walkways over waterbodies, along with such utilities as water pipes, support power cables, and telecommunications lines. There are many examples of bridges that have had dramatic impacts on the areas through which they were built: only three are discussed below.

The Brooklyn Bridge. The Brooklyn Bridge was opened for use on May 24, 1883, crossing the East River in New York City between the boroughs of Brooklyn and Manhattan. As the first bridge over the East River, the Brooklyn Bridge had a major impact on the small, independent city of Brooklyn. The newly energized city soon became closely linked to Manhattan, one of the world's leading commercial, cultural, financial, medical, and tourist centers. By opening a new transportation link, the bridge made possible the rapid growth of Brooklyn.

Golden Gate Bridge. For many years, the only way to cross San Francisco Bay in California was by ferry, and by the early twentieth century the bay was filled with ferries.✳ When the bridge was first designed, an immense engineering challenge was introduced because the area produces winds of up to 100 kilometers (60 miles) per hour, strong ocean currents, and frequent fogging conditions. In addition, the bay lies within a large earthquake zone.

Taking 10 years to complete, the construction of the Golden Gate Bridge was finished in 1937. Despite the many problems with its construction, it

✳ **See "Bays, Gulfs, and Straits" for a photograph of San Francisco Bay.**

effectively opened up the counties to the north of San Francisco. Forty-one million drivers and passengers use the Golden Gate Bridge each year, and roughly 1.6 billion people have used the 2.7-kilometer (1.7-mile) span since it opened.

Confederation Bridge. The 12.9-kilometer (8-mile) Confederation Bridge linked Prince Edward Island to mainland New Brunswick, Canada beginning in June 1997. It is the world's longest bridge over ice-covered waters. The bridge was designed to withstand the harsh waters that flow beneath it.

Researchers will study the bridge's performance using a variety of sophisticated monitoring devices, including 450 thermal sensors, 28 ice-load panels, and 76 vibration sensors. The comprehensive study, which spans a 20-year period that began in 1997, will be the largest data-gathering project ever undertaken in the areas of bridge and marine engineering.

With any structure that is built on or near a waterbody, concerns usually develop about possible impacts on the **environment** near and around the structure. The Confederation Bridge was no exception. Fishermen were worried that the government was ignoring their livelihood by neglecting the impact on the lobster industry. Environmentalists were worried about the effect the bridge would have on the local ecosystem and, especially, about the increased **pollution** of the surrounding environment.

On the other hand, such bridges that connect two separated landmasses can positively impact both areas. The total number of tourist parties visiting Prince Edward Island in 1997 was up by 30 percent over 1996. Expenditures by tourists in 1997 were about $245.9 million, an increase of 63 percent from 1996. Annual increases in tourism are anticipated for the period 2000–2015.

Causeways

A causeway is a raised road or track across low or wet ground. For example, the Lake Pontchartrain Causeway connects the New Orleans coastal area on the southern shore with the northern shore. The causeway is the world's longest highway bridge, a continuous-span beam bridge that is almost 39 kilometers (24 miles) long.

Because the Lake Pontchartrain Causeway travels directly across Lake Pontchartrain, oil, grease, and other pollutants from vehicles using the highway are deposited on the causeway. These contaminants eventually wash off and drain into the lake. Causeways, by their very nature of crossing shallow waterbodies, can generate many types of pollutants that find their way into those waters.

On the other hand, unexpected positive results can occur. Twice a year, about 8 million purple martin birds migrate through southeast Louisiana and use Lake Pontchartrain as a stopover point. During spring and summer, more than 200,000 of these birds have adopted the understructure of the southern end of the Lake Pontchartrain Causeway as their evening roost area. Bird-lovers and spectators gather to watch the birds swoop in and out of the structure. With continuing loss of habitat for such wildlife, the causeway provides an important resting and feeding place for the purple martins as they migrate through the area.

environment: all of the external factors, conditions, and influences that affect the growth, development, and survival of organisms or a community; commonly refers to Earth and its support systems

pollution: any alteration in the character or quality of the environment, including water in waterbodies or geologic formations, which renders the environmental resource unfit or less suited for certain uses

An aerial view shows the parallel roadways of the Lake Ponchartrain Causeway in New Orleans, Louisiana. It is the world's longest road bridge.

A British and a French worker shake hands at the entrance to the English Channel Tunnel upon its completion in 1990. The "Chunnel" spans 50 kilometers (32 miles) and is submerged beneath the seabed at a varied depth of from 45 meters to 75 meters (150 feet to 250 feet).

Underwater Tunnels

An underwater tunnel is a passage, gallery, or roadway beneath a body of water. Underwater tunnels are used for highway traffic, railroads, and subways; to transport water, sewage, oil, and gas; to divert rivers around dam sites while the dam is being built; and for military and civil defense purposes. A few examples are discussed below.

An underground tunnel is located at the Chesapeake Bay. The 28.2-kilometer (17.5-mile) crossing between Norfolk and Cape Charles, Virginia, begins as a bridge, but disappears into the water midway. A combination structure, the Chesapeake Bay Bridge–Tunnel combines two bridges with two tunnels that pass under major shipping channels.

One notable underwater tunnel is the 137-meter (450-foot) Orwigsburg Tunnel (the first tunnel dug in the United States) that was completed in 1821 at Orwigsburg Landing, near Auburn, Pennsylvania. Also impressive are the New York City tunnels: the Holland Tunnel (the world's only three-tube tunnel) and the Lincoln Tunnel (the Hudson River's first tunnel) under the Hudson river; the Queens-Midtown Tunnel under the East River; and the Brooklyn–Battery Tunnel under New York Bay.

The Channel Tunnel, frequently called the "Chunnel," is a 50-kilometer (32-mile) tunnel that provides a railroad link under the Strait of Dover in the English Channel between Cheriton (near Kent), England and Coquelles, France. The tunnel, one of the most impressive civil engineering projects of the twentieth century, has an ultimate design capacity of 600 trains per day each way.

Throughout its history, the English Channel has proven to be very hazardous for marine travel. The Chunnel is delivering a large market share of the transportation industry between England and **continental** Europe,

continental: of or pertaining to the continents

and is doing it in a much safer way than traveling through dangerous ocean waters. SEE ALSO BAYS, GULFS, AND STRAITS; CANALS; ECONOMIC DEVELOPMENT; TRANSPORTATION.

William Arthur Atkins

Bibliography

Brown, David J. *Bridges.* New York: Macmillan; Maxwell Macmillan International, 1993.

Corbett, Scott. *Bridges.* New York: Four Winds Press, 1978.

Epstein, Sam. *Tunnels.* Boston, MA: Little, Brown, 1985.

Kingston, Jeremy. *How Bridges Are Made.* New York: Facts on File, 1985.

Internet Resources

Bridges. WGBH Educational Foundation, PBS Online. <http://www.pbs.org/wgbh/buildingbig/bridge/index.html>.

Geologic Framework and Processes of the Lake Pontchartrain Basin. Coastal and Marine Geology Program, U.S. Geological Survey. <http://coastal.er.usgs.gov/pontchartrain/wetland.html>.

McGloin, John Bernard. *Symphonies in Steel: Bay Bridge and the Golden Gate.* The Museum of the City of San Francisco. <http://www.sfmuseum.org/hist9/mcgloin.html>.

PEI's Confederation Bridge: The Spectacular Confederation Bridge. TourCanada.com. <http://www.tourcanada.com/cbridge.htm>.

Tunnels. WGBH Educational Foundation, PBS Online. <http://www.pbs.org/wgbh/buildingbig/tunnel/index.html>.

Brines, Natural

Natural brines are waters with very high to extremely high concentrations of dissolved constituents—elements, ions, and molecules. Brines are commonly considered to be those waters more saline, or more concentrated in dissolved materials, than sea water (35 grams of dissolved constituents per kilogram of sea water). Brine can contain salt concentrations more than five times greater than the salt content of average sea water. Natural mixtures of brines, sea water, and fresh waters occur at various locations.

Owing to high concentrations of dissolved components such as sodium and magnesium, brines are of commercial interest, especially in the production of table salt. Subsurface caverns (especially those used for the mining of table salt), saline lakes (e.g., the Great Salt Lake, the Dead Sea, the Salton Sea), and the saltwater ocean are three principal sources of brine. Despite their economic value in some circumstances, brines may cause considerable trouble where they leak into potable (drinkable) water supplies or contaminate water for animals, crops, gardens, and other landscaped terrains.

Formation of Ocean Brine

In the ocean, brine is formed by several processes: evaporation, formation of sea ice, and solution of salt domes.

Evaporation.   One of the more common processes is by evaporation. Evaporation is greatest in shallow or stranded regions of sea water, where the energy of the Sun evaporates some water, concentrating the salt. The process where the solvent (water) is removed from the system is known as evaporite formation, and the resulting rock is called an evaporite. Evaporites are common in the geologic record.

Sea Ice.   Another process by which ocean brines arise is through the formation of sea ice. As sea water begins to solidify, some of the saltier, denser water (brine) drains to underlying water. As the ice thickens, the brine can become trapped in pores known as brine pockets. This effect further concentrates the brine. Brine pockets are typically less than half a millimeter in diameter, but can extend downward into the ice for some distance.

The presence of brine pockets influences the mechanical properties of sea ice in ways that are not yet fully understood. As the ice structure changes, more water is extruded from the pores, increasing the salt concentration of the brine in the pore space up to eight times that of typical (liquid) sea water. At this extreme concentration, the sodium and chloride are supersaturated, and so begin to **precipitate** as salt crystals. Concentration processes in the ice pores may continue, resulting in a slurry or a gel. At very high salt concentrations, sodium chloride crystals (halite) form, as can crystals containing chlorides of other salts such as calcium and magnesium.

precipitate: (verb) in a solution, to separate into a relatively clear liquid and a solid substance by a chemical or physical change; (noun) the solid substance resulting from this process

Salt Domes.   Brine can form by the aqueous solution of evaporite deposits such as those found in salt domes. A salt dome is a geological structure where very deep deposits of relatively "plastic" salt flowed upward through the bedrock owing to the great pressure of this overlying rock and sediment. The salt may break through the rock and sediment layer, protruding with a dome-like shape, thus giving the structure its name.

✳ See the frontmatter of this volume for a geologic timescale.

Salt domes are a distinctive feature of the Gulf of Mexico, in particular the central region of the gulf called the Orca basin. The solution at the bottom 150 meters (492 feet) of the Orca basin is not sea water but a highly concentrated brine with little or no free oxygen. A layer of salt formed at the Orca basin during the Jurassic Period of Earth's history.✳ The salt was eventually extruded, under tremendous pressure, through overlying layers of sediment toward the surface, forming salt domes. Oil and gas included in these sediments may be pooled and trapped by salt dome structures and form attractive targets for energy exploration.

There are more than 500 known salt domes in the Gulf Coast region. Some of these originate from the salt layers that are many kilometers underground. In the Orca basin, salt domes on the sea bottom expose the salt to the sea water. Where the salt dome interacts with the sea water, solution of the dome can occur as salt dissolves in water. The extreme salinity of the area immediately surrounding the salt dome, however, will create a pool of salt water that is denser than the surrounding sea. This extremely salty water, or brine, leaks from the area of the salt dome into surrounding depressions on the sea floor, creating brine pools.

Oil Seeps.   The presence of brine, such as in a brine pool, is useful in some regions as an indicator of the presence of an oil seep. Geological features that allow salt to protrude from the seabed in places such as the Gulf of Mexico also are conducive to the leakage of oil and natural gas: the Gulf of Mexico is a significant oil-producing region. The oil seeps in the gulf are common enough that oil slicks are visible from satellites in some places. Hundreds of oil drilling platforms are positioned offshore of Texas and the eastern coast of Mexico to explore these areas.✳

✳See "Petroleum from the Ocean" for a photograph of an offshore oil rig.

Oil-Field Brines

Natural brines are commonly found at depth in the Earth, but they also are found at Earth's surface, most notably as a byproduct of oil and gas test wells and production wells; hence they are known as oil-field brines. As petroleum and gas is commercially produced, brines may be produced in large quantities. In oil fields that have been producing for long periods of time, such as in central and west Texas, wells may produce hundreds of barrels of brine for every barrel of oil.

How do these natural brines form? In most sedimentary rocks (the most common geologic host for oil and gas), the sediments and rocks formed in a marine environment and therefore incorporated sea water in their pores and other interstices. However, subsurface brines are not simply concentrated sea water. (Stranded arms of the sea commonly cause evaporite deposits, where evaporation of pure water from sea water in nearshore marine settings result in the deposition of salt and other evaporitic progeny of sea water, such as gypsum.)

Although the evolution of brines from sea water in sediments and sedimentary rocks is complex and not completely understood, it appears that several processes may be involved:

- Concentration of dissolved constituents through evaporation;

- Retention of dissolved materials through membrane filtration by clay and clay-like minerals;

- Deposition of solids such as halite, dolomite, and anhydrite from the waters;

- Solution of other minerals from adjacent sediment or rock;

- Exchange of cations (positively charged ions) between water and solids;

- Bacterial and other organic processes; and

- Other chemical processes.

Brine Disposal. Oil-field brines must be disposed of in such a way that drinking waters and waters for other uses are not contaminated. Historically, brines would be dumped into a pit and commonly they would appear to "evaporate" or otherwise go away. In too many cases, however, the brines were simply seeping downward into the subsurface rocks, and contaminating the local **aquifer**. Because groundwater in most places moves slowly, perhaps several millimeters a year, many years might pass before nearby water wells became contaminated. Lawsuits commonly followed. SEE ALSO FRESH WATER, PHYSICS AND CHEMISTRY OF; GROUNDWATER; MINERAL RESOURCES FROM FRESH WATER; MINERAL RESOURCES FROM THE OCEAN; OCEAN CHEMICAL PROCESSES; SEA WATER, FREEZING OF; SEA WATER, PHYSICS AND CHEMISTRY OF.

Brian D. Hoyle and E. Julius Dasch

aquifer: a water-saturated, permeable, underground rock formation that can transmit significant quantities of water under ordinary hydraulic gradients to wells and springs

Bibliography

Drever, James I. *The Geochemistry of Natural Waters: Surface and Ground Water*, 3rd ed. Upper Saddle River, NJ: Prentice Hall, 1997.

Holland, Heinrich D. *The Chemistry of the Atmosphere and Oceans*, 2nd ed. New York: Wiley-Interscience, 1984.

Lewis, Richard J. Sr., ed. *Hawley's Condensed Chemical Dictionary*, 13th ed. New York: John Wiley & Sons, 1997.

Bureau of Reclamation, U.S.

The U.S. Bureau of Reclamation, an agency of the Department of the Interior, is one of the principal water management agencies of the federal government. Reclamation was established in 1902 to "reclaim" the **arid** and **semiarid** lands of the seventeen western states for settlement through the development of irrigated agriculture.✳ Over the past century, however, the agency has evolved principally from a developer to a manager of water resources.

Western Water Projects

Irrigation in many areas of the American West is necessary because precipitation is low and alone is insufficient to grow crops. In addition, the highly variable flow of many rivers makes them unreliable as a source of water for irrigation without some regulation. Thus, the U.S. government, through the creation of the Bureau of Reclamation, was tasked with constructing dams to create reservoirs throughout the West. These reservoirs were designed

arid: describes a climate or region where precipitation is exceeded by evaporation; in these regions, agricultural crop production is impractical or impossible without irrigation

semiarid: a climate or region where moisture is normally greater than under arid conditions but still limits the growth of most crops; either dryland farming methods or irrigation generally are required for crop production

✳For a regional map of the Bureau of Reclamation's responsibility, see <http://www.usbr.gov/main/what/regionalmap/index.html>.

Grand Coulee Dam in Washington state is the largest U.S. Bureau of Reclamation dam and reservoir in the Columbia River Basin. It was completed in 1942.

to store sufficient quantities of water to ensure that a reliable water supply was available for irrigated agriculture.

From 1902 to 1907, the Bureau of Reclamation began about thirty projects in the West to provide water for irrigation. Over time, however, it became clear that Reclamation dams and reservoirs could meet other needs as well, and multipurpose projects were developed to provide for flood control, municipal water supply, and hydroelectric power generation in addition to irrigation. The construction of the Hoover Dam, completed in 1936, was Reclamation's first major multipurpose project. The Central Valley Project in California and the Columbia Basin Project in Washington soon followed. The heyday of Reclamation's construction program began during the Great Depression (1929–1939) and continued through the 1970s.

As of 2002, the Bureau of Reclamation operated about 180 water projects, totaling some 600 dams and reservoirs. It is the largest water wholesaler in the country, bringing water to more than 31 million people and irrigating 10 million acres of land. Nearly 140,000 farmers in the West receive water from projects operated by the bureau. These farmers produce

60 percent of the nation's vegetables and 25 percent of its fruits and nuts. Reclamation also operates 58 hydroelectric power plants, generating more than 40 billion kilowatt-hours of electricity annually, enough to serve 6 million homes. In addition, every year more than 90 million people visit 300 recreation sites created by Reclamation projects.

Changing Water Needs

The needs of the West have changed greatly since the early 1900s. Many of the rivers have been overallocated and are straining to meet all the needs that have been identified. While irrigation remains the principal user of water in the West, rapidly growing cities, Native Americans, recreation interests, and environmental protection needs are all demanding their share. This reflects the new western water landscape, and few new federally funded dams are likely to ever be built, owing to the high financial costs and environmental and other concerns.

Without the ability to develop new water supplies to meet all the identified needs, Reclamation must attempt to secure water through other means, in particular through better water management. Reclamation's current program focuses on encouraging water conservation and water reuse, and developing effective partnerships with all water users. Reclamation's mission statement, "to manage, develop, and protect water and related resources in an environmentally and economically sound manner," gives no indication of the complexity and contentiousness that exists in trying to achieve a delicate balance between all the competing needs for a limited supply of water. SEE ALSO AGRICULTURE AND WATER; ARMY CORPS OF ENGINEERS, U.S.; CONSERVATION, WATER; DAMS; HOOVER DAM; IRRIGATION MANAGEMENT; PLANNING AND MANAGEMENT, HISTORY OF WATER RESOURCES; SUPPLY DEVELOPMENT; TENNESSEE VALLEY AUTHORITY.

Richard H. Ives

Bibliography

Robinson, Michael C. *Water for the West, the Bureau of Reclamation 1902–1977.* Chicago, IL: Public Works Historical Society, 1979.

U.S. Bureau of Reclamation. *Written in Water.* Washington, D.C.: U.S. Bureau of Reclamation, 1998.

Internet Resources

"A Brief History of the Bureau of Reclamation." U.S. Bureau of Reclamation. <http://www.usbr.gov/history/borhist.htm>.

California, Water Management in

California and water: the two always have been, and always will be, inextricably linked. No resource is as vital to California's cities, agriculture, industry, recreation, scenic beauty, and environmental preservation as its "liquid gold." And no resource is as steeped in controversy.

The fundamental controversy surrounding California's water supply is one of distribution coupled with conflicts between competing interests over the use of available supplies. Nearly 75 percent of the available water originates in the northern third of the state (north of the city of Sacramento), whereas 80 percent of the demand occurs in the southern two-thirds of the state. The demand for water is highest during the dry summer months when there is little natural precipitation or snowmelt. California's variable climate also leads to extended periods of drought followed by flooding.

Movement of Surface Water from Source to Consumer

The basic problems of California's water supply have been remedied, in large part, by construction of one of the most complex and sophisticated water storage and transport systems in the world. An integrated system of federal, state, and locally owned dams, **reservoirs**, pumping plants, and **aqueducts** transport large portions of the state's surface water hundreds of miles.

These water supply projects include the State Water Project, which originates at Oroville Dam and reservoir (located in the Sierra Nevada foothills 120 kilometers [75 miles] north of Sacramento) on the Feather River. Water from this project is transported all the way to the Los Angeles area via the California Aqueduct. The federal Central Valley Project stretches from Shasta Dam and reservoir in the northern Sacramento Valley to the Bakersfield area in the San Joaquin Valley. Farms in the agriculturally rich Central Valley use 80 percent of its water. Southern California also relies on water from the Colorado River, drawing its supplies from the historic Hoover Dam. Six other states, the Republic of Mexico, and American Indian tribes also share water from the Colorado River.

Groundwater as a Supplementary Supply. Supplementing surface water is **groundwater**, which provides one-third of California's water in an average year. Many homes in rural areas as well as some major cities rely exclusively on groundwater. Contrary to popular belief, groundwater does not exist in underground lakes but in the pores and spaces between **alluvial** materials (such as sand, gravel, silt, or clay) in water-bearing formations called aquifers.

Balancing Diverse Interests

California's rise to preeminence as the nation's most populous state, and sixth largest economy in the world, has largely depended on its ability to develop and manage its water resources. Projects were built to control floods; store water for droughts; produce hydropower, a relatively pollution-free source of electricity; provide water recreation; and supply water to farms and cities.

The negative side of this development is that California's rivers, streams, natural marshlands, and the wildlife inhabiting these areas have been significantly altered or destroyed. Although society once favored such development, public **values** shifted in the 1960s and 1970s as people became aware of environmental changes that had occurred in California and elsewhere: namely, declining wildlife; increasing pollution and urbanization; destruction of stream habitats; and alterations of natural stream flows.

Evolution of Water Management. Congress and the California Legislature responded to environmental concerns by enacting a series of powerful laws designed to protect endangered species, clean up polluted rivers and lakes, and protect and preserve open spaces and wilderness areas. Environmental organizations sued to enforce such laws.

The Mono Lake Controversy. The change in society's values is reflected in the case of Mono Lake, the largest natural lake entirely within California,

reservoir: a pond, lake, basin, or tank for the storage, regulation, and control of water; more commonly refers to artificial impoundments rather than natural ones

aqueduct: long, canal-like or pipe-like structure, either above or below ground, for transporting water some distance

groundwater: generally, all subsurface (underground) water, as distinct from surface water, that supplies natural springs, contributes to permanent streams, and can be tapped by wells; specifically, the water that is in the saturated zone of a defined aquifer

alluvium: a deposit of clay, silt, sand, gravel, or a mixture of these, that has been deposited by a stream or other body of running water in a streambed, on a floodplain, on a delta, or at the base of a mountain

values: abstract concepts of what is right and wrong, and what is desirable and undesirable

U.S. AQUEDUCT SYSTEMS

The most extensive aqueduct system in the world is the one that supplies water to southern California. This aqueduct system of canals, pipelines, and tunnels was begun in the 1960s. Other major aqueduct systems that extensively supply water to major populated areas include the ones located in New York City, Boston, Massachusetts; Baltimore, Maryland; Washington, D.C.; St. Louis, Missouri; and Los Angeles, California.

The California Aqueduct serves millions of urban, rural, and environmental and agricultural users throughout the Golden State. Shown here is the aqueduct and the E-Side Canal near Bakersfield.

and one of the oldest lakes in North America. Throughout its 700,000-year existence, salts and minerals have washed into the lake from streams of the eastern Sierra Nevada. This ancient **saline** lake and its basin supported unique and diverse fish and wildlife populations. Present-day Mono Lake is more than twice as salty as the ocean, and 80 times as alkaline.

In 1940, Los Angeles began to divert water from four of Mono Lake's five **tributary** streams. People knew this would lower the lake's level, but urban water supply had a higher value than the environment. By 1990, the shrinking Mono Lake had doubled in salinity and lost a number of fresh-water habitats such as delta marshes and **brackish** lagoons that formerly provided lake-fringing habitat for millions of waterbirds.

In 1979, environmentalists sued after Mono Lake's level dropped 12.2 meters (40 feet), jeopardizing its bird and brine shrimp populations. In a 1983 landmark decision, the California Supreme Court held that the **public trust** doctrine applied to Los Angeles' diversion, and state officials reduced the amount of water the city could divert. Environmental values had gained precedence and helped transform California's approach to water management. Today the public trust doctrine is being used to protect the natural values of lakes and waterways statewide.

Stakeholders in Water Management. By the 1980s, California's water community was divided into three basic **stakeholder** groups: agriculture, including farmers and irrigation districts; urban, including municipal water suppliers and city officials; and environmental, including conservation groups such as the Sierra Club. While these three groups continue to have major disagreements over water use and restoration of the natural ecosystem, they have made attempts to find solutions that all can accept.

Finding such compromises is one of the biggest challenges facing California water policymakers. The state faces other major challenges such as making sure there is enough water to supply the estimated population boom; reducing the amount of nonpoint pollution (for example, polluted runoff from roads and farm fields); and removing pollutants from drinking water.

saline: describes water containing a high dissolved mineral content; in sea water, the dominant contributor to salinity is sodium chloride

tributary: a smaller stream that flows into a larger stream

brackish: describes water having a salinity from 0.05 to 17 parts per thousand; typically a mixture of sea water and fresh water (e.g., as found in an estuary)

public trust: an historical and presently evolving concept relating to the ownership, protection, and use of essential natural and cultural resources; the purpose of the trust is to preserve resources in a manner that makes them available to the public for certain public uses

stakeholder: an individual or group impacted by a potential decision or action; term is usually associated with a limited number of individuals representing the interests of other like-minded individuals or groups

Calcium-bearing springs below the surface of Mono Lake, California well up through the alkaline lake water, which is rich in carbonates. The calcium and carbonate combine, forming calcite deposits on the lakebed. Over many years, a porous deposit known as tufa accumulates around the mouth of the spring from the ongoing deposition. As the lake waters recede, the tufa formations are exposed, sometimes towering as high as 10 meters (about 30 feet) above the lakebed. Some of the largest tufa towers are between 200 and 900 years old.

Key agencies involved in these water issues include:

- the California Department of Water Resources, which manages state water supplies and conducts water planning;

- the California State Water Resources Control Board, which establishes state pollution-control strategies and oversees water rights;

- the California Department of Heath Services, which develops and enforces regulations for contaminants in drinking water;

- the U.S. Bureau of Reclamation, which operates federal water projects throughout the West, including California's Central Valley Project;

- the U.S. Environmental Protection Agency, which enforces federal water pollution and drinking-water laws;

- the U.S. Fish and Wildlife Service, which protects endangered species; and

- the U.S. Geological Survey, which conducts scientific research into the quality and quantity of streams, lakes, and aquifers. SEE ALSO BALANCING DIVERSE INTERESTS; COLORADO RIVER BASIN; FLORIDA, WATER MANAGEMENT IN; HOOVER DAM; LEGISLATION, STATE AND LOCAL WATER; RIGHTS, PUBLIC WATER.

Sue McClurg

Bibliography

Hart, John. *Storm Over Mono: The Mono Lake Battle and the California Water Future.* Berkeley: University of California Press, 1996.

Hundley, Norris. *The Great Thirst: Californians and Water*, rev. ed. Berkeley: University of California Press, 2001.

McClurg, Sue. *Water and the Shaping of California*. Sacramento: Water Education Foundation and Heyday Books, 2000.

Internet Resources

Mono Lake Web Site. Mono Lake Committee. <http://www.monolake.org>.

California Issues. Water Education Foundation. <http://www.watereducation.org/california.asp>.

Canals

Human societies have long worked on changing nature's waterways for their purposes. Canals are artificial waterways constructed for **irrigation**, drainage, river overflows, water supplies, communications, and navigation, or in connection with power generation from **hydroelectric** dams. The digging of canals for irrigation probably dates to the beginnings of agriculture, with traces of canals found within ancient Chinese, Egyptian, and Babylonian civilizations. Written evidence shows that the Suez Canal, for instance, was excavated prior to 2000 B.C.E. It was documented to be navigable for small vessels by 600 B.C.E. and remained in operation for fourteen centuries as a convenient trade route between the Mediterranean and Red Seas. One of the world's longest canals, the Grand Canal of China, was constructed primarily during the seventh and thirteenth centuries. The 1,900-kilometer (1,200-mile) canal connected the cities of Beijing and Hangzhou, and is often considered the most notable of the early canals.

irrigation: the controlled application of water for agricultural or other purposes through human-made systems; generally refers to water application to soil when rainfall is insufficient to maintain desirable soil moisture for plant growth

hydroelectric: often used synonymously with "hydropower," describes electricity generated by utilizing the power of falling water, as with water flowing through and turning turbines at a dam

Pre-Industrial Canal Era

The regions that built canals during the pre-industrial era were those possessing fairly level landscapes, like Mesopotamia (around Iraq and Iran), Egypt, and China, or where channels were branches of the sea, like in the Netherlands. This pattern occurred because the practice of building **locks** had not yet been invented. Nevertheless, these waterways were not constructed on one continuous level. Evidence shows that the early Egyptian and Chinese canals were adapted to the differing land contours, often using an inclined plane for transferring boats to successive levels. Even today, China uses similar methods on its extensive canal system.

lock: one in a series of gates that allows vessels to pass through multiple water levels

Locks Era

The introduction of locks throughout Europe—primarily for economic, political, and military gains—between the fifteenth and seventeenth centuries spurred rapid canal-building. France was the first to build extensive systems. The greatest work of that period was the Languedoc Canal, connecting the Bay of Biscay with the Mediterranean Sea. The canal, completed in 1681, was an enormous undertaking with its length of 240 kilometers (148 miles), rise of 183 meters (600 feet) above the sea, numerous locks and **aqueducts**, tunnel of more than 213 meters (700 feet), and capacity for floating gigantic barges.

aqueduct: long, canal-like or pipe-like structure, either above or below ground, for transporting water some distance

Industrial Revolution Era

Gangs of laborers (called "navvies" or "navigators") first constructed British canals to provide artificial waterways for more efficient transportation of

Historically, canals were constructed to "extend the sea," thereby connecting the sea with cities, and cities with the countryside. This scene of Hamburg, Germany in 1864 illustrates how canals influenced city life and culture.

goods and materials during the Industrial Revolution of the eighteenth century. Canals served to open up countries to the Industrial Revolution, just as the Internet is opening up the world to the Information Revolution. Waterways afforded a cheap means of transportation, one that could bring input materials to production centers and then take finished products away for mass marketing. Thus, canals played a role in aiding the movement of populations to production centers.

British Isles. Canal building in Ireland, Scotland, and England flourished in the late eighteenth and early nineteenth centuries. Three of the most notable canals were the Grand Canal in Ireland, the Caledonian Canal in Scotland, and the Manchester Ship Canal in England. The Grand Canal was begun in 1756 for trade and passenger transportation, and extended 134 kilometers (83 miles) between Dublin and Shannon Harbor. The Caledonian Canal was completed in 1847 as a 97-kilometer (60-mile) waterway from Inverness to Fort William, to provide a safe route for naval ships during the Napoleonic wars. The Manchester Ship Canal, which was completed in 1894, opened Manchester Port to oceangoing vessels, and contributed to the thriving industrial English economy.

European Mainland. Belgium, France, Holland, and Germany became the first countries in Europe to develop inland waterway systems by using canals

A large cruise ship and another oceangoing vessel pass through the Miraflores Locks of the Panama Canal. This large navigation canal, connecting the Pacific and Atlantic Oceans, is often referred to as the "eighth wonder of the world."

to connect water bodies. For example, the German Kiel Canal was completed in 1895 as the shortest link between the North Sea and the Baltic. Today these countries possess an integrated waterway network such as the Midland Canal, a series of German canals that facilitates east–west transportation of raw materials and manufactured goods.

North America. In 1730, a small excavation was cut across a narrow piece of land in a bend of the Mohawk River near present-day Utica, New York. It is commonly believed that this canal was the first artificial waterway to be created in the United States, and today it symbolizes the beginning of the U.S. canal era.

The first U.S. navigation canal was built in 1793 around the rapids of the Connecticut River at South Hadley, Massachusetts. Two levels that were connected by a water-filled incline transported boats by dragging them with cables operated by waterpower. The construction of the Erie Canal, started in 1817, was largely responsible for opening the American Midwest to settlement. More than 7,250 kilometers (4,500 miles) of water routes, mostly in the middle Atlantic and central states, were created from the seaboard to the inland lakes to help expand a fledgling country.

Navigation Canals

Large canals are primarily built for navigation. Navigation canals were developed after irrigation canals, and for a long time were level, shallow depressions, or had inclined planes in which vessels were hauled between levels. Over the years, such canals have been expanded in width and depth in order to accommodate larger boats, and they have, in some cases, been constructed to form bridges or to pass through tunnels to overcome mountains. Canals were built larger and larger so that water transport could better compete with railway transportation.

Navigation canals usually are classified as either ship canals, which are deep enough to accommodate oceangoing ships, or barge canals, which are shallow and for use mainly by barges.

Barge Canals. On most large, shallow canals, barges are pushed or pulled by tugboats and towboats. Modern barges are designed to carry specific types of cargo: (1) open-hopper barges carry gravel, coal, and large equipment; (2) covered dry-cargo barges carry dry chemicals, grain, and other commodities that must be kept dry; and (3) tank barges carry liquid and petroleum chemicals.

Ship Canals. Some ship canals, such as the Suez and Panama Canals, provide navigational shortcuts by connecting large water bodies. The 64-kilometer (40-mile) long Panama Canal, which goes across the Isthmus of Panama in Central America, allows vessels to travel between the Pacific and Atlantic oceans, avoiding the long voyage around South America. At the time it was constructed, it was estimated that this trip around took approximately 5 to 6 months; the canal reduced the length of the trip to as many weeks.

Other ship canals, such as the Houston Ship Channel (in Texas) and the Manchester Ship Canal (in northwestern England), connect an inland harbor to the ocean. These canals play an important role in the nation's waterborne transportation system.

Construction

Major canals are usually constructed as open-cut excavations with the use of construction tools and machinery. The cuts are often built with masonry to prevent bank erosion. Unlike roads and railways, canals cannot be made to conform to terrain irregularities, but must consist of one or more level stretches. Where different levels meet, vessels are transferred from one stretch to the next by locks. When a boat enters a lock and all gates are secured, the downstream gates open and water flows in. When the level is equal on either side of the downstream gate, water stops flowing, the downstream gate then opens, and the boat continues onto the new water level.

Canalization of Rivers. In the early years of canal building, when important rivers were found to be not **navigable** at certain points, side canals running parallel to the river were built so that vessels could bypass that section and reenter it at a more suitable point. With the invention of power machinery, this practice has generally been discarded in favor of canalization of the river itself; that is, a river is dredged at shallow regions and provided with dams and locks that control the river's level.

In the United States, for example, construction of 40 locks and dams on the Ohio River was completed in 1929; and later modernized with 18 high-lift locks in 1981. Canalization of the upper Mississippi River from Minneapolis, Minnesota to Alton, Illinois (just above St. Louis, Missouri), was completed in 1940.

---

navigable: in general usage, describes a waterbody deep and wide enough to afford passage to small and large vessels; also can be used in the context of a specific statutory or regulatory designation

---

WHO OWNS THE PANAMA CANAL?

The Panama Canal, which crosses the central part of Panama in Central America, was built by the United States from 1904 to 1914. Under a 1903 treaty, the United States controlled as a U.S. territory both the waterway and a 16-kilometer (10-mile) swath across the isthmus known as the Panama Canal Zone.

During most of the twentieth century, the Panamanians resented this arrangement, arguing that their country was unjustly denied canal benefits. Eventually, riots and global pressures led the United States in 1979, under then-president Jimmy Carter, to recognize Panama's eventual ownership of the canal and all the surrounding lands.

Former president Carter and Panamanian president Mireya Moscoso signed documents in December 14, 1999, giving Panama full control of the Panama Canal. The actual transfer to Panama occurred on December 31, along with complete control of canal operations and full possession of the Panama Canal Zone.

In 1954, the U.S. Congress authorized the federal government to join with Canada in the construction of the St. Lawrence Seaway. The United States built two canals, three locks, and various other improvements along the St. Lawrence River from Montreal, Quebec to Ogdensburg, New York.

The Canadian canal system includes the St. Lawrence River canals, the Ottawa River canals, the Chambly Canal, the Rideau Canal, and the Trent Canal (part of the Trent–Severn Waterway). Of these, the St. Lawrence system has long been the most important, because it provides a waterway 4.3 meters (14 feet) deep from the head of Lake Superior to the Gulf of St. Lawrence. As part of the project, completed in 1959, the waterway was deepened to 8.2 meters (27 feet) to permit large oceangoing vessels to sail from the Atlantic Ocean to such ports as Chicago, Illinois, and Duluth, Minnesota. The 3,700-kilometer (2,340-mile) Great Lakes–St. Lawrence Seaway system is the world's longest deep-draft inland waterway, extending from the Atlantic Ocean to Duluth, Minnesota on Lake Superior. SEE ALSO ARMY CORPS OF ENGINEERS, U.S.; LEONARDO DA VINCI; NAVIGATION AT SEA, HISTORY OF; TRANSPORTATION.

William Arthur Atkins

Bibliography

Hadfield, Charles, ed. *World Canals*. Newton Abbot, U.K.: David & Charles, 1986.

Shaw, Ronald E. *Canals for a Nation*. Lexington: University of Kentucky Press, 1990.

Internet Resources

Make the Dirt Fly! The Building of the Panama Canal. Smithsonian Institution Libraries Online Exhibit. <http://www.sil.si.edu/Exhibitions/Make-the-Dirt-Fly>.

Carbon Dioxide in the Ocean and Atmosphere

Carbon dioxide (CO_2) is considered a trace gas in the atmosphere because it is much less abundant than oxygen or nitrogen. However, this trace gas plays a vital role in sustaining life on Earth and in controlling the Earth's climate by trapping heat in the atmosphere.

The oceans play an important role in regulating the amount of CO_2 in the atmosphere because CO_2 can move quickly into and out of the oceans. Once in the oceans, the CO_2 no longer traps heat. CO_2 also moves quickly between the atmosphere and the land biosphere (material that is or was living on land).

Of the three places where carbon is stored—atmosphere, oceans, and land biosphere—approximately 93 percent of the CO_2 is found in the oceans. The atmosphere, at about 750 petagrams of carbon (a petagram [Pg] is 10^{15} grams), has the smallest amount of carbon.

Balances in Carbon Dioxide Levels

Approximately 90 to 100 Pg of carbon moves back and forth between the atmosphere and the oceans, and between the atmosphere and the land biosphere. Although these exchange rates are large relative to the total amount of carbon stored in the atmosphere, the concentration of CO_2 was constant

Marine plants and animals play a role in the uptake and release of carbon dioxide in the ocean. Plants, primarily phytoplankton but also macrophytes such as this seaweed, take up carbon dioxide and release oxygen, which oxygen-dependent animals need to survive.

photosynthesis: the process by which plants manufacture food from sunlight; specifically, the conversion of water and carbon dioxide to complex sugars in plant tissues by the action of chlorophyll driven by solar energy

greenhouse gas: a gas in the atmosphere that traps heat and reflects it back to the planetary body

at 280 parts per million (ppm) by volume for at least 1,000 years prior to the industrial era. Atmospheric concentrations of CO_2 were constant because the carbon being removed from the atmosphere in some places exactly matched the CO_2 being added to the atmosphere in other places.

Today, CO_2 concentrations in the atmosphere are increasing as a direct result of human activities such as deforestation and the burning of fossil fuels (e.g., coal and oil). Over the past 150 years, CO_2 concentrations in the atmosphere have increased by as much as 30 percent (from 280 to 370 ppm).

All trees, nearly all plants from cold climates, and most agricultural crops respond to increasing atmospheric CO_2 levels by increasing the amount of CO_2 they take up for **photosynthesis**. It is believed that the increased uptake in land plants from rising atmospheric CO_2 levels roughly counterbalanced the CO_2 released from cutting down tropical rain forests and other agricultural practices in the decade of the 1980s. In the 1990s, the land biosphere was estimated to take up approximately 1 Pg more CO_2 than it released each year.

Most of the CO_2 released from the burning of fossil fuels and other human activities (e.g., cement manufacturing) is stored either in the atmosphere or in the oceans. The CO_2 that remains in the atmosphere acts as a **greenhouse gas**, absorbing long-wavelength radiation (heat) in the atmosphere. CO_2 taken up by the oceans does not affect the Earth's heat balance, so an understanding of the air–sea exchange of CO_2 is an essential part of understanding the Earth's climate system and the potential impact of future CO_2 emissions.

Regulating Carbon Dioxide Emissions. The potential for anthropogenic (human-derived) CO_2 to adversely affect the Earth's climate has resulted in attempts on the international level to regulate global CO_2 emissions. The Kyoto Protocol, for example, was designed to reduce global CO_2 emissions to 5 percent below 1990 levels. As of late 2002, the Protocol had not been ratified and global emissions have continued to rise. Global emissions in 2001 were roughly 11 percent higher than 1990 levels.

Natural Ocean Carbon Cycle

The oceans contain about 50 times more CO_2 than the atmosphere and 19 times more than the land biosphere. CO_2 moves between the atmosphere and the ocean by **molecular diffusion** when there is a difference between CO_2 gas pressure (pCO_2) between the atmosphere and oceans. For example, when the atmospheric pCO_2 is higher than the surface ocean, CO_2 diffuses across the air–sea boundary into the sea water.

The oceans are able to hold much more carbon than the atmosphere because most of the CO_2 that diffuses into the oceans reacts with the water to form carbonic acid and its **dissociation products**, bicarbonate and carbonate **ions**. The conversion of CO_2 gas into nongaseous forms such as carbonic acid and bicarbonate and carbonate ions effectively reduces the CO_2 gas pressure in the water, thereby allowing more diffusion from the atmosphere.

The oceans are mixed much more slowly than the atmosphere, so there are large horizontal and vertical changes in CO_2 concentration. In general, tropical waters release CO_2 to the atmosphere, whereas high-latitude oceans take up CO_2 from the atmosphere. CO_2 is also about 10 percent higher in the deep ocean than at the surface. The two basic mechanisms that control the distribution of carbon in the oceans are referred to as the solubility pump and the biological pump.

Solubility Pump. The solubility pump is driven by two principal factors. First, more than twice as much CO_2 can dissolve into cold polar waters than in the warm equatorial waters. As major ocean currents (e.g., the Gulf Stream) move waters from the tropics to the poles, they are cooled and can take up more CO_2 from the atmosphere. Second, the high latitude zones are also places where deep waters are formed. As the waters are cooled, they become denser and sink into the ocean's interior, taking with them the CO_2 accumulated at the surface.

Biological Pump. Another process that moves CO_2 away from the surface ocean is called the biological pump. Growth of marine plants (e.g., **phytoplankton**) takes CO_2 and other chemicals from sea water to make plant tissue. Microscopic marine animals, called zooplankton, eat the phytoplankton and provide the basis for the **food web** for all animal life in the sea. Because photosynthesis requires light, phytoplankton only grow in the near-surface ocean, where sufficient light can penetrate.

Although most of the CO_2 taken up by phytoplankton is recycled near the surface, a substantial fraction, perhaps 30 percent, sinks into the deeper waters before being converted back into CO_2 by marine bacteria. Only about 0.1 percent reaches the seafloor to be buried in the sediments.

molecular diffusion: the movement of individual molecules through a solid, liquid, or gas in response to a concentration gradient; molecules will move from where their concentration is higher to where it is lower

dissociation product: individual ions or neutral molecules formed through the chemical disassociation of a single molecule; for example, H_2CO_3 disassociates into H^+ and HCO_3^-

ion: an atom or molecule that carries a net charge (either positive or negative) because of an imbalance between the number of protons and the number of electrons

phytoplankton: microscopic floating plants, mainly algae, that live suspended in bodies of water and that drift about because they cannot move by themselves or because they are too small or too weak to swim effectively against a current

food web: a complex food chain, with several species at each level, so that there is more than one producer and more than one consumer of each type

KYOTO PROTOCOL

In 1997, a United Nations meeting was held in Kyoto, Japan to establish legally binding commitments for reducing future emissions of CO_2 and other greenhouse gases. The goal was for each member country to commit to reducing emissions to 5 percent below 1990 levels by the period 2008–2012. The timeframe 2008–2012 was set for compliance so that member nations could transition to efficient lower-emitting carbon technologies. The Kyoto Protocols will not be binding until 3 months after they have been ratified by at least 55 member nations, including a sufficient number of the developed countries so as to account for 55 percent of the 1990 global emissions.

Scientists research the exchange of carbon dioxide between the atmosphere and ocean. This photograph shows the *Ronald H. Brown,* a research vessel of the National Oceanic and Atmospheric Administration, in the Equatorial Pacific Ocean during the GASEX II expedition in 2001. The floating instrument in the foreground measures a number of parameters associated with the transfer of CO_2 across the air–sea interface.

The CO_2 that is recycled at depth is slowly carried large distances by currents to areas where the waters return to the surface (upwelling regions). When the waters regain contact with the atmosphere, the CO_2 originally taken up by the phytoplankton is returned to the atmosphere. This exchange process helps to control atmospheric CO_2 concentrations over decadal and longer time scales.

Anthropogenic CO_2 Uptake

The constant atmospheric CO_2 concentrations in the centuries prior to the Industrial Revolution suggest that the oceans released a small amount of CO_2 to the atmosphere to balance the carbon input from rivers. Today, this trend is reversed and the oceans must remove CO_2 added to the atmosphere from human activities, known as anthropogenic (human-derived) CO_2.

In the 1980s, the oceans removed an estimated 2.0 ± 0.6 Pg of anthropogenic CO_2 each year. Because humans are producing CO_2 at an ever-increasing rate, the average ocean removal rate increased to 2.4 ± 0.5 Pg of carbon each year in the 1990s.

The uptake of anthropogenic CO_2 by the oceans is driven by the difference in gas pressure in the atmosphere and in the oceans and by the air–sea transfer velocity. Because the pCO_2 is increasing in the atmosphere, CO_2 moves into the ocean in an attempt to balance the oceanic and atmospheric gas pressures.

The mechanisms that control the speed with which the CO_2 gas can move from the atmosphere to the oceans (air–sea transfer velocity) are not well understood today. Recent technological advances are helping scientists to better understand these mechanisms.

The transfer velocity is related to the surface roughness of the ocean and the wind speed. The difference in pCO_2 is related to the amount of carbon that is converted from CO_2 gas to other nongaseous carbon species in the sea water, like bicarbonate and carbonate ions. This so-called "buffer capacity" is what allows the oceans to hold so much carbon.

The relative concentrations of CO_2 (1%), bicarbonate ion (91%) and carbonate ion (8%) control the acidity (pH) of the oceans. Since CO_2 is an acid gas, the uptake of anthropogenic CO_2 uses up carbonate ions and lowers the oceanic pH. The carbonate ion concentration of surface sea water will decrease by an estimated 30 percent with a doubling of atmospheric CO_2 from preindustrial levels (280 to 560 ppm). As the carbonate ion concentration decreases, the buffer capacity of the ocean and its ability to take up CO_2 from the atmosphere is reduced.

Over the long term (millennial timescales), the ocean has the potential to take up approximately 85 percent of the anthropogenic CO_2 that is released to the atmosphere. As long as atmospheric CO_2 concentrations continue to rise, the oceans will continue to take up CO_2. However, this reaction is reversible. If atmospheric CO_2 were to decrease in the future, the oceans will start releasing the accumulated anthropogenic CO_2 back out into the atmosphere.

The ultimate storage place for anthropogenic CO_2 must be reactions that bind the CO_2 in a manner that is not easily reversed. Dissolution of calcium carbonate in the oceans, for example, is a long-term storage place for CO_2. As the oceans continue to take up anthropogenic CO_2, it will penetrate deeper into the water column, lowering the pH and making the waters more corrosive to calcium carbonate. The problem is that carbonate dissolution typically occurs in the deep ocean, well removed from the anthropogenic CO_2 taken up in the surface waters. In portions of the North Atlantic and North Pacific Oceans, however, anthropogenic CO_2 may have already penetrated deep enough to influence the dissolution of calcium carbonate in the water column.

Sediment Burial. Burial of plant and animal material into the sediments can also provide long-term storage of anthropogenic CO_2. Interestingly, almost no phytoplankton seem to grow faster in higher CO_2 environments, unlike many land plants. This is because phytoplankton growth in the oceans is generally limited by the availability of light and chemicals other than CO_2, principally nitrogen and phosphorus but also smaller amounts of iron, zinc, and other micronutrients.

One proposed approach for enhancing carbon removal from the atmosphere is to enhance phytoplankton growth by fertilizing specific regions of the ocean with a relatively inexpensive biologically limiting chemical like iron. The hypothesis is that the resulting bloom of oceanic plants would remove CO_2 from the atmosphere then transport that carbon into the deep ocean or sediments, effectively removing it from the short-term budget. The effectiveness of the "iron hypothesis" is being tested with several research efforts attempting to scale up iron fertilization experiments.

sequester: to remove or render inactive a specific chemical or chemical group from a solution

Other carbon **sequestration** approaches, including direct injection of liquefied CO_2 into the deep ocean, are also being examined. Further research is necessary to determine whether any of these techniques will be effective or economically feasible. Implementation of these approaches may depend, in large part, on policy decisions made at national and international levels. SEE ALSO ALGAL BLOOMS IN THE OCEAN; ECOLOGY, MARINE; GLOBAL WARMING AND THE OCEAN; GLOBAL WARMING: POLICY-MAKING; MICROBES IN THE OCEAN; OCEAN BIOGEOCHEMISTRY; OCEAN CHEMICAL PROCESSES; OCEAN CURRENTS; OCEAN-FLOOR SEDIMENTS; PLANKTON; SEA WATER, GASES IN.

Christopher L. Sabine

Bibliography

Broecker, Wallace S., and Tsung-Hung Peng. *Tracers in the Sea.* Palisades, NY: Eldigio Press, 1982.

Falkowski, Paul G., Richard T. Barber, and Victor Smetacek. "Biogeochemical Controls and Feedbacks on Ocean Primary Production." *Science* 281 (1998): 200–206.

Prentice, I. Colin et al. "The Carbon Cycle and Atmospheric Carbon Dioxide." In *Climate Change: The Scientific Basis—Contribution of Working Group I to the Third Assessment Report of the Intergovernmental Panel on Climate Change,* eds. John T. Houghton et. al., Cambridge, U.K.: Cambridge University Press, (2001):183–237.

Internet Resource

Trends Online: A Compendium of Data on Global Change Carbon Dioxide Information Analysis Center. Oak Ridge National Laboratory, U.S. Department of Energy. <http://cdiac.esd.ornl.gov/trends/trends.htm>.

Careers in Environmental Education

Educating others in environmental principles and theories is a rewarding activity, and one that some individuals pursue as a full-time profession. Environmental education has evolved over the last century from a once-small field of environmental interpretation to a growing discipline with new opportunities steadily arising.

Moreover, environmental issues have become increasingly important worldwide, and crucial decisions must be made with respect to balancing the use of resources, the needs of other organisms, and the economy. Environmental educators can provide an appreciation for the **scientific method** and the data behind these complex issues, leading to a better-informed populace. For example, teaching students and the public how data are collected and interpreted will give them a realistic view of information that influences the decision-making process. An informed public is likely to ask "Where and how were the data collected?" and "What are the assumptions and the alternative hypotheses?"

scientific method: a systematic method of inquiry regarding a specific question or problem that includes the objective collection of data relating to that question, the development of tentative hypotheses or solutions to the problem, collecting more data to test a proposed solution to the problem, and the rational determination of the hypothesis most successful in explaining the problem

From Interpretation to Education

Environmental interpretation was a forerunner of environmental education, and was first undertaken on a broad scale by the National Park Service during the mid-twentieth century. Interpretation is defined as an educational activity that aims to reveal meanings and relationships through the use of natural objects, by first-hand experience, and by illustrative media, rather than simply relating scientific principles in a formal classroom setting.

Fresh-water education encompasses surface waters (e.g., lakes, ponds, streams, and wetlands) and groundwaters (e.g., cave, karst, and aquifer systems). Here a young angler learns from a park naturalist how to bait a hook.

The uniformed park ranger presenting an evening campfire program or an interpretive nature walk was an early form of environmental education. These types of programs were designed for a short-term, passive, noncaptive audience. Most visitors to natural areas simply desired to learn a little about the natural world while in an outdoor or on-site setting.

By the 1970s, traditional educators began to see a need to bring these educational activities into the classroom. The public's knowledge of the natural world was increasing, as well as awareness of the need for environmental protection and stewardship. Most states began to require an environmental education component in their established educational goals and benchmarks for K–12 students. Hence, environmental education came into existence.

Types of Work

Most K–12 science teachers consider themselves multidisciplinary instructors, rather than environmental educators. A need therefore exists for curricula to fulfill state requirements, and workshops that enhance teacher training in environmental sciences as well as in presentation methods.

Environmental education today combines both the principles of interpretation and formal science education. The overall goal is to teach environmental science in ways that are enlightening and enjoyable. This usually requires a combination of classroom work supplemented with outdoor field studies. The integration of traditional science with interpretive techniques is the greatest challenge environmental educators encounter. Many K–12 educators supplement their instruction by bringing in guest speakers who are professionals in environmental disciplines.

Most quality environmental education programs use an inquiry approach to learning. Students learn the basic principles and theories of environmental science and then apply them to the real world through the completion of research projects, field investigations, and hands-on activities. Work is performed outdoors, as well as in the classroom and at visitor centers. Some agencies and private companies have developed programs that offer unique opportunities, including floating classrooms on a research vessel where students can study oceanography, marine biology, and water science. Internships at local, state, and federal agencies may provide additional opportunities.

Employment Opportunities

The employment outlook for environmental educators is good as a result of increasing public awareness and demand for information. The need for up-to-date curricula that educators can use in their classrooms is of prime concern, and many companies and universities hire staff primarily for that purpose.

Field trips are a necessary facet of environmental education. Most aquariums, natural history museums, zoos, and recreation departments have staff and curricula which teachers can access. Many private groups provide field instruction on land as well as on lakes, rivers, and oceans.

Agencies and private companies with an environmental aspect to their activities often utilize public relations staff that can easily relate to the public. Environmental educators are uniquely qualified for such positions. Federal agencies such as the National Park Service, U.S. Forest Service, Bureau of Land Management, U.S. Geological Survey, U.S. Fish and Wildlife Service, and the National Oceanic and Atmospheric Administration have staff and programs that directly serve K–12 education. There are also opportunities for adult environmental education curricula and classes, but these programs are in early stages of development, showing a need for more curricula development in the future.

Academic Preparation

Environmental education is one of only a few professions that consider the Earth as an entire system, and not just the sum of its parts. To prepare for a career in environmental education, students must become well versed in many different disciplines rather than specializing in just one field. Students

Marine education includes activities and facilities ranging from aquariums to beach walks to shipboard excursions. These girls explore a tidepool, a biologically diverse marine habitat, and one that is easily accessible to curious learners.

must concentrate on the biological and physical sciences as they relate to Earth **ecosystems**.

Ecology, chemistry, geology, marine biology, aquatic science, and oceanography are all important if students wish to work in water science education careers. Mathematics is high on the list, as most studies relating to water science involve the use of mathematical formulas and statistics. Computer science and graphic design skills are prerequisites for those wishing to develop environmental education curricula that will satisfy audiences who increasingly prefer visual information. SEE ALSO ECOLOGY, FRESH-WATER; ECOLOGY, MARINE; FISH AND WILDLIFE SERVICE, U.S.; GEOLOGICAL SURVEY, U.S.; NATIONAL PARK SERVICE; NATIONAL OCEANIC AND ATMOSPHERIC ADMINISTRATION; RECREATION; TOURISM.

Ron Crouse

ecosystem: the community of plants and animals within a water or terrestrial habitat interacting together and with their physical and chemical environment

Bibliography

Golley, Frank B. *A Primer for Environmental Literacy.* New Haven, CT: Yale University Press, 1998.

Hale, Monica, ed. *Ecology in Education.* New York: Cambridge University Press, 1993.

Ham, Sam H. *Environmental Interpretation, A Practical Guide.* Golden, CO: North American Press, 1992.

Tilden, Freeman. *Interpreting Our Heritage.* Chapel Hill, NC: University of North Carolina Press, 1997.

Internet Resources

National Environmental Education and Training Foundation. <http://www.neetf.org>.

Environmental Education. U.S. Environmental Protection Agency. <http://www.epa.gov/enviroed>.

Careers in Environmental Science and Engineering

Environmental science as it relates to water may be broadly defined as the study of how fresh-water and marine-water environments are faring in the face of a swelling human population, degradation by pollution and the disturbance of natural habitats, problems with either excess or insufficient water, and threats to the sustainability of living and nonliving resources. Environmental science is interdisciplinary, including aspects of ecology, environmental management, biology, chemistry, microbiology, zoology, geology, soil science, statistics, and land-use planning. The environmental scientist often will work as a part of a team of scientists, engineers, and planners in an effort to better understand how a specific environment works so that its compatibility with changing land use can be evaluated.

Environmental engineering, as it applies to water, is broadly concerned with the design of structures or systems that help protect or solve a problem with water. Two of many career paths in environmental engineering are pollution control and **remediation**. An environmental engineer may be involved with surface water, groundwater, and soil water. Engineered strategies encompass physical, biological, and chemical principles. Hence, training in environmental engineering requires a firm grounding in basic science as well as engineering specialties. As with the environmental scientist, the environmental engineer will need to consult and coordinate with others, particularly scientists, in order to build a structure that is compatible with the environment.

Opportunities

Government agencies such as local, state, and federal environmental protection agencies employ environmental scientists and engineers, where they often deal with regulatory issues. Consulting firms hire scientists and engineers to help their clients meet regulatory criteria. Similarly, utilities, pharmaceutical companies, manufacturing companies, and many other businesses need specialists and engineers to meet environmental protection requirements. Universities and private research institutes conduct research in an array of environmental science subspecialties. International opportunities exist as both developed and developing nations deal with water quality and water quantity concerns. SEE ALSO "CHEMICAL" ENTRIES AND "POLLUTION" ENTRIES.

Brian D. Hoyle

Water sampling provides critical information for environmental scientists. Results can indicate not only the chemical and biological conditions of natural waters, but also the presence of pollutants that may pose environmental or human health concerns.

remediation: the cleanup, through a variety of methods, to remove or contain a toxic spill or hazardous materials from a contaminated site

Bibliography

Doyle, Kevin, Tanya Stubbs, and Sam Heizen. *The Complete Guide to Environmental Careers in the Twenty-First Century.* Washington, D.C.: Island Press, 1998.

Masters, Gilbert M. *Introduction to Environmental Engineering and Science,* 2nd ed. Upper Saddle River, NJ: Prentice Hall, 1998.

Internet Resources

Information about Environmental Engineering Careers. American Academy of Environmental Engineers. <http:www.enviro-engrs.org/newlook/careers.htm>.

Occupational Outlook Handbook: Environmental Scientists and Geoscientists. U.S. Department of Labor, Bureau of Labor Statistics. <http://www.bls.gov/oco/ocos050.htm>.

Careers in Fresh-Water Chemistry

As water reacts with rocks, minerals, or biological materials, or is impacted by **pollution** or a land-use practice, the chemical composition of the water may be changed in a predictable way. Chemical analysis of water allows both natural processes and human-influenced changes to be characterized, and may enable the chemist to determine the "history" of a water parcel. In addition, the analytical results provide a means of comparing the quality of water to a particular chemical and/or biological criteria (for instance, drinking-water standards and ecological indices).

Water chemists are involved in projects such as collecting and analyzing water samples; designing new analytical techniques; evaluating the composition of waters from different watersheds (basins) or from different **aquifers**; monitoring how water from a particular source changes with time; predicting the movement of polluted **groundwater**; using water trapped in minerals or in ice to determine past conditions; and determining the impact of a land-use practice on water composition and the impact it might have on the **environment**.

Water chemists often work as part of an interdisciplinary team with other specialists; for instance, biologists, foresters, geologists, hydrologists, meteorologists, ecologists, and toxicologists. Each of these disciplines requires water analyses that are accurate and representative. Similarly, water resource management often involves careful collection and interpretation of water composition, as do research projects dealing with climatic conditions, the transport of chemicals in water, and the sensitivity of organisms to the composition of water in which they live. Water and wastewater utilities rely on chemical analyses to ensure the safety of their drinking water and the adequate treatment of wastewaters being discharged to the environment. Power plants and various industries monitor the quality of water used in cooling processes and as a manufacturing component.

Chemists commonly find employment with water, wastewater, and power utilities; industries; commercial laboratories; consulting firms; state and federal agencies; and academic and research institutions. With the growing emphasis on the use of water chemistry to assess the overall "health" and "history" of water, career positions in water chemistry will continue to be in demand, and most likely will increase in numbers.

Academic preparation for such a career includes a strong background in the sciences, mathematics, and statistics. In addition to an emphasis on

pollution: any alteration in the character or quality of the environment, including water in waterbodies or geologic formations, which renders the environmental resource unfit or less suited for certain uses

aquifer: a water-saturated, permeable, underground rock formation that can transmit significant quantities of water under ordinary hydraulic gradients to wells and springs

groundwater: generally, all subsurface (underground) water, as distinct from surface water, that supplies natural springs, contributes to permanent streams, and can be tapped by wells; specifically, the water that is in the saturated zone of a defined aquifer

environment: all of the external factors, conditions, and influences that affect the growth, development, and survival of organisms or a community; commonly refers to Earth and its support systems

Chemical analysis of water is the foundation for protecting environmental and public health, and for monitoring industrial–manufacturing processes. Water chemists find employment with utilities, industries, universities, and regulatory agencies.

theoretical and analytical chemistry, many water chemists choose to obtain academic training in one of the sciences in either their undergraduate or graduate work. Having skills in one discipline (for instance, biology, forestry, or geology), while being able to apply chemistry on the job makes one even more desirable to an employer. SEE ALSO CHEMICAL ANALYSIS OF WATER; CHEMICALS FROM AGRICULTURE; CHEMICALS FROM PHARMACEUTICALS AND PERSONAL CARE PRODUCTS; CLEAN WATER ACT; DRINKING-WATER TREATMENT; FRESH WATER, NATURAL COMPOSITION OF; FRESH WATER, NATURAL CONTAMINANTS IN; LAND USE AND WATER QUALITY; POLLUTION SOURCES: POINT AND NONPOINT; SAFE DRINKING WATER ACT; UTILITY MANAGEMENT.

Dennis O. Nelson

Bibliography

Hem, John D. *Study and Interpretation of the Chemical Characteristics of Natural Water*, 3rd ed. Alexandria, VA: Department of the Interior, U.S. Geological Survey, Water-Supply Paper 2254, 1985.

Careers in Fresh-Water Ecology

Fresh-water ecology seeks to understand the relationship between organisms and their environment, and how changes in one part of the system will affect other parts of the system. Many kinds of scientific and communication skills are necessary to understand successfully the ecology of fresh-water **ecosystems**; therefore, career opportunities are numerous.

Broad Scientific Disciplines

Traditionally, many fields of biological expertise, such as fisheries biologists, **entomologists**, and botanists, are required to examine aquatic and terrestrial communities of living organisms associated with lakes, streams, and **wetlands**. Physical scientists, such as hydrologists, meteorologists, chemists,

ecosystem: the community of plants and animals within a water or terrestrial habitat interacting together and with their physical and chemical environment

entomology: the scientific study of insects

wetland: an area that is periodically or permanently saturated or covered by surface water or groundwater, that displays hydric soils, and that typically supports or is capable of supporting hydrophytic vegetation

or toxicologists, also are needed to understand how aquatic ecosystems operate. Scientists with differing emphases on spatial and temporal scales are important. Soil scientists and microbiologists examine organisms at microscopic scales, whereas **ornithologists**, mammalogists, or **herpetologists** must include large spatial ranges to incorporate activities of their study organisms. Geoscientists provide a spatial and temporal (time) perspective and give insight into patterns at regional and even global scales. Other scientists help integrate information: statisticians and theoretical mathematicians assist with analysis and developing abstract models of how the ecosystem functions.

ornithology: the scientific study of birds

herpetology: the scientific study of amphibians and reptiles

Links to Decision-Making

All the professions mentioned above may be pursued in government agencies, with private consultants, or with research institutions such as universities. Many aquatic scientists are researchers and also educators, managers, or consultants to decisionmakers.

Experts trained in both science and relevant policies are important for conserving and restoring fresh-water systems. These might be people with backgrounds in economics, law, geography, or sociology. They help scientists convey information to the public and to lawmakers. As communities become more involved in activities such as restoring populations of threatened species, maintaining vital natural resources, and conducting comprehensive land-use planning, there will be a steady need for fresh-water scientists with good communication and negotiation skills. SEE ALSO ECOLOGY, FRESH-WATER; FISHERIES, FRESH-WATER; FOREST HYDROLOGY; GEOSPATIAL TECHNOLOGIES; LAKE HEALTH, ASSESSING; LAKES: BIOLOGICAL PROCESSES; STREAM HEALTH, ASSESSING; WETLANDS.

Judith Li

Bibliography

Jeffries, Michael, and Derek Henry Mills. *Freshwater Ecology: Principles and Applications.* New York: John Wiley & Sons, 1995.

hydrology: the science that deals with the occurrence, distribution, movement, and physical and chemical properties of water on Earth; also refers to the hydrologic characteristics of a given region

remote sensing: the collection and interpretation of information about an object without being in physical contact with the object; most often, it refers to satellite-based collection of data to map and monitor the environment and resources on Earth

In the computer age, the cartographer's role has become increasingly technological in nature as they work with geographic information system (GIS) software to generate maps and perform environmental analyses. With the inputs from satellite data, the global positioning system (GPS), and remote sensing, maps can be digitally rendered with great precision and detail.

Careers in Geospatial Technologies

A host of technical specialists—geographers, geologists, **hydrologists**, oceanographers, and others—studies the water components of Earth's surface from various points of view. Some of these professionals hold B.S. (Bachelor of Science) degrees in their chosen fields, while others hold graduate-level degrees—either M.S. (Master of Science) or Ph.D. (Doctor of Philosophy). In the last few decades, with the rapid growth of geospatial technologies such as **remote sensing**, the global positioning system (GPS), and geographic information systems (GIS), the work of these specialists has become increasingly interwoven with that of professionals in the information sciences, including programmers, statisticians, and mathematicians.

Diverse Specialties

Most work that makes use of quantitative information about water resources today involves interaction with GIS, which are computer databases dedicated to geographic information. GIS unifies or integrates information from many different sources—geology, biology, satellites, ground observations using the GPS, traditional surveying, census data, and others—and make it available in meaningful forms to a wide variety of users, including engineers, scientists, facility managers, resource planners, lawyers, urban planners, and the military. Data-gathering for GIS is thus a diverse field in itself. Other GIS specialists, such as GIS managers, database administrators, systems analysts, and computer programmers are required to make each system work.

Many of these persons have undergraduate or graduate degrees in computer science with an emphasis on data structures, or in geography with an emphasis on GIS. Those involved with the electronic, aerospace, and other mechanical aspects of geospatial technology (e.g., satellites, aircraft, and sonar) usually have at least B.S. degrees in physics or in electrical, mechanical, nautical, or aeronautic engineering. Many job openings for GIS technicians and specialists call for candidates with B.S. degrees in geography with a GIS emphasis.

Work Environments

Professionals involved with the information-processing and engineering sides of GIS, GPS, and other geographic information technologies usually work in offices or laboratories, and spend much of their time interacting with computers. Those whose direct concern is with the understanding of the Earth's surface, such as geologists and hydrologists, may spend much of their time at sea, in the air, or on the land in quest of samples, observations, measurements, and other data. For these scientists, periods of data-collection generally alternate with periods of analytic deskwork involving computers.

Job Prospects

The federal government conducts research in many aspects of hydrology, ocean sciences, and water resource management. Resource mapping, environmental management, climate modeling, and weather prediction are among the activities carried on at the federal level.

Many states fund their own geological surveys, departments of environmental protection, and programs in water resource management. The responsibilities of these organizations include flood control, pollution control, highway planning, the protection of drinking water, the generation of hydroelectric power, and many other water-science tasks.

At the local and municipal level, community water and wastewater services must be provided. There also are many private corporations specializing in water resource work, often on contract to government bodies.

All such organizations, both governmental and private sector, hire staff with degrees in hydrology, geology, geography, geophysics, and geospatial technologies. Internationally, the United Nations, the World Bank, and most national governments also fund departments or ministries to oversee water-related ecology problems and water resource management.

The U.S. Department of Labor's Bureau of Labor Statistics states in its *Occupational Outlook Handbook* (2002) that "employment of environmental scientists and hydrologists is expected to grow faster than the average for all occupations through 2010, while employment of geoscientists is expected to grow about as fast as average." In other words, job openings for professional environmental scientists devoted to the understanding and control of **pollutants**, waste disposal, water supplies, and the **reclamation** of contaminated resources will grow faster than average, while those for geoscientists who study the composition and structure of Earth will grow at the same rate as most other professions. B.S. degrees in earth-science subfields of physics or in geology suffice to enter some job tracks, but better jobs and more of them are available to those with M.S. or Ph.D. degrees; most entry-level environmental science jobs require a bachelor's degree (or higher degree) in hydrogeology, geochemistry, environmental or civil engineering, or geography. SEE ALSO DATA, DATABASES, AND DECISION-SUPPORT SYSTEMS; GEOSPATIAL TECHNOLOGIES; LAND-USE PLANNING; OCEANOGRAPHY FROM SPACE; SOUND TRANSMISSION IN THE OCEAN

Larry Gilman

pollutant: something that pollutes, especially a waste material that contaminates air, soil, or water

reclamation: in terms of conservation, the process of restoring land to its prior state, such as converting old mineland back to forestland; in historical use, the process of converting land to a more desired use, such as draining a marsh for human development; also refers to treating wastewater in a way it can be reused

Bibliography

Lo, C. P., and Albert K. W. Yeung. *Concepts and Techniques of Geographic Information Systems.* Upper Saddle River, NJ: Prentice Hall, 2002.

Internet Resources

GeoSearch. <http://www.geosearch.com/>.

GIS Jobs Clearinghouse. <http://www.gjc.org/>.

Occupational Outlook Handbook: Environmental Scientists and Geoscientists. U.S. Department of Labor, Bureau of Labor Statistics. <http://www.bls.gov/oco/ocos050.htm>.

Careers in Hydrology

Hydrology is the science of the movement of water through the atmosphere, on the land surface, and underground. It includes the study of the physical, chemical, and biological interaction of water with the rocks and minerals of the Earth, as well as its critical interaction with living organisms.

Hydrologists work on projects as varied as the collection and analysis of water-related data; soil erosion; drought and flood analysis; water chemistry; sediment transport; river channel development; watershed (basin) management; **groundwater** resource evaluation; waste disposal; computer modeling;

groundwater: generally, all subsurface (underground) water, as distinct from surface water, that supplies natural springs, contributes to permanent streams, and can be tapped by wells; specifically, the water that is in the saturated zone of a defined aquifer

Hydrologists study the physical, chemical, and biological properties of fresh water. This hydrologist tests Alaska's Toolik Lake for contamination.

ecosystem: the community of plants and animals within a water or terrestrial habitat interacting together and with their physical and chemical environment

environmental protection; **ecosystem** studies; and construction of dams and roadways. Hydrologists find career opportunities in private business and industry; consulting firms; local, state, and federal agencies; agriculture; forestry; academia; and research-related institutions.

Water management issues, whether related to availability of water or the protection of water quality, have evolved to a more comprehensive view of the relationship between land use and water use. Hydrologists play a key role through fundamental data collection and analysis, resource evaluation, and participation in developing regional or watershed water resource management plans.

Academic preparation for a career in hydrology should include mathematics and science in high school. At the university level, hydrology courses are usually taught in the geology, geography, or civil engineering departments. In addition to these disciplines, academic training in biology, physics, chemistry, mathematics, and computer science is desirable. Many universities offer undergraduate and graduate degrees in hydrology. The completion of a graduate degree in hydrology will continue to offer the greatest career opportunities. SEE ALSO CHEMICAL ANALYSIS OF WATER; DATA, DATA-BASES, AND DECISION-SUPPORT SYSTEMS; DROUGHT MANAGEMENT; ECOLOGY, FRESH-WATER; EROSION AND SEDIMENTATION; FLOODPLAIN MANAGEMENT; GROUNDWATER; GROUNDWATER SUPPLIES, EXPLORATION FOR; HYDROGEO-LOGIC MAPPING; LAKE HEALTH, ASSESSING; MODELING GROUNDWATER FLOW AND TRANSPORT; MODELING STREAMFLOW; STREAM HYDROLOGY.

Dennis O. Nelson

Bibliography

Doyle, Kevin, Tanya Stubbs, and Sam Heizen. *The Complete Guide to Environmental Careers in the Twenty-First Century.* Washington, D.C.: Island Press, 1998.

Internet Resources

Careers in Hydrology. Universities Council on Water Resources. <http://www.uwin.siu.edu/ucowr/hydro/h13.html>.

Occupational Outlook Handbook: Environmental Scientists and Geoscientists. U.S. Department of Labor, Bureau of Labor Statistics. <http://www.bls.gov/oco/ocos050.htm>.

Careers in International Water Resources

Water resources is a dynamic profession worldwide. Every country must deal with water quantity and quality issues, and water affects every individual life on Earth. While international careers in this field are not well documented or studied, an exploration of available opportunities illustrates that career paths, employers, and jobs are quite varied. Furthermore, careers in this field can be rewarding, given the overwhelming international needs for water services and effective water management.

Career Opportunities

Professionals working in international water resources represent a variety of disciplines: engineering, sciences, social sciences, humanities, law, and management. Many professionals work within a particular field of specialization, such as economics or hydrogeology. Increasingly, these specialists are required to work on interdisciplinary teams and need to have a basic understanding of areas outside their discipline.

Because water-related work is so broad and diverse, opportunities can be found in many industries and sectors throughout the world. Employment opportunities include working with water utilities, data collection and analysis, water resources planning, water quality management, drought and flood planning, watershed management, groundwater management, and research and teaching. Nearly any water-related employment opportunity found in the United States also can be found in other geographical regions. Water professionals from the United States may work temporarily on water projects abroad, or may be based in foreign countries through federal agencies, private consulting firms, and nongovernmental organizations.

International Water Management Profession

Developing countries have particular needs that governmental and nongovernmental agencies and private companies try to address. International organizations and governments fund many of these efforts, although private sector involvement is increasing. Water-related issues include water supply, irrigation, watershed management, flood and drought planning, and sewage disposal. The magnitude of needs is clear: more than 1 billion people do not have access to safe drinking water; over 3 billion live without access to adequate sanitation systems; and it is estimated that 20,000 die each day from water-related diseases.

The major international governing bodies have programs dealing with water resources management. The United Nations Educational, Scientific and Cultural Organization (UNESCO) deals with fresh water, engineering, oceans, coasts and small islands, earth sciences, and science policy. It also manages the International Hydrologic Programme, the World Water Assessment Programme, and the Intergovernmental Oceanographic Commission.

The World Bank has a Water Resources Management Group that deals with water policy and strategies, water projects in various regions and issues such as dams, groundwater, transboundary water management, and water supply and sanitation. The regional development banks (e.g., the Asian Development Bank and Inter-American Development Bank) also have

---

ORGANIZATIONS WITH INTERNATIONAL WATER PROGRAMS

American Water Resources Association
<http://www.awra.org/>

Asian Development Bank
<http://www.adb.org/>

Global Environment Facility
<http://www.gefweb.org/>

Global Water Partnership
<http://www.gwpforum.org/>

Inter-American Development Bank
<http://www.iadb.org/>

International Water Association
<http://www.iwahq.org.uk/>

International Water Resources Association
<http://www.iwra.siu.edu>

Leadership for Environment and Development
<http://www.lead.org/>

United Nations Educational, Scientific and Cultural Organization's Natural Sciences Portal
<http://www.unesco.org/science/>

WaterAid
<http://www.wateraid.org.uk/>

World Bank
<http://www.worldbank.org>

Educating local residents in maintaining a safe and adequate drinking-water supply is one of many career opportunities in international water resources. These village women in Tamil Nadu, India were trained by international workers with LEAD (Leadership for Environment and Development) and WaterAid to repair and maintain their own community water pumps. Here the water-pump caretakers pose with pieces of equipment used in the training and demonstrations.

programs that are heavily involved in financing and evaluating water-supply and irrigation projects in their regions.

Increasingly these bodies work with an array of private and nonprofit partners. Multi-sector teams often are employed on water projects and research efforts. Thus, water professionals working internationally can find employment within international agencies, national governments, consulting firms, nongovernmental organizations, nonprofits, and universities. Many professional organizations serve to connect this wide variety of professionals located around the world. Two of the most prominent are the International Water Resources Association (IWRA) and the International Water Association (IWA). Many U.S.-focused associations also have international committees, such as the American Water Resources Association (AWRA).

Educational and Skill Backgrounds

Awareness of environmental issues is increasing around the world and with this awareness comes an increased appreciation of the need for effective water management. The demand for water professionals will multiply in response to this need. Some jobs require no more than a high school diploma and specialized on-the-job training, while others require a Ph.D. in a very specialized area.

In general, students entering the international water resources field need to be well rounded in their knowledge of water resources issues and also develop an area of specialization. Typically a graduate degree, either a Master's or a Ph.D. is required. Each individual must decide which aspect of water resources best suits their interests and skills. Specializations and requirements vary. The Universities Council on Water Resources maintains an online list of available graduate water programs at U.S. universities that can help students research fields of specialization and schools offering those programs (http://www.uwin.siu.edu/ucowr/grad/).

Additional career aids include the following:

Amazing Environmental Organization Web Directory
<http://www.webdirectory.com/>

AWRA Career Center
<http://www.awra.org/service/>

Environmental Careers Organization
<http://www.eco.org/>

Jobs Abroad
<http://www.jobsabroad.com/>

University of Wisconsin's Water Resources Library's Job Listings
<http://wri.wisc.edu/library/finding_jobsall.html#Water%20%20Listings>

Working in International Development (University of Sussex)
<http://www.sussex.ac.uk/Units/CDU/intdev.html>

Any water resources professional working internationally needs to have good written and oral communication skills, an interest in international development and concern for people and the environment, an appreciation for differences in cultures, and solid computer skills. The Internet is a valuable tool for international water management activities, and some teams work "virtually" from different geographical locations. Having a foreign language skill is also an invaluable asset, and sometimes a prerequisite to getting a particular job.

These career options in international water management can be expected to multiply as the international community is setting concrete goals to overcome existing water problems. Careers in the international sector are demanding yet rewarding to those interested in making a difference for the environment and the people who need water to live. SEE ALSO AGRICULTURE AND WATER; DAMS; DEVELOPING COUNTRIES, ISSUES IN; DRINKING WATER AND SOCIETY; FOOD SECURITY; GLOBALIZATION AND WATER; IRRIGATION MANAGEMENT; PORTS AND HARBORS; PUMPS, MODERN; SUPPLY DEVELOPMENT.

Faye Anderson

Careers in Oceanography

Balancing on the deck of a research ship stationed a few miles out to sea; a crewman closes the vault-like door of a submersible. Two biologists share the submarine's rear passenger chamber, and two more share its front chamber. The scientists are preparing to dive 300 meters (1,000 feet) or more

Marine ecologists and conservation biologists study the population biology and diversity of plant and animal communities. The rectangular grid shown here is used to quantify the occurrence of species in a known area.

beneath the water's surface, beyond the world of sunlight and plants, to the realm of darkness.

On their descent to the bottom of the ocean, the deep-sea biologists will see creatures as bizarre as those in the story *Alice in Wonderland*, animals with surprisingly successful adaptations to what for humans would be unimaginably harsh conditions. In this world of eternal darkness, the oceanographers will be awed by creatures living in a netherworld to which few humans have ever traveled.

Oceanographers and Limnologists

Deep-sea biology, the study of life in the ocean's deepest realms, is but one area of research in the field of oceanography. Oceanographers apply the basic sciences to studies of the sea, its contents, and the surrounding environment. Often, oceanographers are chemists, physicists, biologists, or geologists who bring knowledge of those fields to studies of the oceans. Similarly, limnologists study lakes, rivers, ponds, streams, and other freshwater bodies. All these scientists collaborate with one another and with engineers, social scientists, journalists, policymakers, and others on complex, challenging problems as they work to expand knowledge of the world's oceans, lakes, and rivers. Oceanographers work in laboratories ashore, on ships and submersibles at sea, and in coastal environments.

Oceanography is a relatively new science. Research conducted in the twentieth century has given the scientific world the first global glimpse of how the oceans work. It is now known that the oceans, atmosphere, solid Earth, and living organisms are part of an intertwined global system. Many oceanographers and limnologists conduct studies related to changes in this global system, both natural changes and those caused by human activities.

Many oceanographers are currently working on answers to such questions and problems as predicting the impact of increased carbon dioxide and other **greenhouse gas** emissions; increased ultraviolet radiation resulting from ozone depletion; the effects of excess nutrients in coastal waters due to fertilizers, pesticides, or habitat destruction; the short- and long-term effects of increased acidity (acid rain) due to burning of **fossil fuels**; and the impact of various fishing practices on commercially important marine animals like fish and lobsters.

greenhouse gas: a gas in the atmosphere that traps heat and reflects it back to the planetary body

fossil fuel: substance such as coal, oil, or natural gas, found underground in deposits formed from the remains of organisms that lived millions of years ago

Fields of Study

The study of oceanography is traditionally divided into biological oceanography, chemical oceanography, geological and geophysical oceanography, physical oceanography, marine engineering, marine policy, and science journalism. Many of the most exciting fields encompass two or more of these disciplines.

Pursuing a career in a marine-related field requires a good background in at least one area of science or engineering, along with mathematics. In marine policy careers, law, economics, or political science training is usually necessary. In science journalism, knowledge of science and journalism are combined. Specializing in one area too early can be a mistake. It is best to keep all options open, at least through high school and into undergraduate education. Only in graduate school must one begin to make choices.

Biological. Biological oceanographers, marine biologists, and fisheries scientists study marine plants and animals. They are interested in how marine organisms develop, relate to one another, adapt to their environment, and interact with it. Among other things, their work includes developing ecologically sound methods of harvesting seafood, and studying biological responses to **pollution**.

Because marine biology is the best known and often the most popular field of oceanography, it is currently the most competitive. High school students wishing to work with marine mammals, for example, may number in the tens of thousands; even with a graduate degree, however, jobs in that subfield of marine biology are few and far between.

pollution: any alteration in the character or quality of the environment, including water in waterbodies or geologic formations, which renders the environmental resource unfit or less suited for certain uses

Chemical. Chemical oceanographers and marine geochemists conduct research on the chemical composition of sea water, and its interaction with the atmosphere and seafloor. They analyze sea-water components; study the effects of pollutants; look at chemical processes—such as Earth's carbon cycle—that operate in the marine environment; and investigate chemical tracers (small amounts of dissolved substances that give water a certain

Marine scientists specializing in biological and chemical subfields may investigate impacts of environmental change, including pollution, on ocean life. Here, scientists are dissecting a 40-ton, 18-meter-long (60-foot) blue whale to determine why it died off Rhode Island's Narragansett Bay.

seamount: an isolated conical submarine mountain rising 1,000 meters (3,280 feet) or more above the sea floor; most form as submarine volcanoes at spreading centers and are transported to the deep ocean by plate movement

basin (ocean): the topographic low area occupied by oceans; the floor of ocean basins consists of basaltic crust that is more dense than typical continental rocks

signature or set of qualities), helping scientists to understand how sea water flows around the globe, and how the ocean affects climate.

Geological. Geological oceanographers and geophysicists study the ocean floor and its geologic structures, like **seamounts**, ridges, and trenches, to discover how **ocean basins** and other ocean structures are formed. They try to find out about the processes that created these ocean basins, and how the ocean floor and the waters above it interact. Their research on ocean rocks and sediment provides information about Earth's recent and long-ago history.

Physical. Physical oceanographers examine ocean properties like temperature, density of sea water, wave motions, tides, and currents. They conduct research on how the ocean and the atmosphere together influence weather and climate. Physical oceanographers also study how light and sounds are transmitted through sea water.

Engineering. Ocean engineers use scientific and technical information in practical uses like designing instruments for measuring processes in the ocean, and building structures that can withstand currents, waves, tides, and severe storms. Fields in ocean engineering include acoustics; robotics; electrical, mechanical, civil, and chemical engineering; and naval architecture.

Policy. Marine policy experts combine knowledge of oceanography with an understanding of the social sciences, law, or business to devise policies, guidelines, and regulations for the wise use of ocean and coastal resources.

Journalism. Science journalists who specialize in writing about aquatic subjects, whether oceans, lakes, or rivers, meld an understanding of oceanography and limnology with a knowledge of journalism and an ability to write. They may apply their talents in writing for newspapers and magazines, working in broadcast media (television and radio), as science news officers disseminating information about oceanography in government agencies and at universities, and in teaching science journalism.

Employment Opportunities

The marine sciences offer many employment opportunities. Those interested in pursuing research careers will find opportunities in academia, industry, government, nonprofit and nongovernmental organizations, consulting firms, and, in some cases—like aquaculture, the growing of marine life for food and medicines—owning their own businesses. Most consultants, however, have prior experience in some aspect of research or teaching before either venturing out on their own or joining a consulting firm. In an academic setting, most jobs involve conducting research and teaching undergraduate and graduate students, and require at least a master's degree and usually a doctor of philosophy (Ph.D.) degree.

Academic Careers. University oceanographers usually spend at least some time each year engaged in fieldwork, collecting data and samples onboard small boats or large research vessels. They are generally affiliated with professional societies, such as the American Society of Limnology and Oceanography, through which they are able to keep up with the latest advances in their fields, present research results at scientific meetings in the United States and abroad, and build a network of colleagues. When not in the field or at meetings, these oceanographers spend a significant amount of time in the laboratory running experiments, or working on computers to analyze data or develop models. Oceanographers employed at universities also spend some time teaching.

Alternative Careers. While research at a university was once considered the traditional career path for those with graduate-level degrees in the marine sciences, changes in academia and science funding opportunities have made this route far less certain. An increasing number of marine science master's and Ph.D. graduates are choosing so-called "alternative careers" as experts on the marine environment in almost any field where knowledge of the oceans is required. These careers may be found in government agencies at federal, state, and local levels; at places like aquariums; in law firms that need marine experts; in small businesses that seek aquaculturalists and mariculturalists; and in science journalism.

Administrative Jobs. Many oceanographers have administrative jobs, either with academic institutions or with government or private agencies. These oceanographers spend more time in the office, writing reports and giving presentations on their recommendations. They also attend national and international conferences to keep abreast of developments in their fields.

Private Industry. In private industry, insurance companies, for example, rely on oceanographers to predict and understand weather-related hazards and natural disasters. Transportation industries rely on similar information in shipping, whether by air or sea. Jobs in some nonprofit organizations (such as the Sierra Club, the World Wildlife Fund, and The Nature Conservancy) concentrate on environmental advocacy, whereas in other nonprofit institutions oceanographers may develop instruments, systems, and methods for exploring the seas.

Medical Research. A new area in which graduates of oceanography programs, particularly biological oceanography programs, are finding employment is in medical research industries, including biotechnology. Information from current research is setting the stage for development of novel drugs that target a

Marine engineers and technicians are needed to maintain oceanographic observation equipment, such as the complex arrays used in submersibles. Technological advances in instrumentation create cutting-edge job opportunities in the public and private sectors.

variety of human diseases; many of these compounds will likely come from marine sources. One area now on the forefront of biological oceanography is molecular biology and environmental genetics, research on the structure and function of molecules like ribonucleic acid (RNA) and deoxyribonucleic acid (DNA), and the regulation of processes in a cell and by genes.

Key Career Aspects

While academia is still the largest employer for oceanographers, a survey of marine scientists revealed several key aspects to a career in this field. First, oceanographers will likely hold a number of jobs in a variety of sectors, public and private. Second, most oceanographers can expect to change jobs fairly frequently. Finally, many entry-level career possibilities for new graduates, such as internships, externships, traineeships, and teaching and research assistantships, provide knowledge useful and sometimes critical to the next step. These commitments, lasting from several months to two years, will give early career oceanographers an edge over others who lack experience in the field. Volunteering is also an excellent way to break into a career in oceanography or limnology.

In addition to being good scientists, today's oceanographers and limnologists must also be good writers and speakers. Researchers need to submit proposals to funding sources in attempts to acquire financial support for their research, and they must present the results of that research to colleagues, decisionmakers, students, and funding agencies. As one leading oceanographer has said, "Marine science does no good unless it is communicated to others." SEE ALSO ECOLOGY, MARINE; MOORINGS AND PLATFORMS; OCEANOGRAPHY, BIOLOGICAL; OCEANOGRAPHY, CHEMICAL; OCEANOGRAPHY, GEOLOGICAL; OCEANOGRAPHY, PHYSICAL; SUBMARINES AND SUBMERSIBLES.

Cheryl Lyn Dybas

Bibliography

Doyle, Kevin, Tanya Stubbs, and Sam Heizen. *The Complete Guide to Environmental Careers in the Twenty-First Century.* Washington, D.C.: Island Press, 1998.

Kreeger, Karen Young. *Guide to Non-Traditional Careers in Science*. Philadelphia, PA: Taylor & Francis Publishers, 1999.

National Sea Grant College Program. *Marine Science Careers: A Sea Grant Guide to Ocean Opportunities*. National Oceanic and Atmospheric Administration, 2000.

The Oceanography Society. *Careers in Oceanography and Marine-Related Fields*. Washington, D.C.: The Oceanography Society, 1995.

Internet Resources

ASLO. American Society of Limnology and Oceanography. <http://www.aslo.org>.

Sea Grant Marinecareers.net. Woods Hole Oceanographic Institute and New Hampshire Sea Grant Program. <http://www.marinecareers.net>.

Careers in Soil Science

Careers in soil science focus on understanding, managing, and improving soil and water resources. Soil science is a true interdisciplinary science that integrates the use of biology, chemistry, physics, geology, geography, climatology, hydrology, and mathematics to describe, interpret, and manage the soil and water environment.

Traditionally, most soil science jobs were related to agriculture, but today the field has expanded to include forestry, rangelands, and especially environmental concerns in urban ecosystems. Soil is a precious natural resource, and its understanding is paramount to promoting ecosystem sustainability. Because soil is so common, it is often taken for granted. But to soil scientists, interpreting a soil pit is like reading a history book of the landscape—yet much more exciting.

Preparation for Employment

Employment opportunities are found especially in the private sector with environmental and agricultural consulting firms, but jobs also can be found with state, federal, and international agencies and educational institutions. Knowledge of soil properties and processes are important in making environmental and land-use decisions. A strong soil background helps one in making a career in land-use planning; natural resource evaluations; wetland use and protection; soil mapping; farming; forestry; ecology; **sustainable** agriculture; water and agrichemical management; fertilizer technology; environmental site investigations; hazardous waste specialties; geographic information systems; soil and water protection; relative-age dating of land surfaces; and evaluation of septic systems and stormwater facilities.

Academic preparation in soil science can be found in most universities that have an agricultural program. Most of these programs have been expanded to include all the nonagricultural applications of soils. In addition, courses involving soils can be found in geology, geotechnical engineering, environmental science, and geography departments at nonagricultural universities. SEE ALSO CHEMICALS FROM AGRICULTURE; DESERT HYDROLOGY; FOREST HYDROLOGY; GEOSPATIAL TECHNOLOGIES; IRRIGATION MANAGEMENT; LAND-USE PLANNING; RUNOFF, FACTORS AFFECTING; SEPTIC SYSTEM IMPACTS; STREAM EROSION AND LANDSCAPE DEVELOPMENT; WETLANDS.

Scott F. Burns

Soil scientists deal with the complex interactions of soil, its parent materials, and water. Here a scientist for the Navajo Irrigation Project in New Mexico monitors moisture depths in order to determine the optimal irrigation rate.

sustainable: as in "sustainable development," describes efforts that guide economic growth in a manner that meets current needs without compromising the ability of future generations to meet their needs; in terms of natural resources, also encompasses development conducted in an environmentally sound manner, with an emphasis on natural resource conservation, including water and aquatic life

Bibliography

Kohnke, Helmut and D. P. Franzmeier. *Soil Science Simplified.* 4th ed. Prospect Heights, IL: Waveland Press, 1995.

Internet Resources

Soil Science Society of America. <http://www.soils.org>.

Careers in Water Resources Engineering

Although physicians, attorneys, economists, and many other professionals often are primary players in developing and managing water resources, engineers play a significant role in water resources management. Potential employers include large and small businesses; government at all levels; corporations that are local to national and multinational in scope; and schools and universities. Even self-employment as engineering consultants and other technically applied positions is an expanding career option for water resource engineering professionals.

To become an engineer requires a formal education at the college or university level, and advancement in the profession calls for professional registration by state-level agencies. Engineers work alongside, and often supervise, other workers such as technicians, surveyors, draftsmen, and computer programmers.

Engineering and Society

General engineering functions include research, development, design, production, construction, operations, sales, and management. Other engineers are involved in testing, teaching, and consulting. In all these activities, engineers seek to understand the laws of science and mathematics and to put these laws to practical use for the improvement of society and civilization. Engineers seek out and apply practical solutions to technical problems. This role has not changed since the origins of engineering in ancient times; only the objectives pursued, the techniques used, and the tools available for analysis have changed. Advances in developing new materials and in the capabilities of modern computers for analysis and design combine to make many forms of engineering, particularly the specialties in the water sciences, attractive career choices.

Preparing for an Engineering Career

Young people planning careers in engineering should seek the best and most thorough background possible in mathematics and science from their secondary school. Study of algebra, geometry, and trigonometry is essential, and classes in **calculus** and other "higher" mathematics courses are desirable. Other branches of science that are important to water resources engineering include chemistry, physics, and biology. As in every modern career field, familiarity with computer applications is essential; word processing and electronic **spreadsheets** are basic applications, and students will also be introduced to software design and programming of computer code.

The aspiring engineer can expect these subjects to be repeated at advanced levels in college classes, but secondary school study will pave the way

calculus: a branch of mathematics that involves computing or calculating quantities that change as functions of different variables

spreadsheet: computer-based program to facilitate computations and manipulations involving numerical and alphanumeric values

Water resources engineering encompasses many specialties. Here an engineer reads gages at the Hoover Dam.

for success in their college work. Introductory engineering course work is available at most community colleges. However, aspiring engineers will complete their bachelor of science degree work at colleges and universities accredited by the Accreditation Board for Engineering and Technology (ABET), the national agency recognized by the U.S. Department of Education to monitor and evaluate engineering education programs. ABET provides world leadership for quality innovations in engineering, technology, and applied science education.

Engineering Fields Related to Water Sciences

Degree programs that will prepare graduates for engineering careers in the water sciences include civil engineering, environmental engineering, hydrology, water resources management, and others with similar functions. Almost all are nominal 4-year programs, but heavy course loads and the increasing popularity of cooperative degree programs, which alternate periods of study and work, often extend the work beyond 4 years to 5 (or more) years.

The employment market, usually favorable for graduating engineers, was exceptionally good as the twenty-first century began. Young engineering graduates almost always have their choice of several employment opportunities, and signing bonuses and other benefits are not unusual. As in all professional careers, the graduate should investigate and accept employment in positions that offer challenge and the opportunity for meaningful work and advancement, rather than just seeking the highest available salary offer.

Beyond the Bachelor's Degree

Graduate degree work is typically not expected for initial employment with a company or other organization, but is becoming increasingly important for advancement, and is a good choice for all engineers early in their careers. Most employers are supportive, and will usually provide assistance for part-time master's-level study.

Engineering students with a strong undergraduate record can usually study full-time with tuition and fees paid for them while working as teaching or research assistants at research universities. These positions are normally applied for at the schools of the student's choice during the fall months for study beginning the following summer.

Registration as a Professional Engineer (PE) is legally required in most states to be "in responsible charge" of major engineering projects. State registration boards conduct examinations and certify the experience requirement for PE status, which is four years in most states. Students can begin this process by passing the Fundamentals of Engineering (FE) examination during their final year of undergraduate study. SEE ALSO ARMY CORPS OF ENGINEERS, U.S.; CAREERS IN ENVIRONMENTAL SCIENCE AND ENGINEERING.

James R. Groves

Bibliography

Burghardt, M. David. *Introduction to the Engineering Profession*, 2nd ed. New York: HarperCollins, 1995.

National Research Council. *Opportunities in the Hydrologic Sciences*. Washington, D.C.: National Academy Press, 1991.

Oakes, William C. et al. *Engineering Your Future*. Wildwood, MO: Great Lakes Press, 1999.

Wright, Paul H. *Introduction to Engineering*, 2nd ed. New York: John Wiley & Sons, 1994.

Careers in Water Resources Planning and Management

Water resources careers in the early twenty-first century, particularly in planning and management, will offer great interest, large challenges, outstanding opportunities for peer recognition, and great personal satisfaction for young professionals. Rapid population growth, land-use changes, and perhaps global climatic change are among the factors that will place further demands on an already stressed global fresh-water supply and influence career directions of new water resource professionals.

Job Opportunities

Water resources planning and management career opportunities are found with government agencies at the federal, state, and local levels; on the faculties of colleges and universities; in the private sector with environmental or engineering consultants; with environmental groups; and with companies that use significant water resources in their manufacturing or extracting processes.

Depending on the employer, water resources job opportunities involve resource assessment, resource development or utilization, or resource protection. For example, at the federal level, planning or management opportunities may be with the following:

- U.S. Geological Survey or Agricultural Research Service (resource assessment);

- U.S. Bureau of Reclamation, Bureau of Land Management, Army Corps of Engineers, Forest Service, or Natural Resources Conservation Service (resource development or utilization); or

Although employment opportunities are strong in the United States, water planners and managers are needed worldwide. Irrigation projects, such as this one on Senegal's border, are among the resource development and utilization projects that require water resource professionals with various types of expertise.

- U.S. Environmental Protection Agency, Fish and Wildlife Service, or National Park Service (resource protection).

Planning and management opportunities are also available in other countries, both in developed and developing nations.

Qualifications

The qualifications needed for entry into the fields of **watershed** planning and management vary with specific positions and employers. Generally a baccalaureate degree from a college or university in physical science, biological science, engineering, **hydrology**, or forestry will qualify a student for an entry-level position with a consulting firm or government agency. A master of science (M.S.) degree or doctor of philosophy (Ph.D.) degree will assure a student a better starting position, salary, and advancement potential. In most cases, a Ph.D. is required for a position in academia.

The academic background commonly determines the career direction of the student. For example, a career in **floodplain** management may require a civil engineering background, whereas management of a major **aquifer** may require a background in **groundwater** hydrology. Nearly all water resources planning and management careers require computer literacy and many require a background in geographic information systems (GIS).

Other Relevant Disciplines and Experience

Students interested in water resources can approach this field from many disciplines. University departments commonly offering water resources curricula include civil and environmental engineering, geography, geology, fisheries, forestry, soil science, biochemistry, and others. Some programs at the graduate level offer a combination of education and experience to their students by providing them with opportunities to work in the field with practicing nonuniversity water resources professionals.

watershed: the land area drained by a river and its tributaries; also called river basin, drainage basin, catchment, and drainage area

hydrology: the science that deals with the occurrence, distribution, movement, and physical and chemical properties of water on Earth

floodplain: the low-lying land adjoining a river that is sometimes flooded; generally covered by fine-grained sediments (silt and clay) deposited by the river at flood stage

aquifer: a water-saturated, permeable, underground rock formation that can transmit significant quantities of water under ordinary hydraulic gradients to wells and springs

groundwater: generally, all subsurface (underground) water, as distinct from surface water, that supplies natural springs, contributes to permanent streams, and can be tapped by wells; specifically, the water that is in the saturated zone of a defined aquifer

In recent years, water resources planners and managers have found it increasingly necessary to have at least some knowledge of other disciplines including sociology, economics, and law. Students may wish to utilize courses from these disciplines as electives. For example, a career in watershed planning, especially in a developed watershed, may require the planner to deal not only with water resources issues but also with biological issues, and with social, economic, or legal issues of the human population of the watershed. The planner must understand the impact of all issues as they relate to the conservation or development of the water resources of the watershed.

Educating an often skeptical public about the necessity for controversial water resources decisions often becomes a major part of the career of the water resources professional. All water resources professionals must keep the tenet firmly in mind that there is no substitute for being able to explain aspects of science in terms that the public can readily understand.

Rewards

Expectations of personal satisfaction and recognition and respect by the public and by peers are major reasons for considering a career in water resources planning and management. The opportunity to improve the quality of life for persons locally, nationally, or worldwide by providing adequate sources of fresh water for human needs—while being aware of the needs of other plant and animal species—is highly rewarding.

Planning and management professionals contribute greatly to the knowledge base of water resources on a variety of scales from the smallest local basin to the global Earth. Recognition may be based on presentation of research or case studies at scientific meetings, or publication of research and studies in the many journals and publications devoted to water resources. SEE ALSO CAREERS IN INTERNATIONAL WATER RESOURCES; GEOSPATIAL TECHNOLOGIES; PLANNING AND MANAGEMENT, WATER RESOURCES.

Richard A. Engberg

Bibliography

Doyle, Kevin, Tanya Stubbs, and Sam Heizen. *The Complete Guide to Environmental Careers in the Twenty-First Century.* Washington, D.C.: Island Press, 1998.

Internet Resources

Graduate Programs Directory. Universities Council on Water Resources. Southern Illinois University. <http://www.uwin.siu.edu/ucowr/grad/>.

American Water Resources Association: Career Center. <http://www.awra.org/service/career.html>.

Carson, Rachel

American Author, Biologist, and Environmentalist
1907–1964

Rachel Carson made a career of her lifelong fascination with wildlife and the environment around her and became one of the pioneers of the environmental movement in the United States. Her mother taught her to enjoy the outdoors. On graduation from Parnassas High School in Pennsylvania, Carson enrolled in the Pennsylvania College for Women in Pittsburgh, planning to study

English and become a writer. A course in biology rekindled her interest in science and led her to change to a science major.

Carson went on to do postgraduate work at Johns Hopkins University, obtaining a master's degree in 1932. She joined the **zoology** staff at the University of Maryland in 1931. Carson developed a particular interest in the life of the sea, which led her into further postgraduate research at the Woods Hole Marine Biological Laboratory in Massachusetts. In 1936, she accepted a position as an aquatic biologist at the Bureau of Fisheries in Washington, D.C. She went on to be editor in chief at the U.S. Fish and Wildlife Service, the successor to the Bureau of Fisheries. Here she prepared leaflets and informational brochures on conservation and the protection of natural resources.

Early Works

Rachel Carson's first book, *Under the Sea Wind*, appeared in 1941 with the subtitle "a naturalist's picture of ocean life." The book, which grew from Carson's fascination with the seashore and the ocean as a result of vacations on the Atlantic coast, was well received. The narrative told the story of the seashore, the open sea, and the sea bottom.

Carson's important second book, *The Sea Around Us*, was published in 1951. Even more than her previous book, it was acclaimed for its approachable writing style. *The Sea Around Us* provides a layperson's geological guide through time and tide. In this book, Carson explores the mystery and treasures of the hidden world of the oceans, revealing its history and environment to the nonscientists. Carson maps the evolution of planet Earth—the formation of mountains, islands, and oceans—then moves into a more detailed description of the sea, starting with the sea surface and the creatures that live near the surface, descending through the depths to the sea bottom.

The Sea Around Us went to the top of the nonfiction best-seller list in the United States, won the National Book Award for Non-Fiction, was selected for the Book of the Month Club, and was condensed for *Reader's Digest*. It went into nine printings and was translated into thirty-three languages.

Such was the success of *The Sea Around Us* that it enabled Carson to accept a Guggenheim Fellowship and take a leave of absence from her job to start work on a third book, *The Edge of the Sea*, published in 1955. Written as a popular guide to the seashore, this book is a study of the ecological relationship between the Atlantic seashore and the animals that inhabit the coastline. While complementing her previous two books, this work evidences the growth of Carson's interest in the interrelationship of Earth's systems.

Silent Spring

Rachel Carson's lasting reputation as a force in the environmental movement was made with her fourth and final book, *Silent Spring*, published in 1962. The title of the book was inspired by a phrase from a John Keats poem—"And no birds sing." **Pesticides** being sprayed indiscriminately were killing songbirds and thus bringing about the absence of birdsong: a silent spring.

Through her books, Rachel Carson focused attention on marine life and on the dangers of chemical pollution. By educating a wide audience about contaminant hazards, she helped lay the groundwork for the environmental movement.

zoology: the branch of biology that studies animals, including their structure, function, growth, origin, evolution, and distribution

pesticides: a broad group of chemicals that kills or controls plants (herbicides), fungus (fungicides), insects and arachnids (insecticides), rodents (rodenticides), bacteria (bactericides), or other creatures that are considered pests

DDT

The chemical dichlorodiphenyl-trichloroethane, or DDT, is a synthetic organic compound introduced in the 1940s and used as an insecticide. Its continual build-up in the food chain caused concern for human and animal health. As a result, DDT was banned in the U.S. in 1972, 10 years after the publication of *Silent Spring*. DDT remains in use in many countries of the world.

algae: (singular, alga) simple photosynthetic organisms, usually aquatic, containing chlorophyll, and lacking roots, stems, and leaves

In this book, Carson moves away from her focus on the sea and the land-sea interface to describe the interrelationship between communities and modern agricultural and industrial techniques. The book chronicles the disastrous results evident from the widespread use of pesticides, chemical fertilizers, and chemical treatments designed to increase agricultural production or simplify the production process.

As an example, Carson describes streams that became chemical soups, laden with the outpourings of chemical treatment plants. She describes runoff from fields treated with pesticides and chemical fertilizers, killing **algae**, plant life, fish, and animals. With this book, Carson educated the general public about the hazards of environmental contamination and made the case for careful consideration of both short- and long-term impacts of human-generated chemical contamination of our waterways.

The arguments contained in *Silent Spring* were not new. These concerns had been discussed in scientific journals, but Carson's approachable style brought the discussion of environmental management before a much wider general audience. On publication, *Silent Spring* attracted a great deal of adverse criticism, generated mostly by the chemical industry. More balanced reactions were found in the scientific press.

In 1963, the President's Science Advisory Committee concurred with Carson's assessment of the damage wrought by the widespread use of chemicals and the spiral of contamination that resulted from the development of ever more toxic treatments as insects developed resistance to pesticides. Her writing alerted the country to the dangers of chemical pollution to waters and helped transform water resources management. SEE ALSO ENVIRONMENTAL MOVEMENT, ROLE OF WATER IN THE.

Pat Dasch

Bibliography

Bonta, Marcia Myers. *Women in the Field: America's Pioneering Women Naturalists.* College Station: Texas A & M University Press, 1991.

Brooks, Paul. *The House of Life: Rachel Carson at Work.* Boston, MA: Houghton Mifflin, 1972.

Carson, Rachel. *The Edge of the Sea.* Boston, MA: Houghton Mifflin, 1955.

———. *The Sea Around Us.* New York: Oxford University Press, 1951.

———. *Silent Spring.* Boston, MA: Houghton Mifflin, 1962.

———. *Under the Sea Wind.* New York: Viking Penguin, 1941.

Lear, Linda J. *Rachel Carson: Witness for Nature.* New York: Henry Holt, 1972.

Cavern Development

archaeology: the historical study of humans through the excavation of sites and the analysis of artifacts and other physical remains

groundwater: generally, all subsurface (underground) water, as distinct from surface water, that supplies natural springs, contributes to permanent streams, and can be tapped by wells; specifically, the water that is in the saturated zone of a defined aquifer

Throughout time, humankind has been attracted to shelters and the dark mysteries of caverns, or caves. Much of the early evidence of humans and their art comes from **archaeological** sites in caves.

Most solutional caves were formed as weak carbonic acids in **groundwater** dissolved solid rock, especially carbonate rocks (limestone and dolomite) and salt deposits. Caves have rarely formed in sandstone or shale because minerals such as quartz, feldspar, and clay do not react readily with carbonic acid in water.

Coppingers Cave in east-central Tennessee is a solutional cave in an area of karst topography. Dripping and flowing water creates its features, such as this flowstone.

Carbonic acid is the result of the atmospheric gas carbon dioxide (CO_2) reacting with rainwater. When the rainwater enters the soil, it may pick up even more CO_2 from the **organic** material present. The water continues to infiltrate downward until it reaches the saturated zone of the **water table**. Along the way, the water may create openings in the rock where water dissolves soluble minerals. Groundwater flowing through cave systems represents the only true example of so-called "underground rivers;" otherwise, groundwater occurs not in subsurface "rivers" or "lakes" but in small spaces (pores) in rocks and sediments.

organic: pertaining to, or the product of, biological reactions or functions

water table: the upper surface of the zone of saturation in an unconfined aquifer below which all voids in rock, sediment, and other geologic materials are saturated (completely filled) with water

talus cave: cave formed from huge rocks that have fallen from cliffs, leaving spacious chambers within the boulder piles

tectonic cave: a naturally hollowed-out place in the ground formed by any geological force that causes rocks to move apart

precipitate: (verb) the process by which a solution separates into a relatively clear liquid and a solid substance by a chemical or physical change; (noun) the solid substance resulting from this process

sinkhole: a depression in the Earth's surface caused by the collapse of underlying limestone, dolomite, salt, or gypsum

✳ **See "Karst Hydrology" for a photograph of the famous Winter Park, Florida sinkhole.**

karst: topography characterized by closed depressions or sinkholes, caves, and underground drainage formed by dissolution of limestone, dolomite, or gypsum

evaporite: sediments that form as the result of the precipitation of minerals during the evaporation of water, primarily sea water, and that may form sedimentary rock

ice age: a cold period marked by episodes of extensive glaciation alternating with episodes of relative warmth; the formally designated "Ice Age" refers to the most recent glacial period, which occurred during the Pleistocene epoch

Solutional Caves

Caves can form by various mechanisms, and can fall into various categories such as solutional caves, lava tubes, **talus caves**, soil tubes, glacier caves, wind caves, sea caves, and **tectonic caves**. Solutional caves form by the dissolving of rock above or below the water table. If a cave occurs above the water table, water dripping from the roof of the cave may **precipitate** dripstones. Two of the most common dripstone deposits are stalactites and stalagmites. Stalactites form like icicles as minerals slowly precipitate minerals on the ceiling. Stalagmites grow upward from the cave floor where the drops of water land. Eventually, a stalagmite and stalactite may grow together to form a column.

Water flowing over the surface of a wall or floor deposits layers of calcite called flowstone. If the cave forms below the water table, as most caves do, no air is present for the water to drip through; therefore, dripstone and flowstone do not form.

Sinkholes

As caves grow larger, the void space may become so large that the rocks of the cave roof collapse suddenly into the void to form **sinkholes**. Sinkholes commonly need a triggering mechanism to cause their gravitational collapse. These triggers can include heavy rains or floods. Droughts can lower the groundwater levels, triggering collapse, because it is groundwater that often supports a cavity roof. Collapse of sinkholes also may be stimulated by human activity and structures such as ponds, buildings, drainage pattern changes, heavy traffic vibrations, or declines in groundwater level.✳

In areas where extensive limestone formations occur, numerous sinkholes may form an irregular land surface called **karst** topography. Although karst topography is characteristic of humid areas, few surface streams are present because of the underground drainage channels.

Sinkholes also form in areas where underlying layers of **evaporite** minerals (halite and gypsum) dissolve. Evaporites are the most soluble of common rocks. Groundwater rapidly dissolves them and carries the dissolved minerals off in solution. Such high solubility enables subsurface channels and sinkholes to form in a few days, weeks, or years, and catastrophic collapse can result. The Wink Sink of west Texas is an example of a recent sinkhole in salt deposits.

Blue Holes. In some areas, caves that were above the water table have been drowned by the rise in sea following the end of the **ice ages**. The sinkholes providing entrance to these undersea caves are called "blue holes," named for the blue sea water filling them. They are found in Florida, the Bahamas, and other similar areas, and attract adventurous cave divers. The drowned caves often contain stalactites and stalagmites formed thousands of years ago when the caverns were above sea level. These caves may be filled with salt water, fresh water, or both.

Large U.S. Caves

Two of the largest caves in the United States are Mammoth Cave in Kentucky and Carlsbad Caverns in New Mexico. Both consist of passageways dissolved in limestone.

Mammoth Cave is believed to have formed by carbonic acid in water slowly removing limestone, whereas parts of Carlsbad Caverns may have a different origin. In 1980, speleologists (people who study caves) proposed that at least part of Carlsbad Caverns was formed from the bottom up. Hydrogen sulfide, a gas ascending from deep **petroleum reservoirs**, dissolved in groundwater to form sulfuric acid that dissolved huge volumes of rock at the levels of the ancient water table. The added power of this acidic water explains the depth and size of the passageways.

petroleum reservoir: a porous and permeable rock in which petroleum accumulates; primarily marine sedimentary rocks such as sandstone and limestone

Mammoth Cave is the longest recorded cave system in the world with more than 500 kilometers (310 miles) explored and mapped. At a depth of 486 meters (1,594 feet), Carlsbad Caverns is the deepest cave in the United States. The large room at Carlsbad Caverns is 1,200 meters (3,936 feet) long, 200 meters (656 feet) wide, and 100 meter (328 feet) high. SEE ALSO FRESH WATER, NATURAL COMPOSITION OF; FRESH WATER, PHYSICS AND CHEMISTRY OF; GROUNDWATER; KARST HYDROLOGY.

David M. Rohr

Bibliography

Harris, Ann G., and Esther Tuttle. *Geology of National Parks.* Dubuque, IA: Kendall/Hunt Publishing, 1990.

Hill, Carol A. *Geology of Carlsbad Cavern and other Caves in the Guadalupe Mountains, New Mexico and Texas*, Issue 17. Socorro, NM: New Mexico Bureau of Mines and Mineral Resources Bulletin, 1987.

James, Noel P., and Philip W. Choquette, eds. *Paleokarst.* New York: Springer-Verlag, 1988.

Martinez, Joseph D., Kenneth S. Johnson, and James T. Neal. "Sinkholes in Evaporite Rocks." *American Scientist* 86 (1998):38–51.

Internet Resources

Cave Facts: Information on Caves, Karst and Groundwater. American Cave Conservation Association. <http://www.cavern.org/ACCA/ACCA_index.htm>.

Cephalopods

What group of marine invertebrates was celebrated by a Chief Justice of the Supreme Court of the United States? (Answer: cephalopods.) Oliver Wendell Holmes (1809–1894) wrote the poem "The Chambered Nautilus" in 1858 to describe the shell of the cephalopod *Nautilus.*

Nautilus belongs to the cephalopods, a category of mollusks to which the octopus, squid, and cuttlefish octopus also belong. The phylum Mollusca also includes the gastropods (snails and slugs) and bivalves (such as clams and oysters) among others, and is considered one of the most intelligent and successful invertebrate groups in the oceans.

Major Characteristics

All cephalopods live in the marine environment, where they are carnivores. A shared trait of the group are sucker-bearing tentacles used to seize and hold prey. The tentacles range in number from eight in the octopus to more than ninety in *Nautilus.* The tentacles surround a powerful beak-like mouth.

Many living cephalopods (but not *Nautilus*) possess an ink sac capable of ejecting a dark fluid to confound predators. Some octopuses, squids, and

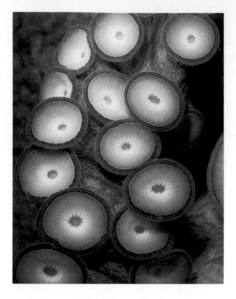

Suction cups on tentacles are used to grasp prey and cling to surfaces. The common octopus has approximately 240 suction cups per tentacle.

cuttlefish have the remarkable ability to change color and color patterns to better blend in with the surrounding seafloor.

While most other mollusks have hard external shells, most cephalopods do not. *Nautilus* has a planispherally coiled external shell, while squids and cuttlefish have a smaller internal skeleton, and octopus has no hard skeleton at all. The cephalopods all have two well-developed eyes used in hunting prey. The octopus spends most of its time scurrying along the seafloor, feeding on other bottom dwellers such as crabs. In contrast, *Nautilus* and squids are active swimmers and also can prey on fish. All cephalopods can move backwards fairly quickly by expelling water in a type of jet propulsion.

Because they are elusive creatures, the habits and ecological details of most species of cephalopods are unknown. Similarly, the population sizes are not well known, making it difficult in many cases to determine if a species is endangered. Overfishing of the most commercially desirable species has occurred in the past. Because of the rapid reproduction of cephalopods, a temporary ban on fishing often is successful in restoring the fishery populations.

Octopuses, Cuttlefish, and Squid

There are approximately two hundred species of octopuses, found throughout the world primarily in shallow coastal waters. The most common species, *Octopus vulgaris*, is approximately 1 meter (3 feet) at adulthood, and lives for up to 18 months. The solitary *O. vulgaris* lives inside a small cave or den on the ocean bottom, and will inhabit tires, barrels, and other hollow spaces in human debris, if available. This habit is exploited by humans who harvest octopuses by setting and retrieving "octopus pots" made of clay or plastic. *O. vulgaris* is the principal commercially harvested octopus.

Cuttlefish are found in the eastern Atlantic Ocean and the Mediterranean Sea. The common cuttlefish, *Sepia officinalis*, is about one-third of a meter long (about 1 foot) as an adult. Ink from the cuttlefish has been used for centuries for writing, and its hard internal shell, the cuttlebone, often is placed in birdcages for beak-sharpening and as a source of calcium.

Octopuses have eight arms, whereas squids have ten, two of which are longer and specialized for feeding. Squids are deemed not as intelligent as octopuses, but are more streamlined and much faster and stronger swimmers, chasing down their prey at top speeds of over 12 kilometers (20 miles) per hour. Squid are fed upon by birds, sea mammals such as sperm whales, and humans. The annual catch of squid is in the hundreds of thousands of metric tons, most of which is caught by Japanese fisherman.

Giant Squid. Perhaps the most spectacular of the living cephalopods is the giant squid. The giant squid, *Architeuthis* (Greek for "ruling squid"), is present in the deep oceans around the world, but most commonly has been found near New Zealand. Living at depths of up to 1,000 meters (about 330 feet), *Architeuthis* probably feeds on fish and other smaller squids. The elusive animal has never been observed alive in its deep-sea habitat, but dead or dying specimens up to 19 meters (60 feet) long have been caught by fishermen, washed up on beaches, or become stranded in shallow waters. Some scientists think strandings may be increasing due to effects of global warming.

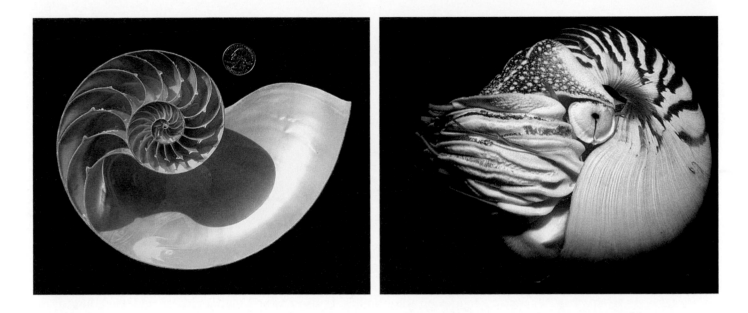

Although the giant squid is one of the largest predators in the ocean, it is considered a tasty meal by an even larger predator, the sperm whale. Remains of the horny beaks of giant squids have been found in the stomachs of sperm whales, and sucker marks from the tentacles of giant squids are found on whales.

Nautilus

Nautilus is found in the southwestern Pacific Ocean and Indian Ocean. It lives at a depth of several hundred meters during the day, but will come up as shallow as 5 meters (16 feet) during the night to hunt. Planispheral shells of the *Nautilus* can be cut into two halves that are bilaterally symmetrical. In contrast, conispheral shells (such as most snails) coil along a vertical axis forming a pointed spire, and are not symmetrical.

As the living *Nautilus* grows, it secretes a larger extension of the shell and seals off the older segments of the shell with thin, curved walls called septa. These concave-forward septa form the chambers of the *Nautilus*. A fleshy cord called the siphuncle connects the chambers. The empty chambers are filled with gas at about atmospheric pressure. The animal can regulate its buoyancy by slowly pumping fluids in and out of the empty chambers through the siphuncle.

The *Nautilus*' shell is thin, only 1 or 2 millimeters (less than a tenth of an inch), but extremely strong. A strong shell is necessary to resist the great pressures experienced at the depth where *Nautilus* lives. Experiments with living *Nautilus* have shown that the shell can endure pressure at depths of up to 600 meters (200 feet) before the shell implodes. SEE ALSO BIVALVES.

David M. Rohr

The cross-section of a modern *Nautilus* (left), the last living genus representing a subclass called the nautiloids, reveals the many chambers, including the latest and largest chamber in which the adult *Nautilus* lives. The same features are seen in the straight, conical shells of fossil ancestors preserved in limestone. On right is a living *Nautilus* in its shell.

Bibliography

Clarkson, Euan N. K. *Invertebrate Palaeontology and Evolution.* Cambridge, U.K.: Blackwell Science, 1998.

Voss, Gilbert L. "Squids: Jet-Powered Torpedoes of the Deep." *National Geographic Magazine* (March, 1967):386–411.

Ward, Peter D., Lewis Greenwald, and Francise Rougerie. "Shell Implosion Depth for Living *Nautilus macromphalus* and Shell Strength of Extinct Cephalopods." *Lethaia* 13 (1980):182.

Internet Resources

Search for the Giant Squid. Smithsonian Institution. <http://partners.si.edu/squid>.

Wood, James B. "The Cephalopod Page." Dalhousie University. http://www.dal.ca/~ceph/TCP/index.html>.

Chemical Analysis of Water

The chemical analysis of water provides considerable insight into the health and workings of lakes, rivers, oceans, and **groundwater**. Water chemistry has helped scientists to define the different currents and circulation of the world's oceans, improved their understanding of water's interactions with Earth's geologic materials, and given insight into the impact of human activities on waterbodies. It also has provided a clearer understanding of the limits of a waterbody's ability to assimilate (take in) some level of **pollution** without harming the water system, its aquatic plants and animals, and humans who may use the water.

Quality Assurance Project Plan

Water monitoring and the chemical analysis of water requires careful planning to achieve valid results. The most important step in any monitoring program is the development of a plan, known as a Quality Assurance Project Plan (QAPP), to bring into focus the purpose of water monitoring efforts, the currently known information about the waterbody, and the intended use of the resulting data. Data may be used for such varied purposes as an educational course requirement, a contribution to a statewide database, or even in a lawsuit. Once this information is known, project managers establish specific parameters to be measured, set the level of quality assurance needed to support the intended data use, and determine the detailed steps of a monitoring program. Note how all these elements build on one another in the following example.

Examples of a QAPP.   Suppose a small river flows down the mountains and through an agricultural area. In recent years, during the late summer months, the river has become murky and ceased to support recreational fishing. As a result, the reduction in tourism has had an impact on the regional economy.

Earlier monitoring by a state environmental agency indicated that the decline in certain **game fish** species was due to extreme daily swings in the **dissolved oxygen** resulting from the respiration and photosynthesis cycles of excessive concentrations of **algae**. It was believed that the algae growth, in turn, was caused by runoff from the agricultural areas that contributed nutrients to the river in the form of nitrates and phosphorus.

The agricultural extension agent worked with the local farmers and proposed that they change their agricultural practices and establish **riparian** buffers along the streambanks to see if they could help improve the water quality of the river in order to restore the prized fishing activity. Together

groundwater: generally, all subsurface (underground) water, as distinct from surface water, that supplies natural springs, contributes to permanent streams, and can be tapped by wells; specifically, the water that is in the saturated zone of a defined aquifer

pollution: any alteration in the character or quality of the environment, including water in waterbodies or geologic formations, which renders the environmental resource unfit or less suited for certain uses

game fish: fish considered to possess sporting qualities on fishing tackle, such as salmon, trout, black bass, and striped bass

dissolved oxygen: concentration of oxygen, expressed in milligrams per liter, dissolved in water and readily available to fish and other aquatic organisms; strongly influenced by temperature, biologic activity, biochemical oxygen demand, and chemical oxygen demand

algae: (singular, alga) simple photosynthetic organisms, usually aquatic, containing chlorophyll, and lacking roots, stems, and leaves

riparian: pertaining to the banks of a river, stream, waterway, or other, typically, flowing body of water as well as to plant and animal communities along these waterbodies

Chemical analyses are used in conjunction with biological and physical parameters to characterize the quality and understand the chemical evolution of fresh water. Standardized analytical methods allow the integration of data collected on disparate waterbodies, regardless of geographic location.

they met with the local community officials, who all agreed to proceed with the proposal. To document the effectiveness of these agricultural changes, the local leaders agreed to form a watershed council to develop and carry out a water monitoring effort.

Once formed, the watershed council set about developing a monitoring plan. The council members documented that the purpose of the monitoring effort was to monitor changes in water quality resulting from changes in agricultural practices. They gathered available historical monitoring data from databases and library searches.

The council members discussed the intended uses of the data that they were proposing to acquire. They knew it was primarily to be used to observe any water quality changes that resulted from the changes in farming activities. Council members also wanted the data to be placed on the state environmental monitoring database where it would be available to university researchers and others who might find it useful. Lastly, they all agreed that because of the voluntary spirit of this venture, the data were not intended to be used for enforcement purposes.

Taking all this into account, the council completed a very specific Quality Assurance Project Plan (QAPP) for this monitoring effort. The parameters to be measured would be as follows:

- Dissolved oxygen (DO) and **pH** (to characterize the oxygen swings);

pH: a measure of the acidity of water; a pH of 7 indicates neutral water, with values between 0 and 7 indicating acidic water (0 is very acidic), and values between 7 and 14 indicating alkaline (basic) water (14 is very alkaline); specifically defined as $-\log_{10}(H^+)$, where (H^+) is the hydrogen ion concentration

grab sample: a water sample collected at a single location and at a single time as opposed to a sample composited over space or time

calibration: the process of correlating the readings of an instrument with those of an established standard in order to check its accuracy of measurement

duplicate: as in duplicate sample, a second sample collected in the same manner and within the same timeframe and analyzed separately from the primary sample in order to determine the precision of the analysis

spike: in chemical analysis, a prepared solution with components or isotopes in known proportion that is added to the sample containing a constituent or an isotope of interest, and used to facilitate the accurate determination of the constituent's or isotope's concentration

accuracy: the exactness or degree to which a measurement or calculation approaches the actual quantity

precision: the reproducibility or repeatability of the results of a test, measurement, or experiment; in a series of tests, refers to the ability to arrive at the same answer each time under the same set of circumstances or sampling criteria

---

CHEMICAL CONCENTRATION UNITS

The concentration of a substance in water is usually expressed as milligrams per liter (mg/L) or micrograms per liter (μg/L), which are more casually referred to as parts per million (ppm) or as parts per billion (ppb), respectively. To appreciate the levels being measured, one ppb is equivalent to one sheet of printer paper in a stack of papers nearly 129 kilometers (80 miles) high, or one drop of water in roughly 95,000 liters (25,000 gallons). It is interesting to note that owing to improvements in the chemical analysis of water, many environmental analyses are measuring well beyond the ppb range and into levels of parts per trillion and even parts per quadrillion.

- Turbidity and chlorophyll (to monitor changes in algae growth); and

- Nitrate and phosphate levels (to monitor the nutrients).

In order to monitor the daily changes in DO and pH, a continuous monitoring probe would be used. Weekly **grab samples** would be taken for the other parameters.

Because the data would be submitted to a state database, quality assurance (QA) requirements were already in place for the chemical analysis methods considered acceptable:

- Direct turbidimeter measurement for turbidity;

- Fluorescence spectrophotometer for chlorophyll;

- Cadmium reduction spectrophotometric method for nitrate; and

- Ascorbic acid spectrophotometric method for phosphate.

Each method in turn specifies the sampling procedures in terms of type of container to be used to collect the sample (plastic or glass); preservation requirements once the sample is collected (acidification or refrigeration); and holding-time limits within which the sample must be analyzed.

The methods also specify the **calibration** procedures and quantitation limits of the method. (In analytical chemistry, "to quantitate" means "to quantify" when referring to measurement processes.) Additional QA requirements indicate how many sample **duplicates** and sample **spikes** must be run; how often the continuous monitors must have a calibration check performed; and how all the data should be reported.

All of these specifications ensure that the analytical results meet the requirements of known data quality in terms of **accuracy** and **precision**. With the decision that the data were not to be used for legal enforcement, the watershed council could forego a formal chain-of-custody record that involves documenting the exact location of the sample at all times to ensure it could not have been tampered with between the time of collection and final analysis.

Short-term and Long-term Results

As this example has shown, the chemical analysis of water involves many steps that are closely linked: planning, sample collection, analytical chemistry, quality assurance, and data management. If these steps are followed, the data can be used for short- and long-term trending, modeling and predicting, and basic research. If necessary, and if chain-of-custody is employed, the data can also be utilized objectively in litigation. SEE ALSO CHEMICALS FROM AGRICULTURE; FRESH WATER, NATURAL COMPOSITION OF; FRESH WATER, PHYSICS AND CHEMISTRY OF.

Richard Gates

Bibliography

Clesceri, Lenore S., Arnold E. Greenberg, and Andrew D. Eaton, eds. *Standard Methods For The Examination of Water and Wastewater*, 20th ed. New York: American Public Health Association, American Water Works Association, and Water Environment Federation, 1998.

Chemicals: Combined Effect on Public Health

In order to protect public health, regulatory agencies set water standards for substances not normally found in natural waters. So far, most standards have been set for individual substances according to their known harmful effects on human health or quality of life. The process to set such a standard involves a complex evaluation of scientific information regarding the probability of human exposure to the substance of concern; its effects on the health of both the general population and sensitive subpopulations (for example, children); the technology available to detect the substance in water; and the impact of regulation on infrastructure and the economy in general.

Only recently and in limited fashion have regulatory agencies looked at the potential interactions between multiple chemicals in water, and how such an interaction can affect public health in a different way than did the individual chemicals alone.

In general, it is believed that low concentration chemical mixtures of similar chemicals could have additive effects similar to the added concentration of one of the chemicals alone. In many cases, this is due in part to the increased probability of interaction between the chemicals and the target tissue. For example, some carcinogens initiate cancer by mutating a DNA (deoxyribonucleic acid) molecule at a particular site. A mixture of several carcinogens may cause cancer even if the individual concentration of each carcinogen in the mixture is low because, in total, there are more molecules of the carcinogen and hence a larger probability of a carcinogen molecule "colliding" with a molecule of DNA and causing a mutation.

The study of complex chemical mixtures is further complicated by the many types of interactions between chemicals, and between chemicals and biological systems. Such interactions may markedly change the toxicity outcome by a number of biological mechanisms, as follows.

- **Absorption.** One chemical may increase or decrease the availability of another chemical in the mixture to be absorbed by organisms.

- **Storage.** Once inside the organism, a chemical may be stored in a particular tissue or have more or less affinity for a target organ. This may be changed by another chemical in the mixture, allowing for either long-term storage of the first chemical or higher availability to interact with diverse organs and tissues.

- **Biotransformation.** Enzymes and other biomolecules that normally occur in the organism may interact with chemicals to either get rid of them (detoxification) or increase their activity and damage to the organism (activation). If a chemical mixture is present, some chemicals may inhibit or activate these biomolecules, changing the normal biotransformation pathways for other chemicals in the mixture.

- **Excretion.** Some chemicals may inhibit or increase the organism's ability to excrete other chemicals.

Any of the biological mechanisms described above may make chemicals mixtures either more or less toxic to the exposed organisms. It is well

Pesticides on lawns are among many chemicals that may ultimately reach waterbodies, posing environmental and human health risks. The potential effects of chemical mixtures are increasingly a concern to scientists, regulators, and decisionmakers.

known from pharmacology that some drugs interact with others to alter the biological mechanisms listed above; therefore, the same alterations can certainly occur with mixtures of environmental pollutants. As with drugs, the resulting combined effect of two or more chemicals may be additive, synergistic, potentiating, or antagonistic.

- **Additive.** The combined effect *equals* the sum of the effects of each chemical alone. (Example: 1 + 1 = 2)

- **Synergistic.** The combined effect *is larger than* the sum of the effects of each chemical alone. (Example: 1 + 1 = 3)

- **Potentiating.** A chemical that normally has no effect will *increase* the effect that another chemical would have alone. (Example: 0 + 1 = 3)

- **Antagonistic.** The combined effect *is less than* the sum of the effects of each chemical alone. (Example: 1 + 1 = 0)

Because the scenarios of chemical mixture interactions are very complex, it is very difficult for regulatory agencies to establish reliable and enforceable standards for chemical mixtures in water. Instead, the problem has been addressed in other ways, mainly by either case-by-case analysis of contaminated sites, or by discharge permits. Such approaches have not yet been applied to drinking-water standards.

Risk Assessments

To determine how to clean up a contaminated property, an analysis known as a risk assessment may be performed in order to protect a nearby stream, **aquifer**, or both. Theoretical concentrations of chemicals in water can be calculated at the site where humans would have contact (for example, a residential well) by taking into consideration all the chemicals polluting the site, their respective concentrations in the soil and water, and the potential of pollutants to move from soil to water. The theoretical concentrations are then compared to known concentrations of the chemicals that would be hazardous to human health.

This analysis is used to establish a cleanup goal, a concentration of chemical to which the soil or groundwater must be cleaned to in order to remove the health hazard. If a mixture of chemicals is present, cleanup goals are established for each chemical, taking into account possible interactions between the chemicals in the mixture. When a cleanup goal cannot be achieved, usually due to technical or economic constraints, water use at the site is restricted according to the predicted risks.

Contaminated site risk assessments are generally done by the party that contaminated the site (for example, a chemical manufacturing company), as required by state or national law, and under the supervision of the state or national environmental agency. Most studies involve only a few hectares of contaminated soil and water.

Risk of Using a Resource. An approach similar to the contaminated site risk assessment is used to determine the risk of using a contaminated body of water (see sidebar). In this case, the area of study may be hundreds or thousands of hectares, usually covering a whole watershed. These studies are done by state or national government agencies under limited budgets, and the large size of the area under study prohibits the detail that can be

aquifer: a water-saturated, permeable, underground rock formation that can transmit significant quantities of water under ordinary hydraulic gradients to wells and springs

afforded in contaminated site risk assessments. Cleanup goals cannot be set since the area would be too large to clean.

To address this problem, government agencies may severely limit discharges to water in the affected area, allowing the pollutants already in the water to be degraded by natural processes. If necessary, restrictions on water resources use (swimming, drinking, and fish consumption) are set and announced to the public. If the contamination problem is too severe, removal of contaminated sediments may be required.

Pollution Permits. A different and most commonly used approach involves the prevention of water pollution by limiting the amounts of pollutants discharged into surface waters. Such an approach involves the regulatory agency reviewing a whole effluent toxicity assessment, which describes the aggregated toxic effect of a discharge of mixed pollutants into a body of water. Such assessments are usually done to protect the health of the water ecosystem affected, and not human health. In general, maintaining a healthy water ecosystem should also protect the health of humans using the waters, even if a human health risk assessment was not performed. The use of the body of water by humans may also be limited to activities that do not pose a threat.

Regulatory Considerations

The methods described above are always applied in a case-by-case scenario rather than as part of a comprehensive regional or national water-quality program. No government agency has yet attempted to develop drinking-water standards that address the possible presence of chemical mixtures. The complexity of such an undertaking is beyond current technology and economic realities. Simply identifying each possible type of chemical mixture in natural waters would be an enormous and complicated undertaking.

Some would argue that the limited resources available to protect waters from pollution are better used by (1) addressing highly contaminated sites on a case-by-case basis, and (2) preventing further contamination by implementing aggressive effluent control and permitting strategies. SEE ALSO POLLUTION SOURCES: POINT AND NONPOINT; SAFE DRINKING WATER ACT; SUPPLIES, PUBLIC AND DOMESTIC WATER.

Minerva Mercado-Feliciano

Bibliography

Amdur, Mary O., John Doull, and Curtis D. Klassen, eds. Casarett and Doull's *Toxicology: the Basic Science of Poisons*, 5th ed. New York: McGraw-Hill Professional, 1998.

Gardner, Henry S. Jr. et al. "Environmental Complex Mixture Toxicity Assessment." *Environmental Health Perspectives* 106 sup. 6 (1998):1299–1305.

Safe Drinking Water Committee, National Research Council. *Drinking Water and Health, Volume 9: Selected Issues in Risk Assessment*. Washington, D.C.: National Academy Press, 1989. Available online at <http://www.nap.edu/catalog/773.html>.

Toussaint, M. W. et al. "Histopathology of Japanese medaka (*Oryzias latipes*) Chronically Exposed to a Complex Environmental Mixture." *Toxicologic Pathology* 27, no. 6 (1999):652–663.

Internet Resources

Middle Willamette River Fish Consumption Study Factsheet. Oregon Department of Environmental Quality and Oregon Department of Human Services. <http://www.deq.state.or.us/wq/wqfact/MidWillFishStudy.pdf>.

RISK ASSESSMENT AT A CONTAMINATED SITE

A 1999 evaluation of risks to humans consuming fish from the Middle Willamette River, Oregon assessed health risks for three target population groups: general public, recreational anglers (fishers), and subsistence anglers. An increased cancer risk was found for the general public, recreational anglers, and subsistence anglers, due primarily to PCBs (polychlorinated biphenyls) and, to a lesser extent, dioxins and the pesticides aldrin, dieldrin, and DDE (the main breakdown product of the pesticide DDT). Subsistence anglers had cancer risks 19 times that of the general population, whereas recreational anglers had cancer risks 2.3 times that of the general public. The study also found that children, women of childbearing age, and adult subsistence anglers had the highest risks of developing immune system or developmental dysfunction, mostly due to exposure to mercury and PCBs.

Because cleaning the whole river basin would be technically impossible, the Oregon Department of Human Services recommended limited use of the fish resources, especially by children and women.

Permit Guide: The "Plain English" Guide to Environmental Permitting. Indiana Department of Environmental Management. <http://www.in.gov/idem/guides/permit/>.

RISC Technical Resource Guidance Document. Indiana Department of Environmental Management. <http://www.in.gov/idem/land/risc/techguide/index.html>.

Setting Standards for Safe Drinking Water. U.S. Environmental Protection Agency, Office of Ground Water and Drinking Water. <http://www.epa.gov/safewater/standard/setting.html>.

"Whole Effluent Toxicity." *National Pollutant Discharge Elimination System (NPDES).* U.S. Environmental Protection Agency. <http://cfpub.epa.gov/npdes/wqbasedpermitting/wet.cfm>.

Chemicals from Agriculture

An important national issue in the United States is the degradation of water quality from **nonpoint sources** of pollution, including the prevalent use of fertilizers and **pesticides** on agricultural land. The issue is of interest to many residents, water resource managers, and policymakers across the nation because of the possible impacts on water uses, such as drinking, **irrigation**, recreation, and sustaining aquatic life.

In sufficient quantities, nutrients from fertilizers encourage abundant growth of **algae**, which leads to low oxygen in streams and the possibility of fish kills. Pesticides and **nitrate** are a potential concern for human health if they affect a drinking-water source or occur where there is recreational use. Elevated concentrations of nitrate have been associated with **methemoglobinemia**, or "blue baby syndrome" in infants, and stomach disorders, and some pesticides have been associated with the potential for causing cancer.

For the protection of drinking water and aquatic life, the U.S. Environmental Protection Agency (EPA), along with the states, have established water-quality standards and criteria for some pesticides and nitrate. These provide widely used benchmarks that serve as starting points for evaluating potential effects of exposure to these chemicals.

Nationwide Sampling Studies

Nationwide sampling of nitrogen, phosphorus, and more than eighty pesticides by the U.S. Geological Survey (USGS) from 1992 to 1996 indicated that streams and **groundwater** in agricultural basins almost always contain complex mixtures of nutrients and pesticides. Concentrations of nitrogen and phosphorus in streams commonly exceeded levels that can contribute to excessive plant growth. Average annual concentrations of phosphorus in three-fourths of seventy-five streams sampled in agricultural areas were greater than the desired EPA goal for preventing nuisance plant growth in streams. Nitrate was most prevalent in shallow groundwater (less than 30.5 meters (100 feet) below land surface) beneath agricultural areas, where about 15 percent of samples collected from 36 different agricultural areas exceeded the EPA drinking-water standard for nitrate.

Herbicides. At least one pesticide was found in almost every water and fish sample collected from forty streams and in over one-half of the more than nine hundred shallow wells sampled in agricultural areas. A relatively small number of heavily used chemicals accounted for most detections. The most

nonpoint source: describes a pollutant release or discharge originating from a land use active over a wide land area (e.g., agriculture) rather than from one specific location (e.g., an outfall pipe from a factory)

pesticides: a broad group of chemicals that kills or controls plants (herbicides), fungus (fungicides), insects and arachnids (insecticides), rodents (rodenticides), bacteria (bactericides), or other creatures that are considered pests

irrigation: the controlled application of water for agricultural or other purposes through human-made systems; generally refers to water application to soil when rainfall is insufficient to maintain desirable soil moisture for plant growth

algae: (singular, alga) simple photosynthetic organisms, usually aquatic, containing chlorophyll, and lacking roots, stems, and leaves

nitrate: the highly leachable form of soil nitrogen taken up by most plants through their roots; it is a common groundwater contaminant, especially in agricultural areas and locations with a high density of septic systems, that is regulated by the U.S. Environmental Protection Agency with a drinking water standard of 10 ppm (parts per million) of nitrogen in the nitrate form

methemoglobinemia: a disease, primarily in infants, caused by the conversion of nitrates to nitrites in the intestines, and which limits the body's ability to receive oxygen

groundwater: generally, all subsurface (underground) water, as distinct from surface water, that supplies natural springs, contributes to permanent streams, and can be tapped by wells; specifically, the water that is in the saturated zone of a defined aquifer

Pesticides applied in plant nurseries and greenhouses are less visible forms of agricultural chemicals than those applied to fields and orchards. But any form of chemical application can potentially contaminate water sources if not managed properly.

frequently detected pesticide compounds in streams and shallow ground-water in agricultural areas were the major **herbicides** atrazine (and its **transformation product** desethylatrazine, or DEA), metolachlor, cyanazine, and alachlor, which ranked in the top five in national herbicide use for agriculture. Transformation products of metolachlor, alachlor, and cyanazine would probably also have been frequently detected if they had been analyzed.

herbicides: a group of chemicals used to kill or reduce the growth of vegetation that is considered undesirable

transformation product: an intermediate breakdown product that occurs during the stepwise breakdown of a chemical in the environment

Insecticides. Compared to herbicides, currently used insecticides were less frequently found in agricultural streams, and even less in groundwater underlying agricultural areas. This results from their relatively low application rates and rapid breakdown in the environment. In contrast, historically used insecticides still persist in agricultural streams because of their resistance to breakdown in the environment.

Dichlorodiphenyltrichloroethane, commonly known as DDT, was the most commonly detected **organochlorine** compound, followed by dieldrin and chlordane. DDT and aldrin (which breaks down rapidly to dieldrin in the environment) were two of the top three insecticides used for agriculture in the 1960s. Because of negative impacts on birds and other species, their uses were restricted in the 1970s; and yet, more than 20 years later, one or more sediment-quality guidelines were exceeded at 15 percent of sampled agricultural sites, and concentrations in whole fish exceeded wildlife guidelines at 20 percent of sampled sites.

organochlorine: any chemical compound that contains carbon and chlorine

Mixtures of Compounds. Most samples with a detectable pesticide contained mixtures of compounds. Nearly half of stream samples collected in agricultural areas contained five or more pesticides compounds, and about 15 percent contained more than ten compounds. Nearly one-third of shallow groundwater samples within agricultural areas had two or more pesticides. Atrazine, DEA, and metolachlor were the most commonly detected compounds in mixtures found in agricultural areas.

Water Quality Criteria. Pesticide concentrations in streams (as annual averages, upon which drinking-water criteria are based) were generally low,

maximum contaminant level: abbreviated as MCL, the allowable level of the specified contaminant in drinking water; established by the federal Environmental Protection Agency, state governments may set lower levels

topography: the shape and contour of a surface, especially the land surface or ocean-floor surface

hydrology: the science that deals with the occurrence, distribution, movement, and physical and chemical properties of water on Earth; also refers to the hydrologic characteristics of a given region

aquifer: a water-saturated, permeable, underground rock formation that can transmit significant quantities of water under ordinary hydraulic gradients to wells and springs

karst: topography characterized by closed depressions or sinkholes, caves, and underground drainage formed by dissolution of limestone, dolomite, or gypsum

only exceeding the EPA **maximum contaminant level** for atrazine in one location. Similarly, pesticide concentrations seldom exceeded the drinking water criteria in wells. Less than one-half of one percent of the sampled shallow wells in agricultural areas had concentrations greater than a criterion (one well for atrazine, one for cyanazine, two for dieldrin, and one for dinoseb).

Geographic Patterns. Analysis of geographic patterns in pesticide use revealed that concentrations of herbicides and insecticides in agricultural streams were highest in those areas of the nation with the greatest agricultural use. Herbicide concentrations were greatest in central U.S. streams, where use is most extensive. The direct relationship between chemical use and chemical concentrations in nearby surface water was demonstrated in some upper Midwest streams in 1994. After a new herbicide, acetochlor, partially replaced alachlor, nearby streams quickly showed increased acetochlor concentrations and decreased alachlor concentrations. For example, in the White River of Indiana, acetochlor was commonly detected, reaching a peak concentration of 2 parts per billion.

Water contamination in agricultural areas is not, however, determined solely by chemical use. Natural features—**topography**, geology, soil type, **hydrology**, and climate—and land-management practices—tile drainage and irrigation and conservation strategies—make some areas more vulnerable to contamination than others. For example, some of the highest concentrations of nutrients and pesticides were in sand and gravel **aquifers** or in **karst** formations consisting of carbonate rocks with large fractures, voids, or conduits. These natural geologic features readily transmit water and are common in various parts of the United States.

In contrast, groundwater contaminants underlying farmland in parts of the upper Midwest were barely detectable, despite similar high rates of chemical use. This is partly because the groundwater is somewhat shielded from surface infiltration of chemicals by relatively impermeable and poorly drained soils and glacial till that cover much of the region. In addition, tile drains and ditches commonly provide quick pathways for chemical transport to streams, which minimize the downward movement of contaminants to groundwater.

Seasonal Patterns. The USGS findings not only documented geographic patterns, but seasonal patterns as well. In streams that drain agricultural areas throughout most of the nation, the highest levels of nutrients and pesticides occurred during spring and summer when recently applied chemicals are washed away by spring rains, snowmelt, and irrigation. In some parts of the country, other patterns were found, such as those in the San Joaquin–Tulare Basins in California where elevated concentrations of the insecticide diazinon occurred in the winter because of the use of pesticide sprays on the region's dormant orchards.

Impact to Drinking Water and Aquatic Life. Although the USGS study results indicate few problems for drinking water, conclusions must be tempered by several considerations, including: (1) criteria are not established for many pesticides, and federal drinking-water standards (administered by the U.S. Environmental Protection Agency) address only a small number of pesticides; (2) mixtures and transformation products are not considered; and (3) effects of seasonal exposure to high concentrations have not been evaluated. Assessment of the pesticide risks to aquatic life is hampered by

Hooded sprayers are among the improvements to chemical application methods. In this photograph, the hoods are directing herbicide just to the areas between rows of grain sorghum.

many of the same issues, but existing water quality criteria were also more often exceeded. For example, the criteria for atrazine was exceeded in nearly 40 percent of sampled agricultural streams.

A Historical Perspective

Agricultural chemicals in water must be assessed not only in terms of scientific findings, but also in the broader context of U.S. agricultural development, a growing conservation ethic, and economics. In the past, farmers focussed primarily on production from their fields, often with little regard to the watershed in which the fields are located. Agricultural chemicals were seen only as scientific marvels; they killed the weeds which reduced crop growth and eliminated the insects that otherwise would have significantly reduced the quality of their crops. The potential impact on the environment, or for that matter, human health, simply was not on the average farmer's mind. Wearing protective clothing while mixing or applying pesticides was unheard of, and concern about runoff to streams or infiltration to groundwater was not considered.

Concern about the potential harm from agricultural chemicals began slowly in the late 1950s and early 1960s and has been growing in both the

RESIDENTIAL USES OF FERTILIZERS AND PESTICIDES

High levels of chemical contamination are not just an agricultural problem. A U.S. Geological Survey study found that insecticides—most commonly diazinon, carbaryl, malathion, and chlorpyrifos—occurred more frequently and usually at higher concentrations in urban streams than in streams in agricultural areas.

About two-thirds of urban streams sampled in the study had concentrations of insecticides that exceeded at least one guideline established to protect aquatic life. In addition, concentrations of total phosphorus generally were as high in urban streams as in agricultural streams, commonly exceeding the desired federal goal to control excessive plant and algae growth.

As in agricultural areas, the types and concentrations of chemicals found in urban streams are closely linked to the chemicals used, such as on lawns, gardens, and in public areas. Reducing the amount of chemicals used and applying these chemicals more efficiently are two effective ways to reduce contaminant levels in both urban and agricultural settings.

public and the agricultural community since. Today, farmers are increasingly aware of the complex interrelationships between agricultural practices and environmental quality. Modern farmers now consider the timing of agricultural chemical application and irrigation, the amount and style of pesticide application, specific crop needs, and local weather conditions in their pesticide and fertilizer use.

In some areas, it was common practice for farmers to apply a heavy load of fertilizer in the fall, reasoning that it would "be ready when the plants needed it in the spring," but not realizing that most of the fertilizer would leach from the soil before the plants began to grow. It was also common to broadcast pesticides by area-wide spraying, covering the ground where the targeted plants were located, as well as ground where they were not.

But today's farmer, with the help of agricultural research, applies fertilizer and pesticide directly on the crop row, reducing the chemical needed and reducing the potential for leaching or runoff. Applying chemicals in a manner so that they do not leach below the root zone before the plant can utilize them is the key to both crop production and environmental protection.

Farmers often check the weather conditions in the morning to adjust the droplet size in the sprayer based on forecasted wind and humidity. It is not uncommon for today's farmer to make use of satellite and GPS (global positioning system) technology to tailor the application of fertilizer and pesticide to the specific crop needs within a single field. Careful consideration of crop needs and the best method to deliver an agricultural chemical to its target has often led to a decrease in chemicals applied per acre, a decrease in the cost to the farmer, and less of a risk to the environment. SEE ALSO AGRICULTURE AND WATER; ALGAL BLOOMS IN FRESH WATER; CARSON, RACHEL; CHEMICALS: COMBINED EFFECT ON PUBLIC HEALTH; CHEMICALS FROM CONSUMERS; CHEMICALS FROM PHARMACEUTICALS AND PERSONAL CARE PRODUCTS; CLEAN WATER ACT; GROUNDWATER; IRRIGATION MANAGEMENT; LAND USE AND WATER QUALITY; NUTRIENTS IN LAKES AND STREAMS; POLLUTION OF GROUNDWATER; POLLUTION SOURCES: POINT AND NONPOINT; SAFE DRINKING WATER ACT; SEPTIC SYSTEM IMPACTS.

Pixie A. Hamilton and Timothy L. Miller
Dennis O. Nelson (Historical Perspective)

Bibliography

Gilliom, Robert J. et al. "Testing Water Quality for Pesticide Pollution." *Environmental Science and Technology* (April 1, 1999):164–169.

Goss, D. W., and R. D. Wauchope. "The SCS/ARS/CES Pesticide Properties Database: Using It with Soils Data in a Screening Procedure." In *Pesticides in the Next Decade: The Challenges Ahead*, ed. D. I. Weigman. Blacksburg, VA: Virginia Water Resources Research Center (1990):471–493.

Kolpin, Dana W., Earl M. Thurman, and S. M. Linhar. "The Environmental Occurrence of Herbicides: The Importance of Degradates in Groundwater." *Arch. Environ. Contam. Toxicol.* 35 (1998):385–390.

Meyer, Michael T., and Earl M. Thurman, eds. "Herbicide Metabolites in Surface Water and Groundwater." ACS Symposium Series 630, American Chemical Society, Washington, D.C., 1996.

U.S. Geological Survey. "Quality of Our Nation's Water—Nutrients and Pesticides." U.S. Geological Survey Circular 1225, 1999.

Chemicals from Consumers

In people's daily lives, numerous consumer products are used inside the home, and the natural and synthetic chemicals in them often end up in the local sewage treatment plant or household septic system. For example, when someone scrubs and disinfects sinks and toilets, chemicals from the cleansers flow down the drain and down the toilet. Similarly, chemicals in toothpaste flow down the sink when someone is brushing. When someone showers after a day at the beach (and hence after a day of applying sunscreen), chemicals in the sunscreen are washed down the drain. When cough medicine is administered to ease cold or flu symptoms, some of the chemicals in the medicine will pass through the body and will be flushed down the toilet. Bacteria in sewage treatment plants and septic systems **metabolize** some of these consumer chemicals, but a small amount are transported into the aquatic **environment**.

Consumer chemicals used outside the house also end up in the aquatic environment. Lawn-watering can carry fertilizers and weed killers into gutters and storm drains. Storm runoff can carry products used in automobiles (e.g., antifreeze, transmission and brake fluid, gasoline, and motor oil) from streets and driveways into storm drains. Soap and detergent used when a car is washed loosen these pollutants from the car. Trace the path of the soapy water to the storm drains: eventually, the soapy water and pollutants in it will end up in nearby lakes and streams. Exhaust from watercraft such as boats and jet skis can carry chemicals used in gasoline into lakes and **reservoirs**. Chemicals in gasoline used in snowmobiles can eventually reach mountain streams when the snow melts.

Although household chemicals in water are being found in extremely low concentrations, much new research is needed to determine what, if anything, needs to be done to protect human health and the environment from these nonconventional pollutants.

Consumer Chemicals in Water and Sewage

Until recently, chemists could not detect consumer chemicals in water samples because the concentrations were so small. But now, consumer chemicals are being found in water samples from all over the world.

For example, triclosan, an antiseptic used in acne creams, has been found in surface water and **groundwater** in the United States. Chemicals used in detergents and household cleansers also have been found in water samples. Limonene, a fragrance that gives a pleasant lemon-like odor to some cleansers, has been found in groundwater. Chemicals called nitromusks are used in most consumer products with fragrance, such as cosmetics, detergents, and toiletries. The **metabolites** of nitromusks have been found in sewage, river water, numerous animals, and even human breast milk. Breakdown products of **nonylphenols**, which are used in detergents, are commonly found in sewage effluent (discharge).

Caffeine from beverages has been commonly found in rivers downstream from sewage treatment plants, and in groundwater near household septic systems. Plastics used in food packaging and other household products are the source of chemicals called **phthalates**, which are commonly found in sewage effluent. MTBE, a chemical used in gasoline to make it burn cleaner,

metabolism: the sum total of biochemical processes that occur within a living organism, or a portion of it, in order to maintain life; the biochemical changes by which energy is provided to living cells and new material is assimilated

environment: all of the external factors, conditions, and influences that affect the growth, development, and survival of organisms or a community; commonly refers to Earth and its support systems

reservoir: a pond, lake, basin, or tank for the storage, regulation, and control of water; more commonly refers to artificial impoundments rather than natural ones

groundwater: generally, all subsurface (underground) water, as distinct from surface water, that supplies natural springs, contributes to permanent streams, and can be tapped by wells; specifically, the water that is in the saturated zone of a defined aquifer

metabolite: any substance produced by metabolism or a metabolic process

nonylphenol: $C_9H_{19}OH$; a surface active agent used as a lube oil additive, and in stabilizers, fungicides, bacteriocides, dyes, drugs, adhesives, rubber chemicals, etc.

phthalate: a derivative of phthalic acid, produced through a reaction of the acid and an alcohol; commonly used as a plasticiser to provide flexibility in plastics; some varieties also are used in synthetic lubricants in the automobile industry

People worldwide have an affinity for coffee. The caffeine it contains can be used as a tracer in fresh waters (e.g., groundwater), because caffeine otherwise is unlikely to enter waterbodies naturally, unless there is an obvious source nearby, such as a coffee bean plantation or processing plant.

acute toxicity: the property of a chemical or microbe enabling it to cause symptoms of illness in a living organism only a short time after exposure

THE CAFFEINE CONNECTION

Caffeine is a stimulant found in high concentrations in coffee, tea, and some soft drinks. A pot of coffee can contain more than a gram of caffeine. Caffeine also is found in sewage because some caffeine passes unmetabolized through the body and because people pour unconsumed beverages down the sink.

Water contaminated by effluent from sewage treatment plants or septic systems often contains small amounts of caffeine. The presence of caffeine proved that people, and not animals, were the cause of nitrate contamination of well water in a Nevada town, because people intuitively understood that horses and cattle don't drink coffee.

was found at high concentrations in Lake Tahoe, California and Nevada, and resulted in watercraft with carbureted two-stroke engines being banned from the lake.

Medicines are designed to persist in the body long enough to have the desired therapeutic effect. Because their chemical structures resist extensive degradation by bacteria, trace amounts of many prescription and non-prescription medicines have been found in water samples. For example, carbamazepine, a medicine used for treatment of seizures, has been detected in surface water and groundwater in Europe, Canada, and the United States. Clofibric acid, a metabolite of drugs used to lower blood lipid and cholesterol levels, has been found in rural lakes in Switzerland, the North Sea, and even in household tap water in Germany. The antibiotics erythromycin and chloramphenicol have been found in sewage effluent and surface water in Germany. The synthetic hormone 17α-ethynylestradiol used in birth-control pills has been found in treated sewage effluent from Germany, Canada, the United States, and Brazil.

Impacts on Humans and Wildlife

Because the concentrations of consumer chemicals in water supplies are so low, **acute toxicity** to humans is unlikely from drinking water containing these chemicals. The concentrations of most drugs that have been found in water are much less than 1 part per billion (ppb), or 0.0000001 percent. To cause acute toxicity, a person would have to drink enormous amounts of water because the concentrations of such chemicals in the environment are much less than the therapeutic dose. Even in the highly unlikely event of acute toxicity, such toxicity is easily detected, and measures can be rapidly taken to mitigate problems.

Because a person probably would not consume enormous amounts of water on a regular basis, it would take a period of time for the person to consume the equivalent of even a single therapeutic dose. For example, a person drinking about 3.8 liters (1 gallon) of water a day that contained 1 ppb of a pharmaceutical would consume the equivalent of one tablet of Ritalin® or Valium® in 3.5 years; one capsule of Benadryl® in 14.5 years; or one tablet of Childrens Tylenol® in 58 years.

The major concern is that long-term exposure to low concentrations of these chemicals may cause subtle, almost imperceptible, effects that could accumulate over time and ultimately have profound effects on both humans and aquatic organisms. For example, hormones work in the body at very low concentrations and can affect sexual development. Natural and synthetic hormones (such as 17α-ethynylestradiol) as well as chemicals that mimic hormones (such as nonylphenols and phthalates) in sewage effluent therefore could cause subtle effects in aquatic animals.

In fact, studies have already revealed effects of low concentrations of hormones. Feminization of wild male fish has been observed in rivers downstream of sewage treatment plants. Male fish exposed to hormones in sewage effluent produce a protein that usually only female fish produce for making eggs. In addition, the testes of male fish may contain ovarian tissue that can even produce eggs.

In humans, the chemical serotonin is a **neurotransmitter** whose metabolism is inhibited by several commonly used antidepressants, including Prozac®. Serotonin is also important in the physiology of invertebrates. In **mollusks**, serotonin regulates spawning and induction of larval metamorphosis. In crustaceans, such as the lobster, it controls aggression and maturation of the ovaries.

Although the active ingredient in Prozac® has not yet been found in natural waters, scientists in the laboratory have found that in low ppb

neurotransmitter: a chemical substance released at the end of a nerve fiber by the arrival of a nerve impulse, enabling the transmission of the impulse between two nerve cells

mollusk: an invertebrate animal with a soft, unsegmented body and usually a shell and a muscular foot; examples are clams, oysters, mussels, and octopuses

concentrations Prozac stimulates spawning behavior in zebra mussels. Subtle changes in an organism's behavior caused by antidepressants in the environment are types of subtle effects that likely would pass unnoticed.

New Research

Early research is underway to answer several important questions. Out of the thousands of chemicals used in consumer products, which ones can make it through stormwater and wastewater treatment facilities, and what are their concentrations in the environment? At these concentrations, what effects on humans or aquatic organisms can be expected from any of these chemicals or combinations of them? What can be done to help prevent their transport to aquatic environments, or what modifications can be made to stormwater and wastewater treatment facilities to increase their effectiveness in removing the chemicals?

Answers to these questions are needed to determine possible measures to protect human health and the aquatic environment from extremely low concentrations of consumer chemicals in water. SEE ALSO CHEMICALS FROM PHARMACEUTICALS AND PERSONAL CARE PRODUCTS; ECOLOGY, FRESH-WATER; LAND USE AND WATER QUALITY; POLLUTION OF GROUNDWATER; POLLUTION OF LAKES AND STREAMS; POLLUTION SOURCES: POINT AND NONPOINT; SAFE DRINKING WATER ACT; SUPPLIES, PUBLIC AND DOMESTIC WATER; WASTEWATER TREATMENT AND MANAGEMENT.

Ralph L. Seiler

Bibliography

Daughton, Christian G., and Thomas A. Ternes. "Pharmaceuticals and Personal Care Products in the Environment: Agents of Subtle Change?" *Environmental Health Perspectives* 107, sup. 6 (1999):907–938.

Halling-Sørensen, Bent et al. "Occurrence, Fate and Effects of Pharmaceutical Substances in the Environment: A Review." *Chemosphere* 36, no. 2 (1998):357–393.

Jobling, Susan et al. "Widespread Sexual Disruption in Wild Fish." *Environmental Science and Technology* 32, no. 17 (1998):2498–2506.

Seiler, Ralph L. et al. "Caffeine and Pharmaceuticals as Indicators of Wastewater Contamination in Wells." *Ground Water* 37, no. 3 (1999):405–410.

Internet Resources

Emerging Water Quality Issues Investigations. U.S. Geological Survey, Toxic Substances Hydrology Program. <http://toxics.usgs.gov/regional/emc.html>.

Chemicals from Pharmaceuticals and Personal Care Products

The use or consumption of natural resources often leads to ecological alteration. These changes can result from exposure of living systems to stressors ranging from physical alteration (such as **habitat** disruption) to chemical **pollution**. Untoward effects on wildlife and humans can range from the aesthetic to increased morbidity and mortality.

This article focuses on a large class of chemicals designed for use by humans and domestic animals; namely, pharmaceuticals and personal care products, or PPCPs. Although the benefits of these chemicals are undisputed

habitat: the environment in which a plant or animal grows or lives; the surroundings include physical factors such as temperature, moisture, and light, together with biological factors such as the presence of food and predators

pollution: any alteration in the character or quality of the environment, including water in waterbodies or geologic formations, which renders the environmental resource unfit or less suited for certain uses

The pharmaceuticals and personal care products found in a single bathroom medicine cabinet, multiplied by untold numbers of medicine cabinets in an urbanized area, hold the potential for substantially affecting environmental quality. The impacts on water quality and aquatic ecology from their mere usage and disposal only now are beginning to be investigated.

and wide-ranging, the consequences of their release or escape to the environment are poorly understood.

Conventional and Nonconventional Pollutants

As early as the 1950s, environmental chemists had focused on **agrochemicals** (for example, dichlorodiphenyltrichloroethane, commonly called DDT), industrial chemicals (for example, polychlorinated biphenyls, or PCBs), and industrial wastes and byproducts (for example, the polychlorinated dioxins). Agriculture and industry were long considered the major sources of chemical pollutants in the environment. Toxic chemicals from these activities are frequently lipophilic (dissolving in fat), persistent (resisting structural breakdown), and volatile (evaporating, subject to atmospheric transport). By virtue of these properties, such "conventional" pollutants have the ability to concentrate in body fat (thereby bioaccumulating in food chains) and to disperse globally.

Despite the long, concerted attention afforded these conventional pollutants, it is not known what portion of total risk due to chemical exposure they comprise. Indeed, many other classes of synthetic and naturally occurring **toxicants** can and do enter the environment. Some of these "nonconventional" pollutants have been long known, whereas others are newly recognized.

agrochemical: a synthetic or naturally derived chemical used in agriculture, such as a fertilizer, pesticide, or hormone

toxicant: a chemical substance that has the potential of causing acute or chronic adverse effects in plants, animals, or humans

(see sidebar)

PROPERLY DISPOSING OF UNUSED AND OUTDATED DRUGS

In addition to excretion and washing, another origin of drugs in the environment is disposal of expired or unwanted drugs to domestic sewage. Flushing down the toilet is used not just by the consumer, but also not infrequently by medical practices, such as nursing homes and physicians (unused medications and expired "physician samples").

Nationwide procedures do not exist in the United States for consumer return of unused drugs to pharmacies, manufacturers, or hazardous waste disposers. In the absence of recommended practices, in the interim it is best for the consumer to dispose of drugs in domestic trash (ensuring that liquids do not leak) targeted for engineered landfills or to save them for periodic curbside or community hazardous waste pickups. The extremely complex topic of lifecycle stewardship of PPCPs has been covered for the first time by Daughton (in press), as cited in the bibliography.

groundwater: generally, all subsurface (underground) water, as distinct from surface water, that supplies natural springs, contributes to permanent streams, and can be tapped by wells

degradation: breakdown of a chemical to yield usually simpler chemical products (molecules) by way of biocatalysis (e.g., metabolism), photolysis (e.g., sunlight), or physicochemical processes (e.g., hydrolysis)

polarity: a relative measure of the distribution of electron density for a molecule; its significance for environmental chemistry is that it determines whether a chemical prefers to associate with water (polar, or hydrophilic) or fat/lipid (nonpolar, or hydrophobic or lipophilic)

Until the 1990s, nonconventional pollutants were largely ignored because their higher water solubility relative to conventional pollutants complicated their chemical analysis, made them more easily degraded, prevented their escape to the atmosphere, and constrained their environmental dispersal to local waters. A significant portion of these chemicals includes PPCPs—a broad, diverse collection of thousands of chemicals, including prescription and over-the-counter therapeutic drugs, diagnostic agents, fragrances, cosmetics, and numerous others, many of which possess profound biochemical activity.

PPCPs in the Environment

PPCPs are applied externally or ingested by humans, and are used for pets and other domestic animals (especially as feed additives). The chemically unaltered, original ("parent") compound together with sometimes many associated transformation ("daughter") products (such as metabolites) have the potential to be excreted (in urine and feces), discharged directly to open waters or into sewage systems, or applied as biosolids (sludge from treated sewage) or washed onto land. Another source is disposal of expired or unwanted PPCPs directly to domestic sewage systems (see sidebar). The potential always exists for migration of PPCPs to, or purposeful introduction to, **groundwaters** (e.g., via septic systems or recharge), where **degradation** is greatly retarded. Other sources exist, as shown in the illustration.

Input of a drug to the environment is a function of the efficiency of human and animal absorption and metabolism coupled with the effectiveness of the technologies employed by municipal sewage treatment works (STWs); furthermore, sewage is often introduced directly to the environment without any treatment by STWs (such as inadvertent "overflow" events or purposeful "straight-piping"). STWs are not specifically engineered to remove PPCPs. The focus of STWs, as historically stipulated by law, is solely on a small number of "criteria" pollutants. While many unregulated pollutants are coincidentally removed during treatment, STW-treated effluents (discharges) can contain a wide spectrum of other chemicals, PPCPs being but one large group.

Occurrence, Fate, and Risk. Compared with the "conventional" pollutants, little is known about PPCPs with regard to potential environmental effects. Even though PPCPs are a more recently recognized group of pollutants, it is reasonable to surmise that the occurrence of PPCPs in waters is not a new phenomenon: many PPCPs probably have existed in the environment for as long as they have been used commercially.

Because of the higher **polarity** of PPCPs, their environmental disposition gravitates to waterbodies hydraulically connected to their origin. This includes all surface waters and groundwaters. Toxicological risks from inadvertent exposure of nontarget organisms in the environment are therefore probably highest for aquatic organisms, especially those occupying locations closest to PPCP discharges. The risks are lower for humans because drinking water usually receives further treatment to remove pollutants.

Furthermore, the risks posed to populations of aquatic organisms accrue from continual lifelong multigenerational exposure, whereas for humans, exposure is via long-term but intermittent consumption of much lower

Origins and Fate of PPCPs† in the Environment

†Pharmaceuticals and Personal Care Products

EPA ORD

U.S. Environmental Protection Agency
Office of Research and Development
National Exposure Research Laboratory
Environmental Sciences Division
Environmental Chemistry Branch

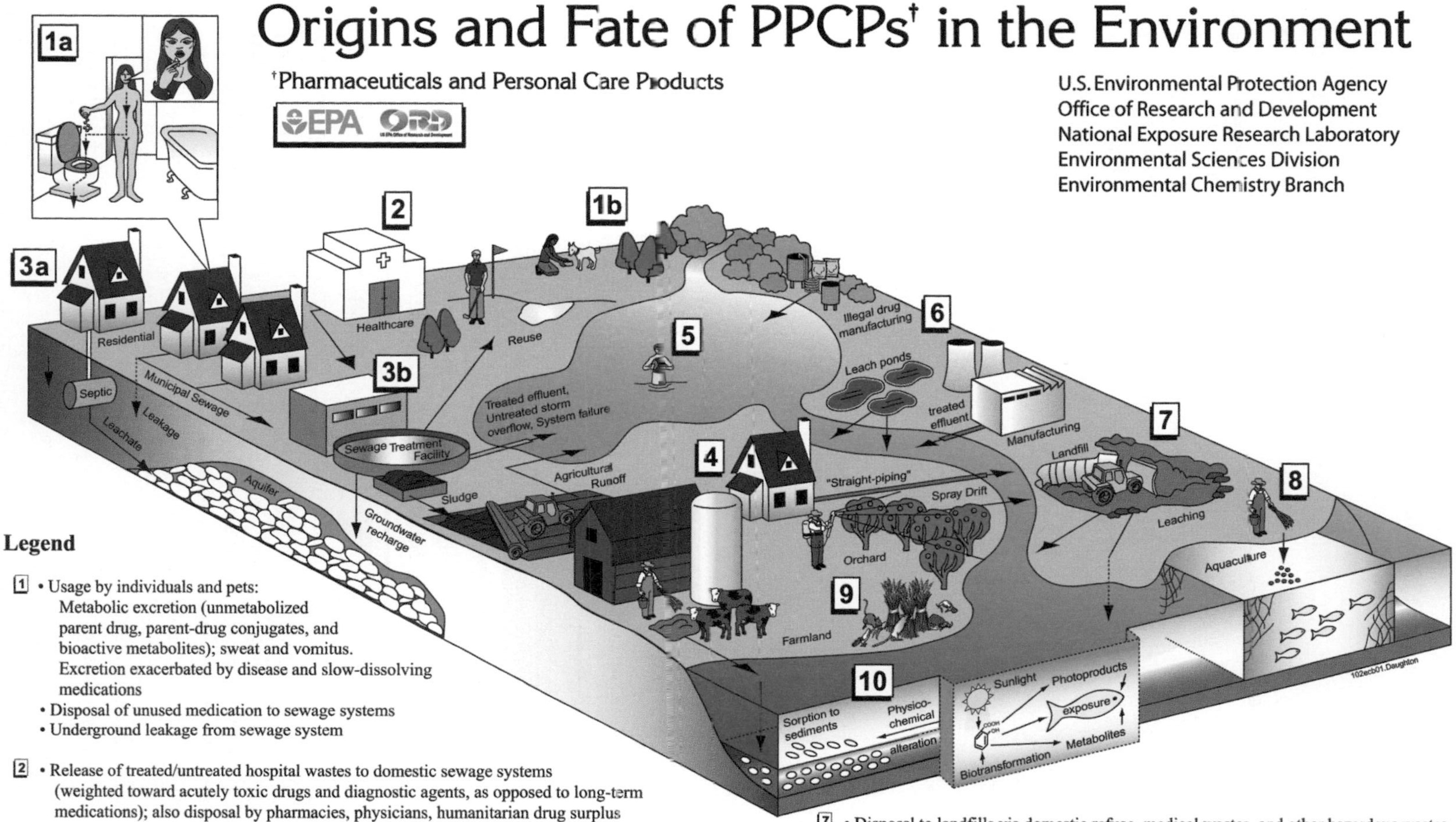

Labels in diagram:

1a
1b
2
3a
3b
4
5
6
7
8
9
10

Residential
Municipal Sewage
Septic
Leakage
Leachate
Healthcare
Sewage Treatment Facility
Sludge
Groundwater recharge
Aquifer
Reuse
Treated effluent, Untreated storm overflow, System failure
Agricultural Runoff
Illegal drug manufacturing
Leach ponds
Treated effluent
Manufacturing
Spray Drift
"Straight-piping"
Orchard
Farmland
Landfill
Leaching
Aquaculture
Sorption to sediments
Physico-chemical alteration
Sunlight
Photoproducts
exposure
Metabolites
Biotransformation

Y06cG01 Daughton

Legend

1 • Usage by individuals and pets:
  Metabolic excretion (unmetabolized parent drug, parent-drug conjugates, and bioactive metabolites); sweat and vomitus. Excretion exacerbated by disease and slow-dissolving medications
  • Disposal of unused medication to sewage systems
  • Underground leakage from sewage system

2 • Release of treated/untreated hospital wastes to domestic sewage systems (weighted toward acutely toxic drugs and diagnostic agents, as opposed to long-term medications); also disposal by pharmacies, physicians, humanitarian drug surplus

3 • Release to private septic/leach fields
  • Treated effluent from domestic sewage treatment plants discharged to surface waters or re-injected into aquifers (recharge)
  • Overflow of untreated sewage from storm events and system failures directly to surface waters

4 • Transfer of sewage solids to land (e.g., soil amendment/fertilization)
  • "Straight-piping" from homes (untreated sewage discharged directly to surface waters)
  • Release from agriculture: spray drift from tree crops (e.g., antibiotics)
  • Dung from medicated domestic animals (e.g., feed) - CAFOs (confined animal feeding operations)

5 • Direct release to open waters via washing/bathing/swimming

6 • Discharge of regulated/controlled industrial manufacturing waste streams
  • Disposal/release from clandestine drug labs

7 • Disposal to landfills via domestic refuse, medical wastes, and other hazardous wastes
  • Leaching from defective (poorly engineered) landfills

8 • Release to open waters from aquaculture (medicated feed and resulting excreta)

9 • Release of drugs that serve double duty as pest control agents:
  examples: 4-aminopyridine experimental multiple sclerosis drug → used as avicide; warfarin anticoagulant → rat poison; azacholesterol antilipidemics → avian/rodent reproductive inhibitors; certain antibiotics → used for orchard pathogens; acetaminophen analgesic → brown tree snake control

10 • Ultimate environmental fate:
  • most PPCPs eventually transported from terrestrial domain to aqueous domain
  • phototransformation (both direct and indirect reactions via UV light)
  • physicochemical alteration, degradation, and ultimate mineralization
  • volatilization (mainly certain anesthetics, fragrances)

For further information on this topic: http://www.epa.gov/nerlesd1/chemistry/pharma/index.htm

Christian G. Daughton, U.S. EPA-Las Vegas   February 2001

concentrations of fewer PPCPs in drinking water. These risks are essentially unknown, largely because the documented concentrations in the environment are extremely low—from sub to hundreds of micrograms per liter (μg/L), or parts per billion (ppb). (One part per billion represents 0.0000001 percent. Detection of a chemical at a concentration of 1 ppb is comparable to searching for one family among the world's entire population.) Moreover, possible effects on nontarget organisms are poorly understood. The occurrence of PPCPs in drinking water is much less frequent and at even lower concentrations than in the environment—nanograms per liter (ng/L), or parts per trillion.

Although these concentrations are very low, they can be perpetual because PPCPs are continually introduced to the aquatic environment. Even PPCPs with short **half-lives** can establish a pseudo-**steady-state** presence because their environmental breakdown is continually balanced by replenishment via fresh sewage effluent. These chemicals are examples of "pseudo-persistent" pollutants.

Biochemical Targets and Nontargets

While personal care products are generally consumed in much larger quantities than pharmaceuticals, drugs are designed expressly to be biologically active, with each therapeutic class having different biochemical targets (although many classes can share one or more targets—or "receptors"). Drugs are designed with the safety of the target organism in mind (humans or domestic animals). Little is therefore known regarding the safety of nontarget organisms, such as aquatic life.

Two classes of drugs have received more attention than any others regarding nontarget effects. The first class is **antibiotics**, where the promotion of **pathogen** resistance is a major concern. (Pathogen resistance can be caused by overuse or misuse in the host and possibly by exposure of microorganisms in the environment.) The second class is the sex **steroids**—both the natural, **endogenous** steroids, especially the estrogens, as well as their synthetic counterparts, such as those used for reproductive control.

Steroidal chemicals such as the sex steroids have the capability of disrupting or modulating hormone (endocrine) systems. Certain other PPCPs, together with various other synthetic chemicals, possess endocrine activity. Collectively, these compounds are known by a number of terms, including endocrine disrupting compounds or hormonally active agents. Their aquatic effects include the feminization of male fish and alteration of the behaviors of either sex at part-per-trillion concentrations. A multitude of other aquatic effects are possible because hormone systems are central to the development, functioning, and reproduction of most organisms.

Antibiotic resistance and hormonal effects are only two of numerous possible untoward outcomes. Others, such as neurobehavioral effects, could be so subtle that they escape our immediate attention, accumulating unnoticed until significant outward effects arise but which cannot be ascribed to a cause.

The Role of Individuals

As of 2002, a growing number of articles were advancing various aspects of the overall issue of PPCPs in the environment. The U.S. Environmental

half-life: the time required for the initial concentration of a radioactive element to decrease, through radioactive decay, by 50 percent; in nonradiochemical usage, the time required for a pollutant to lose one-half of its original concentration (e.g., the half-life of DDT in the environment is 15 years)

steady state: a state of a system in which reactions are occurring or processes are happening, but the system has reached a state of balance such that all components remain at a constant concentration

antibiotic: a substance produced by organisms, especially bacteria and fungi, which passes into the surrounding medium and is toxic to other organisms; for example, penicillin from the mold *Penicillin notatum* destroys many kinds of bacteria

pathogen: a disease-producing agent, usually a living organism, and commonly a microbe (microorganism)

steroid: any of a class of naturally occuring compounds and synthetic analogues, such as sterols, bile acids, sex hormones, or adrenocortical hormones; most have specific physiological action

endogenous: originating from within, as opposed to coming from external sources

Protection Agency maintains a web site devoted to the topic (as referenced in the bibliography). Although the issue of PPCPs in the environment has gained more attention by scientists in many fields, the overall topic will probably continue to generate more questions than answers. A larger lesson, however, resides among the unknowns.

Most PPCPs owe their origin in the environment to the combined actions and behaviors of multitudes of individuals. In contrast to the conventional synthetic pollutants, the origin of PPCPs in the environment has no geographic boundaries or climatic-use limitations; that is, PPCPs are discharged to the environment wherever people live or visit, regardless of the time of year.

Perhaps more so than any other class of pollutants, PPCPs illustrate the immediate, intimate, and inseparable connection of the actions and activities of the individual with the environment. Some scientists feel the importance and significance of the individual in directly contributing to the combined load of synthetic chemicals in the environment has been greatly underappreciated. The continuing, escalating advances in design of new drugs will undoubtedly add to the spectrum of questions regarding the environmental significance of these compounds. SEE ALSO CHEMICALS FROM CONSUMERS; ECOLOGY, FRESH-WATER; LAND USE AND WATER QUALITY; POLLUTION OF GROUNDWATER; POLLUTION OF LAKES AND STREAMS; POLLUTION SOURCES: POINT AND NONPOINT; SAFE DRINKING WATER ACT; SUPPLIES, PUBLIC AND DOMESTIC WATER; WASTEWATER TREATMENT AND MANAGEMENT.

Christian G. Daughton

Bibliography

Daughton, Christian G. "Cradle-to-Cradle Stewardship of Drugs for Minimizing Their Environmental Disposition while Promoting Human Health, Part I: Rationale and Avenues Toward a Green Pharmacy." *Environmental Health Perspectives,* (in press, May 2003).

———. "Cradle-to-Cradle Stewardship of Drugs for Minimizing Their Environmental Disposition while Promoting Human Health, Part II: Drug Disposal, Waste Reduction, and Future Direction." *Environmental Health Perspectives,* (in press, May 2003).

Daughton, Christian G., and Tammy L. Jones-Lepp, eds. *Pharmaceuticals and Personal Care Products in the Environment: Scientific and Regulatory Issues.* American Chemical Society Symposium Series 791. Washington, D.C.: ACS/Oxford University Press, 2001.

Daughton, Christian G., and Thomas A. Ternes. "Pharmaceuticals and Personal Care Products in the Environment: Agents of Subtle Change?" *Environmental Health Perspectives* 107, sup. 6 (1999):907–938.

Dietrich, Daniel R., guest ed. "Toxicology of Musk Fragrances." *Toxicology Letters* 111, no.1–2 (1999):1–187.

Halling-Sørensen Bent, et al. "Occurrence, Fate and Effects of Pharmaceutical Substances in the Environment: A Review." *Chemosphere* 36, no. 2 (1998):357–393.

Hutzinger, Otto. "Drugs in the Environment." Jørgensen, Sven Erik, and Bent Halling-Sørensen, guest eds. *Chemosphere* 40 (2000):691–793.

Kümmerer, Klaus, ed. *Pharmaceuticals in the Environment: Sources, Fate, Effects and Risks.* Heidelberg, Germany: Springer-Verlag, 2001.

Ternes, Thomas, and Rolf-Dieter Wilken, guest eds. "Drugs and Hormones as Pollutants of the Aquatic Environment: Determination and Ecotoxicological Impacts." *The Science of the Total Environment* 225, no.1–2 (1999):1–176.

Internet Resources

"A National Reconnaissance of Pharmaceuticals, Hormones, and Other Organic Wastewater Contaminants in Sources of Drinking Water, 2001." *Emerging Water Quality Issues Investigations Page.* U.S. Geological Survey, Toxic Substances Hydrology Program. <http://toxics.usgs.gov/regional/emc_sourcewater.html>.

Daughton, Christian G., ed. *Pharmaceuticals and Personal Care Products (PPCPs) as Environmental Pollutants: Pollution from Personal Actions, Activities, and Behaviors.* U.S. Environmental Protection Agency. <http://www.epa.gov/nerlesd1/chemistry/pharma/>.

Chesapeake Bay

estuary: a tidally influenced coastal area in which fresh water from a river mixes with sea water, generally at the river mouth; the resulting water is brackish, which results in a unique ecosystem

The Chesapeake Bay is North America's largest **estuary** and has a shoreline of more than 12,800 kilometers (8,000 miles). The bay is a long, narrow arm of the Atlantic Ocean that extends northward into Maryland and cuts the state into two parts. In addition to Maryland, the Chesapeake Bay drainage basin includes parts of the states of West Virginia, Virginia, Pennsylvania, New York, Delaware, and the entire District of Columbia. The cities of Richmond, Virginia; Washington, D.C.; and Annapolis, Maryland lie within its basin boundary.

Commodities have been exported and imported through the Chesapeake Bay since the Jamestown settlers inhabited the area in the early eighteenth century. Exporting and importing a multitude of goods today is a competitive business. Important deep-water **navigable** ports on the bay include Baltimore, Maryland, and Norfolk, Newport News, and Portsmouth in Virginia.

navigable: in general usage, describes a waterbody deep and wide enough to afford passage to small and large vessels; also can be used in the context of a specific statutory or regulatory designation

With deep-sea vessels containing equipment of the latest marine technology, U.S. companies can export large volumes of goods to other countries in a short period of time. The most profitable commodities imported into the Chesapeake Bay area include natural rubber, paper, auto parts, steel, iron, alcoholic beverages, grain, and tobacco. The strongest trade partners for the Chesapeake Bay include Brazil, Colombia, Venezuela, Japan, Greece, the United Kingdom, and Germany.

The Basin and Bay

Chesapeake Bay is approximately 323 kilometers (200 miles) long as it extends from Norfolk, Virginia to Havre de Grace, Maryland. The bay ranges in width from between 5.5 kilometers (3.4 miles) near Aberdeen, Maryland, to 56 kilometers (35 miles) near the mouth of the Potomac River. The mouth of the Chesapeake Bay is a narrow passage—19 kilometers (12 miles) wide—between its northern point (Atlantic side) near Cape Charles, Virginia, and its southern point (inland side) close to Cape Henry, Virginia.

The Chesapeake Bay estuary receives approximately 50 percent of its water from the Atlantic Ocean, in the form of salt water. The other half of the water (fresh water) drains into the bay from a large 165,800-square-kilometer (64,000-square-mile) drainage watershed. Among the 150 major rivers and streams in the Chesapeake Bay drainage basin are the James, Potomac, York, Rappahannock, Patuxent, and Susquehanna. The Susquehanna River, located on the northern shore of the bay, provides about half of the fresh water coming into the bay, an amount totaling about 72 million liters

Cape Hatteras (lower right), Chesapeake Bay (middle), and Delaware Bay (upper right) are visible from this satellite image. The Atlantic Ocean is to the right.

(19 million gallons) of water per minute. The Chesapeake Bay contains on average more than 68 trillion liters (18 trillion gallons) of water.

Chesapeake Bay, the largest of 130 estuaries in the United States, is a complex **ecosystem** that includes important **habitats** and **food chains**. The bay supports more than 3,600 species of animals, plants, and fish, including 348 species of finfish, 173 species of shellfish, and over 2,700 plant species. Fish of all types and sizes either live in the bay and its tributaries, or they use the waters as they migrate along the East Coast. Every year, 1 million waterfowl rest in the bay's basin as they migrate along the Atlantic Migratory Bird Flyway. More than 500,000 Canada geese winter in and near the bay.

The Chesapeake Bay is a commercial and recreational resource for more than 15 million people who live in and near its watershed (drainage basin). The bay produces approximately 500 million pounds of oysters, crabs, and other seafood per year. The richness of its species can be seen in the value of the bay's annual fish harvest, which is estimated at over $100 million. It yields more oysters and soft-shelled crabs than any other region in the

ecosystem: the community of plants and animals within a water or terrestrial habitat interacting together and with their physical and chemical environment

habitat: the environment in which a plant or animal grows or lives; the surroundings include physical factors such as temperature, moisture, and light, together with biological factors such as the presence of food and predators

food chain: the levels of nutrition in an ecosystem, beginning at the bottom with primary producers, which are principally plants, to a series of consumers—herbivores, carnivores, and decomposers

United States. The Chesapeake Bay is the largest producer of blue crabs in the world, although this fishery has recently experienced declines.

Environmental Concerns

Since the early twentieth century, the Chesapeake Bay has experienced serious environmental degradation. Problems include large reductions in sea grass, reduced amounts of **finfish** and shellfish (especially oysters and crab), seasonal depletions in dissolved oxygen, and increases in **sedimentation**.

Environmental concerns were voiced in the 1970s over the damage to key habitats and the decline in water quality. Species in bay waters were being negatively affected, resulting in threats to the commercial and recreational activities.

Most marine scientists believe that these changes are related to ecological stress due to increased human activities. Causes include deforestation, agriculture (including fertilizers), urbanization, **pollution**, and sewage. The Chesapeake Bay Commission predicts that by the year 2020, the population of the bay watershed will increase to 17.4 million. Without additional environment attention on the bay ecosystems, the Commission predict that stress on the natural system will increase dramatically.

Eutrophication. One serious pollution problem in Chesapeake Bay has been **eutrophication** caused by excessive nitrogen and phosphorus. The increased fertility of the bay's waters has caused prolific algal blooms. Algal concentrations in the water column and dense mats of vegetation on the water surface can shade out native aquatic plants. The oxygen depletion resulting from the massive algal die-off disrupts the balance of the ecosystem. The primary sources of nitrogen and phosphorous have been the fertilizers and animal wastes of farmlands in the basin.

Toxic Contamination. **Toxic** chemicals are entering the Chesapeake Bay and its food chain. These poisonous chemicals come from several point and nonpoint sources including industrial discharges, oil spills, agricultural runoff, urban runoff, and rainfall. Metals such as cadmium, copper, chromium, lead, nickel, and zinc are polluting the bay. In 1975, the massive release of the pesticide, Kepone®, into the James River in Virginia was one of the worst toxic inputs into the bay's ecosystem.

Most toxic substances persist in the Chesapeake Bay environment for many years, and have adverse affects throughout its food chain. One factor that complicates this situation is the bay's long **residence time** and low flushing rate. Only 1 percent of the settleable waste that enters the Chesapeake Bay is flushed to the ocean. The remainder settles in the bay's waters to form bottom sediment. Toxic contamination has been a prime suspect in the demise of several species in the bay.

Blue Crab. One particular ecological concern is the blue crab, a popular commercial fish within the Chesapeake Bay. The 2001 Chesapeake Bay commercial blue crab harvest of approximately 52 million pounds was well below the average of about 75 million pounds that has annually occurred from 1968 to 2001.

Analysis of long-term fishery independent surveys conducted in the Chesapeake Bay indicate that the blue crab population is approaching a record low after declining in recent years. The low numbers places the blue

finfish: an aquatic animal with a backbone and fins, as opposed to a shellfish, an aquatic animal without a backbone and with a shell

sedimentation: in geology and geomorphology, a process in which sediment is transported and deposited in a new location; in water treatment, the settling of solids or of flocculated or coagulated particles

pollution: any alteration in the character or quality of the environment, including water in waterbodies or geologic formations, which renders the environmental resource unfit or less suited for certain uses

eutrophication: the process by which lakes and streams become enriched, to varying degrees, by concentrations of nutrients such as nitrogen and phosphorus; enrichment results in increased plant growth (principally algae) and decay, the latter of which reduces the dissolved oxygen content; highly eutrophic conditions may be considered undesirable depending on the human use of the waterbody

toxic: describes chemical substances that are or may become harmful to plants, animals, or humans when the toxicant is present in sufficient concentrations

residence time: the average time an element spends in a given environment between the time it arrived and the time it is removed by some process; in the ocean, residence time is defined as the concentration in sea water relative to the amount delivered to the ocean per year

Chesapeake Bay is the world's largest producer of blue crabs. Generations continue to enjoy this seafood favorite.

crab at increased risk for not rebounding. With low population numbers combined with a high fishing catch rate, the blue crab continues to be a great concern.

Mute Swans.   Mute swans, native to Europe and Asia, were transported to North America in the late nineteenth century by European immigrants. Some swans eventually escaped or were deliberately released into the wild. In Maryland, the mute swan population grew from five captive swans that escaped in 1962 to more than four thousand swans as of 2000.

Because mute swans did not evolve with the native species in Chesapeake Bay, these aggressive invaders have caused many problems. Mute swans are suspected of causing a 30-percent decline in Maryland's wintering population of tundra swans. In the early 1990s, mute swans caused a colony of least terns and black skimmers (both threatened species in Maryland) to abandon their nesting site. Mute swans overgraze bay grasses, eliminating habitats for crabs, fish, and other species.

Some mute swans are aggressive and will attack humans, including small children, in defense of their nest territory and cygnets (their offspring). This territorial behavior can be a nuisance, and renders some land and water areas inaccessible to people during the swan nesting and brood-rearing season. Swans have even been documented killing mallard ducklings and Canada goose goslings.

Since the mid-1990s, the Maryland Department of Natural Resources, along with some federal agencies, has taken measures to control mute swan populations. In 1998, Maryland's governor appointed a committee to develop mute swan management recommendations. In 2002, the management plan was in its public comment period. The recommendations combine lethal and nonlethal methods intended to reduce the mute swan populations to levels compatible with native wildlife, natural ecosystems, and human environments.

Saving the Bay

Due to impacts from serious environmental threats, the U.S. Environmental Protection Agency (EPA) recognized the Chesapeake Bay as a damaged ecosystem. The EPA conducted a $27 million research study from 1976 to 1983. This study concluded that immediate and intensive efforts were needed to save this estuary and restore its ecological health. In 1983, the Chesapeake Bay Agreement was signed and the federal government and the states of Maryland, Virginia, and Pennsylvania, and the District of Columbia pledged to take action to reverse its environmental deterioration.

These actions included upgrading sewage treatment plants, controlling urban runoff, controlling manure and fertilizer runoff, reducing soil erosion, issuing stricter discharge permits, and banning the use of phosphorous detergents. This agreement outlined the goal of reducing the amounts of nitrogen and phosphorus entering the bay by 40 percent by the year 2000. These strategies have had some measurable success in saving the bay. The Chesapeake Bay Agreement has been amended in 1987, 1992, and 2000. These agreements reflect the ongoing political process of strengthening regional efforts to save the bay.

Two important organizations working toward an improved Chesapeake Bay environment are the Chesapeake Bay Program and the Small Watershed Grants Program.

Chesapeake Bay Program. The Chesapeake Bay Program is a partnership among the states of Maryland, Virginia, Pennsylvania, the District of Columbia; along with the Chesapeake Bay Commission and the federal government. It was formed in 1983 as a result of the first Chesapeake Bay Agreement. The partnership has stated a number of bay protection and restoration goals, and it strives to mobilize the resources of the governmental sector with the private sector to achieve its goals. The Chesapeake Bay Program operates as a voluntary, collaborative resource management program. It has set goals related to fisheries, **wetlands**, submerged grasses, **nutrient** reduction, toxins, sustainable development, and citizen involvement.

Small Watershed Grants Program. The Small Watershed Grants Program provides grants to organizations working on a local level to protect and improve watersheds in the Chesapeake Bay basin, while building citizen-based resource stewardship. The purpose of the grants program is to emphasize the water quality and living resource needs of the Chesapeake Bay ecosystem. The Small Watershed Grants Program has been designed to encourage the development and sharing of innovative ideas among the many different types of organizations involved in watershed protection activities.

Concerted efforts are being made to improve the ecological health of the Chesapeake Bay. While progress has been made, the recovery of this resource will require long-term effort and the active participation of all six states and the District of Columbia lying within its drainage basin. Given projected population increases, these efforts to control nutrient and chemical discharges into its rivers and to improve waste treatment technologies are vital to protecting the water, habitat, and species of this estuary ecosystem.

wetland: an area that is periodically or permanently saturated or covered by surface water or groundwater, that displays hydric soils, and that typically supports or is capable of supporting hydrophytic vegetation

nutrients: a group of chemical elements or compounds needed for all plant and animal life; nitrogen and phosphorus are the primary nutrients; excessive or imbalanced nutrients in water may cause problems such as accelerated eutrophication

SEE ALSO ALGAL BLOOMS IN FRESH WATER; ALGAL BLOOMS IN THE OCEAN; BAYS, GULFS, AND STRAITS; CRUSTACEANS; ECOLOGY, MARINE; ESTUARIES; POLLUTION BY INVASIVE SPECIES; PORTS AND HARBORS; RIVER BASIN PLANNING; TRANSPORTATION; WATERSHED, RESTORATION OF A.

William Arthur Atkins and Faye Anderson

Bibliography

Dorbin, Ann E. *Saving the Bay: People Working for the Future of the Chesapeake.* Baltimore, MD: Johns Hopkins University Press, 2001.

Internet Resources

Chesapeake Bay Blue Crab Advisory Report 2002. Chesapeake Bay Stock Assessment Committee. <http://www.fisheries.vims.edu/bcar/>.

Chesapeake Bay Commission. <http://www.chesbay.state.va.us/>.

Chesapeake Bay Program: America's Premiere Watershed Restoration Partnership. Chesapeake Bay Program, Chesapeake Information Management System. <http://www.chesapeakebay.net/>.

Ecosystem Trends and Response: Chesapeake Bay. U.S. Geological Survey. <http://geochange.er.usgs.gov/pub/info/facts/chesapeake/>.

EPA Chesapeake Bay Program Office. <http://www.epa.gov/r3chespk/>.

Clean Air Act   *See Acid Rain.*

Clean Water Act

The Federal Water Pollution Control Act Amendments of 1972, commonly referred to as the Clean Water Act, is one of the most important and far-reaching environmental statutes ever passed by the U.S. Congress. It is still one of the most controversial pieces of legislation ever passed. More than 30 years since its passage, key provisions of the act continue to be debated at all governmental levels, and lawsuits frequently are brought to federal courts under the act. To understand why the Clean Water Act remains controversial, it is necessary to review the history of the legislation, its goals, and its methods of achieving those objectives.

Water Quality as a National Interest

The 1972 Clean Water Act represented a radical departure from previous federal water quality legislation. Beginning in 1948, Congress declared it to be in the "national interest" to assure a high level of water quality throughout the United States. It passed additional water **pollution** control laws in 1956, 1961, 1965, 1966, and 1970.

While each subsequent act was more stringent than the previous ones, they all contained the philosophy that water quality was primarily the responsibility of the states. It was the role of the federal government to assist the states financially, to conduct basic water research, and to maintain water quality in interstate waters. But the creation and enforcement of quality standards for most of the waters in the United States—intrastate lakes, rivers, streams, **wetlands**, and ponds—were left to state and local governments.

Federal Responsibility. The 1972 Clean Water Act abandoned the approach that state and local governments were primarily responsible for ensuring water quality. In the midst of a national environmental movement, whose

pollution: any alteration in the character or quality of the environment, including water in waterbodies or geologic formations, which renders the environmental resource unfit or less suited for certain uses

wetland: an area that is periodically or permanently saturated or covered by surface water or groundwater, that displays hydric soils, and that typically supports or is capable of supporting hydrophytic vegetation

The Federal Water Pollution Control Act Amendments of 1972 (the Clean Water Act) regulates the release of pollutants into U.S. waterways, such as this stream degraded by chemical contaminants and silt. The legislation signaled a new way of dealing with the nation's water pollution by prohibiting the discharge of pollutants unless the discharger first obtains a permit from the government.

leaders claimed that virtually nothing had been achieved by relying on state action to reduce water pollution, the 92nd Congress embarked upon a bold new course. Although the 1972 act incorporated some elements contained in previous legislation, such as generous financial assistance to state, tribal, and local governments to construct wastewater treatment facilities, it also charted new waters in federal regulatory policy, and in relations between the federal government and the states.

Regulatory Objectives

The regulatory philosophy contained in the Clean Water Act is referred to as the command-and-control, or standards-and-enforcement, method. No longer would the federal government wait for the states to devise their own water quality standards, since few had done so when given the opportunity. Rather, Congress gave this responsibility to a new federal agency, the Environmental Protection Agency (EPA). Under authority contained in the 1972 legislation, the EPA had primary responsibility for implementing the ambitious and optimistic goals of ensuring that all waters of the United States be "fishable" and "swimmable" by 1983, 10 years after the act's passage.

The 1972 Clean Water Act also set as a lofty goal the "zero discharge" of **pollutants** into the nation's waters by 1985. Congress passed related legislation also at this time to ensure that its intent to cover *all* waters of the United States was clear. In 1972, Congress passed the Marine Protection, Research, and Sanctuaries Act, known as the Ocean Dumping Act, and in 1974 the Safe Drinking Water Act. The EPA was given authority to implement these acts as well.

Rigorous Demands.   In order to make as much progress as possible in cleaning up the nation's waters in a short period of time, the EPA embarked upon what is called a "technology-forcing" regulatory strategy. That is, the agency placed rigorous and rigid demands on those who were regulated by the statute—mainly municipalities and industries at first—to achieve increasingly higher levels of pollution abatement. Industries were told to install the "best practicable control technology" by 1977, and municipalities were told to achieve secondary treatment of their wastewater by that date.

Federal Construction Grants.   To assist local governments in meeting these deadlines, the 1972 act also provided for a generous federal grant program to construct modern treatment facilities. Indeed, much of the nation's water quality infrastructure was built in the 1970s, and an issue for today's politicians in Washington, D.C., is whether to make a similar investment in bringing an aging system up-to-date. The EPA has estimated that it could cost as much as $140 billion to accomplish that objective.

Amendments

The 1972 Clean Water Act has been amended three times: in 1977; in 1981 when Congress passed the Municipal Wastewater Treatment Construction Grants Amendments; and in 1987 with the Water Quality Act. All of these statutes reaffirmed the federal interest in assuring water quality in the United States, but they also recognized the difficulty of achieving the goals set forth in the 1972 act within the time period specified. Thus, timelines were pushed forward, and the rigid command-and-control regulatory approach was modified. It was replaced, in part, by a more flexible approach that stressed partnerships between the federal government and the states, tribal governments, and municipalities in achieving common purposes.

Sources of Pollution.   Another important distinction between the original act and the 1987 revision was in its emphasis on the *sources* of water pollution in the United States. Prior to 1987 most programs were directed at eliminating what is called point-source pollution: that is, discharges into water that are more or less easily tracked to their sources. Pipes and other outfalls are examples of point-source pollution.

By 1987, however, it became clear that a great deal of pollution was coming from nonpoint sources. It was estimated that over 50 percent of the nation's remaining water pollution problems was coming from sources that are not easily identified, such as runoff from agricultural lands, construction sites, urban areas, and even forests.

Under Section 319 of the 1987 legislation, Congress authorized measures to address these diffuse sources of pollution by directing states to develop

pollutant: something that pollutes, especially a waste material that contaminates air, soil, or water

---

WHAT IS A WATER PERMIT?

The 1972 Clean Water Act contained the philosophy that all discharges into the nation's waters are unlawful unless specifically authorized by a permit obtained from the Environmental Protection Agency (EPA). Under Section 402 of the act, the National Pollutant Discharge Elimination System (NPDES) was created, covering more than 65,000 industrial and municipal dischargers.

An NPDES permit requires industries to attain the best practicable control technology applicable to each pollutant discharged, and for municipalities at least secondary treatment of their discharges. Permits are issued for 5 years and must be renewed to allow for continued discharges. Permit holders must maintain records of their activities, and they must carry out effluent monitoring.

The NPDES permit, containing effluent limitations on what may be discharged by any single source, is the principal enforcement tool of the Clean Water Act. The EPA may issue compliance orders, or bring civil suits in U.S. District Court against persons who violate the terms of their permit. Penalties for noncompliance can range from $25,000 per day to as much as $250,000 a day, 15 years in prison for "knowing endangerment" of public health, or both. In addition, individuals may bring a citizen suit in district court against persons who are suspected of violating the NPDES permit process.

and implement management programs targeting their major nonpoint sources. Federal grants, covering up to 60 percent of the program costs, also were authorized to assist states in tackling this difficult pollution problem.

Overdue Reassessment?

There has not been a major revision to the Clean Water Act since 1987, and many feel that a comprehensive reassessment of accomplishments and failures is long overdue. The reason that such legislation has been stalled in Congress for so long is that the original 1972 act contained a few highly controversial programs, the most contentious of which may be the national wetlands protection program. Also known as the Section 404 Program, the 1972 act declared a federal interest in the protection of all wetlands in the United States. It set up a complex regulatory program administered jointly by the U.S. Army Corps of Engineers and the EPA under which anyone planning to dredge, drain, or fill a wetland must first secure a permit from the Corps.

The EPA exercises veto authority over Corps decisions, while other federal agencies, in particular the U.S. Fish and Wildlife Service, provide additional input to the process. Although the process has been streamlined and simplified since its inception, it remains controversial for property owners wishing to alter their lands. Certain states, too, have claimed that the program is an unwarranted intrusion into their domain; in contrast, most environmental organizations solidly support it.

Issues of Contention. Over the years, numerous court cases have addressed various issues concerning the wetlands protection program. A 2001 Supreme Court case, *Solid Waste Agency of Cook County, Illinois, v. U.S. Army Corps of Engineers*, found that federal jurisdiction did not extend to isolated wetlands such as the one Cook County planned to alter. With this important decision, the scope of the national wetlands protection program is reduced and returned to what it was some 30 years ago—at least until Congress revisits this aspect of the Clean Water Act.

Another contentious issue arising out of the Clean Water Act and its revisions involves the setting of precise water quality standards by the states and the EPA. The original act required states to identify pollution-impaired water areas and then develop "total maximum daily loads" (TMDLs) for each waterbody. TMDLs are the maximum amount of pollution that a waterbody can receive without violating water quality standards. If the state fails to act, then the EPA is required to undertake this time-consuming and technologically challenging determination.

Most states have lacked the resources to undertake this task, and the EPA has been reluctant to step in and assume responsibility, in part because it, too, lacks the necessary personnel to do the job nationwide. Consequently, since the late 1980s, citizen groups have filed more than forty lawsuits in thirty-eight states against the EPA and the states for failing to implement the TMDL requirement. During the Clinton administration, the EPA attempted to strengthen the enforcement of this program, but with the change in the presidency after the 2000 election, that proposal has been tabled. As with the wetlands issue, scholars and other interested parties note that the time has come for the U.S. Congress to revisit the Clean Water Act of 1972.

This ironic juxtaposition of two signs on a public beach reveals the complex task that society faces in protecting both land and water quality. The U.S. Environmental Protection Agency has established National Beach Guidance and Performance Criteria for Recreational Waters designed to ensure the public's health and improve environmental protection for beaches. The Clean Water Act restricts discharges of pollutants into the nation's waterways.

Aspirations and Deficiencies

If and when Congress reconsiders this historic piece of legislation, it will want to look closely at what has been accomplished, and by what means. The Clean Water Act is not without its critics. Even the EPA acknowledges that the results are mixed: Today, 40 percent of the waters surveyed by the states fail to meet national water quality standards.

Although the Clean Water Act was well intentioned, some scholars have found it to be an instance of flawed public policy-making. Cornell University political scientist Theodore Lowi wrote in 1979 that Congress knew nothing about water pollution when it was writing the act, and so simply mandated a regulatory agency, the EPA, to do whatever it saw fit. This was a recipe for political chaos, Lowi charged, which inevitably would result in the federal courts becoming deeply involved in the water pollution control policy process. Indeed they have, as noted earlier.

Another critic of federal pollution control policy, Barry Commoner, a scientist and spokesperson for the environmental movement for nearly 50 years, wrote in a 1990 book that both the Clean Water and Clean Air Acts relied far too much on "control" and too little on "prevention." Noting that waste, once produced, has to go somewhere, the federal approach has been largely to try to control the effects of municipal, industrial, and agricultural waste production. The EPA should have spent more time working on the causes; that is, in preventing it in the first place, through such measures as recycling, reducing, and reusing (known as "the three Rs" of conservation).

The Clean Water Act of 1972 and its revisions spoke to the highest aspirations of the American people with regard to the environment they wished to inhabit. Although deficient in a number of ways, it nevertheless pointed the direction society needed to take to insure the continuance of a healthy and productive natural environment. The task of politicians today is to discover more efficient means, including the development of new technologies, in order to achieve the objectives set forth in 1972. SEE ALSO ENVIRONMENTAL MOVEMENT, ROLE OF WATER IN THE; ENVIRONMENTAL PROTECTION AGENCY, U.S.; FISH AND WILDLIFE SERVICE, U.S.; LEGISLATION, FEDERAL WATER; POLLUTION OF LAKES AND STREAMS; POLLUTION SOURCES: POINT AND NONPOINT; SAFE DRINKING WATER ACT; WASTEWATER TREATMENT AND MANAGEMENT.

Jeanne Nienaber Clarke

Bibliography

Adler, Robert W., J. C. Landman, and D. M. Cameron. *The Clean Water Act: 20 Years Later.* Washington, D.C.: Island Press, 1993.

Commoner, Barry. *Making Peace with the Planet.* New York: Pantheon, 1990.

Loeb, Penny. "Very Troubled Waters." *U.S. News and World Report* 125, no. 12 (September 28, 1998):39, 41–42.

Schneider, Paul. "Clear Progress, 25 Years of the Clean Water Act." *Audubon* (September/October 1997):36–47, 106–107.

Internet Resources

EPA Beach Watch Webpage. U.S. Environmental Protection Agency. <http://www.epa.gov/waterscience/beaches/>.

U.S. Code Chapter 26: Water Pollution Prevention and Control. Legal Information Institute, Cornell Law School. <http://www4.law.cornell.edu/uscode/33/ch26.html>.

30th Anniversary of the Clean Water Act. Year of Clean Water 2002. <http://www.yearofcleanwater.org/>.

Climate and the Ocean

Weather is defined as the state of the atmosphere at a specific place and time, whereas climate is a long-term average of weather in a region. Many factors combine to create the different climates found throughout the world, such as the amount of solar radiation an area receives, local terrain, nearby large bodies of water, and changing geological and biological conditions. Small changes in Earth's orbital pattern around the Sun also can have major effects on climate.

Meteorologists have achieved some success at predicting weather patterns in part because they are of a localized nature and of short duration. Climate, however, takes into account weather factors over a larger region and a longer timespan, and hence is much harder to predict.

Factors Affecting Earth's Climate

The primary factor that affects climate is solar radiation. About half of the Sun's energy radiated towards Earth is absorbed, but this energy is not evenly distributed across the surface. Factors that influence absorption are the transparency of the atmosphere, the angle of the Sun above Earth's surface, and the reflectivity of that surface.

The angle of the Sun above the horizon, known as the angle of incidence, determines the amount of energy striking Earth. If the angle of incidence is high, as it is in the equatorial region, with the Sun nearly perpendicular to Earth's surface, maximum energy will be spread over a small surface area with little reflection. As the angle of incidence drops, as when nearing the poles, the same amount of energy is spread over a much larger area due to the increased angle. More solar energy is reflected out of Earth's system if it comes in at an angle.

The absorption of solar energy is also influenced by Earth's orbital inclination. Because Earth is tilted on its rotational axis 23.5 degrees relative to its orbital plane around the Sun (the ecliptic), middle latitudes of the Northern Hemisphere receive about three times more solar radiation in June than in December. As Earth orbits the Sun, first the Northern Hemisphere, then the Southern Hemisphere is tilted closer to the Sun, creating the seasons. On June 21, the Sun is directly overhead at noon at the Tropic of Cancer. This date is the summer solstice of the Northern Hemisphere. By December 21, southern hemisphere solstice, the Sun is directly over the Tropic of Capricorn at 23.5 degrees south latitude.

This uneven solar heating has created climatic regions of the open ocean that run parallel to the lines of latitude. These climatic regions are relatively stable and are only slightly influenced by surface currents.

Heat Transfer. If the heat from the Sun were not redistributed, the poles would be much colder and the equator much hotter than they are. Moving currents of air and ocean water redistribute the heat over Earth. Evaporation of water at the equator adds **latent heat of vaporization** to the atmosphere. The hot, humid air rises at the equator, forming two circulation cells, one on each side.

The influence of Earth's spin causes the velocity at the equator to be much greater than the velocity near the poles. This creates the Coriolis

The world's oceans play a major role in absorbing and releasing solar energy, and providing moisture to the atmosphere. They also absorb huge amounts of carbon dioxide gas from the atmosphere.

latent heat of vaporization: the energy required to vaporize 1 gram of water, or 540 to 640 calories per gram, depending on the water temperature ranging from 100°C to 0°C

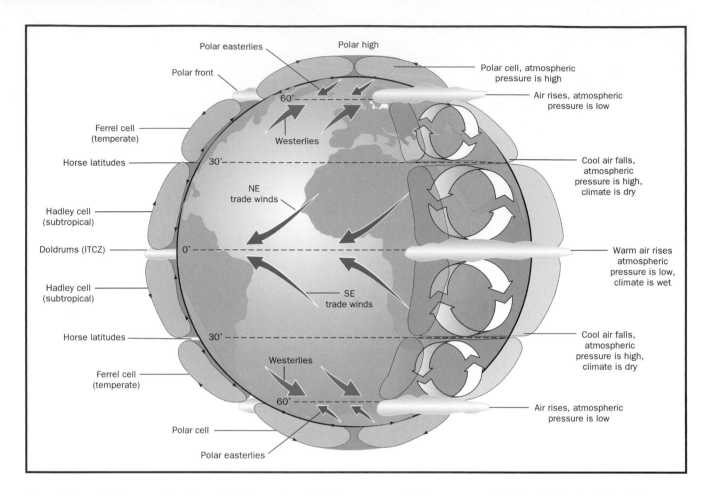

Figure 1. Atmospheric convection cells and winds on a hypothetical water-covered Earth are arranged in latitudinal bands, although they are modified by the influence of land masses. The Coriolis effect deflects air masses, either to the east (if moving away from the equator) or west (if moving toward the equator). Upwelling occurs at the equator and polar fronts, and downwelling at the poles and in mid-latitudes.

effect, deflecting moving fluids to the right in the Northern Hemisphere, and to the left in the Southern Hemisphere. The resulting complications cause each hemisphere to have three atmospheric circulation cells instead of only one.

The Hadley cells consist of hot air rising at the equator, becoming cooler and denser with movement upward and poleward, and sinking at about 30 degrees north and south latitude. Poleward of the Hadley cells, atmospheric circulation is governed by the Ferrell and Polar circulation cells (see Figure 1). The air rising and sinking at the junctures between these cells governs surface winds and atmospheric pressure across Earth.

Climate Zones

The equatorial region receives the maximum amount of solar radiation. The warm air is capable of evaporating and storing large amounts of water vapor. The warm air begins to rise, causing weak, variable surface winds, known by sailors as the "doldrums." This moist, rising air cools with altitude, generating rain showers almost daily.

Tropical regions extend north and south from the narrow equatorial region to about the Tropic of Cancer and the Tropic of Capricorn, respectively.

altitude: in navigational usage, the angle measured from the horizon to a celestial body, such as the Sun, Moon, or stars; in general usage, the height above the ground surface, called elevation if referring to height above sea level

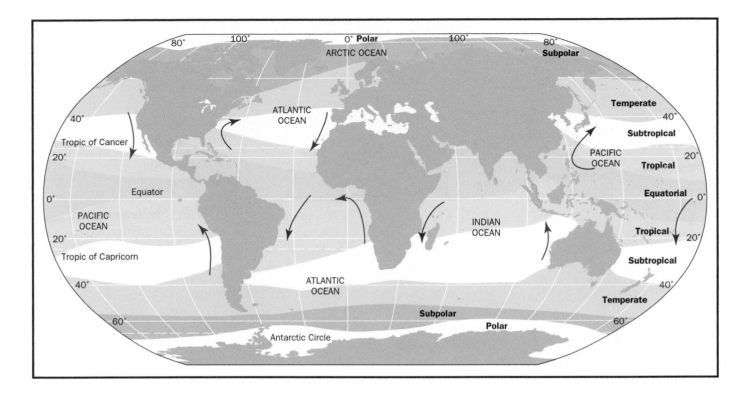

Figure 2. Equatorial, tropical, subtropical, temperate, subpolar, and polar zones are the result of uneven heating of the Earth's surface.

This is the area of trade winds, favored by early sailors where consistent winds maintain the strong equatorial currents. Rising heat and water vapor generate the tropical storms and cyclones for which this region is well known.

North and south of the tropics lies a band of hot, dry air known as the subtropical regions. Descending air creates a high-pressure belt with low precipitation, and as in the equatorial region, minimal ocean currents and weak winds. These are the so-called "horse latitudes," where the hot, dry air evaporates the ocean water at an accelerated rate.

The temperate regions lie above 40 degrees North and South latitude. The prevailing westerlies dominate this region with strong winds and unstable weather. As on land, this region is well known for storms of great size and intensity, especially when hot, moist air, as in a tropical cyclone, mixes with the cooler air of the temperate region.

The subpolar regions have predominately low pressure and areas of high precipitation. Sea-surface temperatures reach a summer high of only 5°C (41°F). This allows sea ice to form during winter months and completely cover the ocean until the spring thaw.

The polar regions constantly have high-pressure conditions and very little precipitation. Temperatures rarely rise above freezing and remain below zero most of the year. These regions have the harshest conditions on Earth. Winds seldom cease and the year is divided into six months of light, followed by six months of darkness. Only a few areas in Antarctica briefly escape the lock of the ice.

Climate Change

The study of **fossil** records indicates that Earth's climate has shifted numerous times in the geologic past. Many plant and animal species have

fossil: a preserved plant or animal imprint or remains

evolved and then disappeared throughout Earth's past. Climate change has been suggested as a possible cause for some of these mass extinctions.

Climate changes may be caused by several factors: a sudden decrease in amount of available sunlight; variations in Earth's orbit around the Sun; major changes in circulation patterns of the ocean; and changes in the amount of infrared-absorbing **greenhouse gases** in the atmosphere. The interaction of all these causes, and positive and negative feedbacks among them, make climate predictions very difficult.

greenhouse gas: a gas in the atmosphere that traps heat and reflects it back to the planetary body

Evidence additionally confirms that erupting volcanoes (e.g., Krakatoa, Pinatubo) and impacting asteroids have altered Earth's climate by filling the atmosphere with particulate matter. This is seen in the study of terrestrial outcrops of rock, and of core samples from ocean-floor sediments. If solar energy is severely restricted for an extended period, a drastic change in Earth's climate will result.

Changes in Earth's orbit may create climate changes. The tilt of the rotation axis oscillates between 22.1 and 24.5 degrees over a 40,000-year period. The shape of the orbit changes between an ellipse and a circle over a 100,000 year span. And this spin axis wobbles with an 11,000-year cycle.

Major changes in ocean circulation have important effects on global climate. For example, the geologic closing of the Isthmus of Panama caused a reorganization of currents 4 million years ago. As the Atlantic surface currents pass through the Trade Wind Belt they become saltier by evaporation of water. Instead of moving westward into the Pacific Ocean, the salty water is now blocked by Panama and flows into the North Atlantic. There it is chilled and becomes quite dense, forming the sinking North Atlantic Deep Water that begins the deep-current conveyer belt. If the surface water were fresher, it would be less dense. Instead of sinking, it might flow into polar regions and warm them. Sinking of this water initiated an **ice age**; changes in the sinking rate appear to have been closely linked to glacial and interglacial changes in the Northern Hemisphere.

ice age: a cold period marked by episodes of extensive glaciation alternating with episodes of relative warmth; the formally designated "Ice Age" refers to the most recent glacial period, which occurred during the Pleistocene epoch

glacier: a huge mass of ice, formed on land by the compaction and recrystallization of snow, which moves slowly downslope or outward owing to its own weight

Glacial and Interglacial Periods.   During long periods of cooling, snow and ice could not melt as fast as they accumulated. Over time, **glaciers** began to form and grow, causing weather changes over the huge ice masses covering the poles. Water evaporated from the oceans and was locked up as snow and ice at the higher latitudes. Because Earth holds only a finite amount of water, ocean levels began to drop. At the height of the last glacial age about 18,000 years ago, the oceans may have been as low as 150 meters (500 feet) below their present level.

Warming climates would melt glacial ice faster than it was being created, slowly recharging the ocean basins. These periods of interglaciation generally exhibited mild enough conditions to push back the polar glaciers and allow for migration and distribution of both marine and terrestrial species, including humans.

Global Warming.   Global warming will be a point of research and debate for the foreseeable future. Global warming is part of a natural cycle in the broader climate-change scenario, which is confirmed in the fossil and geologic record. However, human activity has had an impact that, if not causing global warming, is at least helping to accelerate it. Records of atmospheric CO_2 in glacial ice over time show a correlation between high CO_2 content and warming of the global climate.

Researchers agree that global warming will produce changes, but do not agree as to what exactly those changes will be or their intensity. An increase in tropical storms, heat waves, and precipitation has been suggested. The rise in global temperatures may influence the ocean's deep-water circulation patterns, which can cause rapid climate change, which in turn would affect the global distribution of plant and animal species.

Another possible change would be accelerated melting of the polar ice caps. Water released from the melting ice would cause a rise in sea level, flooding low-lying coastal areas. SEE ALSO CARBON DIOXIDE IN THE OCEAN AND ATMOSPHERE; EL NIÑO AND LA NIÑA; GLACIERS, ICE SHEETS, AND CLIMATE CHANGE; GLOBAL WARMING AND THE HYDROLOGIC CYCLE; GLOBAL WARMING AND THE OCEAN; ICE AT SEA; OCEAN CURRENTS; OCEANS, POLAR; OCEANS, TROPICAL; WEATHER AND THE OCEAN.

Ron Crouse

Bibliography

Ahrens, C. Donald. *Essentials of Meteorology, An Invitation to the Atmosphere.* Minneapolis/St. Paul, MN: West Publishing Company, 1993.

Charlson, Robert J. "The Coupling of Biogeochemical Cycles and Climate: Forcings, Feedbacks, and Responses." In *Earth System Science From Biogeochemical Cycles to Global Changes*, eds. Michael Jacobson, et al. San Diego, CA: Academic Press, 2000.

Garrison, Tom. *Oceanography, An Invitation to Marine Science.* New York: Wadsworth Publishing Company, 1996.

Philander, S. George. *Is the Temperature Rising? The Uncertain Science of Global Warming.* Princeton, NJ: Princeton University Press, 1998.

Stanley, Steven M. "Ocean Circulation: Conveyer of Past and Future Climate." In *The Earth Around Us*, ed. Jill S. Schneiderman. New York. W.H. Freeman and Company, 2000.

Thurman, Harold V., and Alan P. Trujillo. *Essentials of Oceanography.* Upper Saddle River, NJ: Prentice Hall, 1999.

Internet Resources

National Climatic Data Center. National Oceanic and Atmospheric Administration. <http://lwf.ncdc.noaa.gov/oa/ncdc.html>.

Climate Change
See Carbon Dioxide in the Ocean and Atmosphere; Climate and the Ocean; El Niño and La Niña; Glaciers, Ice Sheets, and Climate Change; Global Warming and the Hydrologic Cycle; Global Warming and the Ocean; Global Warming: Policy-Making; Ice Ages; Ice at Sea; Ice Cores and Ancient Climatic Conditions.

Climate Moderator, Water as a

Water at the Earth's surface and in the atmosphere exerts a strong moderating effect on climate. Generally speaking, the higher the water content in the air, the more moderate (less extreme) the climate.

Prince Edward Island exemplifies a region with a maritime climate, moderated by the presence of the Gulf of St. Lawrence. The mild climate makes the area suitable for growing grain crops (shown here) and potatoes.

Water Content in the Air

Proximity to water bodies causes humidity to be higher due to evaporation of water from the water surface. All other things being equal, the greater the distance from a major waterbody, the drier the air.

The ability for air to hold water in the form of water vapor varies with temperature. Hot air can have a very large water vapor content, while cold air holds very little. One measure of the actual amount of water vapor in the air is vapor pressure, which is a measure of the number of water molecules in the air compared with the number of molecules of other constituent gases in the air. Another term, saturation vapor pressure, indicates the maximum amount of water vapor that the air could hold; this is strictly a function of temperature. Relative humidity is the percentage of the actual water vapor content compared with the saturation vapor pressure. Saturated air has a relative humidity of 100 percent, whereas totally dry air (which never occurs in the atmosphere) would have a relative humidity of 0 percent.

Orographic Lifting and Rain Shadows. When air moves up and over a mountain or ridge, in a process called orographic lifting, it cools as it rises. (As the pressure decreases, the air "expands," and the air molecules move more slowly). If the rising air cools enough, its temperature will reach the dew point, the temperature at which air is saturated. At that temperature, condensation will begin; this is the point at which water vapor begins to be converted to liquid water, the result being clouds and precipitation.

Because a steep mountainside can force air upward very quickly over a short distance, orographic lift can produce heavy rain or snow along the side of the mountain range that faces the wind, if enough moisture is present in the air. In the western United States, some mountain ranges are aligned north-to-south, with their western slopes facing the Pacific Ocean and its abundant moisture. Ski resorts in the Cascade Range of Washington and Oregon, and the Lake Tahoe region in the Sierra Nevada, for example, benefit from orographically produced snowfall.

Moist air moving up the side of a mountain facing the prevailing wind causes precipitation to fall in a process known as orographic lifting. On the lee side, a rain shadow occurs, and precipitation is sparse.

When the air rises to and passes over a mountain or ridge, it begins to descend down the other side. Descending air warms, and as it does, the saturation vapor pressure increases. But because no water is being added to the air, the actual vapor pressure stays the same. Thus the relative humidity becomes lower, and the air gets drier. This process causes the lee side of the mountains (i.e., the side away from the prevailing winds) to be a zone of limited precipitation known as a rain shadow. Rain shadows are major contributors to the climate of certain parts of the world. In the example above, the regions east of the Cascades in Oregon and Washington, and east of the Sierra Nevada Mountains in California, are **arid** as a result of the rain shadow effect.

arid: describes a climate or region where precipitation is exceeded by evaporation; in these regions, agricultural crop production is impractical or impossible without irrigation

Lake-Effect Snow. Lake-effect snow is a localized, and sometimes heavy, snow that develops downwind of large lakes. In the United States, it is most common south and east of the Great Lakes, where residents experience the highest annual snowfall totals anywhere east of the Rocky Mountains. A related phenomenon, called sea-effect snow, occurs in coastal regions when cold air spreads over warmer ocean water.

In these processes, the air passing over water picks up moisture, which rises and forms clouds that produce snow. At least 80 kilometers (50 miles) of fetch (the length of lake over which air travels) is required for a significant lake-effect snow. A greater temperature difference between the air and water enhances the cloud-forming and snow-forming process, as does steeply rising terrain downwind of a lake. Wind direction also affects the snow intensity.

Although a lake-effect process may not always produce snow, the amount of snow that can fall in these events can be enormous, reaching rates of 12.5 centimeters (5 inches) per hour. Parts of the Tug Hill Plateau in upstate New York receive an average of 625 centimeters (250 inches) of snow each winter, more than six times the typical amount in areas not in lake-effect regions.

greenhouse effect: the phenomenon whereby a planetary body's atmosphere traps solar radiation; caused by the presence in the atmosphere of gases such as carbon dioxide, water vapor, and methane, that allow incoming sunlight to pass through but trap heat radiated back from the body's surface

Moderation of Air Temperature

Water vapor is the main reason for the greenhouse effect, in which certain gases in the atmosphere allow sunlight to pass through, but absorb heat released from the Earth (when sunlight strikes the Earth it changes from visible light to infrared radiation, or heat). Without this effect the Earth would be about 33°C cooler than it is at present (that is, 60°F cooler). Human-caused emissions, leading to increased levels of carbon dioxide (CO_2) and other gases in the atmosphere may accelerate the **greenhouse effect**.

Water vapor absorbs heat and releases it slowly. At night, when the humidity is high, the atmosphere retains more heat, and nighttime temperatures stay somewhat high. On dry nights, however, with little water vapor to absorb heat, the atmosphere cools off rapidly.

Clouds act in much the same way as high humidity. The presence of clouds means humid atmospheric conditions, and this promotes greater heat retention, and higher nighttime temperatures, than on a clear (dry) night.

Liquid water at the surface also can play a significant role in climate moderation. Water takes much longer than air to heat up, and also longer to cool, because it has much higher specific heat. Thus, on hot days, water (oceans, lakes, and rivers) absorbs heat, keeping the air somewhat cooler. When the air gets cool, however, water slowly releases heat to the atmosphere, raising air temperatures. This is why temperatures along coastlines are cooler in summer and warmer in winter relative to inland areas (see sidebar). Temperature vary more the farther inland one travels. There is some moderation of climate because condensation is an exothermic process, and warms the atmosphere, particularly in wet coastal areas (i.e., downwind from the ocean).

As an example of how distance from the ocean influences air temperature, consider the states of Oregon and Washington. The Cascades Range divides the two states into a western region, west of the mountains, and an eastern region, east of the mountains. The climate of the western region is moderated by the Pacific Ocean, and is mild and moist. But the eastern region is relatively dry (the rainshadow effect) and warm, even hot.

The coastal city of Astoria, Oregon experiences warmer daily minimum temperatures and cooler maximum temperatures than Pendleton, Oregon which is about 400 kilometers (250 miles) inland, and separated from the ocean by the Cascades. Astoria's average monthly temperatures also exhibit a smaller range: 5.5°C (41.9°F) in January, the coolest month (compared to Pendleton's 0.8°C [33.5°F]) and 16°C (60.9°F) in the hottest month, August (compared to Pendleton's 22.7°C [72.9°F] in July, its hottest month).

Ironically, although higher humidities mean more moderate temperatures, to human and animals they feel more extreme. A 32°C-day (90°F) in Arizona feels hot, but the same temperature on a humid summer day in Washington, D.C. feels stifling. Similarly, a cold, dry day feels less extreme than a humid day at the same temperature. These effects, again, are due to water's specific heat—its ability to conduct heat (or cold) compared to dry air. SEE ALSO AGRICULTURE AND WATER; CLIMATE AND THE OCEAN; FRESH WATER, PHYSICS AND CHEMISTRY OF; PRECIPITATION, GLOBAL DISTRIBUTION OF.

George H. Taylor

SEA AND LAND BREEZES

A sea breeze occurs in the daytime along the shore of an ocean or large lake when air over the sun-heated land becomes warmer than air over the adjacent, relatively cool ocean. The heated air over land rises, creating a localized low pressure zone into which the cooler sea air moves (because air moves from higher to lower pressure). A sea breeze helps keep daytime coastal temperature pleasantly mild, even though inland areas may be hot.

At night, the air over the rapidly cooling land becomes cooler than the air over the relatively warm ocean. Because the lower air pressure is now over the ocean, the wind blows from land to water in what is known as a land breeze.

Bibliography

Schneider, Stephen Henry. *Encyclopedia of Climate and Weather.* New York: Oxford University Press, 1996.

Stein, Paul. *Macmillan Encyclopedia of Weather.* New York: Macmillan Reference USA, 2001.

Internet Resources

National Weather Service, National Oceanic and Atmospheric Administration. <http://www.nws.noaa.gov>.

Clouds *See Precipitation and Clouds, Formation of.*

Coastal Ocean

When you take a waterfront vacation, do you say you are going to the beach or going to the coast? Both the beach and the coast are places where the land meets the sea, but the names reflect the variety of features and conditions that may exist there. Sandy beaches, rocky cliffs, tidal flats, or barrier islands may develop depending on the coastal geology and **topography**, the size of the waves, the range of the tides, and the climate.

The coastal zone represents a small area compared to the whole world ocean, but it is a dynamic setting, and it is where the most people come in contact with ocean processes. The often rapid natural changes that occur on the coast have an immediate effect on human-made structures and recreation.

Beaches

Sandy beaches exist along much of the East and Gulf Coasts of the United States. Sandy beaches develop where the tidal range is not too great (less than about 2 meters or 6.5 feet), and waves from the open ocean strike the shore.

A rugged, rocky coastline like that found in Maine or along parts of the West Coast of the United States may have no beach at all. Erosion of the cliffs may produce smaller beaches in coves, sometimes consisting of gravel and cobbles instead of sand. The dominant process in these areas is erosion of the existing coastline by wave action. Plants and animals living along rocky coastlines must be adapted to deal with the high turbulence by clinging tightly to the rocks or hiding under them.

Beach Sands. Most beaches in North America are composed of quartz sand along with a few other minor mineral grains. However, in the southernmost areas where the climate is warmer, calcium carbonate ($CaCO_3$) sands form. These sands are commonly much whiter and comprise the beaches of parts of Florida and the Bahamas. Calcium carbonate sands are made of shell and coral fragments as well as **ooids** precipitated directly from sea water. Warm, tropical seas are supersaturated with dissolved calcium carbonate; therefore, the mineral **precipitates** much more readily than in northern climates. Shorelines with calcium carbonate sediments are still affected by waves and currents and can also be molded into beaches, barrier islands, and tidal flats. Many ancient limestones originated in this type of setting.

topography: the shape and contour of a surface, especially the land surface

ooid: a small (0.5 to 2 millimeter), spherical object composed of concentric layers of calcium carbonate that has grown in concentric rings, often around some kind of nucleus such as a quartz grain

precipitate: (verb) the process by which a solution separates into a relatively clear liquid and a solid substance by a chemical or physical change; (noun) the solid substance resulting from this process

Rocky shorelines like this one in Oregon are dominated by wave erosion and may have few sandy beaches. Here the headlands are composed of resistant basalt.

weathering: the decay or breakdown of rocks and minerals through a complex interaction of physical, chemical, and biological processes; water is the most important agent of weathering; soil is formed through weathering processes

Beaches surrounding volcanic islands such as Hawaii may have black and green sands. Black sands are produced by the action of surf pounding black basaltic lava flows into sand-sized fragments. Less common are green sands composed of the mineral olivine. Olivine is an iron-rich mineral common in basalts. It is an unstable mineral at surface **weathering** conditions, and can only accumulate as sand when an abundant source of basalt is present.

Beach Zones. A typical beach can be separated into three zones: the supratidal, intertidal, and subtidal. The supratidal zone is normally above the level of the ocean except during large storms such as hurricanes. Dry sand blown from lower on the beach accumulates in dunes paralleling the shore and may be stabilized by dune vegetation. The intertidal zone is a sloping, nearly planar surface between the high and low tide marks. This is the swash zone where waves break onto the beach. The size of the intertidal zone depends on the tidal range; the greater the tidal range, the larger the intertidal zone. Because of the constant wave action in the intertidal zone, few animals can live on the surface. Burrowers such as bivalves and crabs live in protected tunnels in the sand.

The subtidal part of the beach is the shallow area just offshore that is never exposed by tides. It typically has a series of submarine sandbars that parallel the shoreline. The sandbars tend to move offshore in the winter when there are more storms and onshore in the calmer summers. The subtidal beach is strongly affected by waves as well as longshore drift.

Longshore Drift. Longshore drift is the movement of sand along the shoreface by shallow currents. These longshore currents are generated because waves do not normally strike the shore exactly perpendicular. The result of countless waves striking at an oblique angle moves ocean water along the beach and transports sand grains. This slow drift of sand parallel to the beach is the reason many shorelines are so straight or smoothly curved. When human-made structures such as groins are placed along the beach,

A black lava sand beach in Hawaii contrasts with a white calcium carbonate sand beach, such as found in Florida and the Bahamas. Beach materials can derive from erosion of rocks and coral reefs by ocean waves, from delivery of sediments by rivers intersecting the coastline, and from other processes.

the flow of sand is interrupted. **Dredging** and pumping of sand often are required to artificially restore beaches.

dredging: the process of excavating sediments and other materials, usually from underwater locations, for the purpose of mining aggregate (sand and gravel), constructing new waterways, or maintaining existing waterway cross-sections

Barrier Islands

In some areas such as the Carolinas and Texas, the beaches are separated from the land by lagoons. These lagoons are shallow bodies of water that are protected from open-ocean waves by a barrier island. A barrier island may be only a few hundred meters wide, but dissipates the wave energy, so that the lagoons generally have small waves and accumulate finer sediments such as silt. Otherwise, the seaward side of a barrier island is the same as a normal beach. Human-made structures on barrier islands, as well as the islands themselves, are very susceptible to the forces of hurricanes.

Because the lagoons are affected by tides, the water must flow in and out from the ocean through tidal inlets that cut the barrier island. The number of inlets is related to the tidal range and how much water moves through them daily.

Tides

The greatest tidal range on the planet is the Bay of Fundy in eastern Canada, where the tides rise and drop 15 meters (nearly 50 feet) every day. Areas where the tidal range is more than 4 meters (13 feet) are called macrotidal. Along a macrotidal shoreline such as near Anchorage, Alaska, the intertidal zone is so wide that a tidal flat forms instead of a beach. The ebb and flow of the tides generate tidal currents that move sediment across the tidal flats in tidal creeks. The creeks have tributaries and look much like a river system, except that water flows in both directions.

Even a small barrier island helps dissipate wave energy before it reaches the shore. This narrow arc of land may be a temporary feature, because it can easily be eroded or inundated.

The tidal range varies from one region to another, but it also varies at the same point during the month. Because the tides are due to the gravitational pull of the Moon, and to a lesser extent the Sun, the Sun and Moon will align with the Earth and act together to produce *spring tides*, or will counteract each other at right angles to generate *neap tides*. Spring tides have a greater range (higher high tides and lower low tides) and occur when the Moon is in the full and new phases. Neap tides have a lesser range and occur at the first and third quarter phases of the Moon. Many marine organisms such as turtles and horseshoe crabs acutely tune their time of breeding to the spring tides. SEE ALSO ALGAL BLOOMS IN THE OCEAN; BEACHES; BIVALVES; CLIMATE AND THE OCEAN; COASTAL WATERS MANAGEMENT; CORALS AND CORAL REEFS; CRUSTACEANS; ESTUARIES; HUMAN HEALTH AND THE OCEAN; OCEANOGRAPHY, GEOLOGICAL; OIL SPILLS: IMPACT ON THE OCEAN; TIDES; WAVES; WEATHER AND THE OCEAN.

David M. Rohr

Bibliography

Duxbury, Alyn C., Alison B. Duxbury, and Keith A. Sverdrup. *An Introduction to the World's Oceans, 6th ed.* Boston, MA: McGraw-Hill, 2000.

Kaufman, Wallace, and Orrin H. Pilkey. *The Beaches Are Moving: The Drowning of America's Shoreline.* Durham, NC: Duke University Press, 1983.

Scholle, Peter, and Darwin Spearing. *Sandstone Depositional Environments.* Tulsa, OK: American Association of Petroleum Geologists, 1982.

Scholle, Peter, Don Bebout, and Clyde Moore. *Carbonate Depositional Environments.* Tulsa, OK: American Association of Petroleum Geologists, 1983.

Coastal Waters Management

Americans love the seashore and the water. Nearly half of all the construction in the United States since the 1970s has been on the seacoast. By the year 2000, 80 percent of Americans lived an hour's drive or less from the seashore. The National Oceanic and Atmospheric Administration, the primary federal agency responsible for managing the oceans, has projected that by 2010 half of all Americans will be living in coastal counties. Globally almost two-thirds of the world's largest cities are coastal. Sixty percent of people on Earth live within 97 kilometers (60 miles) of the sea.

The reasons why so many humans are coastal dwellers are that coastal areas and oceans have provided a large part of the food that people eat, and have served as the major transportation highways long before there were adequate roads, railroads, or airplanes. The coasts are desirable places to live, offering recreational opportunities such as swimming, boating, fishing, snorkeling, and diving. Coastal areas also are home to marine mammals and other sea life, and can be rich in minerals and other energy sources.

The Need for Coastal Management

This massive habitation at and growing migration to the ocean's edge has brought with it serious side effects. More people have increased the need for infrastructure such as roads, sewers, sewage treatment facilities, bridges,

Coastal zone management programs seek to protect rugged and remote shorelines as well as heavily used beaches. All coastal habitats are vulnerable to pollution and overdevelopment.

People flock to beaches and coasts for recreation, business, and home ownership. Coordinated management is needed to protect the land and water quality of coastal environments.

brackish: describes water having a salinity from 0.05 to 17 parts per thousand; typically a mixture of sea water and fresh water (e.g., as found in an estuary)

ecosystem: the community of plants and animals within a water or terrestrial habitat interacting together and with their physical and chemical environment

global warming: an increase in the average temperature of the Earth's atmosphere, especially a sustained increase sufficient to cause climatic change

fresh-water sources, and solid waste (garbage) disposal. The increased human activity has strained the ability of nature to replenish and clean itself. Therefore, Americans have gradually established regulations to guide how the seashore is developed and how coastal waters are managed. The three major water resources to examine are (1) the ocean itself, (2) **brackish** waters, and (3) fresh waters.

Ocean.   The ocean itself is often considered the planet's most vital **ecosystem** for making life possible. Oceans comprise 97 percent by volume of all the Earth's living space for plants, animals, and humans. The oceans contain vast living and nonliving resources. Reefs, beaches, and other areas are among the ocean environments directly affected by the quality and temperature of the water. Moreover, coastal areas have served as the entry and exit point for what has always been and still is the major mode of commercial transportation: marine shipping.

Ocean temperatures and the flow of currents are vitally important in regulating climate. Many scientists have shown that the rising temperature of the oceans could be contributing to **global warming**. In addition, warming temperatures may cause polar ice to melt, which would raise the level of the oceans and cause vast flooding in the heavily populated seaside areas.

The ground under oceans, especially near coastal areas, contains enormous oil and gas resources. As easy and ample supplies of these hydrocarbons so necessary for an energy-intensive economy and society such as the United States become scarce, pressure increases to commercialize these suboceanic sources of energy.

Drilling for, pumping, and transporting ocean-based oil and gas resources to onshore refineries without creating serious damage to the water and marine life is a delicate process. Both federal and state laws regulating offshore drilling are constantly being reexamined. The interests of oil companies, electric power-generating plants, consumers who enjoy affordable energy, and environmentalists can sometimes collide.

Brackish Waters.   Rivers and their coastal **estuaries** supply coastal areas with brackish water. Estuaries are extremely important habitats for a wide variety of animal and plant life. Turtles, fish, crabs, clams, mussels, and other sea life (including coastal mammals) all benefit from healthy estuaries and other coastal **wetlands** that often are the nurseries for young animals.

Coastal wetlands and marshes also act as sponges and filters, retaining water and slowing or preventing it from rushing uncontrollably downstream, which would produce erosion. These wetlands also slowly filter out **sediments** and chemical **contaminants** that otherwise would reach the ocean.

Development as well as contamination from pesticides and herbicides, industrial pollutants, sewage spills, and other sources of pollution are degrading the quality of coastal ecosystems. For example, in the 1990s a huge area deemed the "Dead Zone" was discovered in the Gulf of Mexico at the mouth of the Mississippi River. This area, covering 12,800 square kilometers (5,000 square miles), is almost devoid of any life as a result of runoff containing **nitrates** (a component of some fertilizers), pesticides, herbicides, and other chemicals from farms and industries upriver. The Dead Zone threatens fish, shrimp, and other commercial seafood, as well as recreational fishing, and is a potential risk to tourism.

Fresh Waters.   Construction and intensive development are threatening fresh **groundwater** that is especially vulnerable at sea level. Streams, springs, and **aquifers** easily can be contaminated by runoff from streets and parking lots. Fresh-water issues also include proper management of the Great Lakes, which are considered part of the coastal zones of the United States because of their vast sizes.

One of the most serious fresh-water problems is infiltration by sea (salt) water, often known as salt-water intrusion. Fresh water is in short supply in most areas of the United States, but it is especially precious in coastal zones because of the demand for fresh water for drinking, cooking, bathing, irrigation of crops and lawns, and industrial uses. In April 2001, for example, the state of Florida asked for a waiver of federal law, which would allow the state to pump untreated rainwater into underground aquifers that were being depleted at rates much faster than natural seepage could replace them.

Coastal Zone Management Act

In order to protect the salt-water and fresh-water resources of the American coastal areas described above, numerous federal laws have been enacted. The most important is the Coastal Zone Management Act (CZMA) of 1972. This law resulted from several studies that showed extensive pollution of the nation's estuaries and that recommended action to clean these up. The legislation also was the result of a growing awareness of environmental problems in the United States, and active pressure from environmental groups such as the Sierra Club, the Audubon Society, and groups such as the Friends of the Earth and the Natural Resources Defense Council.

The CZMA provides for a wide range of programs and regulations of which the following are the most significant:

• Protection of the estuaries and coastal wetlands;

• Protection of beaches, dunes, bluffs, and rocky shores;

estuary: a tidally influenced coastal area in which fresh water from a river mixes with sea water, generally at the river mouth; the resulting water is brackish, which results in a unique ecosystem

wetland: an area that is periodically or permanently saturated or covered by surface water or groundwater, that displays hydric soils, and that typically supports or is capable of supporting hydrophytic vegetation

sediment: rock particles and other earth materials that are transported and deposited over time by geologic agents such as running water, wind, glaciers, and gravity; sediments may be exposed on dry land and are common on ocean and lake bottoms and river beds

contaminant: as defined by the U.S. Environmental Protection Agency, any physical, chemical, biological, or radiological substance in water, including constituents that may not be harmful to the environment or human health

nitrate: the highly leachable form of soil nitrogen taken up by most plants through their roots; it is a common groundwater contaminant, especially in agricultural areas and locations with a high density of septic systems, that is regulated by the U.S. Environmental Protection Agency with a drinking water standard of 10 ppm (parts per million) of nitrogen in the nitrate form

groundwater: generally, all subsurface (underground) water, as distinct from surface water, that supplies natural springs, contributes to permanent streams, and can be tapped by wells; specifically, the water that is in the saturated zone of a defined aquifer

aquifer: a water-saturated, permeable, underground rock formation that can transmit significant quantities of water under ordinary hydraulic gradients to wells and springs

- Regulation of seaport development; and

- Redevelopment of urban ports.

Today over 97 percent of the U.S. shoreline is under the CZMA program.

Over the years, the CZMA has been strengthened and expanded. Moreover, additional specialized laws and regulations have been enacted that extend the management of water and coastal resources. The objective of these laws directed at the waters and lands along the seacoast is to lay out a strategic land-use policy that will protect coastal water resources and beaches. The objective of land-use policy is to achieve sustainable development of these coastal resources; that is, using them so that they do not deteriorate but instead have a chance to replenish themselves for future generations.

Clearly, coastal water management is a vitally important process for the future prosperity, continued enjoyment, and effective economic use of oceans, beaches, seashores, and coastal waters. SEE ALSO ARTIFICIAL RECHARGE; BALANCING DIVERSE INTERESTS; COASTAL OCEAN; ESTUARIES; LAND-USE PLANNING; MINERAL RESOURCES FROM THE OCEAN; NATIONAL OCEANIC AND ATMOSPHERIC ADMINISTRATION; OCEAN HEALTH, ASSESSING; PETROLEUM FROM THE OCEAN; POLLUTION OF GROUNDWATER; POLLUTION OF LAKES AND STREAMS; POLLUTION OF THE OCEAN BY PLASTIC AND TRASH; PORTS AND HARBORS; TRANSPORTATION.

Steffen W. Schmidt

Bibliography

Barker, Rodney. *And the Waters Turned to Blood: The Ultimate Biological Threat.* New York: Simon & Schuster, 1997.

Cicin-Sain, Biliana, and Robert W. Knecht *The Future of U.S. Ocean Policy: Choices for the New Century.* Washington, D.C.: Island Press, 2000.

Dean, Cornelia. *Against the Tide.* New York: Columbia University Press, 1999.

Internet Resources

Celebrating 30 Years of the Coastal Zone Management Act. Office of Ocean and Coastal Resource Management, National Ocean Service, National Oceanic and Atmospheric Administration. <http://www.ocrm.nos.noaa.gov/czm/>.

EPA Action Plan for Beaches and Recreational Waters. U.S. Environmental Protection Agency. <http://www.epa.gov/ORD/WebPubs/beaches/>.

Gulf of Mexico Hypoxia Assessment. National Ocean Service. <http://www.nos.noaa.gov/products/pubs_hypox.html>.

headwaters: the source or upper reaches of a stream; also the upper reaches of a reservoir

irrigation: the controlled application of water for agricultural or other purposes through human-made systems; generally refers to water application to soil when rainfall is insufficient to maintain desirable soil moisture for plant growth

hydroelectric: often used synonymously with "hydropower," describes electricity generated by utilizing the power of falling water, as with water flowing through and turning turbines at a dam

Colorado River Basin

Located in the southwestern United States and northwestern Mexico, the Colorado River is a 2,330-kilometer (1,450-mile) river with its **headwaters** in the Rocky Mountain National Park in north-central Colorado. The river is the primary source of water for a region that receives little annual rainfall.

More than 1,000 years ago, Native Americans irrigated their crops with the waters from the river. Today, the Colorado River is still used for **irrigation,** but it is also used to generate **hydroelectric** power and to supply water to distant urban areas.

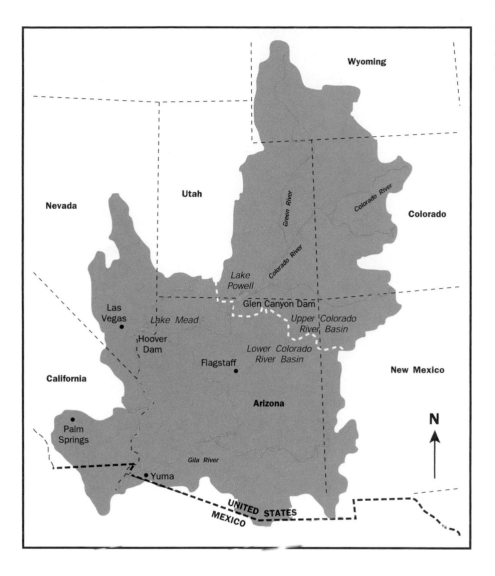

The Colorado River has been a central feature in the history and development of the American West. Management efforts in the Colorado River Basin embody society's struggle to overcome conflicts between competing interests over a shared water resource.

The Basin

The Colorado River system, including the Colorado River, its **tributaries**, and the lands that these waters drain, is called the Colorado River basin, or watershed. It drains an area of 637,000 square kilometers (246,000 square miles), including parts of seven western U.S. states (Wyoming, Colorado, Utah, New Mexico, Nevada, Arizona, California) and Mexico. Three-fourths of the Colorado basin is federal land comprised of national forests, national parks, and Indian reservations. The drainage basin's total runoff is about 700 cubic meters (24,700 cubic feet) per second. It is the international boundary for 27 kilometers (17 miles) between Arizona and Mexico.

tributary: a smaller stream that flows into a larger stream

Water Resources.   The Colorado River Basin offers a major renewable water supply in the southwestern United States. About two-thirds of the water flowing in the Colorado River and its tributaries is used for irrigation, and the other one-third supplies urban areas, evaporates into the atmosphere, or provides water to riparian (streamside) vegetation. Without Colorado River water, the region would support few crops, and major cities such as Las Vegas, Nevada, and Phoenix, Arizona, would not have grown so rapidly.

A young member of the Cocopah Indians of northern Mexico plays in a dried-up arm of the Colorado River near the town of El Mayor, Mexico. The Colorado River, on which the Cocopah people fished and farmed for about 2,000 years, is often drained dry by upstream demand before reaching this part of Baja, California.

Today nearly 17 million people depend on the Colorado's waters. The basin population has expanded dramatically in recent years, with most growth occurring in urban areas, where about 80 percent of the region's residents live. Phoenix and Tucson, Arizona, and Las Vegas, Nevada are the largest cities in the basin, and they use the Colorado River and its tributaries as their primary source of water.

Water from the Colorado River is taken from its primary route and transported to locations far from the Colorado River Basin. For example, water is diverted eastward across the Rocky Mountains to Denver and other cities in Colorado. The Colorado River Aqueduct carries water to metropolitan Los Angeles, and the Central Arizona Project supplies the Phoenix and Tucson areas. The All-American Canal provides water for the Imperial Valley of southern California, a productive agricultural region converted from a desert.

Multipurpose Dams. Numerous dams were built on the Colorado and its tributaries during the twentieth century. The purpose of these dams was primarily to generate electricity, control floods, and provide recreational opportunities. They also store water during wet times for use during the dry months and, in some cases, during dry years.

The basin dams are able to store more than 86 billion cubic meters (3,037 billion cubic feet) of water, which is about four times the Colorado River's average annual runoff. The largest of these facilities, completed in 1936, is Hoover Dam, located on the border between Nevada and Arizona. The second largest dam is Glen Canyon Dam, which is in north-central

Arizona and began operating in 1964. These two dams provide about 80 percent of the water-storage capacity in the basin.

The Morelos Diversion Dam, located on the Mexico–Arizona border, is the southernmost dam on the Colorado River. It sends nearly all of the remaining water to irrigation canals in the Mexicali Valley and to the Mexican towns of Mexicali and Tijuana. As a result, the river rarely reaches the Gulf of California, normally the river's mouth. Consequently, the vast wetlands at the mouth of the Colorado River have been reduced to just a fraction of their former size, affecting vegetation and wildlife. Before the construction of a number of dams along its reach, the Colorado flowed 129 kilometers (80 miles) through Mexico to the Gulf of California.

Hydroelectric generation from water stored at dam sites along the Colorado River totals about 12 billion kilowatt-hours per year, which is roughly equivalent to one-sixth of the electricity consumed in Arizona each year. This power is shared among several western states.

The dams of the Colorado River are used to control flooding and to permit development of flood-prone land along lower reaches. In addition, some of the **reservoirs** created by dams have been formed into national recreational areas comprising spectacular engineered wonders amidst natural landscapes. For example, Lake Mead National Recreation Area is made up of Lake Mead, formed by Hoover Dam, and Lake Mohave, formed by Davis Dam, while the Glen Canyon National Recreation Area includes Lake Powell.

reservoir: a pond, lake, basin, or tank for the storage, regulation, and control of water; more commonly refers to artificial impoundments rather than natural ones

Management Efforts

The Colorado Basin states were anxious about their shares of the Colorado River as early as the 1900s. Then as now, growth within the state of California was viewed with concern, as burgeoning expansion meant increased water demands. The signing of the Colorado River Compact in 1922 was an important milestone in the management of the Colorado River and became the foundation for the law of the river. This compact included the seven Colorado River Basin states, and apportioned water from the Colorado River between the Upper and Lower Basin states. The parties to the Colorado River compact were not unduly concerned with Indian water rights, nor did the Compact include provisions to protect the environment.

In 1963, a U.S. Supreme Court decision stated the amount of water to be apportioned among the lower-basin states, as well as the amounts that had been historically reserved for Indian tribes and federal public lands. Because of this landmark case, tribes are now considered to have the best water rights along the Lower Colorado River. The competition for water in the Colorado River Basin continues to be severe, as is shown by the increasing numbers of lawsuits that are within the court system. Water projects must now thoroughly research various environmental-impact studies in accordance with federal environmental protection legislation.

The apportionment of the waters of Colorado River has been cause for a great deal of controversy. The impact of dams and canals along the Colorado has spawned widespread debate on river development and the ecological role of instream flows. Given projected growth in its region, these controversies and debates will continue for some time.

Salinity. A water quality problem that has grown in importance within the Colorado River is salinity, or the amount of solids (mostly salt) in the water. A variety of sources bring such dissolved salts into the river. The majority of salts run naturally off of soils and rocks. When river water is used for irrigation, some salts evaporate, and become concentrated in the remaining water that returns to the river. The salt problem is also caused by evaporation from reservoir surfaces and water use by plants along the river. The concentration of salt in the water of the lower river valley is so high that it cannot be used for human consumption without treatment. As a result, a desalinization plant near the border with Mexico removes salt from the river and allows the United States to provide Mexico with usable water.

Significant water quality problems occur in the Colorado River Basin, primarily because the river carries an estimated 9 million tons of salts annually. This amount is expected to increase in the future because of increased human use. Even worse, the lower Colorado River contains about 2,000 pounds of salts per acre-foot. Salinity increases downstream primarily owing to agriculture, evaporation, and the leaching of salts from soils. High salinity levels also originate in several tributaries, especially the Virgin River that flows through Arizona into Nevada. Environmental groups study the high salinity in the Colorado River and regularly meet to address this issue and other related water quality problems. SEE ALSO DAMS; DESALINIZATION; HOOVER DAM; INSTREAM WATER ISSUES; PLANNING AND MANAGEMENT, WATER RESOURCES; POWELL, JOHN WESLEY; PRIOR APPROPRIATION; RESERVOIRS, MULTIPURPOSE; RIGHTS, PUBLIC WATER; RIVER BASIN PLANNING; SUPPLY DEVELOPMENT.

William Arthur Atkins

Bibliography

Graf, William L. *The Colorado River: Instability and Basin Management.* Washington D.C.: Association of American Geographers, 1985.

Waters, Frank. *The Colorado.* New York: Rinehart, 1946.

Internet Resources

Colorado River Basin Salinity Control Program. Bureau of Reclamation, U.S. Department of the Interior. <http://www.uc.usbr.gov/progact/salinity/>.

Colorado River Water Dispute (COLORADO Case). American University, Washington, D.C. <http://www.american.edu/ted/COLORADO.HTM>.

Gillon, Kara (Defenders of Wildlife). *The Lower Colorado River Basin: Challenges of Transboundary Ecosystem Management.* Border Information and Outreach Service (BIOS), Interhemispheric Resource Center (IRC). <http://www.us-mex.org/borderlines/2000/bl68/bl68rivbasin.html>.

The Colorado River: Lifeline of the Southwest. DesertUSA.com, Digital West Media, Inc. <http://www.desertusa.com/colorado/coloriv/du_coloriv.html>.

Columbia River Basin

The Columbia River is one of the most dominant environmental features of the Pacific Northwest. Beginning high in the mountains of southeastern British Columbia, the Columbia River flows 2,000 kilometers (1,243 miles) through alpine and subalpine environments, montane forests, lava fields, **semiarid** grasslands, and low-elevation rainforests before entering the Pacific Ocean.

semiarid: a climate or region where moisture is normally greater than under arid conditions but still limits the growth of most crops; either dryland farming methods or irrigation generally are required for crop production

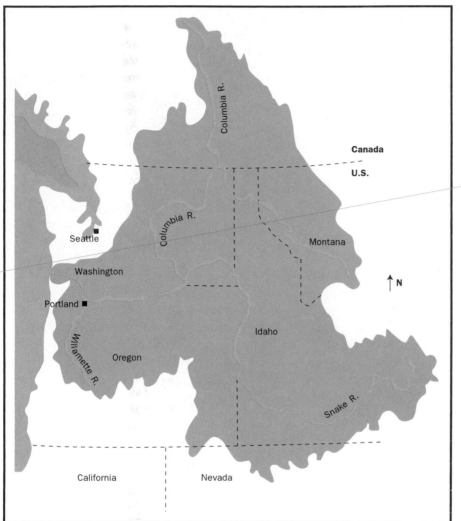

The Columbia River Basin embodies the major challenges of river basin planning and management in the twenty-first century. It is particularly known for its vast network of hydroelectric dams and the environmental and cultural controversies surrounding them.

Draining more than 671,000 square kilometers (259,100 square miles), the Columbia River Basin is the fourth largest river basin in the United States. It encompasses seven states (Washington, Oregon, Idaho, Montana, Wyoming, Nevada, and Utah) and one Canadian province (British Columbia), more than a dozen Indian reservations, and numerous local jurisdictions. This complex physical and jurisdictional landscape makes managing the Great River of the West an exceptional challenge.

Native and Non-Native Settlement

Archaeologists have found evidence of human occupation of the Columbia River Basin dating back more than 10,000 years, though many of the basin's Native peoples argue that they have always been in the region. The Columbia River was and still is a central feature in the life of Native peoples, providing food, water, and transportation. Salmon was a keystone resource, providing a significant percentage of their protein; it was also an important trade item. Despite thousands of years of heavy use, under Native peoples' stewardship the Columbia River remained a diverse, highly productive **ecosystem** well into the nineteenth century.

ecosystem: the community of plants and animals within a water or terrestrial habitat interacting together and with their physical and chemical environment

Non-Native peoples began moving into the basin in notable numbers during the 1840s and 1850s, pushing Native peoples onto reservations and imposing a radically different management regime on the river. Early non-Native use of the river paralleled that of the Indians'—fishing for salmon, using the river as a transportation conduit, locating settlements on the flat, fertile floodplains. But as technology evolved and the basin's population expanded in the latter half of the nineteenth century, demands on the river greatly increased. Irrigation ditches, **hydroelectric** dams, commercial fisheries, the **dredging** of navigation channels, and the input of pollutants had all effected major changes in the river's physical and biological characteristics by the early twentieth century.

While many of the Columbia's **tributaries** were dammed and ditched in the late nineteenth and early twentieth centuries, it was not until the 1930s that the mainstem of the Columbia was developed. Responding to the Great Depression, the U.S. government built Bonneville and Grand Coulee dams, the latter of which was the largest dam in the world at the time and is still the country's largest single power producer. Today there are more than 400 dams in the basin, including 14 on the mainstem—projects that generate an average of 12,000 **megawatts** a year, accounting for about 40 percent of the United States' hydroelectric power and for up to 75 percent in the Pacific Northwest. The total hydropower production of the Columbia system roughly equals 20 nuclear power plants running full-time.

Impacts of Dams

The dams on the Columbia River and its major tributaries form the backbone of the Pacific Northwest's economy, providing power to homes and industry, controlling floodwaters, irrigating hundreds of thousands of **hectares** of farmland, and forming an extensive navigation system. However, these benefits have come at an exceptionally high environmental cost.

Annual runs of Columbia River salmon have declined from an estimated 8 to 16 million to an average of fewer than 1 million, and a dozen **stocks** have been listed as either threatened or endangered under the U.S. Endangered Species Act. In addition to blocking access to spawning grounds, dams alter the seasonal flow of the river, prevent juvenile salmon from migrating downstream to the ocean, increase the abundance of fish predators, and change water quality by raising the temperature and increasing the amount of nitrogen in the water.

Though dams are a major factor in the decline of salmon, they are not the only one. Overfishing, logging, irrigation withdrawals, urban pollution, **channelization**, road construction, the introduction of nonnative fish, and other activities have also contributed to the decline of salmon and other native fish populations.

Institutional Complexities

While river management in the Columbia River Basin historically focused on the creation of economic benefits (e.g., hydroelectric power and flood control), the focus in recent years has shifted to ecosystem management and restoration. Salmon have been at the center of this important shift in management philosophy, but a variety of obstacles have stood in the way of effective restoration.

hydroelectric: often used synonymously with "hydropower," describes electricity generated by utilizing the power of falling water, as with water flowing through and turning turbines at a dam

dredging: the process of excavating sediments and other materials, usually from underwater locations, for the purpose of mining aggregate (sand and gravel), constructing new waterways, or maintaining existing waterway cross-sections

tributary: a smaller stream that flows into a larger stream

megawatt: a unit of power equal to one million watts, where the watt corresponds to the rate of energy in an electric circuit

hectare: a metric unit of area equal to 10,000 square meters (107,639 square feet or 2.471 acres)

stock: (noun) a distinct population of fish or aquatic resource, defined on the basis of population biology and commonly used in the context of conservation biology and the particular fishery; (verb) to add fish or aquatic animals to a waterbody for the purpose of either conservation or sport

channelization: any excavation and construction activities intended to widen, deepen, straighten, or relocate a natural river channel; the term does not include maintenance activities on existing channels, such as the clearing of debris or dredging of accumulated sediments

Native tribes in the Canadian and U.S. portions of the Columbia River Basin still rely on its fish and wildlife for sustenance, economic benefit, and cultural preservation. Salmon restoration continues to be the most far-reaching challenge for managers, scientists, politicians, and legal experts.

Some argue that one of the most significant obstacles to successful integrated ecosystem management is institutional fragmentation. The Columbia River Basin is under the jurisdiction of two countries, several states, more than a dozen tribes, and numerous local agencies. Even among federal river managers there is a substantial amount of institutional fragmentation. The Bonneville Power Administration, for instance, markets power produced at dams built and managed by the U.S. Army Corps of Engineers and the Bureau of Reclamation, while the Federal Energy Regulatory Commission oversees nonfederal dams (those built by private companies and public utility districts).

The National Marine Fisheries Service and the U.S. Fish and Wildlife Service manage the river's fish and oversee the implementation of the Endangered Species Act; the former manages marine fish and wildlife, the latter manages fresh-water fish and wildlife. The Environmental Protection Agency is charged with implementing the Clean Water Act, ensuring that federal agencies and other entities meet water quality standards in the Columbia and its tributaries. The Bureau of Indian Affairs ensures that tribal rights are recognized, especially the 1855 treaty right to take fish at usual and accustomed fishing places. The U.S. Forest Service and the Bureau of Land Management manage a large portion of the basin's land, overseeing logging, grazing, recreation, and other land-based activities, many of which have direct impacts on aquatic habitats.

Finally, the Northwest Power Planning Council, a unique regional agency that is neither federal nor state-based but rather somewhere in between, helps plan power production, energy conservation, and fish and wildlife restoration activities throughout the basin. Add in the dozens of state agencies, tribal agencies, and local agencies, and one gets a picture of the complexity of the institutional landscape and the challenges river managers face in trying to restore the region's fish and wildlife populations to healthy levels.

It took 150 years for the health of the Columbia River to decline to the condition it is in today. Hundreds of dams impound the river and its tributaries, more than half a dozen fish species are at risk of extinction, and pollutants ranging from human sewage to radioactive wastes flow through the river and into the ocean. Private, local, state, and federal management activities, while undoubtedly providing many benefits, are directly responsible for this state of affairs. The recent shift to restoration and ecosystem management is largely in response to this decline in ecosystem health, but these new management approaches are still in their infancies and face many difficult challenges in the years to come. Only time will tell if they will be as socially and politically successful as more traditional management approaches. SEE ALSO ARMY CORPS OF ENGINEERS, U.S.; BUREAU OF RECLAMATION, U.S.; CLEAN WATER ACT; DAMS; ENDANGERED SPECIES ACT; FISH AND WILDLIFE SERVICE, U.S.; FISHERIES, MARINE; HYDROELECTRIC POWER; LEWIS, MERIWETHER AND WILLIAM CLARK; PLANNING AND MANAGEMENT, HISTORY OF WATER RESOURCES; PLANNING AND MANAGEMENT, WATER RESOURCES; RIVER BASIN PLANNING; SALMON DECLINE AND RECOVERY; TRANSPORTATION.

Cain Allen

Bibliography

Blumm, Michael C., and Brett M. Swift, eds. *A Survey of Columbia River Basin Water Law Institutions and Policies: Report to the Western Water Policy Review Advisory Commission.* Portland, OR: Northwestern School of Law, 1997. Available online at <http://www.waterinthewest.org/reading/readingfiles/fedreportfiles/col2.pdf>.

Cone, Joseph, and Sandy Ridlington, eds. *The Northwest Salmon Crisis: A Documentary History.* Corvallis: Oregon State University Press, 1996.

Dietrich, William. *Northwest Passage: The Great Columbia River.* Seattle: University of Washington Press, 1995.

Federal Caucus. *Conservation of Columbia Basin Fish: Building a Conceptual Recovery Plan.* Spokane, WA: Federal Caucus, December 1999. Available online at <http://www.salmonrecovery.gov>.

Independent Scientific Group. *Return to the River: Restoration of Salmonid Fishes in the Columbia River Ecosystem.* Portland, OR: Northwest Power Planning Council, 2000. Available online at <http://www.nwcouncil.org/library/return/2000–12.htm>.

Lang, William L., and Robert C. Carriker, eds. *Great River of the West: Essays on the Columbia River.* Seattle: University of Washington Press, 1999.

White, Richard. *The Organic Machine: Remaking of the Columbia River.* New York: Hill & Wang, 1995.

Internet Resources

Center for Columbia River History. <http://www.ccrh.org>.

carbonaceous chondrites: one of the three major groups of chondrites; little-altered, primitive meteorites containing significant amounts of carbon, water, and other volatile constituents

asteroid: a rocky body, much smaller than a planet, that orbits the Sun; asteroidal means pertaining to or originating from an asteroid

meteorite: a solid body that has fallen from space to the surface of the Earth or another planet; meteoritic means pertaining to or originating from a meteorite

Comets and Meteorites, Water in

An understanding of the earliest composition of the solar system is derived from analyses of the Sun, comets, and the little-altered **carbonaceous chondrites**. Most of these measurements have come from analyzing the spectra of light that originates from the Sun or that is reflected by bodies such as comets and **asteroids**, the presumed source of most **meteorites**. Many chemical analyses of meteorites have been made in laboratories on Earth and, increasingly, from spacecraft that encounter comets, asteroids, and the Sun's atmosphere.

Comets comprise a huge reservoir of water in Earth's solar system. Shown here is Halley's Comet, which crossed Earth's orbit in 1986 but was barely visible to the naked eye in much of the world.

Solar Components of Water

Because the great mass of matter in the solar system (nearly 99.9 percent) resides in the Sun, solar hydrogen (H), oxygen (O), and the water molecule (H_2O) must be considered when discussing **extraterrestrial** water.

extraterrestrial: from beyond the Earth and its atmosphere

The Sun, with an average surface temperature of about 6,000 kelvin (approximately 5,727°C or 10,340°F), would seem to be a poor place to look for water. However, scientists know that the constituents of water are enormously abundant in the Sun: hydrogen is its most abundant component, and oxygen also is a major component. Although tiny in amount, traces of the water molecule have been reported in cooler parts of the Sun's atmosphere.

Comets

Earth's solar system is believed to be about 4.6 billion years old, based in part on the age-dating of many **chondrites**. The Sun is slightly older. Comets, consisting of ice and grains of minerals and rocks—the "dirty snowballs" of astronomer Fred Whipple—are thought to be the oldest, least altered of any of the components of the solar system. They contain mainly water ice, but other icy components have been measured as well, such as carbon monoxide, carbon dioxide, sulfur, hydrogen sulfide, methane, and hydrogen cyanide. (The term "water ice" is not redundant because in space, some gases can change to ice on the surface of planetary bodies.) Comets may have rocky cores as well as interspersed grains of material. The interspersed granular character extends to comet tails, which form by **ablation** as comets approach the Sun and the ice heats up.

chondrites: primitive meteorites with origins in the solar nebula

ablation: processes that remove snow or ice from glaciers, including melting, evaporation, wind erosion, and sublimation

These materials are minor components, however, compared to water ice. Comets thus account for a very significant fraction of water in the solar system: although small, there are many of them. The **Oort Cloud** of comets and the more recently described **Kuiper Belt** of comets account for untold numbers of comets and therefore comprise a huge reservoir of water. Many planetary scientists believe that cometary impacts early in Earth's history could have supplied much of the water for its oceans.

Oort Cloud: a spherical cloud of comets around the Sun at a distance far from Neptune's orbit, extending from approximately 50,000 to 100,000 astronomical units (AU) from the Sun

Kuiper Belt: a disk-shaped region past the orbit of Neptune roughly 30 to 50 astronomical units (AU) from the Sun, containing many small icy bodies; considered the source of the short-period comets

---

LIFE'S TWO REQUIREMENTS

Where water is found on Earth, life is also found, even in the most extreme physical and chemical environments. Although there is no direct evidence that life was transported to Earth by way of comets or meteorites, cometary and meteoritic transport certainly delivered the components required for the development of life: water and organic (carbon-containing) compounds.

The most common surficial features of most planets and moons are impact craters, so water and organic compounds also have been transported to all other solar system bodies via the impacts of comets and asteroids. Where heat or other sources of energy exist, along with water and organic compounds, the potential for the development of life is high.

---

mantle: the region of the Earth between the molten core and the outer crust, composed mainly of silicate rock, and around 2,900 kilometers (1,800 miles) thick; also the interior of another planet, moon, or large asteroid between the core and the crust

volcanism: the activity and phenomena of volcanoes on Earth

igneous: rock that solidified from molten (magma) material; the rock is extrusive (or volcanic) if it solidifies on the surface and intrusive (or plutonic) if it solidifies beneath the surface

volatile: easily vaporized at moderate temperatures and pressures

hydrosphere: liquid water and ice on the surface of the Earth and in underground reservoirs

asteroid belt: the area between the orbits of Mars and Jupiter that contains most of the asteroids found orbiting the Sun

metamorphism: the changes in the mineral assemblage and texture of a rock subjected to temperatures and pressures that are significantly different than the conditions under which the rock orginally formed; significantly enhanced by the presence of water; changes occur without melting the rock

weathering: the decay or breakdown of rocks and minerals through a complex interaction of physical, chemical, and biological processes; water is the most important agent of weathering; soil is formed through weathering processes

Meteorites

Though small in amount compared to cometary water, meteoritic and asteroidal water is important in understanding water-rich Earth. Earth accumulated early in the history of the solar system by the sweeping up and accumulating of enormous amounts of debris as the early Earth orbited the Sun. These materials contributed their contained water to the growing Earth.

As Earth grew, it evolved into a core, an intermediate **mantle**, and an external crust. Water played a critical part, especially through the process of melting of the mantle and crust, with resulting **volcanism** and other **igneous** activity. Owing to volcanism, water and other **volatile** components were expelled to the surface, forming, along with possibly significant additions of cometary water, Earth's **hydrosphere**.

Meteorites fall to Earth continuously and are studied intensively for the information they provide about the earliest solar system and Earth. Until the return of rocks from the Moon, meteorites were the only known samples of extraterrestrial materials. Most meteorites are believed to come from the **asteroid belt**, which contains numerous rocky objects that orbit the Sun, mainly between the orbits of Mars and Jupiter. Some asteroids may have originated as comets, with icy exteriors that were vaporized by the Sun, leaving the rocky core.

Meteorites and asteroids have been extensively studied for their chemical composition, including water. Carbonaceous chondrites, which are the most fundamental and least modified type of meteorites, and are chemically most like the composition of the Sun, have several percent of water, primarily chemically combined in their mineral structures. The amount of contained water may decrease or increase as meteorites are altered, such as through **metamorphism**, melting, or **weathering** or impacts. SEE ALSO ASTROBIOLOGY: WATER AND THE POTENTIAL FOR EXTRATERRESTRIAL LIFE; EARTH: THE WATER PLANET; EARTH'S INTERIOR, WATER IN THE; MARS, WATER ON; SOLAR SYSTEM, WATER IN THE; VOLCANOES AND WATER.

E. Julius Dasch

Bibliography

Chaisson, Eric J. *Astronomy*. 2nd ed. Upper Saddle River, NJ: Prentice Hall, 1997.

Commerce, Waterborne *See Canals; Ports and Harbors; Transportation.*

Composition of Water   *See Fresh Water, Natural Composition of; Fresh Water, Natural Contaminants in; Fresh Water, Physics and Chemistry of; Ocean Biogeochemistry; Ocean Chemical Processes; Sea Water, Gases in; Sea Water, Physics and Chemistry of.*

Computers and Technology   *See Data, Databases, and Decision-Support Systems; Geospatial Technologies; Modeling Groundwater Flow and Transport; Modeling Streamflow.*

Conflict and Water

Water resources management increasingly requires compromise and consensus if solutions to problems are to be formulated and implemented. As issues of competing uses intensify, water decisionmakers are increasingly called upon to manage people as well as the water resource itself.

The Nature of Conflict

Conflict can be defined as disagreement over the appropriate course of action to be taken in a particular situation. Conflict abounds as individuals and groups have different **values**, priorities, **interests**, and hopes for the future. Conflicts take place between neighbors, communities, states, regions, and nations. Areas of severe water conflict correlate with water scarcity; hence, the regions with the greatest conflict and potential for conflict are the Middle East, the Indian subcontinent, and the former Soviet Union.

Water is a **fugitive resource**. As water moves through the **hydrologic cycle**, it does not pay any attention to political boundaries and conflicts that often result between differing political units. These types of conflicts are referred to as transboundary water issues. Conflicts also arise between different groups in society, such as business interests and environmental groups, or between parties located upstream and downstream.

The ultimate conflict is armed conflict. Many fears have been expressed that water wars will occur in the future as water becomes more and more scarce. Historical studies have not supported this hypothesis that water disputes lead to war. There are only a couple of documented situations in all of history where war broke out over water. Although most water conflicts are nonviolent, they still have serious implications for societal welfare.

Sources of Conflict

Conflict can result from many factors. The sources of conflicts must be understood in order to manage water resources effectively. Three basic sources of conflict are conflicting goals, factual disagreements, and ineffective relationships (distrust and power struggles).

Conflicting Goals. Water planning and management activities are undertaken for the purpose of solving problems such as inadequate water supplies or poor water quality. For water planning efforts to be undertaken, the problem to be solved must be clearly identified and understood. Once a problem is identified, possible courses of action to address the problem can be enumerated and then the best course of action can be chosen and implemented.

values: abstract concepts of what is right and wrong, and what is desirable and undesirable

interests: as in "business interests" or "environmental interests," the vested opinions, perspectives, and positions of stakeholders regarding gains and losses, real or perceived, stemming from decision-making outcomes

fugitive resource: a natural resource such as water that moves from one location and one state (liquid, gas, or solid) to another

hydrologic cycle: the solar-driven circulation of water on and in the Earth, characterized by the ongoing transfer of water among the oceans, atmosphere, surface waters (lakes, streams, and wetlands), and groundwaters

Conflicts over water often emerge when different groups of people have different goals. Here, New Delhi women carrying traditional water pots protest in May 2000 over an ongoing shortage of water and electricity in the Indian capital and surrounding areas.

hydropower: power, typically electrical energy, produced by utilizing falling water

stakeholder: an individual or group impacted by a potential decision or action; the term is usually associated with a limited number of individuals representing the interests of other like-minded individuals or groups

In reality, however, the preferred course of action to solve a problem depends on goals, values, and objectives. Goals are statements of a desired future situation, where stated goals then function as criteria for evaluating alternative courses of action. Thus, the process of goal-setting actually serves to influence the ultimate actions taken to achieve these goals. Goals are related to the decision-making participants' interests and values.

Conflicting goals are common in water management scenarios. For example, dam-building is controversial around the world. Several large dam projects have engendered conflict with local peoples over the best ways to provide water supplies, protect the environment, and the rights of relocated groups to their homes. These conflicts are local, but have also attracted international attention from environmental and human rights groups. These groups work together in order to influence the local government to stop building the dam, and to persuade the banks to eliminate loan money to fund the dam. These types of conflicts over dam-building are currently seen in India, Turkey, China, and many other countries needing to meet the rising water demands of their large populations.

The clashing desires to achieve different goals lead to much conflict in the water management process. In the example above, the conflict is between the goals of water supply and **hydropower** versus the goals of social and environmental preservation. In such instances, it is difficult to resolve conflicting goals. In these cases, the parties may agree on the effects of certain actions but disagree on the desirability of these effects, and therefore fundamentally disagree on the desirability of the action itself. Thus, goal-setting is an important water management activity requiring the participation of all relevant **stakeholders**.

Factual Disagreements. Sometimes, differences over the preferred course of action to solve water problems stem from disagreements over the facts, or perceived facts, of the situation. These disagreements are often genuine differences of opinion, and can be related to the poor quality of information or to a lack of data. For example, in the previous example of dam-building, factual disagreements may arise over the exact **sediment load** of the river, the actual need for additional water supplies, the ability to finance the project, or the legal rights the local people have according to national laws. In practice, facts are rarely clear-cut pieces of information; on the contrary, they often are infused with information stemming from individual or group values and interests.

Several factors can lead to factual disagreements. First, facts are rarely completely certain and their degree of uncertainty can influence how much conflict may result. This uncertainty exists because human knowledge is incomplete or imperfect. Furthermore, there are limitations to science and scientific methods. For example, people may not completely understand how **contaminants** travel through a specific **groundwater** system, nor how water is actually used in a given locality. Often assumptions are substituted for agreed-upon facts. This lack of information constrains decision-making processes and opens up room for parties to debate the facts utilized in decision-making.

Second, factual disagreements can stem from the situation in which the parties have different information. Many times, parties rely on completely different sets of information for their decision-making, and may not share or discuss the information with the conflicting party. For example, hydropower providers tend to look at the quantity, cost, and profit level of power to potentially be generated. Yet local environmental groups tend to look at the state of water systems, and threats to those systems. Each group has its own network from which they collect information. Sometimes groups may even exaggerate factual disagreements to achieve their own desired goals in the decision-making process.

Third, factual disagreements can arise from limitations of parties' abilities to process information. Many water management problems are very complex. Psychological research often shows that both the expert and average citizen can use only a few pieces of information when drawing conclusions in decision-making. Which pieces are actually used and the weight attached to them differs widely from individual to individual. And sometimes, people are not consistent in decision-making. All these factors help explain many seemingly factual disagreements between parties in water management processes.

Distrust and Power Struggles. The third source of conflict stems from the state of the ongoing relationship between the disagreeing parties, particularly issues of distrust and power struggles. A situation of distrust breeds conflict, as parties have no foundation for communication and collaborative problem-solving activities. Distrust is often the result of poor communication and can often lead to further misunderstandings. These tensions often cause parties to be less willing or even unwilling to cooperate with each other. Sometimes distrust is the result of personality conflicts or historical circumstances.

Power struggles are related to distrust and take the form of competition over various sources of power related to the decision-making process, such as financial resources, access to the media, and access to information. Parties are struggling for power rather than attending to solving the water problem at hand.

sediment load: the combination of bed load, suspended load, and dissolved load carried by a stream

contaminant: as defined by the U.S. Environmental Protection Agency, any physical, chemical, biological, or radiological substance in water, including constituents that may not be harmful to the environment or human health

groundwater: generally, all subsurface (underground) water, as distinct from surface water, that supplies natural springs, contributes to permanent streams, and can be tapped by wells; specifically, the water that is in the saturated zone of a defined aquifer

Protestors in front of the Pakistan embassy in Washington, D.C. in 2000 wave placards against the proposed Kalabagh Dam on the Indus River. Their concerns included the displacement of people, environmental impacts, and the ultimate distribution of water. The Pakistani government was compelled to cancel its construction plans because of these stakeholder conflicts.

WHAT IS ALTERNATIVE DISPUTE RESOLUTION?

Alternative dispute resolution (ADR) emerged in response to perceived problems relating to resolving all conflicts in the court system. ADR approaches try to avoid the adversarial nature of the legal system's winner–loser outcomes and try to promote win–win solutions.

There are several different types of ADR. Under alternative dispute resolution processes involving mediation, the parties in conflict come together along with a mediator to find ways to resolve their conflict. The mediator is a trained, neutral third party who has no stake in the outcome of the process. The mediator enables the parties to discuss their interests, listen to the other parties, and understand the facts and the areas of common ground where win-win type solutions may be built. The parties in conflict have no obligation to abide by the outcomes of the mediation, unless it is a process called binding arbitration.

It is difficult to resolve power struggles, and parties often find themselves locked into these types of conflicts. Sometimes these parties will refuse to accept workable solutions because the power struggle becomes more important than solving the actual problem, and they might be perceived as weak for accepting a compromise. These relationship-based factors among the stakeholders can generate conflict in water management scenarios.

Conflict Resolution

More than one source of conflict may be present in any water management situation. Due to these prevalent sources of conflict, conflict resolution is an essential component of current water management activities around the world. Many conflicts are taken to court systems where they can be costly to resolve, in terms of both time and money. Some disputes are repeatedly taken to the courts and thus are never truly resolved.

Resolving conflict requires compromise. And compromise often involves (1) a willingness to accept the validity of another party to hold a different perspective; (2) an attempt to understand other perspectives even when those perspectives are not accepted; and (3) a search for solutions that will accommodate diverse interests.

In the past, water management issues were often viewed as technical problems that could be "cured" by structural solutions such as reservoirs, dams, and levees. Satisfying water demands was the primary goal.

But today, water resources are increasingly scarce, populations have grown, and water management is much more complex. Financial considerations have grown in importance, given society's tight budgets and the major expenses of water-related infrastructure. Environmental considerations are more prominent with greater societal awareness and concern for detrimental impacts to the environment.

All of these factors have increased the potential for conflict in water management activities. Hence, conflict resolution techniques have grown in importance as water managers increasingly are called upon to resolve conflicts.

Methods that water managers can use to resolve specific types of conflict include the following.

Conflicting Goals

- Developing a common vision of the future among stakeholders
- Educating stakeholders and conducting public awareness activities
- Finding **win-win solutions**
- Compensating those who will experience losses stemming from a solution
- Promoting holistic understandings of water problems

win-win solution: the collaborative outcome where the conflicting parties each feel like they gain something from the decision-making outcome (and do not "lose" due to the decision)

Factual Disagreements

- Promoting effective communication over areas of genuine disagreement
- Undertaking additional research to generate better data
- Promoting joint research or research performed by the third party

Distrust and Power Struggles

- Developing better relationships between the parties
- Taking parties out of their familiar environments
- Getting parties to listen to each other
- Finding common ground or self-interests
- Bringing in a **mediator**

mediator: a person who is trained to help parties resolve their own conflicts by using established conflict resolution techniques

These types of solutions can be valuable in resolving conflict and promoting effective long-term answers to water problems. Conflict is not necessarily a bad or undesirable thing, and it often presents an opportunity for much-needed dialogue. Conflict can also help identify where things need to be done better.

The challenge for water managers is to ensure that conflict is a constructive force in decision-making processes and that it does not become destructive. Ignoring conflict can lead to greater conflict in the future and thus impairs the implementation of potential solutions to water-related problems. Water managers must effectively deal with conflict if water management is to be successful and benefit society. SEE ALSO HYDROPOLITICS; INTERNATIONAL COOPERATION; LAW, WATER; PLANNING AND MANAGEMENT, WATER RESOURCES; TRANSBOUNDARY WATER TREATIES; USES OF WATER.

Faye Anderson

Bibliography

Mitchell, Bruce. *Resource and Environmental Management.* Essex, U.K.: Addison Wesley Longman Limited, 1997.

Internet Resources

Conflict Prevention and Resolution Center. U.S. Environmental Protection Agency. <http://www.epa.gov/adr/>.

CRInfo: Conflict Resolution Information Source. University of Colorado at Boulder. <http://www.Colorado.edu/conflict/>.

Mediation Information and Resource Center. Resourceful Internet Solutions, Inc. <http://www.mediate.com/>.

Resolve. Center for Environmental and Public Policy Dispute Resolution. <http://www.resolv.org/>.

Wolf, Aaron T. *Transboundary Freshwater Dispute Database*. Department of Geosciences, Oregon State University. <http://www.transboundarywaters.orst.edu>.

Conservation, Water

The term *conservation* emerged in the late nineteenth century to refer to the management—basically for economic reasons—of such valued natural resources as minerals, pastureland, timber, and topsoil. Conservation became part of U.S. government policy with the creation in 1871 of a U.S. commissioner of fish and fisheries. The conservation school of thought, with its focus on the wise use of resources, often conflicted with the preservation school of thought that sought to preserve resources for their intrinsic values.

Conserving Water Resources

Today, conservation of natural resources encircles the general idea of conserving the Earth itself by protecting its capacity for self-renewal. The most fundamental and essential of all these natural resources is water. Without water, life on Earth would not exist.

Water conservation is defined as those activities designed to reduce the demand for water, improve the efficiency of its use, and reduce losses and waste. The purpose of conservation is to protect water resources and to achieve, at lower costs, the benefits from its use. This is achieved through measures such as water-saving devices, water-efficient processes, water demand management, and water rationing. A key to water conservation is getting people to recognize the value of water and not using it as if it were a free good.

Almost every country in the world faces a growing challenge to meet the increasing demand for water that is driven by expanding populations and economic growth. Water supplies are affected by more industrialization, mechanization, urbanization, and their polluting byproducts. Water conservation is playing a greater role in water resources planning due to the difficulties of developing new water sources, trends of increasing frequencies of droughts, increased environmental concerns, and legislative mandates such as the Safe Drinking Water Act.

Conservation Planning

Most U.S. states are continuing to develop and implement comprehensive water resource management plans. These plans serve as guidelines for overall water resource management and set targets for smaller, local utilities to provide adequate water supplies. Comprehensive plans are increasingly popular as a method of combining supply and conservation projects.

Historical. Water conservation practices have been advocated since the 1960s. As early as 1965, the federal government made water conservation a goal with the Water Resources Planning Act. In 1980, the U.S. Water Resources Council defined conservation as "activities designed to reduce the demand for water, improve efficiency in use and reduce losses and waste of

One of Santa Clara's (California) water conservation measures is participation in the South Bay Water Recycling program, which captures treated wastewater from eight communities in Santa Clara that would otherwise be discharged into San Francisco Bay. The reclaimed wastewater is used to irrigate golf courses, parks, schools, and agricultural land, as well as for industrial processes.

WAYS TO CONSERVE WATER AT HOME

- Turn off the faucet while shaving and brushing teeth
- Take quick showers and eliminate unnecessary showers
- Chill drinking water in the refrigerator rather than running the tap until the water cools
- Clean fruits and vegetables in a water basin rather than under running tap water
- Thaw frozen foods in the refrigerator rather than under running tap water
- Add food wastes to the compost bin instead of the in-sink garbage disposal
- Use full loads in automatic dishwashers and washing machines
- Install low-flow appliances
- Never use the toilet as a wastebasket

- Avoid toxic cleaning materials, which can pollute water
- Check faucets and pipes for leaks
- Avoid purchasing toys that require a constant water stream.
- Avoid using fertilizers and pesticides
- Place mulch around trees and shrubs to reduce evapotranspiration
- Water lawns only when needed
- Plant native, drought-resistant trees and plants
- Raise the cutting level of lawnmowers; longer grass blades reduce evapotranspiration
- Use a bucket or spring-loaded nozzle to wash the car
- Use a broom, not a hose, to clean driveways
- Use sand, not salt, to de-ice walkways

water, or improve land management practices to conserve water." Historically, local conservation has been a valuable part of water resource plans because small savings can add up to large volumes of water saved.

Benefits. Conservation benefits to the customer include reduced water bills and greater water supplies that help in better economic development. Environmental benefits include **ecosystem** and **habitat** protection. Decreased water demand also has positive implications for tourism, especially for the recreational use of waterways. Water conservation can be achieved through stronger plumbing codes, promotion of conservation devices, pricing levels, and public education. These practices have all shown positive results in the United States.

Common Characteristics. Innovative water conservation programs have been enacted throughout the United States. Although each state program is distinctive with regards to particular geographic, hydrologic, and political characteristics, each contains features common to all. The major characteristics include:

- Needs to simplify and coordinate resource planning efforts;
- Efforts to extend limited supplies prior to initiating new source development projects;
- Reductions in residential, industrial, and agricultural demand; and
- Improvements in the efficiency of older supply **infrastructure**.

Demand Management

Conservation measures are services that are desired by customers while, at the same time, use less water than traditional practices. An example of a

ecosystem: the community of plants and animals within a water or terrestrial habitat interacting together and with their physical and chemical environment

habitat: the environment in which a plant or animal grows or lives; the surroundings include physical factors such as temperature, moisture, and light, together with biological factors such as the presence of food and predators

infrastructure: the permanent constructed system (e.g., pipes and other structures) that enables the treatment and delivery of water to support human habitation and activity, or that supports manufacturing activities and water projects (e.g., desalinization and hydropower plants)

irrigation: the controlled application of water for agricultural or other purposes through human-made systems; generally refers to water application to soil when rainfall is insufficient to maintain desirable soil moisture for plant growth

conservation measure is the requirement for low-flush toilets to work as well as older, high-flow toilets. Measures that achieve long-term, permanent reductions in water use by changing behavioral activities are called demand management. A water conservation plan that emphasizes demand management frequently includes the following practices and technologies.

Irrigation Hours Ordinance. Communities may enact a minimum rule that limits lawn and garden **irrigation** to restricted hours, generally during early morning or late evening when less sunlight and winds minimize water evaporation.

Xeriscape Landscape. Xeriscape, or "dry gardening," is defined as a method of improving the character of land that maximizes water conservation by the use of site-appropriate plants and an efficient watering system.

The principles of Xeriscape include:

- Developing plans and designs that consider exposure, slope, view, and soils;

- Creating practical turf areas with type and location determined by landscape purpose and function;

- Evaluating and improving soils, and when appropriate, adding peat moss or compost to improve root development, water penetration, and water retention;

- Using appropriate plant selection according to water needs so minimum usage will allow maximum conservation;

- Watering efficiently with properly designed irrigation systems and with well managed plant groupings of similar watering needs; and

- Using organic mulch that minimizes **evapotranspiration**, reduces weed growth, slows erosion, and helps reduce soil temperature fluctuations.

evapotranspiration: water discharged to the atmosphere as a result of evaporation from the soil and surface-water bodies and by plant transpiration

Ultra-Low-Volume Fixtures. The installation of ultra-low-volume (ULV) plumbing fixtures in new construction is often required to save water while still providing desired services. Permit regulations usually specify that fixtures possess a maximum flow volume when pressure is (for instance) 80 pounds per square inch. In this case, the maximum flow volume is normally 1.6 gallons per flush for toilets; 2.0 gallons per minute for faucets; and 2.5 gallons per minute for showerheads. The goal is to attain ongoing savings without behavioral changes.

Rain Sensor Device. This measure requires that any person purchasing or installing an automatic sprinkler system must install and operate a rain sensor device or an automatic switch. This equipment will override the irrigation cycle of the sprinkler system when adequate rainfall has occurred.

Water Conservation-Based Rate Structure. A conservation rate structure is a pricing system used by utilities that provides financial incentives for users to reduce their water demands. Rates generally entail one of the following:

- Increasing block rates, where the marginal cost to users increases in two or more steps as use increases; or

- Seasonal pricing, in which water consumed in the peak demand season is charged a higher rate than in the off-peak season.

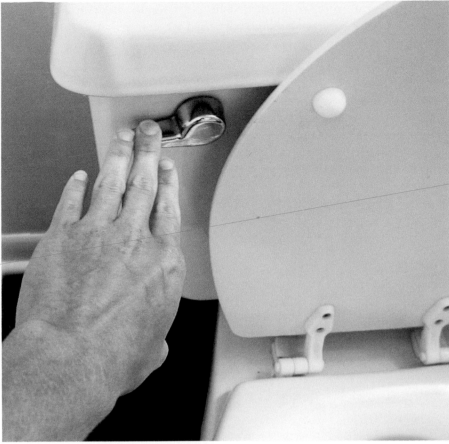

Toilet flushing is the largest indoor household use of water. Replacing an older toilet with a water-saving one is a good investment.

Leak Detection and Repair Program.   Public water supply systems desire to attain a 10 percent or less unaccounted-for water loss. When actual loss is greater, then the implementation of leak detection programs is required. The program must include auditing procedures, and in-field leak detection and repair efforts.

Public Education Program.   Public information will inform citizens of opportunities to reduce water use, give reasons why they should choose to practice conservation, and publicize the conservation options being promoted. Nearly all users can be affected by public information efforts, although they are typically targeted at the uses with the broadest participation.

Commercial and Industrial Users.   All individual commercial and industrial users submit a conservation plan that generally includes: audits of water use; implementation of cost-effective conservation measures; employee conservation awareness programs; and feasibility studies of using reclaimed water.

Social Acceptability

Water conservation is not an isolated activity and its social acceptability is related to many factors such as the characteristics of the utility market; the pricing system; and economic, political, technological, and willingness to conserve. By the time that water conservation is necessary, the public has already developed established use patterns and may be resistant to changing these patterns. To change social consciousness about water resources, an understanding of all the issues is critical. Public perception often is influenced by an effective campaign to highlight the positives of these new decisions. Drought situations often highlight the need for conservation measures and increase social acceptability.

Water conservation has financial advantages for both customers and utilities. The consumer benefits from the efforts at reducing water use through lower bills. For utilities, conservation reduces the magnitude of, and delays the need for, costly infrastructure development projects. For society and the natural environment as a whole, water conservation efforts can minimize the alteration of the natural landscape, thereby benefiting recreational activities, the aesthetic quality of surroundings, as well as the preservation of wetlands and wildlife habitats. SEE ALSO DEMAND MANAGEMENT; POPULATION AND WATER RESOURCES; PRICING, WATER; RAINWATER HARVESTING; RECLAMATION AND REUSE; SUPPLY DEVELOPMENT; USES OF WATER.

William Arthur Atkins

Bibliography

Broydo, Leora. "The Great Xeriscape: Low-water Landscaping, Includes other Household Environmental Tips." *Mother Jones* vol. 22 (May 15, 1997):21.

Gibbons, Whit. "Whither Our Air and Water?" *The World & I* vol. 14, issue 6 (June 01, 1999):184.

Gleick, Peter H. "Safeguarding Our Water: Making Every Drop Count." *Scientific American* vol. 284, no. 2 (February 01, 2001):38.

Vickers, Amy. *Water Use and Conservation: Homes, Landscapes, Industries, Businesses, Farms.* Amherst, MA: WaterPlow Press, 2001.

Internet Resources

Guidelines for Water Conservation Plans. U.S. Environmental Protection Agency, Office of Water, Office of Wastewater Management. <http://www.epa.gov/owm/factsheet.pdf>.

"Using Effective Water Conservation Measures can Save Millions of Taxpayer Dollars" Within *Water Conservation Program.* Federal Energy Management Program. <http://www.eren.doe.gov/femp/techassist/waterconserve.html>.

Water Conservation. Municipal Research and Services Center of Washington. <http://www.mrsc.org/subject/environment/water/wc-conservation.aspx>.

Water Efficiency Measures for Residents. State of Connecticut Drought Response, information provided by U.S. Environmental Protection Agency. <http://www.drought.state.ct.us/efficiency.htm>.

WaterWiser: The Water Efficiency Clearinghouse. American Water Works Association. <http://www.waterwiser.org/>.

Contamination *See "Chemicals" and "Pollution" entries.*

Cook, Captain James

British Explorer
1728–1779

Captain James Cook added more to early knowledge of the southern Pacific Ocean and the western North American coast than any other person. Among his contributions, he surveyed the St. Lawrence River, the transit of Venus across the Sun's disk from Tahiti, and the unexplored east coast of Australia (then claimed British possession); explored the southern oceans in search of a continental land mass (Antarctica); discovered New Caledonia, Norfolk Island, and the Sandwich Islands (Hawaii); and showed that a

Northwest Passage from the Pacific to the Atlantic did not exist south of the Arctic. Cook was the first navigator to apply the scientific method to exploration.

Early Life

Cook was born near Whitby, Yorkshire, England, and received a limited education. After apprenticeships with a storekeeper and with ship owners at Whitby, he joined the British Navy and rose in rank rapidly. As a navigator, he surveyed the St. Lawrence River and played a significant role in the capture of Quebec. He spent the summers from 1763 to 1767 surveying the coastline of Newfoundland. The Royal Society took interest in Cook after his observations of a solar eclipse in 1766 helped establish the longitude of Newfoundland.

Life's Work

Cook's first voyage in command began in 1768, when he was appointed commander of an expedition to Tahiti to observe the transit of Venus across the disk of the Sun and, clandestinely, to look for new lands in the southern Pacific between Chile and New Zealand. His ship, the *Endeavour*, surveyed the coasts of New Zealand and reached the unexplored coast of Australia. He named the region New South Wales. The *Endeavour* sailed inland of the Great Barrier Reef, nearly wrecking on coral, and explored the coast of Queensland.

Soon after the first voyage, Cook sailed as captain of the *Resolution*, accompanied by Tobias Furneaux and the *Adventure*, to explore the southern oceans and the mythical southern land mass as near to the South Pole as possible. They crossed the Antarctic Circle in 1773 before turning northward to Tahiti for supplies and respite from the bitter cold. Cook thereafter lost contact with the *Adventure*, which returned to England by way of the first west–east circumnavigation of Earth. Cook continued his search for a southern continent (Antarctica), making numerous island discoveries.

In 1776, Cook set out on the *Resolution*, later accompanied by the *Discovery*, commanded by Charles Clerke. They went in search of the vaunted Northwest Passage, which was thought to exist between the Pacific and Atlantic Oceans. En route, the ships revisited New Zealand, Tonga, and Tahiti. In 1778, Cook found and named the Sandwich (Hawaiian) Islands. He then sailed to the coast of North America, which he followed northward through the Bering Strait and into the Arctic Ocean. Returning to the Hawaiian Islands for supplies in 1779, Cook was murdered by natives over a dispute involving a stolen boat. Both ships continued, without success, to look for a passage south of the Arctic Circle between the Pacific and Atlantic Oceans before returning to England. SEE ALSO NAVIGATION AT SEA, HISTORY OF.

E. Julius Dasch

Captain James Cook is considered one of the world's greatest explorers. His voyages took him around the world.

Bibliography

Cook, James. *Explorations of Captain James Cook in the Pacific As Told by Selections of His Own Journals, 1768–1779*, ed. A. Grenfell Price. Mineola, NY: Dover Publications, 1971.

Hough, Richard. *Captain James Cook*. New York: W. W. Norton & Company, 1997.

Corals and Coral Reefs

A coral reef is a structure in the sea constructed by coral skeletons and limestone debris that remains in place after the plant or animal dies. The structure is geological, the communities include plants and animals, and they are controlled by meteorological and oceanographic conditions.

Distribution and Roles of Coral Reefs

Coral reefs include shallow-water tropical reefs, such as the Great Barrier Reef off the east coast of Australia, and deep-water reefs, such as Sula Bank off Norway. Tropical reef diversity (the number of different plants and animals) is high, with complexity similar to tropical rain forests.

Natural and Human Values. Coral reefs function as living breakwaters. For example, on Bikini Atoll, Marshall Islands, the wave energy that strikes this reef amounts to 20 horsepower per surge channel per wave (waves arrive at the surge channel at a rate of one wave approximately every 8 seconds).

A cross section of a reef shows that it is built by multiple generations of corals and that there is significant void space. This empty space provides refuge for plants and animals. A coral cut in half would reveal small tunnels and galleries created by boring sponges, clams, and other animals that provide homes for worms, shrimp, and fish.

The tourism and fisheries industries supported by coral reefs are important to the economies of tropical areas, as well as the economies of the countries from which the tourists travel. Conservation efforts have been aided by the high visibility of reefs and their biocommunities.

Coral: Simple Animals. Corals exist at the tissue level: they do not have organs, such as a heart. On the evolutionary ladder, corals are one step above the sponges. They are the simplest animals to have nervous and connected muscular systems and a dedicated reproductive system. They belong to the phylum Cnidaria, which also includes the jellyfish.

Tetiaroa in French Polynesia's Society Islands is an atoll reef that formed at the edge of an old submerged volcano. It forms an irregular ring around a shallow central lagoon, and its outside edges drop steeply to the ocean floor.

Tentacles and sticky mucus help coral polyps trap plankton. Coral are simple animals in the same phylum as jellyfish.

Each coral animal consists of an individual sac-like body called a polyp. Tentacles radiate from the mouth end of the polyp and bristle with tiny hairs; these are the triggering devices for a microscopic harpoon called a nematocyst. The harpoon includes a barb for injecting neurotoxin, and a tube to connect the barb and the toxin's reservoir. Corals are colonial animals, and multiples of polyps form a colony.

Types of Coral

The more common corals include hydrocorals, octocorals (polyps with eight tentacles), and scleractinian corals (polyps with six, or multiples of six, tentacles).

Hydrocorals. The hydrocorals include the fire corals (genus *Millepora*). *Millepora* is common on shallow, tropical–subtropical reefs in the Caribbean and the Pacific. Hydrocorals have a life cycle of alternating sexual and asexual generations known as metagenesis. The hydroid asexual generation attaches itself to the reef and produces a medusa offspring by budding. The medusa generation sends eggs and sperm into the water, and the product of this union, a free-swimming larva, settles on the bottom and grows into a new hydroid coral. The upward growth for *Millepora* is about 1 centimeter (2.5 inches) annually.

Octocorals. Octocorals include sea fans, plumes, mats, and rods. They are flexible and sway to and fro in the waves. The octocoral skeleton is a matrix of limestone structures called spicules and an organic connective material. Spicules provide strength like bones, and the connective material holds the spicules together.

(Top) Pillar coral, *Dendrogyra cylindrus,* is a Caribbean coral species noted for its cathedral-like columns or pillars. (Bottom) A coral species from the family Mussidae is shown here exhibiting the septa, a feature of the skeleton (thin plates); the red color is contributed by plant pigments in the zooxanthellae.

Octocorals reproduce sexually, with eggs and sperm released in the water column. Following fertilization, the larvae may remain in the water column for days or weeks before settling and attaching to the sea floor. An individual larva settles and grows into an adult. Octocorals in the western Atlantic grow from 1 to 4 centimeters (2.5 to 10 inches) annually.

Scleractinian Corals. The scleractinian corals have many growth forms: branching, hemispheres, columns, sheets, mushrooms, and tubes. Because of the strength and persistence of their limestone skeletons, these corals are the principal reef architects.

Reproduction in the scleractinian corals is either by broadcasting eggs and sperm into the water or by internal fertilization and brooding of larva. Some corals have female and male sex organs in the same polyp and are capable of self-fertilization. Larvae either live in the water column or crawl along the bottom.

Branching corals have relatively rapid growth (15 centimeters, or 6 inches, per year). The boulder corals grow 1.2 to 2.5 centimeters (0.5 to 1 inch) per year. Branching corals are more fragile, often breaking during storms and generating fragments that in turn can grow into new coral colonies. Boulder corals generally do not fragment.

Symbiosis: Living Together

Nearly all the shallow-water corals and related Cnidarians have a microscopic symbiotic algae living in the tissues. The alga, called zooxanthellae, is an important partner in the success of tropical coral reefs. Zooxanthellae provide the means for corals to sustain high growth and reproduction rates in waters that are low in **nutrients**. Metabolic wastes generated by animal tissues are used by the alga; the corals use the fats, oils, and sugars synthesized by the alga during photosynthesis.

For the process to function optimally, three things are necessary: sufficient light, clear water, and temperatures that range from 20 to 30°C (68 to 86°F). The process of photosynthesis is conceptualized as follows.

Carbon Dioxide + Water$^{\text{light energy}}$ → Sugar + Water + Oxygen + Energy

The energy provided by photosynthesis enhances coral growth. Corals grow by taking in calcium **ions** from the sea and combining them with bicarbonate ions. The result, calcium carbonate, bonds as a single crystal onto other crystals, creating the limestone skeleton. Energy generated from photosynthesis expedites the calcium carbonate movement from the tissues to the skeleton. The steps follow.

Calcium bicarbonate formation: $Ca^{2+} + 2HCO_3^- \rightarrow Ca(HCO_3)_2$

Calcium carbonate and carbonic acid formation:
$Ca(HCO_3)_2 \rightarrow CaCO_3 + H_2CO_3$

Carbonic acid ionization: $H_2CO_3 \rightarrow H^+ + HCO_3^-$

Conversion to water and carbon dioxide: $H_2CO_3 \rightarrow H_2O + CO_2$

Examples of Coral Reef Types

Reefs in the Pacific Island chains (Hawaii, French Polynesia, and the Marshall Islands) initially are formed on the sides of old volcanic mountains and are called fringing reefs. In the process of **tectonic plate** movement, the plate carries the mountain into deeper water, and the reef becomes a ring that surrounds the mountain but is separated from it by a body of water called a lagoon. The reef is now called a barrier reef. Over thousands of years, the mountain submerges, leaving a ring of reef and a few low islands called an atoll. The terms "fringing," "barrier," and "atoll" were first used in 1834 by Charles Darwin in his book about coral reefs.

Norway. Deep-water coral assemblages include those off the coast of Norway. Because they live in darkness, deep-water corals do not have the

nutrients: a group of chemical elements or compounds needed for all plant and animal life; nitrogen and phosphorus are the primary nutrients; excessive or imbalanced nutrients in water may cause problems such as accelerated eutrophication

ion: an atom or molecule that carries a net charge (either positive or negative) because of an imbalance between the number of protons and the number of electrons

tectonic plate: a section of the lithosphere that acts as a single mass and interacts with other plates; lithospheric plates are created at spreading centers and destroyed at subduction zones

Coralline algae produce calcium carbonate skeletons that assist in building reefs. The coralline algae typically are found in areas with heavy wave surge.

food web: a complex food chain, with several species at each level, so that there is more than one producer and more than one consumer of each type

---

CORALS AS HISTORIC RECORDKEEPERS

Just as tree rings or layers of sediment provide environmental records of past events, skeletons of massive corals provide records that are useful in climate research. Each year, the coral precipitates calcium carbonate in two density layers that, if X-rayed, provide relative growth rates and coral age. Isotopes from the skeleton yield information on temperature and salinity. Corals exposed to floods of fresh water have fluorescent bands (seen under black light) because they retain humic and fulvic acids in their skeletons.

---

symbiotic zooxanthellae that are common to the shallow reefs. The reefs are built up from the sea floor by a branching coral, *Lophelia pertusa*.

These coral banks are often associated with petroleum gas seeps that are surrounded by bacterial mats. The biological productivity (chemosynthesis) from these mats supports a **food web** somewhat similar to deep-sea thermal vent communities: high biomass and productivity without the influence of light. Corals, presumably, obtain small prey animals (crustaceans, worms, and mollusks) that feed on the bacterial mats.

Lophelia pertusa banks are often miles long, up to 30 meters (100 feet) high, and equally wide. The maze of twisted and interlocking branches provides refuge for resident fish populations.

Nova Scotia. Off the coast of Nova Scotia, on the fishing banks, most corals are large octocorals; some old and large colonies are up to 5 meters (about 16 feet) high. *Paragorgia arborea*, a common coral, is pink to orange in color with branches ending in blunt bundles resembling a wad of gum, living up to its common name—bubblegum coral. Although this coral is not well studied, its presumed ecological value is as a refuge for juvenile fish. This is a region that in the past had large populations of codfish; however, overfishing has decimated the fishery.

Florida. Off the central east coast of Florida, another branching coral, *Oculina varicosa*, builds banks upward from the sea floor. *Oculina* banks are a refuge area for a variety of fish, such as the snowy grouper. These deep-water coral reefs exemplify two common themes of deep-water corals: one species builds the framework, and photosynthesis is not a major energy source.

Physical and Biological Controls

Tropical cyclones are the most important natural force controlling reef development. Storms generate massive waves that break up coral formations, heavy rains that reduce salinity, and silt deposits in reefs close to high

The crown-of-thorns starfish (or acanthaster) eats coral polyps. If present in sufficient numbers, this voracious starfish can decimate coral populations.

islands. Damage and recovery depends on storm strength, wind direction, duration, and the frequency of events.

Crown-of-Thorns Starfish.   The biological controls on coral reefs generally are not as catastrophic as a tropical cyclone; however, a number of reefs have been virtually picked clean of coral thanks to a voracious predator. In the Pacific and Indian Oceans, a starfish called the crown-of-thorns (*Acanthaster planci*), has a history of population explosions. When the crown-of-thorns (COT) reaches abundances of several per square meter, they will eat virtually every coral in sight.

In the 1970s, conventional wisdom held that COT outbreaks were related to insufficient predators to control them. In Australia and Guam, a bounty of $1 per COT collected was instituted. Others placed the blame on pollution.

However, geologists sampled deep sediments on the reefs and found pockets of COT spines. Determining the age of these spines indicated that COT population explosions occurred thousands of years before the arrival of Europeans in Australia. The COT outbreaks seem to be related to the typhoons that occasionally strike the east coast of Australia. The torrential rainfall from the typhoon causes heavy flooding, bringing nutrients into the near-shore waters around the Great Barrier Reef.

The COT starfish usually lays millions of eggs, which develop into floating (planktonic) larvae. Normally, the larvae would have a poor chance for survival because of a lack of food. After a flood event with the enriched water, phytoplankton blooms occur. Such blooms are key to COT larval survival. The COT larvae thrive on the rich soup of plankton, and when they **metamorphose** into the adult COT, huge swarms of COT begin feeding on coral.

metamorphosis: the biological process of transformation from an immature form to an adult form in two or more separate stages

If a COT event occurs approximately once per decade, there is sufficient time for the coral to recover before the next COT disturbance. However, if a COT event occurs every three years, the reef does not have sufficient time for the coral larvae to settle and grow and replace the lost corals.

Long-Black-Spine Sea Urchin.   The concept of **keystone species** for coral reefs is not subscribed to universally; however, there is some validity to the

keystone species: a species on which the persistence of a large number of other species in the ecosystem depends

idea. In western Atlantic coral reefs prior to 1983, a prodigious algae grazer was held up as the keystone for controlling the algal growth on the reefs and for creating space for the coral larvae to settle. Studies have documented the value of the long-black-spine sea urchin in removing algae and enhancing coral **recruitment** on Caribbean reefs.

recruitment: the increase in a natural population as offspring grow and immigrants arrive

In 1983 and 1984, a pandemic disease killed 99 percent of the urchins on reefs from Barbados to Panama. Since that disease event, the urchin has not recovered to reclaim its role as a major **herbivore**. Today, most Caribbean reefs have moderate to high algal cover. There is continuing debate as to whether the algal cover seen today is the result of higher levels of nutrients in the waters, or whether it is due to the lack of grazing.

herbivore: an animal that feeds mostly on plants

Hazards and Global Stresses

Various environmental hazards can threaten coral reefs. Some stresses are natural, whereas others are magnified by human activities.

Thermal Stress. Elevated surface sea-water temperatures cause coral bleaching at the time of seasonal maximum heating (late summer to early fall). This thermal stress results in the expulsion of the zooxanthellae (symbiotic alga), causing the corals and similar reef inhabitants to turn white and, in severe cases, to die. Loss of the zooxanthellae results in reduced or no growth, no reproduction, and susceptibility to disease.

Corals in shallow tropical reefs are at the near-margin of upper thermal tolerance. Most corals will tolerate water of 30°C (86°F); however, if the temperature reaches 32°C (90°F), corals will bleach.

Factors that affect temperature include tide, wind, time of year, cloud cover, and currents. In the 1960s and 1970s, bleaching events were rare, occurring about once a decade in a region. By the 1990s, bleaching events were occurring every other year or every third year. The magnitude of the events (oceanwide and the extended duration of the episode) resulted in massive coral mortalities in reefs in the Indian Ocean and western Pacific. An El Niño event could have played a major role in a vast coral bleaching event in French Polynesia's Rangiroa Atoll in 1998.

Global temperature is rising, and this in turn elevates surface sea-water temperatures. Global warming is believed to be the result of increased greenhouse gases (such as carbon dioxide) and an increase in ultraviolet radiation due to the loss of ozone in the atmosphere caused by the release of chlorofluorocarbon compounds (CFCs).

❋ See "Ocean-Floor Sediments" for a photograph of a dust storm over the Red Sea.

Dust. Satellite images show the movement of dust across the oceans from other continents.❋ African dusts from the sub-Saharan region are entrained in the upper winds and carried across the Atlantic. The dust includes spores from bacteria and fungi, and mineral elements such as iron, copper, mercury, and arsenic. A well-documented disease in a Caribbean sea fan (*Gorgonia ventalina*) is caused by a fungus whose spores are carried in African dust. The ocean, land, and atmosphere are interconnected; no part of the global community is insulated from influences that come from other continents or oceans.

Fish and Agriculture. Reefs are under siege in some places by destructive fishing practices: dynamite, chemicals, dredging, poor land-use practices, slash-and-burn agriculture on hillslopes, and fishing efforts beyond maximum

Tropical settings and a diversity of easily viewable biota make snorkeling a popular tourist activity on shallow-water coral reefs. Deep-water reefs are less accessible and hence have not captured as much popular appeal.

sustainable yield. The recent trend in protecting reefs is to designate large areas as parks or reserves and not to allow the harvest of any plant or animal. This maximizes conservation of the entire reef community.

Preserving Coral Reefs. Marine protected areas (MPAs) permit visitors to look at, but not take, anything; these areas therefore are a reasonable way to protect reef resources. An MPA protects the habitat and the target species that the fishers are harvesting.

The Florida Keys National Marine Sanctuary and the Great Barrier Reef Marine Park in Australia have created "no-take" zones to protect all the plants and animals. The spillover effect provides a source of animals to replenish other areas; that is, as the MPA becomes saturated, some animals move away. Within 2 years of creating the Florida Keys no-take zones, populations of grouper, snapper (fish), and lobster increased dramatically. SEE ALSO BIODIVERSITY; EL NIÑO AND LA NIÑA; GLOBAL WARMING AND THE OCEAN; LAND-USE PLANNING; LIFE IN WATER; OCEANS, TROPICAL.

Walter C. Jaap

Bibliography

Connell, Joseph H. "Diversity in Tropical Rain Forests and Coral Reefs." *Science* 199 (1978):1302–1310.

Jaap, Walter C., and Pamela Hallock. "Coral Reefs." In *Ecosystems of Florida*, eds. Ronald L. Myers and John J. Ewel. Orlando: University of Central Florida Press, 1990.

Littler, Dianne S., and Mark M. Littler. *Caribbean Reef Plants*. Washington, D.C.: OffShore Graphics, 2000.

Thorne-Miller, Boyce, and John G. Catena. *The Living Ocean: Understanding and Protecting Marine Biodiversity*. Washington, D.C.: Island Press, 1991.

Veron, John E. *Corals of the World*, Vols. 1–3. Townsville: Australian Institute of Marine Science, 2000.

Wells, Sue, and Nick Hanna. *The Greenpeace Book of Coral Reefs*. London, U.K.: Blanford, 1992.

Internet Resources

Corals. Australian Institute of Marine Science. <http://www.aims.gov.au/pages/search/search-corals.html>.

NOAA's Coral Health and Monitoring Program. National Oceanic and Atmospheric Administration. <http://www.coral.noaa.gov>.

Cost–Benefit Analysis

Since being mandated in the Flood Control Act of 1936 (PL 74–738), cost–benefit analysis has been used routinely in evaluating water projects. Cost–benefit analysis gives decisionmakers a method for evaluating investments in water projects, judging alternative projects, and estimating the impact of various regulatory changes. The basic principle of cost–benefit analysis is that the benefits of a water project must exceed the costs. Therefore, the issue is to measure all the benefits and costs attributable to a project accurately and completely. The application of this principle becomes difficult because of the uncertainty inherent in dealing with projects over time.

The Value of Nonmarket Goods

When conducting project analysis, it should be remembered that all projects will have benefits and costs to the environment not directly accounted for in the planning. These spillovers should be considered so that decisionmakers are aware of such costs. Whenever a large public spending program exists, there are both winners and losers.

A major shortcoming of cost–benefit analysis is the difficulty in valuing **nonmarket goods**. Water projects, by nature, will affect the fish and wildlife habitats in an area as well as recreational and other environmental amenities. Since these benefits and costs are not priced in the market, they are often not included in a project analysis. However, note should be taken of these issues to give decision makers the ability to consider such nonmarket values while evaluating a project.

nonmarket good: a product or service that is not traded in a market and which does not have a market price that reveals how consumers value the good; examples include air and water quality, some parks and recreation amenities, endangered species, and some natural resources such as wetlands

Valuing the benefit of pollution control is also difficult in cost–benefit analysis and often leads to controversy when studies are publicly released. Economists have no formula for valuing the avoided damage to humans and the environment of pollution control. What is the value of extending life or reducing illness? Still, economics can be useful in determining whether the same water quality improvements might have been achieved at a lower cost or whether the same investment could have purchased greater quality improvements.

Practical Economic Analysis

Despite the difficulty in assigning economic value to certain environmental or human factors, economists and analysts nonetheless can provide decisionmakers with what might be called second-best or practical cost–benefit analysis. Economist John Krutilla summarized the role of economics as follows: "Economic analysis of benefits and costs of long-lived investments involve as much art as science. There is a need to project the relevant course of events within the area of project influence over a very long period of time, and getting to understand human responses to changes in the social and physical environment does not come easily."

Several items must be considered before beginning an analysis of any water project, investment, or spending decision. For example, construction of a public flood-control project or a reservoir often does not consider the effect on fish, wildlife, wetlands, or surrounding watersheds. Or, the evaluation of a water conservation project may not include the effects on the recreational use of a lake or reservoir. Consequently, the fully informed decisionmaker must first determine the scope of the costs and benefits to be taken into account. This way, managers can assure the public that the major relevant factors were considered before making a decision.

Another question concerns the entity to be maximized: Returns to the system? Rate payer benefits? Water use? Environmental concerns? Whether a project is a net benefit to the system, the community, or the environment will depend on the objective that is being sought.

Third, analysts must know the investment criteria. Whether one project is chosen over another or no investment is made depends on the criteria for ranking projects.

Fourth is the relevant timeframe for the project. A period of analysis must be chosen. For example, how long is a reservoir to last? The analyst must also remember that different projects have different cash flows over time; some have early returns, others more distant returns.

Evaluating Dollars Over Time

In project evaluation, benefits and costs clearly accrue over many years. Thus, it is necessary to discount the present value of a project over time: $1,000 is worth more today than it will be 5 years from now. A method is needed to take future costs and benefits and put them into today's dollars.

Planners "discount" future dollars to take into account the time value of money. By using a **discount rate**, planners can compare today's costs and benefits to those in the future. The discounted net present value is the discounted sum of benefits minus costs. Only projects where net present value is positive would be economically feasible. SEE ALSO ECONOMIC DEVELOPMENT; ETHICS AND PROFESSIONALISM; PLANNING AND MANAGEMENT, WATER RESOURCES.

Jeffrey L. Jordan

Bibliography

Frederick, K. D. "The Economics of Risk in Water Resource Planning." In *Water Resources Administration in the United States: Policy, Practice, and Emerging Issues.* Martin Reuss, editor. East Lansing: Michigan State University Press, 1993.

Krutilla, John V. "The Use of Economics in Project Evaluation." In *Transitions of the 40th North American Wildlife and Natural Resources Conference.* Washington, D.C., 1975.

Schmid, A. Allan. *Benefit-Cost Analysis: A Political Economy Approach.* Boulder, CO: Westview, 1989.

PORK BARREL PROJECTS

The term "pork barrel" dates from just after the American Civil War (1861–1865) and comes from the plantation owners' practice of distributing rations of salt pork to slaves from wooden barrels. The term "pork barrel spending" can be traced to about 1905, defining such spending as "a government appropriation . . . that provides funds for local improvements designed to ingratiate legislators with their constituents." Such spending implies federal legislation filled with special projects for members of Congress to give to the voters back home paid for by federal taxpayers.

Most pork barrel projects, also referred to as line-item, or "earmark," projects, are infrastructure spending on items such as roads, airports, government buildings, and often water projects. However, "ear marks" are not evaluated competitively. Pork barrel projects are often seen as a growing trend for Congress to become heavily involved in local and states affairs through the "power of the purse."

---

discount rate: the discount rate is a factor that translates future monetary values into today's values; in cost–benefit analysis, is represented as r in the discounting formula $1/(1 + r)^t$ when t is the number of years in a water project

Cousteau, Jacques

French Oceanographer
1910–1997

Jacques-Yves Cousteau, born in Saint-Andre-de-Cubzac, France, on June 11, 1910, explored the depths of the ocean and educated the world on what he found there. Being an environmentalist, Cousteau strove to persuade people to take care of the Earth, especially the oceans.

Early Years

Cousteau's interest with the sea began when he was a child. Although he suffered from poor health, he became an avid swimmer. Throughout his youth, he explored the bottoms of pools and lakes and practiced holding his breath underwater. Breathing underwater would become a challenge for Cousteau to solve later in life.

Cousteau graduated from high school in 1929, and in 1930 he joined the French Navy. After completing his mandatory world tour with the navy, Cousteau decided he wanted to become a naval aviator and began training for it. Unfortunately, he was involved in a serious car accident that ended his hopes of becoming a flier. The accident did not end his naval career, however; he went to sea instead.

The Aqualung

Cousteau enjoyed exploring the sea and wanted to examine what was below its surface. Remembering lessons learned in his youth about breathing underwater, he knew he had to develop a breathing apparatus if he was to stay underwater for longer periods of time.

Since the sixteenth century, inventors had been trying to meet the challenge of breathing underwater for long periods of time. Various apparatuses were invented for meeting this challenge. One such apparatus was a headpiece attached to a long breathing tube, but the tube was awkward to wear because it did not allow divers to dive very deep, and it was heavy. Another apparatus was a tank of oxygen not unlike today's **aqualung**. The early oxygen tank could not compress and regulate air the way it was needed for deep-sea diving. The air pressure in a diver's lungs has to be the same as the water pressure acting upon the diver's body.

Dr. Christian Lambertsen designed an apparatus for the United States military in 1939 that he called the "Self-Contained Underwater Oxygen Breathing Apparatus." The military called it "SCUBA."

However, scuba gear proved useful only for shallow dives. Cousteau wanted the freedom to explore the ocean at great depths but knew the available equipment would not allow him to make such dives, because he had experimented with these traditional breathing apparatuses. He joined French engineer Émile Gagnan in designing a breathing apparatus that would appropriately regulate air pressure at varying water depths.

In 1943, after several experiments, Cousteau and Gagnan finally invented the demand regulator, solving the problem of equalizing air pressure in the lungs with the water pressure acting upon the diver's body. They attached the regulator to three cylinders of air. The complete set of equipment was called the "aqualung" and would enable divers to dive deeper for longer periods of time. Through this accomplishment, Cousteau and Gagnan had modernized scuba diving. Cousteau could now explore the depths of the ocean more freely. Eventually he would record and film what he saw below the ocean's surface and share his findings with both the scientific community and the general public.

Jacques Cousteau developed, with Émile Gagnan, the first aqualung in 1943. For the next 50 years, he explored the world's oceans.

aqualung: equipment used by a person as an air supply while underwater; developed in 1943 by Jacques-Yves Cousteau and French engineer Émile Gagnan

War and Post–War Years

While Cousteau worked on the aqualung, he continued performing his naval duties. France was involved in World War II (1939–1945) against Nazi Germany during this time. Cousteau aided France's war efforts through his resistance work. The French resistance would secretly battle the Nazis by conducting spy missions, sabotage, and by aiding people who fled persecution. One of Cousteau's resistance roles included spying on Italian naval forces.

Calypso. After the Allied victory in World War II, Cousteau once again concentrated on exploring the depths of the ocean. In 1950, with the financial help of a friend, Cousteau bought a minesweeper called *Calypso* and converted it into a research vessel. *Calypso* transported Cousteau, his wife Simone, and a research crew around the world to such places as Easter Island, Mexico, California, and the Antarctic Circle.

Conshelf. In the early 1960s, Cousteau experimented with underwater living by developing the Conshelf living stations in which divers, on three separate occasions, stayed for periods of one week to nearly a month. The divers tested living conditions and conducted ocean experiments. Through these experiments, Cousteau gave the world a better understanding of the ocean.

Films, Books, and Later Life

Jacques Cousteau made films of ocean life and sunken ships that were havens for fish and plant life. The 1955 film, *The Silent World*, and the 1964 film, *World without Sun*, are two of his most famous movies. *The Silent World* won an Oscar and the Cannes International Film Festival's prestigious Palme d'Or award.

Cousteau also wrote many books including *The Silent World* (1953), *World without Sun* (1965), and *The Whale* (1972). Educating the world about ocean life was Cousteau's focus. This focus was apparent on the television series that ran from 1968 to 1975, *The Undersea World of Jacques Cousteau*. Cousteau studied sharks, squid, dolphins, penguins, and many other sea creatures and invited the viewing audience to learn with him.

In his later years, Cousteau continued to learn about the sea and share his knowledge with the world. He started the Cousteau Society and became an active environmentalist. Jacques Cousteau died in June 1997 at the age of 87. SEE ALSO CAREERS IN OCEANOGRAPHY; EARLE, SYLVIA; SUBMARINES AND SUBMERSIBLES.

Marie Scheessele

Bibliography

Munson, Richard. *Cousteau: The Captain and His World.* New York: William Morrow and Company, Inc., 1989.

Reef, Catherine. *Jacques Cousteau: Champion of the Sea.* Frederick, MD: Twenty-First Century Books, 1992.

Internet Resources

Bellis, Mary. "Inventors of Scuba Diving Equipment." About, Inc. <http://www.inventors.about.com/library/inventors/blscuba.htm>.

"Cousteau People: Jacques-Yves Cousteau, Founder." *About TCS.* The Cousteau Society. <http://www.cousteausociety.org/tcs_people.html>.

Crustaceans

Crustaceans include crabs, lobsters, shrimp, krill, barnacles, and related species. There are approximately 40,000 crustacean species, the great majority of which are aquatic. Crustaceans are the only primarily aquatic group in the phylum Arthropoda, which also includes the insects and spiders. A few crustaceans, such as the familiar pillbug, have invaded terrestrial (land-based) habitats.

Like other arthropods, crustaceans are characterized by a segmented body, jointed appendages, and an external skeleton that offers protection from predators. The external skeleton, called a cuticle, is made of **chitin**. The cuticle is periodically molted in order to allow for growth. The period after molting can be a dangerous one, because the new shell is still soft and affords little protection.

Crabs

There are nearly 5,000 crab species. Most are marine, although terrestrial species exist as well. Crabs have ten jointed appendages, including two large claws for food capture called chelipeds, and eight walking legs that are used for walking sideways. An elliptical carapace protects the rest of the body.

Crabs have two stalked eyes and a pair of sensory antennae. Respiration occurs via gills, and special jointed mouthparts process food. Crabs have diverse diets: some are **scavengers**; others are **predators** on clams and snails; and still others are **herbivores**, feeding on vegetation. The largest crab species reach sizes up to 3.7 meters (12 feet) across, including the legs. Crabs are an important seafood species.

Hermits and Fiddlers. Two familiar crab groups are hermit crabs and fiddler crabs. Hermit crabs have the unique life history strategy of using discarded snail shells for protection. These crabs find new shells to inhabit as they grow.

Fiddler crabs are known for their asymmetry in claw size—one claw is much larger than the other. The large claw is used to communicate with other individuals—males raise and wave their claws in order to defend their

chitin: a nitrogen-containing polysaccharide (carbohydrate whose molecules consist of a number of sugar molecules bonded together) forming a hard outer layer in many invertebrates, especially insects; also found in the cell walls of many fungi

scavenger: an animal that eats animal wastes, dead plant material, and dead bodies of animals not killed by itself

predator: an animal that hunts and kills other animals for food

herbivore: an animal that feeds mostly on plants

The ghost crab, native to the eastern United States, spends most of its life on land. Ghost crabs can be seen scurrying down to the water in order to wet their gills, which must be kept moist in order to breathe.

The lobster's large claw can crush crabs, clams, mussels, and human fingers. The largest lobster ever caught weighed 17 kilograms (37.4 pounds) and was 0.6 meters (2 feet) long.

territories, intimidate other males, or attract females. These displays allow competition to be resolved without dangerous physical combat.

Lobsters

Like crabs, lobsters have ten appendages, two claws and eight walking legs. A lobster can also snap its tail to propel itself quickly backward—this is most often used as an escape response when confronted with potential predators.

Lobsters have compound, stalked eyes, chemosensory antennae, and sensory hairs on various parts of the body to detect touch and motion. The antennae are particularly sensitive, responding to environmental chemical cues regarding food, potential mates, and predators.

Lobsters are predatory, and use their large claws to attack prey such as clams. The two claws of lobsters are adapted to different tasks—the crusher claw is used to break shells, whereas the ripper claw, which has finer teeth, is used to tear flesh. Legs and jointed mouthparts are used to manipulate prey items.

There are both marine and fresh-water lobster species. The largest lobsters grow to lengths of 1.2 to 1.5 meters (4 to 5 feet) and may live over 100 years. Like crabs, lobsters are considered a delicacy and represent an important seafood species.

Shrimp

Shrimp are small crustaceans that, like crabs and lobsters, have ten jointed legs. However, shrimp also have special swimmerets, small appendages along the abdomen, which enable them to swim. In addition, shrimp use sweeping motions of the tail to propel themselves backwards.

Shrimp species are marine or fresh-water. The shrimp's chitinous external skeleton is thinner than that of crabs and lobsters and is shed as the animal grows. The largest species reach nearly 23 centimeters (9 inches). By weight, more shrimp are eaten by humans worldwide than any other crustacean.

Barnacles

Barnacles are commonly seen attached to solid substrates such as piers, boats, or rocks, and are sometimes mistaken for **mollusks** because of their shells and sedentary lifestyle. Barnacles live in the high **intertidal** zone and filter small food particles from the water.

Before they attach permanently to a substrate, barnacles go through a mobile larval stage. Larvae then attach head first and begin to secrete shells of chitin, which are expanded as they grow. These shells are kept closed when the tide is out in order to prevent drying out. When submerged, barnacles open their shells and filter-feed by waving their legs to capture **plankton**.

Respiration occurs through gills on the legs. Many barnacles are hermaphrodites, producing both eggs and sperm.

Krill

Krill are small crustaceans that form large, dense swarms in Antarctic waters. They are intimately associated with sea ice. Krill are important in the diet of numerous Antarctic species, including fish, whales, seals, and penguins.✳

Krill are **filter feeders** that feed at night on the water surface. Their diet consists primarily of phytoplankton and algae.

Like all crustaceans and arthropods, krill shed their exoskeleton over time. Unlike other crustaceans however, shedding is not always the result of growth—krill sometimes shrink in size, using their own body resources for metabolism during the long, dark Antarctic winter when food availability is low.

The largest krill species attain lengths of up to 14 centimeters (5.5 inches). Krill are consumed by humans in some parts of the world.

Other Aquatic Arthropods

The horseshoe crab is not technically a crustacean—rather, it is an arthropod distantly related to spiders, which are arachnids. Horseshoe crabs have a large carapace and long tail. They eat clams and other invertebrates, crushing shells with their legs. Mating and egg-laying occur on beaches. Horseshoe crabs sometimes are described as "living fossils" because they do not appear to have evolved much in the last 400 million years.

There are numerous species of aquatic insects and arachnids. Many insects play important roles in aquatic ecosystems, including as crucial elements of the food chain. For example, mayflies spend a lengthy larval period in the water, living either in the water column or in the muddy bottoms. Mayflies are detritivores (animals that feed on dead organic matter), and play an important role in breaking down nutrients.

Dragonflies and damselflies are also found in aquatic habitats—their larvae are aquatic and highly predatory, capturing worms, small fish, and small amphibians. Insects such as mosquitoes are also characterized by an aquatic larval stage. Aquatic spiders feed on aquatic insects or small fish.

---

mollusk: an invertebrate animal with a soft, unsegmented body and usually a shell and a muscular foot; examples are clams, oysters, mussels, and octopuses

intertidal: coastal land that is covered by water at high tide and uncovered at low tide

plankton: an assemblage of small, often microscopic aquatic organisms encompassing aquatic plants (phytoplankton) and aquatic animals (zooplankton) that float or drift passively with water currents, having no or very limited powers of locomotion

✳ **See "Ecology, Marine" for a photograph of a krill swarm.**

filter feeder: an aquatic animal that feeds by filtering particulate organic material from water

The shells (carapaces) of horseshoe crabs sometimes are found on beaches. If this were a live animal, picking it up by the tail could cause injury to the crab.

Some aquatic spiders maintain an underwater air pocket to which they repeatedly transport fresh air. SEE ALSO FOOD FROM THE SEA; MARICULTURE; OCEANOGRAPHY, BIOLOGICAL.

Jennifer Yeh

Bibliography

Brusca, Richard C., and Gary J. Brusca. *Invertebrates.* Sunderland, MA: Sinauer Associates, 1990.

Gould, James L., and William T. Keeton, with Carol Grant Gould. *Biological Science,* 6th ed. New York: W. W. Norton & Co., 1996.

Hickman, Cleveland P., Larry S. Roberts, and Allan Larson. *Animal Diversity.* Dubuque, IA: Wm. C. Brown, 1994.

Internet Resource

The Lobster Conservancy. <http://www.lobsters.org>.

Dams

Dams are structural barriers built to obstruct or control the flow of water in rivers and streams. They are designed to serve two broad functions. The first is the storage of water to compensate for fluctuations in river discharge (flow) or in demand for water and energy. The second is the increase of **hydraulic head**, or the difference in height between water levels in the lake created upstream of the dam and the downstream river.

hydraulic head: the potential energy of water as a result of its elevation and weight of overlying water; it is the driving force for natural water movement

By creating additional storage and head, dams can serve one or more purposes:

- Generating electricity;
- Supplying water for agricultural, industrial, and household needs;
- Controlling the impact of floodwaters; and
- Enhancing river navigation.

They can be operated in a manner that simultaneously augments downstream water quality, enhances fish and wildlife habitat, and provides for a variety of recreational activities, such as fishing, boating, and swimming.

Classes of Dams

Four major classes of dams are based on the type of construction and materials used: embankment, gravity, arch, and buttress.

Embankment.   Embankment dams typically are constructed of compacted earth, rock, or both, making them less expensive than others that are constructed of concrete. Consequently, more than 80 percent of all large dams are of this type. Embankment dams have a triangular-shaped profile and typically are used to retain water across broad rivers.

Gravity.   Gravity dams consist of thick, vertical walls of concrete built across relatively narrow river valleys with firm bedrock. Their weight alone is great enough to resist overturning or sliding tendencies due to horizontal loads imposed by the upstream water.

Arch.   Arch dams, also constructed of concrete, are designed to transfer these loads to adjacent rock formations. As a result, arch dams are limited

The 37-meter-high Pen–y–Garreg Reservoir Dam and three associated dams were constructed on the government-owned Elan Valley Estate in mid-Wales (United Kingdom) at the turn of the twentieth century to provide a safe water supply for the city of Birmingham. By the close of the twentieth century, new hydroelectric turbines had been installed below ground at the base of the historic dams to provide small-scale power generation while safeguarding the habitats of the estate's diverse plant and bird species.

to narrow canyons with strong rock walls that can resist the arch thrust at the foundation and sides of the dam.

Buttress.   Buttress dams are essentially hollow gravity dams constructed of steel-reinforced concrete or timber.

Planning for Dams

Careful planning throughout the siting, design, and construction of dams is necessary for optimal utilization of rivers and for preventing catastrophic **dam failure**. These planning phases require input from engineers, geologists, hydrologists, ecologists, financiers, and a number of other professionals.

Designers must first evaluate alternative solutions and designs for meeting the same desired objective, whether the goal is to allocate water supply, improve flood control, or generate electricity. Each alternative requires a comprehensive cost–benefit analysis and feasibility study for evaluating its physical, economic, ecological, and social impact.

dam failure: the collapse of a dam or a portion of its components, often as a result of structural weaknesses that develop over time, of improper design or operation, or of larger-than-anticipated flood events

Once an alternative has been selected, a number of important considerations enter into the design and construction of the dam. These include:

- Hydrological evaluation of climate and streamflows;

- Geologic investigation for the foundation design;

- Assessment of the area to be inundated by the upstream lake (also called a reservoir) and its associated environmental and ecological impacts;

- Selection of materials and construction techniques;

- Designation of methods for diverting stream flow during construction of the dam;

- Evaluation of the potential for **sediments** to accumulate on the reservoir bottom and subsequently reduce storage capacity; and

- Analysis of dam safety and failure concerns.

When a dam is put into operation, or commissioned, water is released from the upstream reservoir over a spillway or through gates in a manner to satisfy intended objectives. Operating rules for maximizing power generation, for example, include maintaining hydraulic head. In contrast, water levels in flood control reservoirs must be periodically reduced to allow for new storage during anticipated periods of flood hazard. Operating issues, however, can easily become complex and highly politicized and may be difficult to resolve. This is particularly true for river systems containing several reservoirs, for dams serving multiple purposes, and in cases where adverse social, ecological, and environmental impacts are significant.

Overview of Dam-Building

The first dam for which reliable records exist was built on the Nile River sometime before 4000 B.C.E. near the ancient city of Memphis. Remains of other historic dams have been located at numerous sites bordering the Mediterranean Sea and throughout the Middle East, China, and Central America. The oldest continuously operating dam still in use is the Kofini Dam, which was constructed in 1260 B.C.E. on the Lakissa River in Greece.

Today, there are approximately 850,000 dams located around the world. Of the more than 40,000 that are categorized as large dams, more than half are located in China and India. It is estimated that 24 countries currently generate more than 90 percent of their electrical power from dams, and 70 countries rely on dams for flood control.

Dams in the United States. Large-scale construction of dams occurred in the United States during the post–World War II years and reached its peak in the 1960s. The organizations that have been primarily responsible for dam-building are the U.S. Army Corps of Engineers, the Bureau of Reclamation (part of the U.S. Department of the Interior), and a number of public and private utility developers.

Since the nineteenth century, the U.S. Army Corps of Engineers has been engineering rivers to accommodate river traffic, control floods, produce electricity, and provide irrigation waters. Four of the largest dams

sediment: rock particles and other earth materials that are transported and deposited over time by geologic agents such as running water, wind, glaciers, and gravity; sediments may be exposed on dry land and are common on ocean and lake bottoms and river beds

BIG DAMS

The world's two tallest dams are located in Tajikistan in the city of Vakhsh where they tower over 335 meters, or 1,100 feet tall (Rogun) and 300 meters, or 985 feet tall (Nurek). The Three Gorges Dam in China, a concrete gravity dam scheduled for completion in 2009, will be 175 meters tall (574 feet), the equivalent of a 48-story building.

When completed, Three Gorges Dam will be the world's largest hydropower facility with a generation capacity of 18,200 megawatts. It will simultaneously supply flood storage and enhance navigation along the Yangtze River. The structure will create a reservoir more than 600 kilometers long and 1,100 meters wide, capable of storing 39.3 billion cubic meters of water.

Construction of the dam, which began in 1993, requires the inundation of 632 square kilometers of existing land and will cause the permanent relocation of over 1.2 million people.

Arizona's Glen Canyon Dam on the Colorado River shows the curvature in arch dams that provides structural stability. The rock walls of the deep canyon absorb a majority of forces that result from the upstream reservoir, Lake Powell.

decommissioning (dams): the process by which a dam is permanently taken out of operation

constructed by the Corps include Garrison, Oahe, Fort Peck, and Fort Randall Dams.

The second group, the Bureau of Reclamation, was established in 1902, when Congress passed the National Reclamation Act. The Bureau was initially charged with developing irrigation and power projects in seventeen western states and has been responsible for the construction of more than six hundred dams and reservoirs, including the massive Hoover, Shasta, Glen Canyon, and Grand Coulee Dams.

The third organization responsible for dam construction encompasses various power administrations, such as the Tennessee Valley Authority, the largest public power company in the United States, as well as others operating under the Federal Power Act of 1920, which provided for the licensing of privately built dams to produce electric power. In part because of this mid-twentieth-century dam-building era, the U.S. dam population has approached 75,000. More recently, however, the rate of dam construction in the United States is exceeded by the rate of **decommissioning**. In many cases, maintenance costs for aging infrastructure, significant social and ecological impacts, high construction costs, and the reduced availability of suitable sites have made alternatives to dams more viable. SEE ALSO ARMY CORPS OF ENGINEERS, U.S.; BUREAU OF RECLAMATION, U.S.; COST–BENEFIT ANALYSIS; HOOVER DAM; HYDROELECTRIC POWER; RECREATION; RESERVOIRS, MULTIPURPOSE; SUPPLY DEVELOPMENT; TENNESSEE VALLEY AUTHORITY.

John W. Nicklow

Bibliography

Linsley, Ray K. et al. *Water Resources Engineering*, 4th ed. New York: McGraw-Hill, 1992.

Mays, Larry W. *Water Resources Engineering*. New York: John Wiley & Sons, 2001.

Morris, Gregory L., and Jiahua Fan. *Reservoir Sedimentation Handbook*. New York: McGraw-Hill, 1998.

U.S. Department of Interior, Bureau of Reclamation. *Design of Small Dams*, 3rd ed. Denver, CO: U.S. Government Printing Office, 1987.

World Commission on Dams. *Final Report: Dams and Development—A New Framework for Decision-Making.* Cape Town, South Africa: World Commission on Dams, 2000.

Internet Resources

The World Commission on Dams. <http://www.dams.org>.

Darcy, Henry

French Hydraulic Engineer
1803–1858

No other name is more closely associated with the field of **hydrology** than that of Henry Darcy. His expression for the movement of water through an **aquifer**, known as Darcy's Law, is still used today.

Henry Philibert Gaspard Darcy was born in Dijon, France, the capital of the Department of Côte d'Or. In 1826, Darcy received his degree in Civil Engineering from the School of Bridges and Roads in Paris, a specialty institution of the Corps of Bridges and Roads. Upon graduating in the top tier of his class, he was appointed to the prestigious Corps as an engineer, and soon accepted a position in his hometown.

Creating a Water Supply System

Upon his return to Dijon, Darcy undertook the task of creating a sanitary, efficient public water-supply system for the city and his proposal was accepted with no modifications. The plan included: the Rosoir **spring** as the water source; an underground **aqueduct** through which the water would travel over 12 kilometers (7.4 miles); two **reservoirs**; 28,000 meters (91,800 feet) of underground pipes; and 142 public street fountains.

The project was completed in 1844, by which time Darcy had received the Legion of Honor award and the appointment of Chief Engineer for the Department of Côte d'Or. He was offered 55,000 francs as compensation for his project, but declined the payment and instead accepted only a gold medal and free water for the rest of his life. The public water system was a tremendous achievement not only because it greatly increased the quality of life for an entire city, but also because it was completed 20 years before anything of its kind in Paris.

Other Projects. In the next few years Darcy moved on to several railroad and canal projects. Before long, during the revolution, he was exiled from Dijon because of his affiliation with the former government. He moved to Paris, but soon poor health forced him to resign from his engineering duties and he again returned to Dijon. He devoted his last years to performing laboratory experiments on the flow of water through sand columns and pipes.

Appendix D and Darcy's Law

In 1856, Darcy published "The Public Fountains of the City of Dijon," a report detailing the engineering that was used for Dijon's water supply, with the results of the sand column experiments included in the report's Appendix D. The experiments with pipes resulted in the Darcy–Weisbach friction

hydrology: the science that deals with the occurrence, distribution, movement, and physical and chemical properties of water on Earth; also refers to the hydrologic characteristics of a given region

aquifer: a water-saturated, permeable, underground rock formation that can transmit significant quantities of water under ordinary hydraulic gradients to wells and springs

spring: location where a concentrated, natural discharge of groundwater emerges from the Earth's subsurface as a definite flow onto the surface of the land or into a body of surface water, such as a lake, river, or ocean

aqueduct: long, canal-like or pipe-like structure, either above or below ground, for transporting water some distance

reservoir: a pond, lake, basin, or tank for the storage, regulation, and control of water; more commonly refers to artificial impoundments rather than natural ones

coefficient, a value used to account for resistance to flow through an individual pipe.

Found only at the end of his report, Appendix D contained the groundbreaking work for which Darcy is best known: Darcy's Law. Simplified, this linear rule demonstrates that the rate of flow of water through a porous medium is proportional to the slope between two points of water at different heights, and that it flows from the higher to the lower point. Darcy's Law also takes into consideration the area of the medium and its ability to transport water (i.e., its permeability). Scientists now use this analytical approach to hydrology worldwide.

In 1858, Henry Darcy died of pneumonia and was buried in Dijon. The next day, to honor one of the most important, selfless contributors to the life of Dijon and the world of science, the Town Square was renamed to Place Darcy. SEE ALSO AQUIFER CHARACTERISTICS; GROUNDWATER; GROUNDWATER, AGE OF; MODELING GROUNDWATER FLOW AND TRANSPORT.

Amy B. Parmenter

Bibliography

Freeze, R. Allen. "Henry Darcy and the Fountains of Dijon." *Ground Water* 32, no.1 (1994): 23–30.

Philip, J. R. "Desperately Seeking Darcy in Dijon." *Soil Science Society of America Journal* 59, no. 2 (1995): 319–324.

Internet Resources

Henry Darcy and His Law. Oklahoma State University. <http://biosystems.okstate.edu/darcy/>.

Data, Databases, and Decision-Support Systems

Databases are critical to the successful use of computer-based models that help to identify, compare, and evaluate various impacts of alternative management policies for specific **watersheds**. Menu-driven, graphics-based computer programs that permit the interactive use of these impact prediction models and their databases support the iterative (sequentially repetitive), explorative, participatory and adaptive decision-making processes that typify water resources management.

Water resources data, which are stored, accessed, manipulated, and managed electronically within databases, are numbers, text, and images that characterize the quantity, quality, and spatial and temporal distributions of the supply of, and demand for, water. Data also identify and describe the physical, social, legal, economic, and institutional factors that affect how water resources are managed.

Types of Data

Water resources management requires a knowledge of the resources being managed. Such water resources assessments are based on measurements of physical and **hydrologic** conditions over time and space. The needed degree of spatial and temporal detail (that is, the resolution) and the level of accuracy of these measurements will depend on the particular management

watershed: the land area drained by a river and its tributaries; also called river basin, drainage basin, catchment, and drainage area

hydrology: the science that deals with the occurrence, distribution, movement, and physical and chemical properties of water on Earth; also refers to the hydrologic characteristics of a given region

Proper data collection, analysis, and interpretation are the foundation of effective water resources management. Decision-makers rely on information that often is provided to them by scientific and data-gathering organizations.

issues and problems being addressed. The data required for prediction and management studies for the quantity and quality of water flows in watersheds typically include:

- Climatic factors such as temperature, wind, solar radiation, and rainfall;

- **Geomorphic** and land-use information such as slopes, drainage density, geology, soils, land covers, channel cross-sections, and **groundwater** depths;

- Hydrologic data that include flows, water levels, depths, and velocities;

- Point pollutant loads from point sources such as large industries, cities, and wastewater treatment plants that discharge their wastes into surface waters at a specific locations;

- Diffuse loads from nonpoint sources that enter surface waters along an entire stretch of the river;

- Ecological attributes including an inventory of existing habitats and their condition;

- Water quantity and quality demands over time and space that in some cases can be compatible and in other cases conflicting; and

- Information on the institutional framework in which management decisions are to be made, such as laws pertaining to the **allocation** of water to various users and the various standards set by public health and environmental agencies.

geomorphology: the scientific study of the physical characteristics of the land surface and landforms that are the result of specific geologic processes; also refers to the geomorphological characteristics of a given region

groundwater: generally, all subsurface (underground) water, as distinct from surface water, that supplies natural springs, contributes to permanent streams, and can be tapped by wells; specifically, the water that is in the saturated zone of a defined aquifer

allocate: to distribute resources for a particular purpose

Data Collection

International organizations, governmental agencies, and private companies collect and store data to support local watershed and regional river basin management activities, as well as ongoing research on more global issues related to possible climate change impacts,. These data are needed to perform the assessments used in planning and decision-making devoted to various goals:

- Meeting agricultural, industrial, and municipal demands;
- Reducing waterborne diseases;
- Producing hydroelectric energy;
- Providing for increased navigation, recreation, and environmental protection;
- Coping with natural hazards of floods and droughts; and
- Restoring the aquatic and **riparian** ecosystems.

riparian: pertaining to the banks of a river, stream, waterway, or other, typically, flowing body of water as well as to plant and animal communities along these waterbodies

Because of the variability of water supplies over time, these assessments are based on systematic measurement programs carried out in the past. This is why it is important today to maintain and improve networks of monitoring stations and data collection organizations.

Long-Term Data. Determining trends in water availability and quality, due to human activities and trends in climate, requires consistent data resulting from standard measurements made regularly over the long term. Long-term systematic measurement programs are normally undertaken by government agencies as part of the information infrastructure needed for national or regional development.

In many countries, there exists a single agency responsible for water measurements for all purposes. International agencies, such as the World Meteorological Organization, work toward the standardization of instruments, methods of observation and terminology, design of instrument networks, water quantity and quality monitoring, technology transfer, and local training. As in any other systematic monitoring program, it is not enough just to make the observations. The data must be quality controlled, stored, analyzed, and made available for use by many different clients. Today the Internet provides a primary access to many such databases.

Large-Scale Data. The improvement of water resource measurements and assessments is needed not only for national purposes and management, but also to understand global and large-scale regional processes. For example, the water budget of the oceans, fed largely by rivers and precipitation, is critical in assessing the reasons for the observed rise in mean sea level over the past century and the likely rate of rise in a projected warming climate. Determining the sources of pollution of the seas and oceans requires information on the quality of river discharges. Yet many of the largest rivers, which carry over half of the continental water and sediments to the oceans, are inadequately measured. Evaporation and precipitation processes transfer both water and energy through components of the global climate system and must be better understood on a large scale in order to model and predict trends in the climate.

Databases and Decision-Support Systems

remote sensing: the collection and interpretation of information about an object without being in physical contact with the object; most often, it refers to satellite-based collection of data to map and monitor the environment and resources on Earth

A considerable amount of data used in water resources assessments required for planning and management are now available from public agencies through the Internet. Today, one can obtain a variety of mapping and **remotely sensed** data, including scanned and rescaled aerial photos (Digital

Databases, once housed on computers accessible only to limited number of users, increasingly are available via the Internet. Their accessibility helps increase the transparency of the data analysis process and allows for increased stakeholder involvement.

Orthophoto Quadrangles), scanned topographic maps (Digital Raster Graphics), boundary lines, water systems, transportation networks, land cover, cultural information in computer-compatible form (Digital Line Graphs), and terrain elevations for ground positions at regularly spaced intervals (Digital Elevation Models). The Internet provides access to streamflow and water quality data for numerous gaging sites, sometimes in real time.

In the United States, water resources data can be obtained from the websites of federal agencies such as the U.S. Geological Survey (usgs.gov), the Environmental Protection Agency (epa.gov), the U.S. Fish and Wildlife Service (fws.gov), the U.S. Army Corps of Engineers (usace.army.mil), the U.S. Bureau of Reclamation (usbr.gov), the U.S. Department of Agriculture (usda.gov), the National Aeronautics and Space Administration (nasa.gov), the National Oceanic and Atmospheric Administration (noaa.gov), and the Central Intelligence Agency (cia.gov).

Decision-Support Systems. Data are not very useful if they cannot be used effectively. Decision-support systems (DSS) are interactive graphics-based, menu-driven computer programs that link databases to models. They are designed to facilitate the input and editing of data, the execution of models desired or required (for example, to identify the economic, environmental, ecological, and social impacts of different alternatives), and the display of the results in meaningful, understandable formats.

Developments in information and computer technology, electronic communication, remote sensing, geographic information systems, instrumentation, control, and modeling are having a significant impact on research, operation, planning, environmental impact assessment, and decision-making. Visual and multimedia tools are becoming more and more useful in transferring technical knowledge to decisionmakers and policymakers as well as to the public. DSS plays an important role in water resources management.

EXAMPLES OF FEDERAL DATABASES

A few examples of federal databases illustrate the types of applications afforded by computer and geospatial technologies. The USDA's National Resources Inventory is a sample of land-use and natural resource conditions and trends on U.S. nonfederal lands. It is the most comprehensive database of its kind ever attempted anywhere in the world.

The U.S. EPA's Watershed Atlas is a catalog of geospatial displays and analyses of information and data important for watershed protection and restoration.

EPA's home webpage provides databases and software that apply to specific environmental media (for example, water, air, land); geographic information systems in support of mapping of environmental data; and models for predicting environmental impacts and increasing the level of understanding about natural systems and the way in which they react to varying conditions.

The EPA's Environmental Information Management System accesses descriptive information (metadata) for datasets, databases, documents, models, projects, and spatial data.

SEE ALSO GEOSPATIAL TECHNOLOGIES; LAND-USE PLANNING; PLANNING AND MANAGEMENT, WATER RESOURCES.

Daniel P. Loucks

Bibliography

Guariso, Giorgio, and Werthner, H. *Environmental Decision Support Systems*. Chichester, U.K.: Ellis Horwood Limited, 1989.

Loucks, Daniel P., and J. R. da Costa, eds. *Decision Support Systems: Water Resources Planning*. NATO ASI Series G, Vol. 26. Berlin, Germany: Springer-Verlag, 1991.

Sprague Jr., Ralph H., and Eric D. Carlson. *Building Effective Decision Support Systems*. Englewood Cliffs, NJ: Prentice Hall, 1982.

Davis, William Morris

American Geomorphologist
1850–1934

William Morris Davis is a major historical figure in geomorphology, the scientific study of landforms. Davis is especially known for his theory of landscape development—called the geographical cycle—that was the leading geomorphic theory from 1890 to 1950. He is also considered the father of American academic **geography** because of his role in establishing geography as an independent professional field. Today, geomorphology constitutes part of the subject matter of both geography and **geology**, and this dual affiliation exists largely because throughout his career Davis maintained strong ties to both disciplines.

Landscape Evolution

Davis attended Harvard University, where he studied geology (bachelor of science in 1869) and mining engineering (master of science in 1870) at a time when geography was taught only as part of other subjects. In 1878, Davis was hired by Harvard's geology department to teach physical geography courses, including landforms and **meteorology**.

Combining field observations in Montana in the summer of 1883 with his knowledge of the geomorphic literature, Davis began developing his theory of landscape evolution. He theorized that the geomorphic appearance of a given landscape is controlled by the combination of the following three variables.

- Structure: Structure involves rock resistance to weathering and erosion, and whether strata (rock layers) have been deformed into relief elements (areas of variable elevation) like fault blocks or folds.

- Process: Landforming processes include weathering as well as erosion and deposition by such agents as gravity and streams.

- Stage: Youth, maturity, and old age constitute the principal stages of development, an indication of how long the processes have been acting.

Davis first developed his theory for stream-dominated, humid, midlatitude settings, but geographical cycles were eventually proposed for other environments. The great popularity of the geographical cycle propelled Davis into the forefront of landform studies and the emerging discipline of

geography: the science of the Earth and life, especially the description of land, sea, air, and the distribution of plant and animal life, including humankind and its industries, with reference to the mutual relations among these diverse elements

geology: the scientific study of the Earth, its form and composition, and the physical, chemical, and biological processes that affect it; includes the study of ancient life on the planet

meteorology: the science that deals with the atmosphere, especially with regard to climate and weather

geography. Throughout his career Davis remained a professor in Harvard University's geology department and a tireless champion of geography. SEE ALSO STREAM EROSION AND LANDSCAPE DEVELOPMENT.

Dorothy Sack

Bibliography

Chorley, Richard J., Robert P. Beckinsale, and Antony J. Dunn. "The Life and Work of William Morris Davis." London, U.K.: Methuen, 1973.

Demand Management

Demand management is the purposeful and beneficial manipulation of the level and timing of water usage. Demand management deploys various techniques for conserving water and improving the efficient use of water by end users. Improvements to economic efficiency are achieved whenever the total benefits of a measure are outweighed by the total costs of implementation. Demand management evolved in the context of least-cost or integrated resource planning, which balanced supply and demand management considerations. Managing demand can complement or supplant traditional and emerging supply-management options for water utilities.

Demand management involves measures that promote the efficient use of water, including **load management** and load reduction or conservation. Water conservation also can be understood as the economically and/or socially beneficial reduction of water withdrawals, water use, or water waste. Conservation can forestall future supply-capacity needs; it can be implemented on the supply side as well as the demand side; and it can consist of both temporary measures used during emergencies and permanent measures used to improve long-term efficiency. Reductions in water usage can be beneficial to both water utilities and wastewater utilities in terms of flow reduction.

load management: steps taken to reduce water demand at peak load times, such as shifting some of it to off-peak times; may refer to peak hours or peak days

Demand management or strategic load management complements supply management because controlling the level and timing of demand can improve overall efficiency of system operations and help eliminate, reduce, or defer the need for an investment in new capacity by the water utility. Reductions in peak and off-peak demand affect the total capacity requirements of the utility system and thus the total cost of providing water service.

All demand management activities that decrease the demand for utility services tend to affect supply management since existing system capacity is released for other customers and other uses. That is, the freed or redirected utility capacity can be compared to that provided by more traditional means. Thus, the benefits of demand management can be measured in terms of avoided costs, or the incremental savings associated with not having to produce additional units of water or water service. Avoided cost can be used to compare demand management and supply management options and encourage utilities to seek out least-cost alternatives for meeting future water needs.

Although demand management should not be equated with drought management, the experience of water utilities and customers in implementing efficiency practices can be beneficial during periods of water shortage. Some of the basic demand management techniques can be accelerated during supply emergencies or droughts.

A sign warns residents that they may no longer water their lawns because of drought conditions. Lack of rain in conjunction with high temperatures can lead communities and even states to enact water-use restrictions in an attempt to control water demand.

Water Demand

Several factors influence the residential and nonresidential demand for water. In the aggregate, per capita water demand is very stable. Residential water usage is largely a function of basic demographics, particularly household size, property size, and income. Nonresidential water varies substantially according to type of industry. The production of some goods (such as food and beverages, paper products, and microchips) is highly water intensive.

The demand for water, like the demand for other goods and services, can be represented by a downward-sloping curve where price is represented on the *y*-axis and quantity demanded on the *x*-axis, as shown in the figure below. However, compared with many other goods and services, water demand is relatively price inelastic; that is, changes in price generally do not induce large changes in water use. Nonresidential (large-volume) water use and outdoor residential water use (such as summer lawn watering) are generally more price responsive than indoor water use.

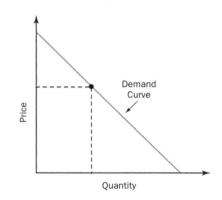

Tools and Techniques

Demand management techniques include conservation-oriented pricing, water-fixture plumbing standards and retrofitting, water-efficient landscaping, changes in water-use practices, and public education. Combining demand and management measures can prove to be effective. For example, a public education program can enhance the effectiveness of a conservation-oriented rate structure.

Despite water's relative price inelasticity, price is considered an essential tool of demand management because it sends customers an essential signal about the value of water. Water metering is a basic demand management measure because it allows the utility to charge a variable price (that is, a per unit rate) so that a customer's bill varies with the level of water usage. Some methods of rate design are particularly efficiency oriented. These include increasing-block rates (where unit rates are increased at higher levels of usage), seasonal rates (where unit rates are higher during peak usage periods), and water budget and excess-use rates (where unit rates are higher for usage above a specified level).

Utility Programs

Some demand management measures can be implemented by consumers on their own, while others can be implemented through utility-sponsored programs. High water and energy prices can induce customers to invest in water-efficient fixtures and appliances as well as to change water-use behavior. Utility programs can help consumers provide more informed choices as well as provide specific incentives for engaging in demand management. Some programs have helped utilities reduce operating costs (water, energy, and chemicals) and postpone or avoid capital costs (treatment plants and other facilities). Both water and wastewater systems can benefit from utility-sponsored demand management programs.

Utility demand management programs can range from very passive to very active. Passive approaches include the distribution of educational materials and low-cost conservation devices (such as leak detection tablets and faucet aerators). More active methods include water audits and rebates to households that purchase replace fixtures (such as toilets). An even more active approach is for the water utility to directly perform onsite retrofits. Program elements can be designed specifically for the needs of residential and nonresidential customers. Utilities can work directly with large-volume users in identifying methods for reducing or shifting loads.

Program design and implementation are critical to the success of a conservation program.

Attention must be paid to the characteristics, needs, and preferences of water users. Utilities can partner with other local utilities, government agencies, or community groups. A pilot program can be useful for developing an effective program. Utilities often collect data throughout the course of implementation in order to assess program effectiveness. The program can be refined over time to ensure that program goals are met. SEE ALSO CONSERVATION, WATER; INTEGRATED WATER RESOURCES MANAGEMENT; PLANNING AND MANAGEMENT, WATER RESOURCES; POPULATION AND WATER RESOURCES; PRICING, WATER; USES OF WATER.

Janice A. Beecher

Bibliography

Baumann, Duane D., John J. Boland, and W. Michael Hanemann. *Urban Water Demand Management and Planning*. New York: McGraw-Hill, 1998.

Billings, R. Bruce, and C. Vaughn Jones. *Forecasting Urban Water Demand*. Denver, CO: American Water Works Association, 1996.

Desalinization

Because only 1 percent of the Earth's water is fresh, it is useful to utilize the oceans as a means of supplementing the fresh-water supply. To be potable (drinkable), however, salt and other chemicals must first be removed from the sea water. This process of salt removal, known as desalinization (also called desalination), has been practiced since ancient times. Today, a number of technologies are used.

Heat Distillation

Over 60 percent of the world's desalinated water is produced using heat to distill fresh water from sea water. The distillation process mimics the natural **hydrologic cycle** in that sea water is heated, producing water vapor, which is in turn condensed to form fresh water.

hydrologic cycle: the solar-driven circulation of water on and in the Earth, characterized by the ongoing transfer of water among the oceans, atmosphere, surface waters (lakes, streams, and wetlands), and groundwaters

vaporization: the change of a substance from a liquid or solid state to the gaseous state

carbonate: carbonates are common minerals and are the principal constituents of sedimentary rocks such as limestone and dolostones; the most widespread carbonate minerals are calcite, aragonite, and dolomite

sulfate: a combination of sulfur in the oxidized state (S^{6+}) and oxygen, and a part of naturally occurring minerals in some soil and rock formations; a common constituent in groundwater and surface water; sulfate minerals tend to be highly soluble

ion: an atom or molecule that carries a net charge (either positive or negative) because of an imbalance between the number of protons and the number of electrons

brackish: describes water having a salinity from 0.05 to 17 parts per thousand; typically a mixture of sea water and fresh water (e.g., as found in an estuary)

In a desalinization plant, sea water is heated to its boiling point to allow maximum **vaporization**. For this to be done economically, the boiling point is lowered by reducing the atmospheric pressure. The reduction of the boiling point is important for two reasons: it allows multiple boiling that results in lower energy requirements, and it controls the buildup of **carbonate** and **sulfate** scale production on the apparatus. The distillation process is used successfully in many locations around the world.

Ion Extraction

Another method of desalinization is **ion** extraction, in which the ionized salts found in sea water are extracted through chemical or electrical means.

Ion Exchange. The chemical method is called ion exchange. In this method, granules of commercially prepared resin remove the positive ions from the sea water and replace them with ions that are loosely bound in the molecular structure of the resin. Other beds of resin are able to exchange negative ions. However this process is too expensive to be used to desalinate large quantities of sea water.

Electrodialysis. In contrast to the chemical method, the electrical mechanism of ion removal, commercially introduced in the early 1960s, is much cheaper. It is called electrodialysis, since electric current pulls the ions through membranes that are permeable to only the positive or negative ions. Alternating positive or negative membranes, which number in the hundreds, are bound by a frame and form narrow compartments to trap the ions. When a direct electric current is applied, the positively charged ions tend to migrate through the membranes permeable to positive ions and the negatively charged ions tend to migrate through the membranes permeable to negative ions. By this process, ions move between the compartments and become more concentrated.

The distance the liquid flows in the compartments, the intensity of the current flow, the permeability of the membranes used, and the distance that the membranes are apart govern the efficiency of electrodialysis. The cost depends on the concentration of salts in the sea water, since the electrical power used varies directly with the number of ions to be removed and their electrochemical characteristics. Usually, the electrical power required to separate the ions from the water would be cheaper than the resin and chemicals used in ion exchange. Even then, it is usually so high that only **brackish** water, less salty than sea water, can be desalinated economically by electrodialysis for large-scale use.

In both ion extraction procedures, sediments and other impurities in the water can greatly reduce the success rate. Careful pre-treatment of the water to remove undesirable materials is usually necessary.

Freezing Desalinization

Extensive work was done in the 1950s and 1960s to develop freezing desalinization. During the process of freezing, dissolved salts are naturally excluded from the lattice structure of ice crystals. Cooling the water to form ice under controlled conditions can desalinate sea water. Before the entire mass of water has been frozen, the ice is removed and rinsed to remove any salts adhering to the ice surface. It is then melted to produce fresh water.

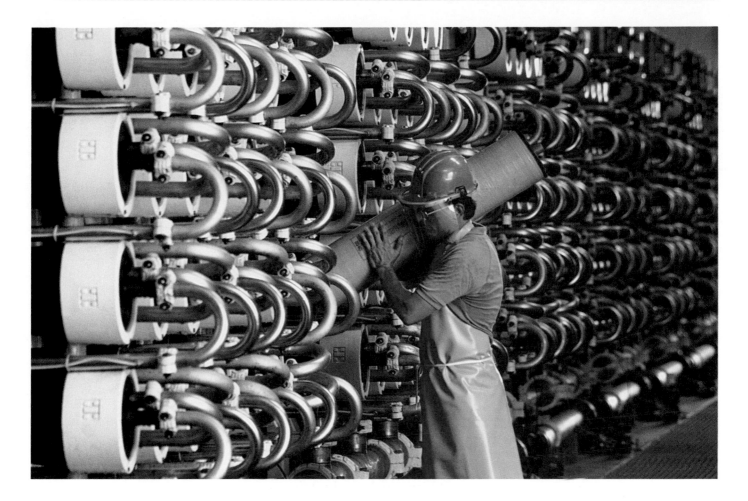

Theoretically, freezing has some advantages over distillation, including a lower energy requirement, little scaling or **precipitation**, and minimal potential for corrosion. The disadvantage is that it involves handling ice and water mixtures that are difficult to move and process.

Solar Humidification

The use of direct solar energy for desalinating sea water has been investigated and used for some time. During World War II (from 1939 to 1945), small solar stills were developed for use on life rafts. These devices imitate the natural hydrologic cycle in that the Sun's rays heat the sea water so that the production of water vapor (humidification) increases. The water vapor is then condensed on a cool surface, and the condensate collected as fresh water. An example of this type of process is the solar greenhouse in Porto Santo, Portugal, in which the sea water is heated in basins, resulting in the condensation of water vapor on the sloping glass roof that covers the basins.

Although the thermal energy may be free, the stills are expensive to construct, additional energy is needed to pump the water to and from the facility, vapor can leak from the stills, and careful operation and maintenance is needed to prevent scale formation. Generally, these types of solar humidification units have been used for desalinating sea water on a small scale, where solar energy is abundant but electricity is not.

Reverse osmosis, one of several desalinization technologies, removes impurities and salt from sea water to make it potable (drinkable). Shown here is a reverse osmosis water treatment plant in Cape Coral, Florida.

precipitation: in chemistry, the separation of a solid phase (precipitate) from solution (dissolved state)

Reverse Osmosis

Reverse osmosis (RO) is relatively new, with successful commercialization occurring in the early 1970s. In RO, sea water is forced through a membrane. As a portion of the water passes through the membrane, the remaining "feed water" increases in salt concentration. Some of the feed water is discharged without passing through the membrane to prevent precipitation of supersaturated salts and increased pressure at the membrane surface. Pretreatment is important in RO because the membranes are fine; suspended solids must be removed and the water pre-treated so that salt precipitation or **microorganism** growth does not occur on the membranes. Usually the pretreatment consists of fine filtration and the addition of acid or other chemicals to inhibit precipitation. During the 1990s, the development of membranes that can operate efficiently with lower pressures and energy recovery devices has greatly reduced operating costs.

microorganism: a microscopic organism

Iceberg Towing

Using icebergs as a source of fresh water is not a new idea. Captain James Cook used icebergs to replenish fresh water supplies aboard his ship *The Resolution* in 1773. However, it was not until the 1950s that serious consideration was given to towing icebergs from Antarctica to **arid** regions of the world.

arid: describes a climate or region where precipitation is exceeded by evaporation; in these regions, agricultural crop production is impractical or impossible without irrigation

Today, satellites could be used to find suitably sized icebergs that optimize the trade-off between handling costs and ice volume. Once located, a bow could be cut in the iceberg and a Kevlar sheet wrapped around it to prevent melting. Powerful tugboats could tow the iceberg along favorable ocean currents to its destination. A trip to Southern California is estimated to take one year and result in a 20-percent loss due to melting.

At present, the cost of transporting icebergs is prohibitive, and many technological barriers remain. Although towed icebergs would avoid major shipping lanes, towing large icebergs for long distances is not yet possible, and most icebergs are too thick to be towed into shallow seas and ports. Instead, other options for drinking water (like desalinization) are more practical. SEE ALSO COOK, CAPTAIN JAMES; DRINKING-WATER TREATMENT; ICE AT SEA; SEA WATER, FREEZING OF; SEA WATER, PHYSICS AND CHEMISTRY OF.

Alison Cridland Schutt

Bibliography

Levine, S. N. *Selected Papers on Desalination and Ocean Technology.* Gloucester, U.K.: Peter Smith Publisher, 1990.

Speigler, K. S., and Y. M. El-Sayed. *A Desalination Primer.* L'Aquila, Italy: Balaban Publishers, 1994.

Desert Hydrology

Deserts are arid regions, generally receiving less than 25 centimeters (10 inches) of precipitation a year, or regions where the potential evaporation rate is significantly greater than the precipitation. In most cases, deserts possess a high average temperature with large differences between daytime and nighttime temperatures. Arid regions can also be defined as environments in which water is the limiting factor for **biosystems**. This means that sur-

biosystem: a biologically based system for the maintainable production and processing of biological materials (such as food) in parallel with the efficient utilization of natural and renewable resources

This desert in Valley of the Tsauchab, Namibia illustrates the vegetation, desert crust, and occasionally pooled water that characterize these arid regions. Annual rainfall in Namibia's coastal desert is 50 millimeters (about 2 inches).

vival of life in these regions involves a constant struggle to obtain this limited commodity and to draw the maximum benefit from it.

The world's deserts are divided into four categories. *Subtropical deserts* are the hottest, with parched terrain and rapid evaporation. Although cool *coastal deserts* are located within the same latitudes as subtropical deserts, the average temperature is much cooler because of frigid offshore ocean currents. Cold *winter deserts* are marked by stark temperature differences from season to season, ranging from 38°C (100°F) in the summer to minus 12°C (10°F) in the winter. *Polar regions* are also considered to be deserts because nearly all moisture in these areas is locked up in the form of ice.

Hydrologic Aspects of Deserts

Several basic conditions distinguish between desert regions and others from a **hydrological** point of view.

- A few, often intensive, rain events with a low amount of overall precipitation, which causes most of the small rivers to be active only a few months every year, and sometimes only once every few years.

- Development of "desert crust" on the land surface.

- A thick vadose zone (the zone between the **water table** and the land surface) resulting in a deep water table.

- The salinization problems of both **groundwater** and soils.

hydrology: the science that deals with the occurrence, distribution, movement, and physical and chemical properties of water on Earth; also refers to the hydrologic characteristics of a given region

water table: the upper surface of the zone of saturation in an unconfined aquifer below which all voids in rock, sediment, and other geologic materials are saturated (completely filled) with water

groundwater: generally, all subsurface (underground) water, as distinct from surface water, that supplies natural springs, contributes to permanent streams, and can be tapped by wells; specifically, the water that is in the saturated zone of a defined aquifer

infiltration rate: the rate at which water from precipitation enters the soil; the maximum rate is known as infiltration capacity

ephemeral stream: a stream that flows only in direct response to precipitation, and thus discontinues its flow during dry seasons; in ephemeral wetlands, refers to holding water from weeks to months but not year-round

fissured sediment: fractured (or cracked) sediments with distinct separation along the crack surfaces; fissures may be filled with mineral-bearing materials; in terms of water flow, water will infiltrate more rapidly along fissures than through porous sediment

contaminant: as defined by the U.S. Environmental Protection Agency, any physical, chemical, biological, or radiological substance in water, including constituents that may not be harmful to the environment or human health

radioactive: describes a substance such as uranium or plutonium that emits energy in the form of streams of particles because of the decay of its unstable atoms

macropore: an opening or zone of high permeability that provides a zone of rapid transport of water (and potentially waterborne contaminants) into the subsurface; examples include animal burrows and tree roots

evapotranspiration: water discharged to the atmosphere as a result of evaporation from the soil and surface-water bodies and by plant transpiration

subsurface: of, relating to, or situated in an area beneath a surface, especially the surface of the Earth or of a body of water

Desert Crust. Vast areas of bare soils, low annual precipitation, and few high intensity rainfall events with high kinetic energy characterize arid zones. Bare soils exposed to rainfall are subjected to physical and chemical processes that change the hydraulic properties of the soil near the surface. When dried, a hard layer is formed in the soil surface that is often called "desert crust," commonly enriched in calcite or silica.

Desert crust decreases the **infiltration rate** of soils, thereby increasing runoff and soil erosion, reducing the availability of water to the root zone, and impeding seedling and plant growth. Understanding the formation and properties of such a crust, as well as developing engineering methods to break it, are essential to control the runoff–infiltration (recharge) ratio and to maintain successful agricultural activities.

Vegetation Control. Vegetation may be the most important control on water movement in desert soils. Because vegetation in arid regions is opportunistic, when the water application rate is increased, plant growth increases as it uses up the excess water.

The opportunistic nature of desert vegetation is shown by a significantly higher concentration of vegetation in areas of increased water flow, such as in **ephemeral streams** and in **fissured sediments**. Where the water supply is limited, plant activity decreases until the water-supply rate increases. The importance of vegetation on a local scale has been shown in several field studies. For instance, it was found that the presence of plants greatly reduced deep drainage in comparison to bare soils.

Vadose Zone Studies. In the past, studies of the unsaturated zone, or vadose zone, in arid settings were conducted primarily for water resources evaluation. In the last two decades of the twentieth century, however, emphasis shifted from water resources to waste disposal and the transport of **contaminants**.

Arid areas are being proposed for low-level and high-level **radioactive** waste disposal. Most of the studies related to the vadose zone in arid settings were conducted in the western United States in regions that are designated as waste facilities. Some of these sites include Hanford, Washington; Sandia, New Mexico; Ward Valley, California; Eagle Flat, Texas; and Nevada test site and Yucca Mountain, Nevada.

The increasing interest in the desert environment for waste facilities, in general, and radioactive waste, in particular, raises the need to understand the practical importance of preferential flow in the subsurface. One could assume that a thick vadose zone combined with low precipitation promotes the safest possible environment for waste disposal. However, fast flow via fractures, cracks, and **macropores** had been suggested as a major mechanism leading to contaminant transport much faster than anticipated by models that predicted transport based on average soil properties.

Salt Accumulation. A significant issue to consider in arid environment is the salinization of both soils and groundwater. The low precipitation, combined with high **evapotranspiration** and often-slow flow rates in the **subsurface**, result in higher concentrations of salts. Human-induced salinization has a long history. A major source of salts accumulating in the upper vadose zone is irrigation water, which is essential for sustaining agriculture in arid lands.

More than one-third of the developed agricultural lands in arid and semiarid regions reflect some degree of salt accumulation. High salinity in agricultural lands imposes stress on the growing crops that can lead to decreased yield and in some cases complete crop failure. This problem emphasizes the need for careful management of desert land and water balance.

Water Management Issues

Despite the difficulties for plants, animals, and humans to live in desert regions, they are increasingly being utilized because of pressure from world population growth. This problem is expressed in the expansion of agricultural activities onto desert lands as well as by the formation and rapid growth of urban and industrial centers. These trends not only result in a growing demand for usable water, but also for the increased disposal of vast amounts of wastewater and solid wastes (e.g., radioactive wastes, hazardous wastes, and municipal solid wastes).

In several cases, international conflicts have developed due to water rights in arid regions. Large rivers crossing desert regions are often the only potential source for water that is essential for agriculture, industrial use, and drinking water. For example, the rights to use the water of large rivers in Africa (e.g., the Nile) and in the Middle East (e.g., the Euphrates and Jordan) remain one of the major issues that govern the relations and conflicts between the countries upstream, where most of the river water discharges, and the countries that use the river water downstream.

Desalinization. **Desalinization** of either deep saline groundwater or sea water is an important alternative source for water in arid regions. However, the cost of desalinization remains higher than most other alternatives. A complex **infrastructure** is required, and the need for a close source of saline water makes this alternative impractical in many arid environments. The world's largest desalinization projects are in the Arabian Gulf (Saudi Arabia, United Arab Emirates, Kuwait), United States, and Japan; all which are wealthy countries with long seashores. SEE ALSO ARTIFICIAL RECHARGE;

desalinization: also spelled desalination, the process of removing salts and other dissolved solids from sea water or saline (salty) water, usually to make it drinkable

infrastructure: the permanent constructed system (e.g., pipes and other structures) that enables the treatment and delivery of water to support human habitation and activity, or that supports manufacturing activities and water projects (e.g., desalinization and hydropower plants)

HYDROLOGIC CYCLE; HYDROPOLITICS; INTERNATIONAL COOPERATION; PRE-CIPITATION AND CLOUDS, FORMATION OF; RADIOACTIVE CHEMICALS; RUNOFF, FACTORS AFFECTING; TRANSBOUNDARY WATER TREATIES.

Noam Weisbrod

Bibliography

Gleick, Peter H. *The World's Water: The Biennial Report on Freshwater Resources 2000–2001.* Washington, D.C.: Island Press, 2000.

Issar, Arie S., and Sol D. Resnick. *1996: Runoff, Infiltration and Subsurface Flow of Water in Arid and Semi-Arid Regions.* Water Science and Technology Library. Dordrecht, The Netherlands: Kluwer Academic Press.

Scanlon, Bridget R., Scott W. Tyler, and Peter J. Wirrenga. "1997: Hydrologic Issues in Arid Unsaturated Systems and Implication for Contaminant Transport." *Reviews in Geophysics* 35, no. 4, 461–490.

Weisbrod, Noam et al. "Salt Accumulation and Flushing in Unsaturated Fractures in an Arid Environment." *Groundwater* 38, no. 3, 452–461.

Developing Countries, Issues in

Water resource issues and problems in the world's developing countries, or lesser developed countries, present special management challenges. These issues and problems include inadequate drinking-water supply and sanitation facilities, water pollution, floods, the siltation of river systems, and the management of rivers and large dams. These problems are more severe and widespread in the developing countries than in the world's wealthier, industrialized ones. Barriers to addressing water problems in developing nations include poverty, illiteracy, rapid population growth, and ineffective institutions and policies for developing, distributing, pricing, and conserving water resources.

The complex patterns of these problems in the developing countries are shaped by differences in wealth, environment, and political systems. For example, extreme poverty in much of sub-Saharan Africa limits access to quality water services. Bangladesh's location at the confluence of the Ganges and Brahmaputra Rivers makes it one of the world's most flood-prone nations. The political system of apartheid in South Africa for years limited the access of rural blacks to adequate water resources. Such differences and patterns must be considered when evaluating water resource problems in the developing nations.

Inadequate Supply and Sanitation

The United Nations designated the 1980s as the International Drinking Water Supply and Sanitation Decade. Despite this commitment and the resources devoted to improving water services, inadequate drinking-water supplies and sanitation facilities constitute a key water resource problem in the developing countries. Nearly 1 billion of the world's people do not have an "adequate" supply of water, and roughly 2 billion do not have access to "adequate" sanitation facilities (with "adequate" defined as a single water tap shared among hundreds of people). Most of these people are in the world's developing nations.

The lack of adequate water services is the cause of much disease and illness in the developing nations. For example, the World Health Organization of the United Nations estimates that 900 million people each year suffer from diarrheal illnesses or other diseases spread by contaminated water, such as typhoid and cholera. According to the World Bank, the use of polluted water for human consumption is the principal cause of health problems that kill more than 2 million people each year—most of them children—and make another billion sick.

The shortage of drinking-water facilities means that open bodies of water are often used as drinking-water sources. Standing, open water bodies make attractive breeding grounds for mosquitoes, which may transmit malaria. Standing water also may host snails, which may carry schistosomiasis, a tropical disease that affects the urinary and intestinal systems. Poor public health conditions reduce human productivity and result in economic losses that poor countries can ill afford.

One barrier to improving water services in the developing nations is the high cost of upgrading and constructing **infrastructure**. Increased demand and intensive use of water (as caused by population increases) often create the need for additional water treatment because water in new source areas tends to be of lower quality; in addition, the original supplies have diminished or their quality has been degraded. In Mexico City, for example, water is pumped over an elevation of 1,000 meters (about 3,280 feet) into the Mexico Valley. This is 55 percent higher than the former source, the Mexico Valley **aquifer**. A newly designed water supply project for the city, to be pumped over an elevation of 2,000 meters (about 6,562 feet), is expected to be even more costly.

Water Pollution

Water pollution in the developing nations is caused by animal and human waste, overapplication of fertilizers, industrial chemicals, urban runoff, and a general lack of pollution prevention laws and their enforcement. Access to adequate wastewater treatment facilities in the developing countries is very limited. For example, only 209 of India's 3,119 towns and cities—less than one in ten—have even partial sewage systems and treatment facilities. As a result, waterbodies in the developing nations are often used as open sewers for human waste products and garbage.✳

An example of this degradation is in Bangkok, Thailand, a city crossed by thousands of canals and referred to as "The Venice of the East." Biochemical oxygen demand (BOD) is a measure of water quality. Pristine streams exhibit high levels of BOD, and low BOD levels indicate degraded water quality. The water in Bangkok's canals is so polluted that levels of BOD in Bangkok's canals are equivalent to BOD levels in sewage.✳

Floods

Floods convey both dangers and benefits to people in the developing nations. Floods account for about 40 percent of all deaths caused by natural disasters, most of which are in the developing nations. For example, 3.7 million people were killed in a 1931 flood on China's Yangtze River. In 2000, four of the world's five largest natural disasters were floods.

Floods also convey environmental and social benefits. Floods carry sediments and nutrients downstream and into floodplains. This natural process is important to river ecology and for agricultural production. Many farmers

A girl in Dhaka, Bangladesh bathes in water leaking from a giant pipe on March 22, 2000, which ironically was designated World Water Day. Inadequate water supply in this city of 9 million has forced many residents to drink and bathe from derelict surface-water sources.

infrastructure: the permanent constructed system (e.g., pipes and other structures) that enables the treatment and delivery of water to support human habitation and activity

aquifer: a water-saturated, permeable, underground rock formation that can transmit significant quantities of water under ordinary hydraulic gradients to wells and springs

✳ **See the "Pollution of Streams by Garbage and Trash" for a photograph of household garbage and rubbish being dumped into a creek.**

✳ **See "Nutrients in Lakes and Streams" for a photograph of the prolific water-weed growth in a Bangkok waterway.**

Women in Ethiopia carry water from a lake (in background) back to their homes. The time spent hauling water can be significant in areas where sources of domestic water supply are limited.

in the developing nations depend on recession agriculture, a practice in which crops are planted in soils saturated by receding floodwaters.

Floods provide reproductive cues to fishes and allow them to swim into floodplains and feast on submerged floodplain vegetation. (Fish are a critical source of animal protein for many people in the lesser developed countries.) Programs for flood management should consider and seek to balance these hazardous and beneficial aspects of floods.

Irrigation

Irrigated agriculture is important in the developing nations, as it constitutes about 80 percent of water uses. Many varieties of irrigated agriculture are practiced in the developing nations, ranging from gravity irrigation canal systems to small tanks and tube wells. Some of these systems are highly efficient, whereas others are affected by problems such as leaky delivery systems, salinization, fouled water supplies (including groundwater, an important source of irrigation), and inflexible delivery schedules.

A boy in West Bengal, India pumps water from a well in a flooded area. Floodwaters can contaminate cisterns and improperly designed wells, compounding problems caused by the river currents and inundation.

Deforestation

Throughout the developing countries, deforestation is being caused by a combination of overpopulation, inappropriate land use practices, and inadequate environmental regulations and enforcement. Soil erosion is a natural process, but deforestation and other human activities have resulted in a fivefold increase in the average levels of sediment carried in the world's rivers. Excess sediment in rivers can damage aquatic ecosystems and fisheries, affecting the people who directly depend on them. For example, deforestation in the **watershed** surrounding Cambodia's Great Lake—the nation's most important fishery—is causing parts of the lake to fill in and is threatening the fishery's long-term viability.

watershed: the land area drained by a river and its tributaries; also called river basin, drainage basin, catchment, and drainage area

Dams

The developing nations have constructed thousands of large dams to reduce flood damages, to generate **hydroelectricity**, and to increase and stabilize water supplies. These dams have provided significant benefits to the developing countries but have also caused complex physical, biological, and societal changes.

hydroelectric: often used synonymously with "hydropower," describes electricity generated by utilizing the power of falling water, as with water flowing through and turning turbines at a dam

The creation of a reservoir submerges a river's bottomlands. These floodplains have rich soils, and their high productivity often supports large human populations. Reservoirs thus often require the resettlement of large numbers of people. For example, China is building the Three Gorges Dam, scheduled for completion in 2009; the reservoir behind the dam will require the resettlement of more than one million people. As a result of the social and environmental changes they have caused, large dams have also been a source of controversy—sometimes violent—in the developing nations.

Aspects of Problem-Solving

In order to better understand these effects and help resolve some of the controversies, in 1997 the World Bank appointed the World Commission on Dams to review the record of dam construction and management and the social, economic, and environmental impacts. The commission released its report in 2000. One of its conclusions was that although dams clearly have made many significant contributions, unacceptable costs have too often been borne to secure those benefits, especially in the form of environmental impacts and by people who lived downstream.

Many barriers to better water management in the developing countries are rooted in economic, institutional, and policy issues. One of these economic problems is overpriced drinking water. For example, people in Port-au-Prince, Haiti, spend 20 percent of their income on water; in Nigeria, the figure is roughly 18 percent. Ironically, problems may also arise if water is priced too low. If fees are set too low, the costs of providing the services are not recaptured; thus, the finances necessary to continue providing services are inadequate, which sets off a cycle of declining quality of services and customers unwilling to pay for them.

Governments in the developing nations, as well as donor nations and organizations, should strengthen efforts to provide adequate water services for their citizens. Although drinking-water and sanitation facilities lack the glamour of larger, more visible projects, the public health problems caused by the lack of these facilities stifle economic and social progress. Additional efforts toward stabilizing population growth rates would reduce demands on limited water and environmental resources. Water planning programs and policies should be better integrated than in the past; for example, water projects must consider ecological and human factors along with hydrologic and engineering principles. While these problems can be lessened with the assistance of donor nations, approaches should be tailored to local and regional settings through cooperation between external experts and local scientists and people (such information exchanges also often prove to be mutually beneficial). While the key to addressing these issues ultimately lies within the developing nations themselves, the means for merging local, indigenous knowledge with experiences from the developed nations should be explored. SEE ALSO AGRICULTURE AND WATER; CONFLICT AND WATER; DAMS; DRINKING WATER AND SOCIETY; DROUGHT MANAGEMENT; ECONOMIC DEVELOPMENT; FISHERIES, FRESH-WATER; FLOODPLAIN MANAGEMENT; FOOD SECURITY; HUMAN HEALTH AND WATER; IRRIGATION MANAGEMENT; POPULATION AND WATER RESOURCES; PRICING, WATER; SUPPLY DEVELOPMENT; SURVIVAL NEEDS; SUSTAINABLE DEVELOPMENT.

Jeffrey W. Jacobs

Bibliography

"Ecology of Large Rivers." *Bioscience* 45, no. 3 (1995):134–203.

Economic and Social Commission for Asia and the Pacific. *State of the Environment in Asia and the Pacific 1990.* Bangkok: United Nations, 1992.

Lansing, J. Stephen. *Priests and Programmers: Technologies of Power in the Engineered Landscapes of Bali.* Princeton, NJ: Princeton University Press, 1991.

Scudder, Thayer. "Recent Experiences with River Basin Development in the Tropics and Subtropics." *Natural Resources Forum* 18, no. 2 (1994):101–113.

"Survey on Development and the Environment." *The Economist* 21 (March 1998):1–16.

"The Beautiful and the Dammed." *The Economist* 28 (March 1992):93–97.

World Bank. *Water Resources Management: A World Bank Policy Paper.* Washington, D.C.: World Bank, 1993.

Internet Resources

Dams and Development: A New Framework for Decision-Making. The Report of the World Commission on Dams, 2000. The World Commission on Dams. <http://www.dams.org>.

Disease, Waterborne.   *See Drinking Water and Society; Human Health and the Ocean; Human Health and Water; Microbes in Groundwater; Microbes in Lakes and Streams; Microbes in the Ocean.*

Douglas, Marjory Stoneman

American Conservationist
1890–1998

From sunrise discoveries of the Florida Everglades in the early 1920s to promoting a national park, Marjory Stoneman Douglas informed Americans and the world of the splendor, uniqueness, fragility, and importance of this region—the only subtropical wetland in the United States.

Douglas was the pen and the voice of South Florida's environmental movement. Her book *The Everglades: River of Grass* is the preeminent work on the subject. Published the same year that Everglades National Park was dedicated (1947), Douglas's work articulates the workings of America's unique subtropical ecosystem.

The greater Everglades ecosystem stretches from above the headwaters of the Kissimmee River near Orlando south to the end of the peninsula and encompasses from one-third to more than half the state's width. Douglas recognized that the flow of fresh, clean water sustained huge bird and fish populations, unique plant communities, and **endangered** species.

Had Douglas simply described the natural environment, *The Everglades* would have been a beautiful book. Her inclusion of the social environment (the people, politics, and money) of the region elevated the work to one of historic importance.

In *The Everglades*, Douglas wove together the water, grass, rock and muck, animals, and people of South Florida. She was not the first to recognize the relationship of water to the environment, but she eloquently described the "river of grass." Douglas was one of the first writers to document the fact that the Everglades is not a swamp but a broad, shallow wetland and waterway spanning an area about 160 kilometers (100 miles) wide and 320 kilometers (200 miles) long.

Whereas her written words captivated readers, her spoken words invigorated listeners to action. In 1970, Douglas organized and led the Friends of the Everglades citizens' action group, which by 2000 had grown to more than six thousand members and is an influential player in all environmental issues affecting the Everglades ecosystem.

Marjory Stoneman Douglas, until her death at 108, remained devoted to environmental activism to protect and restore the Everglades. Here she poses at age 96 with her best-known book.

endangered: describes a plant or animal species threatened with extinction by human-made or natural changes throughout all or a significant area of its range; designated in accordance with the 1973 Endangered Species Act

Early Years

Douglas was born April 7, 1890, in Minneapolis, Minnesota. She grew up in a house of adults, separated from her father. Because of her mother's mental illness, she lived with her maternal grandparents and aunt. Graduating in 1912 with a degree in English literature from Wellesley College, Douglas was named class orator.

Soon after Douglas's graduation, her mother died, and Douglas was free to be independent, but lacked direction. For 3 years she wandered through a series of department store jobs; relocations to Boston, St. Louis, and Newark; and a failed marriage. In 1915, she reunited with her father in Miami. Except for 2 years (1918 to 1920) she spent as a Red Cross worker in Europe, Douglas experienced and documented South Florida's explosive growth and the environmental consequences of that growth over the course of 80 years.

Transition to Writing and Leadership. Above all, Douglas aspired to be a writer. Beginning with essays in high school, she moved on to a career as a journalist and assistant editor with the *Miami Herald* and as a freelance writer. She produced thirteen novels and books of short stories, hundreds of newspaper and magazine articles, three plays, poems, and numerous contributions to other authors' works. Acknowledging that *The Everglades* was her best work, Douglas felt that her single most important accomplishment was achieved through poetry.

Her oratory skills served Douglas well. Considered bookish, she was also confident and outspoken. Douglas was a women's rights, civil rights, and human rights activist long before completing her legacy as an environmental leader. She urged the Florida legislature to pass the women's suffrage amendment, and she began speaking out on issues, especially about the Everglades.

By her own admission, she would talk at the drop of a hat, often telling listeners more than they may have wanted to know. She lectured, cajoled, scolded, and inspired public officials, farmers, ranchers, developers, and everyday citizens. Challenged to do something more and believing in the power of organizations, Douglas founded the Friends of the Everglades. Initially begun to defeat a proposed Everglades jetport, the group continues to epitomize Douglas's belief in action, that each individual citizen has to do something.

Contributions to the Everglades

Through her writing, Douglas gave a forum for scientists to describe how draining the Everglades, interrupting the sheet flow of water with roads and canals, and **channelizing** the Kissimmee River changed the Everglades. She gave a remote, often harsh environment a personality; explained the basic science and processes; and bluntly pointed out the effects of altering the environment. In addition, she provided others with a vehicle to explain the importance of the system's hydrological cycle, sheet flow mechanics, surface-water runoff, and soil subsidence and to make the necessary scientific case for restoring the natural systems.

Pioneering Everglades environmentalist Art Marshall told Douglas that with three words ("river of grass") she had changed people's perceptions and

channelization: any excavation and construction activities intended to widen, deepen, straighten, or relocate a natural river channel; the term does not include maintenance activities on existing channels, such as the clearing of debris or dredging of accumulated sediments

---

DOUGLAS'S LEGACY

A prolific writer, Douglas contributed many books about Florida, the Everglades, and the environment. Among her books are: *Alligator Crossing: A Novel* (1959); *Florida: The Long Frontier* (1967); *Joys of Bird Watching in Florida* (1969); *Adventures in a Green World: The Story of David Fairchild and Barbour Lathrop* (1973); *Freedom River* (1994); and *River in Flood, and Other Florida Stories* (1998).

also educated the world about the true nature of the Everglades. Douglas died May 14, 1998, in Miami, Florida at the age of 108. She was cremated and her ashes were spread over the Everglades. SEE ALSO EVERGLADES; FLORIDA, WATER MANAGEMENT IN.

Terry C. Dodge

Bibliography

Breton, Mary Joy. *Women Pioneers for the Environment.* Boston, MA: Northeastern University Press, 1998.

Byers, Stephen W. "Don't Mess with Her Wetlands." *New York Times Magazine* v. 6 (1999):46–47.

Douglas, Marjory Stoneman. *The Everglades: River of Grass.* 50th Anniversary Edition. Sarasota, FL: Pineapple Press, 1997.

Douglas, Marjory Stoneman, and John Rothchild. *Voice of the River.* Sarasota, FL: Pineapple Press, 1987.

Internet Resources

Marjory Stoneman Douglas Page. Friends of the Everglades. <http://www.everglades.org/msd.html>.

Drinking Water and Society

The course of world society in the twenty-first century is likely to be substantially influenced by a single resource: drinking water. The first and most obvious fact is that water is an absolute necessity. Without water, life—animal, plant, or human—cannot exist. Water comprises approximately 75 percent of the human body. Without adequate water, the body ceases to function. Depending on one's exertion level and weather conditions, the average adult should consume a minimum of eight 8-ounce glasses (or about 2 liters) of water daily.

One might think that drinking water should not be a problem in the twenty-first century, but it can be. Several related factors define the challenges. First, quantities of water on planet Earth suitable for drinking are extremely limited. Less than 1 percent of all water on Earth is available as **groundwater** and **surface water** suitable for human uses such as drinking and cooking. The remainder is either salt water (97 percent) or is locked up in ice (just over 2 percent).

Second, precipitation, which replenishes groundwater and surface-water resources, does not fall evenly over the face of the Earth. Additionally, some times of the year are rainy, other times dry. Thus, water resources are bountiful at some times and in some places, but extremely sparse in others.

Third, for more than a billion people in developing countries, water is scarce and frequently contaminated, thereby posing a health risk. In these parts of the world, contaminated drinking water along with primitive (or nonexistent) sanitation systems annually result in widespread illness and millions of deaths annually. The majority of the victims are children.

Infrastructure Versus the Search for Water

In the United States and other industrialized nations, access to clean, safe water for the majority of the population is achieved through a public water-supply **infrastructure**. In the United States, federal, state, and local laws

groundwater: generally, all subsurface (underground) water, as distinct from surface water, that supplies natural springs, contributes to permanent streams, and can be tapped by wells; specifically, the water that is in the saturated zone of a defined aquifer

surface water: water found above ground and open to the atmosphere, such as the oceans, lakes, ponds, wetlands, rivers, and streams

infrastructure: the permanent constructed system (e.g., pipes and other structures) that enables the treatment and delivery of water to support human habitation and activity, or that supports manufacturing activities and water projects (e.g., desalinization and hydropower plants)

Societies in Arctic and subarctic regions often struggle to find adequate supplies of drinking water. Ice and snow may be the only source of domestic self-supply, as shown by this resident of Quaanaq, Greenland.

toxic: describes chemical substances that are or may become harmful to plants, animals, or humans when the toxicant is present in sufficient concentrations

and regulations tightly govern most public drinking-water supplies. The U.S. Environmental Protection Agency is principally responsible for establishing standards for public water supplies and overseeing their enforcement. The agency defines water as "safe" if it contains no harmful bacteria or other pathogenic (disease-causing) microorganisms, and the concentrations of individually regulated **toxic** chemicals are below drinking-water standards.

Yet supplying water conforming to this criterion is expected to become increasingly difficult. The U.S. drinking-water infrastructure (collection, holding, treatment, and distribution systems) is aging. Much of it has been in place for most of the twentieth century, and is becoming subject to frequent failures. Recent federal government studies indicate that repairs to, and replacement of, the drinking-water infrastructure will become a multi-billion-dollar item in federal, state, and local budgets.

Moreover, competition for water for domestic, industrial, and agricultural needs can only be expected to accelerate in the years ahead. Increasing urbanization and development compete with nonurban uses such as agriculture; often, these very different land and water uses adjoin one other geographically. Lawmakers and resource planners worldwide face a daunting challenge to meet ever-increasing needs for adequate drinking-water supplies.

Developing Countries. The situation is quite different in less developed countries. A water-supply infrastructure often does not exist. International assistance may provide a community well; but in many cases, people drink dirty and contaminated water because no other options are available in their communities. People typically gather water from the nearest source, which often is the same one used for bathing and washing activities, waste disposal, and perhaps even a watering source for local livestock. These varied uses of the same water source frequently lead to the spread of diseases.

More than 1 billion of the world's people lack access to safe water, and nearly 2 billion people lack safe sanitation. Over 3 million people annually die from avoidable water-related diseases. Dirty water from unsanitary conditions is the leading cause of death of children in Asia, and globally claims the life of one child every 30 seconds.

The search for water is a daily way of life for many people in developing countries, especially in most countries of the African continent, and numerous areas within Asia and South and Central America. A 2000 report by the Asian Development Bank stated that of the 300 million people living in the Asia–Pacific region, one person out of three have no access to sources of safe drinking water within 200 meters (655 feet) of their homes. Whether in cold or hot climates, the constant search for safe drinking water is often difficult and time consuming. This situation can worsen during droughts (and other adverse weather conditions), conflicts, and wars. Women and children most often carry out the task of gathering water.

Compounding the problem are demographers' predictions that the world population will increase by approximately 33 percent over the first 25 years of the twenty-first century. As this century opened, the world population was just over 6 billion. At present growth rates, it will top 7 billion by 2013 and 8 billion by 2028. Much of this growth is expected to take place in developing countries, many of which are already burdened with serious drinking-water problems.

International aid programs provide safe drinking water for key localities in developing countries. Here a child in Gabisi, Ghana balances a water bucket after visiting the WaterAid pump.

Examples of Inadequate Water Supplies

With 40 percent of the world's population facing water scarcity, United Nations Secretary-General Kofi Annan identified water as one of the key discussions for the 2002 World Summit on Sustainable Development held in Johannesburg, South Africa. The summit identified the limited availability of fresh-water resources—along with economic growth, industrialization, population growth, and urbanization—as the major factors that have contributed to water scarcity. This condition is not limited to certain regions, but extends throughout the world, as the following three examples illustrate.

Burkina Faso. The isolated city of Liptougou in the western African country of Burkina Faso (formerly Upper Volta) lacks the basic infrastructure of a regular water supply, along with schools, roads, and health facilities. One of the main problems confronting all citizens is insufficient drinkable water sources. This necessitates that women fetch water for their families' needs during most of the day, which in turn restricts their ability to perform other necessary tasks.

Nepal. Nepal is a small mountain country that lies north of India and south of China, and near Mount Everest, the highest point on Earth. Most of the country's 20 million people have no water, no electricity, and limited access to health facilities. Women spend much of their time walking narrow paths in treacherous terrain to the nearest water source. The hike for water is difficult because some women must carry 50-pound jugs full of water for up to an hour.

Honduras. Honduras is a developing nation in Central America with an economy that has never been stable and with large areas of poverty and subsistence farming. More than 81 percent of families have no access to drinkable water, electricity, or schools.

Water is necessary for human survival, and the search for and transport of water still characterizes daily life for much of the world's population,

In developing countries, people (usually women and children) often must walk long distances to find water. These village women from Pakistan's southern Sindh province embark on a water search, carrying traditional earthenware pots in addition to their small children.

particularly the poor. Their lack of access to adequate and safe drinking-water supplies affects health and economic opportunities. To address this ongoing global challenge, the 2002 Johannesburg Summit pledged the goal of halving the proportion of people without access to safe drinking water by 2015. SEE ALSO CONFLICT AND WATER; DEVELOPING COUNTRIES, ISSUES IN; GROUNDWATER SUPPLIES, EXPLORATION FOR; HUMAN HEALTH AND WATER; INFRASTRUCTURE, WATER-SUPPLY; POPULATION AND WATER RESOURCES; RAINWATER HARVESTING; SAFE DRINKING WATER ACT; SUPPLIES, PUBLIC AND DOMESTIC WATER; SUPPLY DEVELOPMENT; SURVIVAL NEEDS; SUSTAINABLE DEVELOPMENT; USES OF WATER; WAR AND WATER.

Edward F. Vitzthum and William Arthur Atkins

Bibliography

de Zuane, John. *Handbook of Drinking Water Quality*, 2nd ed. New York: John Wiley & Sons, 1997.

Gleick, Peter H. *The World's Water: The Biennial Report on Freshwater Resources 2000–2001*. Washington, D.C.: Island Press, 2000.

Ingram, Colin. *The Drinking Water Book: A Complete Guide to Safe Drinking Water*. Berkeley, CA: Ten Speed Press, 1991.

Tobin, Richard J. "Environment, Population, and the Developing World." In *Environmental Policy* (4th ed.). eds. Norman J. Vig and Michael E. Kraft. Washington, D.C.: CQ Press, 2000.

Internet Resources

Allie, Mohammed. *South Africa Flounders In Its Search For Free Water*. Panos Institute. <http://www.panos.org.uk/news/February2002/south_africa_water.htm>.

Campaign for Safe and Affordable Drinking Water. <http://www.safe-drinking-water .org/>.

EPA Ground Water and Drinking Water. U.S. Environmental Protection Agency. <http://www.epa.gov/safewater>.

Water for People. <http://www.water4people.org>.

Water in Africa. Volunteers of the Peace Corps and World Wide Schools. <http://www.peacecorps.gov/wws/water/africa/resources/index.html>.

Water Supply and Sanitation. The World Bank Group. <http://www.worldbank.org/ watsan/>.

Drinking-Water Supplies *See Groundwater Supplies, Exploration for; Safe Drinking Water Act; Supplies, Protecting Public Drinking-Water; Supplies, Public and Domestic Water.*

Drinking-Water Treatment

Public water systems vary in the treatment of water that is delivered to the consumer, depending on whether the system uses a **groundwater** source or a **surface-water** source. Some public water systems, primarily those that utilize groundwater wells, deliver untreated water directly to the customer's tap. Groundwater is usually less susceptible to **contamination** than surface water, and therefore requires little or no treatment.

Many large public water systems, however, draw their water from surface sources such as lakes, rivers, and streams, which are vulnerable to many types of contamination. Hence, a multiple-barrier approach to water treatment is most effective in producing drinking water that is free of health risks, meets regulatory requirements, and is palatable (acceptable in taste) to the consumer.

Groundwater

Although groundwater generally is less likely to be contaminated than surface water, it nonetheless may require contaminant removal. Possible groundwater contaminants include naturally occurring **inorganic** chemicals such as arsenic, fluoride, and nitrate, as well as human-made chemicals (from solvents, fuels and pesticides, for example) that have found their way into the **aquifer**. Other contaminants that present aesthetic concerns are calcium and magnesium (which produce hardness); iron and manganese (which cause staining of laundry and plumbing fixtures); and hydrogen sulfide gas (which produces the unforgettable "rotten-egg" smell). The word "contaminant" includes any substance in water, including those that are not harmful, even though popular usage often refers only to harmful pollutants.

Hard water is usually treated with the water "softening" method, which utilizes a resin-coated **media** that exchanges its **ion** (usually sodium) for the calcium and magnesium ions that are responsible for hardness. The water-softening media must be regenerated periodically with a brine (very salty) solution.

Even if the water is not hard, inorganic chemicals such as iron and manganese can cause problems that require treatment. Iron and manganese can be oxidized, or brought out of solution, by chemicals such as chlorine

groundwater: generally, all subsurface (underground) water, as distinct from surface water, that supplies natural springs, contributes to permanent streams, and can be tapped by wells; specifically, the water that is in the saturated zone of a defined aquifer

surface water: water found above ground and open to the atmosphere, such as the oceans, lakes, ponds, wetlands, rivers, and streams

contamination: impairment of the quality of water by natural or human-made substances to a degree that is considered undesirable for certain uses; this term usually implies a human or environmental health threat, but some types of contamination are merely nonaesthetic rather than harmful

inorganic: an element, molecule, or substance that did not form as the direct result of biologic activity

aquifer: a water-saturated, permeable, underground rock formation that can transmit significant quantities of water under ordinary hydraulic gradients to wells and springs

hard water: water that forms a precipitate with soap due to the abundance of calcium, magnesium, or ferrous ions in solution

media: as in water treatment, the sand, gravel, small plastic beads, or other material designed for water filtration

ion: an atom or molecule that carries a net charge (either positive or negative) because of an imbalance between the number of protons and the number of electrons

Settling tanks at a water treatment plant allow coagulated particles to settle to the bottom of the tank. The settled material is periodically drained and collected for eventual disposal in a landfill.

ozone: a chemical compound composed of three oxygen atoms (triatomic oxygen), used in water treatment; a blue, gaseous allotrope of oxygen O_3, formed naturally from diatomic oxygen by electric discharge or exposure to ultraviolet radiation

volatile organic compounds: organic compounds that can be isolated from the water phase of a sample by purging the water sample with inert gas, such as helium, and subsequently analyzed by gas chromatography

turbidity: a measure of the cloudiness (reduced transparency) of water, determined by the amount of light reflected by particulate matter in the water

algae: (singular, alga) simple photosynthetic organisms, usually aquatic, containing chlorophyll, and lacking roots, stems, and leaves

coagulant: flocculant; a substance that, when in a fluid, coagulates or flocculates (comes together in a coherent mass); contaminants such as microbes are attracted to the flocculant and are filtered out of the water

pH: a measure of the acidity of water; a pH of 7 indicates neutral water, with values between 0 and 7 indicating acidic water (0 is very acidic), and values between 7 and 14 indicating alkaline (basic) water (14 is very alkaline); specifically defined as $-\log_{10}(H^+)$, where (H^+) is the hydrogen ion concentration

or potassium permanganate. The oxidized metals can then be filtered out as the water passes through a sand media. A zeolite sand, commonly known as manganese greensand, is usually used for this filtration.

Some groundwaters have taste and odor problems that require treatment in order for the water to be palatable to the user. Chlorine and **ozone** are effective in reducing hydrogen sulfide odors, and simple aeration can rid the water of some **volatile organic compounds**, such as solvents or petroleum byproducts.

Surface Water

Many large cities are served by surface-water sources; most of these surface waters are exposed to a variety of contaminants. Common contaminant sources are untreated sewage and runoff from fertilized fields, parking lots, or unprotected watersheds. The primary contaminants of concern are microbes, including *Giardia* and *Cryptosporidium*. Effective surface water treatment therefore relies on the multiple-barrier approach, involving a sequence of processes from among the following options.

Pre-Treatment.   Simple screens over intake pipes in lakes or rivers can prevent large debris, such as leaves, sticks, or small fish from entering the treatment plant. Waters that exhibit seasonal changes in **turbidity** or **algae** growth may require an oxidant such as chlorine, potassium permanganate, or ozone for pre-treatment.

Chemical Feed and Rapid Mix.   **Coagulants** such as alum, ferric chloride, or synthetic polymers are added to the raw water and mixed rapidly. Chemicals to adjust the **pH** may also be added at this point. The effectiveness of further treatment depends partly on raw water chemical characteristics such as pH, temperature, and alkalinity.

Coagulation, Flocculation, and Sedimentation.   The coagulant chemicals, by the process of coagulation, neutralize the electrical charges of the sediment particles, allowing the binding together of small particles into larger

Small filters made of pleated paper, carbon, or synthetic resins often are used by consumers. Pleated paper filters can remove sand, dirt, and some iron. Carbon filters are effective against chlorine and organic chemicals such as herbicides and pesticides, and can also remove objectionable tastes and odors. Some manufacturers of resin-type filters claim a high removal of lead or other inorganic chemicals.

particles that can then be settled or filtered. This process is known as flocculation. The sedimentation process then allows the larger "floc" particles to settle in a basin. The cleaner water at the top of the sedimentation basin flows onto the filter.

Filtration. The filter media is usually a mixture of carefully graded and specified gravels and sands, specifically designed for particle retention. These removed particles include turbidity and biological contaminants such as *Giardia* and *Cryptosporidium*. Inorganic chemicals such as arsenic and mercury are also removed by proper coagulation and filtration.

Disinfection. This process is designed to kill disease-causing microorganisms such as bacteria, viruses, and protozoa. Chlorine is most commonly used for this purpose, although ozone and ultraviolet light are increasingly being used in public water systems. The single-celled protozoa (*Giardia* and *Cryptosporidium*), which can cause severe intestinal illness, are more resistant to traditional disinfectants than bacteria or viruses, and the disinfection process must therefore be closely monitored.

Other Treatment Technologies

A number of other treatment technologies are employed both by the public and private sector, depending on the needs and desires of the water users. Granular-activated carbon is used for the elimination of objectionable tastes and odors, as well as for removal of organic chemicals such as pesticides and herbicides. Sodium carbonate, commonly known as soda ash, can be used to raise the pH of the water to make it less corrosive to pipes and plumbing fixtures. Some public water systems add small amounts of fluoride in order to aid in the prevention of dental cavities in children.

In addition, many small water treatment units, designed to fit under the kitchen sink or in any other convenient location, are used by individual homeowners regardless of the water source. Cartridge filters, membrane

reverse osmosis: process in which dissolved substances are removed from water by forcing water, but not dissolved salts, through a semipermeable membrane under high pressure; commonly used to treat contaminated drinking water or process water; in desalinization, reverse osmosis is used to extract fresh water from salty water

filters, and **reverse osmosis** units are all able to filter out most contaminants that cause health risks and aesthetic concerns. Water softeners are often necessary to treat hard water. Small ozone or ultraviolet-light disinfection units are becoming popular with homeowners who depend on private water supplies of questionable quality.

Many different types of water treatment units are designed for the individual homeowner. When considering the purchase of such a unit, the homeowner should have the water tested to determine exactly what type of contaminants are in the water, and what, if anything, needs to be removed. No one filter works for all contaminants. A filter that removes iron and manganese, for example, will probably not remove herbicides or pesticides. It is also important to remember that all treatment units require regular maintenance to keep them functioning properly and to prevent the buildup and possible breakthrough of the unwanted contaminants. SEE ALSO FRESH WATER, NATURAL COMPOSITION OF; FRESH WATER, NATURAL CONTAMINANTS IN; POLLUTION OF GROUNDWATER; POLLUTION OF LAKES AND STREAMS; SAFE DRINKING WATER ACT; SUPPLIES, PUBLIC AND DOMESTIC WATER.

Scott G. Curry

Bibliography

Peavy, Howard S., and Donald R. Rowe. *Environmental Engineering.* New York: McGraw-Hill, 1985.

Viessman Jr., Warren, and Mark J. Hammer. *Water Supply and Pollution Control.* New York: Harper & Row, 1985.

Drought Management

natural hazard: a hazard event arising from geophysical processes or biological agents—such as those creating earthquakes, hurricanes, floods, or locust infestations—that affect the lives, livelihood, and property of people

Drought is a subtle, insidious **natural hazard** that is a normal part of the climate of virtually all regions of the world. Its occurrence results in a myriad of economic, social, and environmental impacts in developed as well as developing nations, although the characteristics of its impacts differ considerably between the two settings.

Drought is considered by many to be the most complex but least understood of all natural hazards, affecting more people than any other. It is a normal feature of climate and its recurrence is inevitable. However, there remains much confusion about its characteristics. It is precisely this confusion that explains, to some extent, the lack of emphasis on proactive drought management efforts in most parts of the world. Through an improved understanding of the inevitability and characteristics of drought, as well as its differences from other natural hazards, scientists, policymakers, and the public will be better equipped to establish much-needed policies and plans whereby future vulnerability to drought can be reduced.

Drought as a Natural Hazard

Drought differs from other natural hazards in several ways. First, drought is a slow-onset, creeping natural hazard. Its effects often accumulate slowly over a considerable period of time and may linger for years after the termination of the drought event. Second, the absence of a precise and universally accepted definition of drought adds to the confusion about whether a drought exists and, if it does, its degree of severity. Third, the impacts of

During the Dust Bowl of the 1930s, nearly two-thirds of the U.S. land area experienced severe to extreme drought conditions. This ruined farm is buried under layers of dirt and sand blown across the landscape.

drought are nonstructural and typically are spread over a larger geographical area than are damages resulting from other natural hazards. These characteristics of drought have hindered the development of accurate, reliable, and timely estimates of severity and impacts and, ultimately, the formulation of effective drought preparedness plans.

Drought Characteristics and Definition

Drought results from a deficiency of precipitation from statistically normal (long-term average) amounts that, when extended over a season or especially over a longer period of time, is insufficient to meet the demands of human activities. All types of drought originate from a deficiency of precipitation that results in water shortages for some activity (such as crop production) or for some group (such as farmers). The incidence of drought in the United States during the period from 1895 to early 2002 is shown in the figure on page 262.

Droughts differ from one another in three essential characteristics: intensity, duration, and spatial coverage. Moreover, many disciplinary perspectives of drought exist. Because of these numerous and diverse disciplinary views, considerable confusion often exists over exactly what constitutes a drought. Regardless of such disparate views, the overriding feature of drought is its negative impacts on people and the environment.

This graph shows the percent area of the United States in severe and extreme drought during the twentieth century.

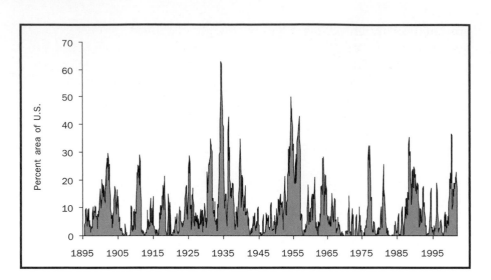

Types of Drought

Drought is normally grouped by type: meteorological, hydrological, agricultural, and socioeconomic. The impacts associated with drought usually take 3 months or more to develop, but this time period can vary considerably, depending on the timing of the initiation of the precipitation deficiency.

Meteorological. Meteorological drought is expressed solely on the basis of the degree of dryness in comparison to some normal or average amount and the duration of the dry period. Thus, intensity and duration are the key characteristics of this type of drought.

Agricultural. Agriculture is usually the first economic sector to be affected by drought because soil moisture content is often quickly depleted, especially if the period of moisture deficiency is associated with high temperatures and windy conditions. Agricultural drought links various characteristics of meteorological drought to agricultural impacts, focusing on precipitation shortages, differences between actual and **potential evapotranspiration**, and soil water deficits. A thorough definition of agricultural drought should account for the variable susceptibility of crops at different stages of development.

potential evapotranspiration: the maximum quantity of water capable of being evaporated from the soil and transpired from the vegetation of a specified region in a given time interval under existing climatic conditions; expressed as a depth of water (e.g., centimeters)

groundwater: generally, all subsurface (underground) water, as distinct from surface water, that supplies natural springs, contributes to permanent streams, and can be tapped by wells; specifically, the water that is in the saturated zone of a defined aquifer

Hydrological. Hydrological droughts are associated with the effects of periods of precipitation shortfall on surface or subsurface water supply (for example, streamflow, reservoir and lake levels, and **groundwater**) rather than with precipitation shortfalls. Hydrological droughts usually lag the occurrence of meteorological and agricultural droughts because more time elapses before precipitation deficiencies are detected in reservoirs, groundwater, and other components of the hydrologic system. As a result, impacts of hydrological drought are out of phase with impacts of other drought types. Also, water in hydrological storage systems such as reservoirs, rivers, and groundwater often is used for multiple and competing purposes, further complicating the sequence and quantification of impacts. Water uses affected by drought can include purposes as varied as power generation, flood control, irrigation, drinking water, industry, and recreation.

Socioeconomic. Socioeconomic drought associates the supply and demand of some economic good or service with elements of meteorological, hydrological, and agricultural drought. In socioeconomic drought, deficiencies of precipitation are linked directly to the supply of some commodity or economic good (for example, water, hay, or hydroelectric power). Increases in population can alter substantially the demand for these economic goods over time. The incidence of socioeconomic drought can increase because of a change in the frequency of meteorological drought, a change in societal vulnerability to water shortages, or both. For example, poor land-use practices such as overgrazing can decrease animal **carrying capacity** and increase soil erosion, which exacerbates the impacts of, and vulnerability to, future droughts.

carrying capacity (animal): the maximum population that can be supported by the natural resources

The Impacts of Drought

The impacts of drought are diverse and often ripple through the economy. Thus, impacts are often referred to as either direct or indirect. A loss of yield resulting from drought is a direct or first-order impact of drought. However, the consequences of that impact (for example, loss of income, farm foreclosures, and government relief programs) are secondary or even tertiary impacts.

The impacts of drought appear to be increasing in both developing and developed countries, which in many cases reflects the persistence of non-sustainable development and population growth. Lessening the impacts of future drought events will require nations to pursue development of drought policies that emphasize a wide range of **risk management** techniques, including improved monitoring and early warning systems, preparedness plans, and appropriate **mitigation** actions and programs.

risk management: process of evaluating and selecting regulatory and nonregulatory responses to environmental risks

mitigation: actions designed to lessen or reduce adverse impacts; frequently used in the context of environmental assessment

The impacts of drought that must be addressed can be classified into one of three principal types: economic, environmental, and social.

Economic Losses. Economic impacts range from direct losses in the broad agricultural and agriculturally related sectors (including forestry and fishing), to losses in recreation, transportation, banking, and energy sectors. Other economic impacts would include added unemployment and loss of revenue to local, state, and federal government.

Environmental Impacts. Environmental losses include damages to plant and animal species, wildlife habitat, and air and water quality; forest and range fires; degradation of landscape quality; and soil erosion. These losses are difficult to quantify, but growing public awareness and concern for environmental quality has forced public officials to focus greater attention on them.

Impacts on Society. Social impacts mainly involve public safety, health, conflicts between water users, and inequities in the distribution of impacts and disaster relief programs. As with all natural hazards, the economic impacts of drought are highly variable within and between economic sectors and geographic regions, producing a complex assortment of winners and losers with the occurrence of each disaster.

Drought Preparedness and Mitigation

Drought is considered by many people to be strictly a natural or physical event. This view of drought provides little, if any, opportunity to alter the impact of drought through the application of appropriate drought management techniques. In reality, drought has both physical and social components, and it is essential that water managers and decisionmakers understand

---

WHAT DOES DROUGHT COST?

Because of the number of affected groups and sectors associated with drought, its spatial extent, and the difficulties connected with quantifying environmental damages and personal hardships, the accurate determination of the financial costs of drought is an arduous task. It has been estimated that the average annual impacts of drought in the United States are between $6 and $8 billion. However, during the drought years of 1976 to 1977 and 1988, government estimates of impacts were $36 billion and $40 billion, respectively.

A prolonged drought in the eastern United States in 1999 lowered the water level of the Lehigh River approximately 5 feet. The much-reduced flow affected municipal and industrial uses along the river, including the Bethlehem Steel Plant (background).

both components if they are to make progress in reducing the risks associated with drought for future generations.

It is critical that the people inhabiting each geographic region understand their exposure to the drought hazard: for example, the probability of drought occurrence at various severity levels. However, the risks associated with drought for any region are products of both the region's exposure to the event and the vulnerability of its society to a drought at that point in time. Vulnerability, unlike the natural event, is determined by varied social factors. Examples include:

- Population changes;
- Population shifts (region to region and rural to urban);
- Demographic characteristics;
- Environmental awareness (or lack thereof);
- Level of technology;
- Wisdom and applicability of government policies;
- Land management practices; and
- Social behavior.

These factors change over time and thus vulnerability is likely to increase or decrease in response to these changes. Subsequent droughts in the same region will have different effects, even if they are identical in intensity, duration, and spatial characteristics, because societal characteristics will have changed. However, much can be done to lessen societal vulnerability to drought through the development of preparedness plans that emphasize risk management and the adoption of appropriate mitigation actions and programs.

Management Alternatives During Drought. Many of the management alternatives available to water suppliers to prepare for and respond to drought events fall into two broad categories: demand management and supply augmentation.

Demand Management

- Public information and education campaigns

- Emergency conservation programs

- Water service restrictions

- Restrictions on nonessential uses of water

- Prohibition of selected commercial uses

- Drought emergency pricing

- Water rationing programs

Supply Augmentation

- Improvements in water systems (for example, leak detection, lining of transmission canals)

- Emergency sources of supply (for example, emergency interconnections, drilling new wells)

- Management of available water resources (for example, emergency water banks, overdrafting of groundwater aquifers)

- Search for new supplies of water

In summary, increased emphasis can and should be placed on **drought mitigation** and preparedness, as well as prediction and early warning capabilities, if society is to reduce the economic and environmental damages associated with drought and its personal hardships. This will require interdisciplinary cooperation and a collaborative effort with policymakers at all levels. SEE ALSO AGRICULTURE AND WATER; CONSERVATION, WATER; DEMAND MANAGEMENT; SUPPLY DEVELOPMENT.

Donald A. Wilhite

drought mitigation: actions designed to lessen or reduce adverse impacts of drought events on individuals and communities

Bibliography

Riebsame, William E., Stanley A. Changnon Jr., and Thomas R. Karl. *Drought and Natural Resources Management in the United States: Impacts and Implications of the 1987–89 Drought.* Boulder, CO: Westview Press, 1991.

Wilhite, Donald A., ed. *Drought: A Global Assessment (Volumes 1 and 2).* London, U.K.: Routledge, 2000.

Wilhite, Donald A., and Michael H. Glantz. "Understanding the Drought Phenomenon: The Role of Definitions." *Water International* 10 (1985):111–120.

Wilhite, Donald A., and Olga Vanyarkho. "Drought: Pervasive Impacts of a Creeping Phenomenon," (Chapter 18). In *Drought: A Global Assessment,* ed. Donald A. Wilhite. London, U.K.: Routledge, 2000.

Wilhite, Donald A. et al. "Planning for Drought: Moving from Crisis to Risk Management." *Journal of American Water Resources Association* 36 (2000):697–710.

Photo and Illustration Credits

The illustrations and tables featured in Water: Science and Issues *were created by GGS Information Services. The photographs appearing in the text were reproduced by permission of the following sources:*

Volume 1

Photograph © Charles E. Rotkin/CORBIS: 2; Photograph © Joseph Sohm. ChromoSohm Inc./CORBIS: 6, 16, 173, 206; Photograph © Ted Spiegel/CORBIS: 8, 131; The Library of Congress: 11, 222; Photograph by Caroline Penn/CORBIS: 13, 248; Photograph © Galen Rowell/CORBIS: 17, 122; Photograph by Andrew Johnston. *Outdoor Indiana* Magazine, Indiana Department of Natural Resources: 23; Photograph by Mike Hutchings. © Reuters NewMedia Inc./CORBIS: 25; Photograph courtesy NASA/GSFC/LaRC/JPL, MISR Team: 27; Image by D. Grant Hokit: 30; Photograph by Craig Line. AP/Wide World Photos: 31; Photograph © David Samuel Robbins/CORBIS: 32; Photograph by Richard Fields. *Outdoor Indiana* Magazine, Indiana Department of Natural Resources: 33, 84; Photograph © Paul A. Souders/CORBIS: 35, 38, 130; Image © Lake County Museum/CORBIS: 37; OAR/National Undersea Research Program (NURP), National Oceanic and Atmospheric Administration: 43, 79 (top), 225; AP/Wide World Photos: 44, 128; Photograph © Jonathan Blair/CORBIS: 46; Photograph © Phil Schermeister/CORBIS: 48, 102; Corbis-Bettmann: 55, 211; Photograph by Cindy Clendenon: 56, 72, 73, 76, 79 (bottom), 180, 184, 187; The Kobal Collection: 57; Illustration by Don Davis. NASA: 59; Photograph by David Crisp and

the WFPC2 Science Team (JPL/Caltech): 60; Photograph by Mark Wheeler. U.S. Army Corps of Engineers: 64; Photograph by Sherwin Crasto. AP/Wide World Photos: 66; Photograph by Robert J. Huffman. Field Mark Publications: 67, 81; © NASA/CORBIS: 68; Image provided by Orbimage. © Orbital Imaging Corporation; processing by NASA Goddard Space Center: 70; Photograph by Richard B. Mieremet. National Oceanic and Atmospheric Administration: 74; Florida Keys National Marine Sanctuary: 78; Photograph © Wolfgang Kaehler/CORBIS: 83; Photograph © Kelly A. Quin: 87, 147, 156, 157, 159, 209, 219, 259; Photograph © Robert Holmes/CORBIS: 92; Reuters/ Archive Photos, Inc.: 93; Photograph © Jim Cummins/CORBIS: 95; Photograph by D. Walsh. U.S. Bureau of Reclamation: Pacific Northwest Region: 98; Photograph © Yann Arthus-Bertrand/CORBIS: 101; © The Mariners' Museum/CORBIS: 104; Photograph by Susan D. Rock: 105; Photograph © Chris Rainier/CORBIS: 108; Photograph by Christopher Sabine: 110; Photograph by John Maxwell. *Outdoor Indiana* Magazine, Indiana Department of Natural Resources: 113; Photograph by Ronald Crouse: 115; Photograph © John Zoiner/ CORBIS: 116; Photograph © Roger Ressmeyer/CORBIS: 118; Photograph © Natalie Fobes/CORBIS: 119; Roger Ressmeyer/CORBIS: 120; Photograph © Caroline Penn/CORBIS: 124; Photograph by Animals Animals/© L. Gould—OSF: 126; Photograph © Robert Maass/CORBIS: 133; Photograph © Carl and Ann Purcell/ CORBIS: 135; UPI/Bettmann Newsphotos:

137; Photograph by Jeffrey L. Clendenon: 139; Photograph © Stuart Westmorland/CORBIS: 142; Photograph by David M. Rohr: 143 (left); Photograph by Amos Nachoum/CORBIS: 143 (right); Photograph © George B. Diebold/CORBIS: 145; Photograph by Ed Young/CORBIS: 151; Photograph by Jack Dykinga. Courtesy of the Agricultural Research Service, USDA: 153; Illustration by Dr. Christian G. Daughton. U.S. Environmental Protection Agency (EPA): 161; National Oceanic and Atmospheric Administration, Department of Commerce: 165; Photograph by Mary Hollinger. National Oceanic and Atmospheric Administration, Department of Commerce: 167, 226; Photograph by John Wilkinson. © Ecoscene/CORBIS: 170; © ESA/PLI/CORBIS: 175; Photograph by Commander John Bortniak. NOAA Corps (ret.), National Oceanic and Atmospheric Administration: 185; Photograph by Annie Griffiths-Bell/CORBIS: 186; Photograph by Cydney Conger/CORBIS: 188; Photograph by Gregory Bull. AP/WideWorld Photos: 192; Photograph © Vince Streano/CORBIS: 197; CORBIS: 199; Photograph by Raveendran. © AFP/Corbis-Bettmann: 202; Photograph by Stephen Jaffe. © AFP/Corbis-Bettmann: 204; Photograph by Douglas Peebles/CORBIS: 212; Photo collection of Dr. James P. McVey. National Oceanic and Atmospheric Administration, Department of Commerce: 213; Photograph by William Harrigan. Florida Keys National Marine Sanctuary: 214 (top); Photograph by Anthony R. Picciolo. National Oceanic and Atmospheric Administration, Department of Commerce: 214 (bottom); Photograph by Dr. James P. McVey. National Oceanic and Atmospheric Administration, Department of Commerce: 216, 217; Sapelo Island National Estuarine Research Reserve: 224; Photograph by Peter Hulme. © Ecoscene/CORBIS: 228; Photograph © George D. Lepp/CORBIS: 230; Photograph by Martha Tabor/Working Images Photographs: 233, 235; Photograph by Jeff Christensen/Newsmakers. Getty Images: 237; Photograph © Kevin Fleming/CORBIS: 241; Photograph © Winifred Wisniewski. Frank Lane Picture Agency/CORBIS: 243;

Photograph by Roger Ressmeyer/CORBIS: 245; Photograph by Rafiqur Rahman. © Reuters NewMedia Inc./CORBIS: 247; AFP/Corbis-Bettmann: 249; Photograph by Kathy Willens. AP/Wide World Photos: 251; Photograph by Michael Lewis/CORBIS: 254; Photograph © Caroline Penn/CORBIS: 255; © AFP/Corbis-Bettmann: 256; Photograph by Alan Towse. © Ecoscene/CORBIS: 258; National Archives and Records Administration: 261; Photograph by Tom Mihalek/Newsmakers. Getty Images: 264.

Volume 2

OAR/National Undersea Research Program (NURP), National Oceanic and Atmospheric Administration: 2, 50, 170; Photograph © Firefly Productions/CORBIS: 4; Photograph © James L. Amos/CORBIS: 6; Photograph. © Niall Benvie/CORBIS: 8; Photograph by Peter Johnson/CORBIS: 11; Image © Lake County Museum/CORBIS: 16; Photograph © Bates Littlehales/Corbis-Bettmann: 18; NASA JPL: 19 (left and right); Photograph by Richard Fields. *Outdoor Indiana* Magazine, Indiana Department of Natural Resources: 22, 57, 98; U.S. Fish and Wildlife Service: 23; Photograph © Robert Holmes/CORBIS: 25; Photograph © David Pu'u/CORBIS: 26; © AFP/Corbis-Bettmann: 28, 121, 184, 227; © Bettman/Corbis: 30, 161; Photograph © Mug Shots/CORBIS: 32; Photograph by Commander John Bortniak. NOAA Corps (ret.), National Oceanic and Atmospheric Administration: 34; Photograph by Cindy Clendenon: 35, 35, 79, 104, 144, 203, 268; Photograph by William Folsom. National Oceanic and Atmospheric Administration, Department of Commerce: 36; Photograph by April Bahen. National Oceanic and Atmospheric Administration, Department of Commerce: 38; Photograph by David Muench/CORBIS: 40; Photograph © Kelly A. Quin: 43; Photograph © Carl and Ann Purcell/CORBIS: 45; Photograph by Jeffrey L. Rotman/CORBIS: 49; Photograph by Jeffrey L. Clendenon: 51, 166; Photograph by Mary Hollinger. National Oceanic and Atmospheric Administration, Department of Commerce: 53; Photograph by Matthew Cavanaugh. AP/Wide World Photos: 55;

Photograph © Natalie Fobes/CORBIS: 59; Photograph © Gunter Marx Photography/CORBIS: 62; National Oceanic and Atmospheric Administration, Department of Commerce: 64; Alaska Fisheries Science Center, Marine Observer Program: 66; Photograph by Robyn Beck. © AFP/Corbis-Bettmann: 68; Photograph © Ivor Fulcher/CORBIS: 70; Photograph © AFP/Corbis-Bettmann: 71, 201; Photograph by Maury Tannen. © AFP/Corbis-Bettmann: 72; U.S. Army Corps of Engineers: 75; Photograph © Kevin Fleming/CORBIS: 77; Photograph © Yann Arthus-Bertrand/CORBIS: 80, 86, 264; Photograph by Savita Kirloskar. © Reuters NewMedia Inc./CORBIS: 82; Photograph by Grant A. Meyer: 88; Photograph © Robert Landau/CORBIS: 93; Photograph © Raymond Gehman/CORBIS: 95; Photograph © Layne Kennedy/CORBIS: 102; Photograph © Roger Ressmeyer/CORBIS: 106; Photograph created at University of Miami by Bob Evans, Peter Minnett, and coworkers. NASA: 108; AFP/Corbis-Bettmann: 110, 127; Photograph © Catherine Karnow/CORBIS: 113; Photograph © Joseph Sohm. ChromoSohm Inc./CORBIS: 114; Photograph by John Bortniak. National Oceanic and Atmospheric Administration, Department of Commerce: 115, 117; Photograph by Bernard Edmaier. Science Photo Library/Photo Researchers, Inc.: 119; Photograph by Giuseppe Zibordi. National Oceanic and Atmospheric Administration, Department of Commerce: 124; Photograph by Scott Bauer. Courtesy of the Agricultural Research Service, USDA: 128, 252; Photograph © Michael Weiss/CORBIS: 133; Photograph by Aizawa Toshiyuki. Hulton/Archive: 135; Photograph © Lester Lefkowitz/CORBIS: 138; Photograph © Mike Zens/CORBIS: 140; Photograph by Dan Newell. Illustration © 2002 Mark D. Heckman: 148; Photograph © Ted Spiegel/CORBIS: 159, 216; © Corbis-Bettmann: 164; National Undersea Research Program: 172; © Japack Company/Corbis: 176; Photograph © Stuart Westmorland/CORBIS: 177; Photograph by Commander Richard Behn. NOAA Corps, National Oceanic and Atmospheric Administration:

179, 209; Photograph © Liba Taylor/CORBIS: 182; Photograph by Susan D. Rock: 183; U.S. Geological Survey: 187; Photograph. © Bob Rowan, Progressive Image/CORBIS: 188; U.S. Army Corps of Engineers: 189; Photograph © Douglas Peebles/CORBIS: 196; Illustration courtesy of Oregon State University, Department of Geosciences: 199; Photograph by Michael Van Woert. National Oceanic and Atmospheric Administration, Department of Commerce: 204, 207, 211; Photograph by Tas Van Ommen: 212; Photograph © Gary Braasch/CORBIS: 219; Photograph. © Bojan Breceli/CORBIS: 224; Photograph by Robert van der Hilst/CORBIS: 228; Photograph © Adam Woolfitt/CORBIS: 230; Hulton/Archive: 233; Photograph by George H. Huey/CORBIS: 236; Photograph by Jonathan Blair/CORBIS: 238; AP/Wide World Photos: 245; Photograph provided by the Earth Sciences and Image Analysis Laboratory, Johnson Space Center: 249; Photograph © Kevin Schafer/CORBIS: 257; Photograph © Peter Turnley/CORBIS: 266 (top and bottom).

Volume 3

Photograph © Joseph Sohm. ChromoSohm Inc./CORBIS: 4; Photograph by Richard Fields. *Outdoor Indiana* Magazine, Indiana Department of Natural Resources: 5, 245; AP/Wide World Photos: 8, 49, 64, 121; Photograph © James A. Sugar/CORBIS: 13, 118; Photograph by Daniel Aguilar. © Reuters NewMedia Inc./CORBIS: 15; Photograph © Robert Holmes/CORBIS: 20; AP/Wide World Photos/Yonhap: 25; Photograph © Alan Schein Photography/CORBIS: 27; Photograph by Marc Muench/CORBIS: 29; Photograph by Paul B. Southerland. AP/Wide World Photos: 33; Image © Seth Joel/CORBIS: 36, 36; UCB: 38; Alfred Russell. Corbis-Bettmann: 40; Photograph © Raymond Gehman/CORBIS: 45; Photograph by I. McDonald. OAR/National Undersea Research Program (NURP), National Oceanic and Atmospheric Administration: 47; OAR/National Undersea Research Program (NURP), National Oceanic and Atmospheric Administration: 50 (top and bottom), 80, 130; Photograph by Anthony Bannister. CORBIS/Anthony Bannister; ABPL: 51; Image provided by Orbimage. © Orbital Imaging Corporation; processing by NASA Goddard Space Center: 55, 81, 147; Photograph by Cindy Clendenon: 59, 164, 213, 252; Photograph. © Bojan Breceli/CORBIS: 60; Photograph by Kevin Schafer/CORBIS: 61; Photograph by Commander Richard Behn. NOAA Corps, National Oceanic and Atmospheric Administration: 62; Photograph by Brandon D. Cole/CORBIS: 62; Photograph by Budd Christman. National Oceanic and Atmospheric Administration, Department of Commerce: 63; Image © AFP/Corbis-Bettmann: 68; AFP/Corbis-Bettmann: 70; Photograph © Ed Young/CORBIS: 72; Photograph © Custom Medical Stock Photo: 74; Photo Researchers, Inc.: 74; Photograph © Darrell Gulin/CORBIS: 76; Photograph © Layne Kennedy/CORBIS: 78, 230; Photograph © Roger Ressmeyer/CORBIS: 79; Photograph © Ralph White/CORBIS: 82; Photograph © Marie Tharp: 84; Photograph © Anthony Cooper. Ecoscene/CORBIS: 86; Photograph by Kevin Schafer. CORBIS Corporation (Bellevue): 89; Photograph. © Ed Kashi/CORBIS: 92; Image © Lake County Museum/CORBIS: 93; Photograph © Annie Griffiths Bell/CORBIS: 94; North Carolina Aquarium at Pine Knoll Shores: 95; Photograph © Macduff Everton/CORBIS: 96; Photograph by Cliff Schiappa. AP/Wide World Photos: 101; National Oceanic and Atmospheric Administration: 107, 112, 149; Photograph by Michael Van Woert. National Oceanic and Atmospheric Administration, Department of Commerce: 109, 168; UPI/Corbis-Bettmann: 111; Photograph by Robert J. Huffman. Field Mark Publications: 113; Photograph by Allen M. Shimada. NMFS: 115; Photograph by Richard T. Nowitz/CORBIS: 120; Photograph by Emmanuel Durand © AFP/Corbis-Bettmann: 124; Photograph by Jae-Hwan Kim. © AFP/Corbis-Bettmann: 125; Photograph © Tom Van Sant/CORBIS: 128; Engraving by James Poupard. National Oceanic and Atmospheric Administration: 137; Photograph by Mychele Daniau. © AFP/Corbis-Bettmann: 145; Photograph © Lowell Georgia/CORBIS: 153;

NASA: 155; Photograph © Paul A. Souders/CORBIS: 158, 160, 232; © CORBIS: 162, 182; Photograph by William Van Woert. National Oceanic and Atmospheric Administration, Department of Commerce: 166; Photograph by Wolfgang Kaehler. Wolfgang Kaehler/Corbis-Bettmann: 171; Photograph © M. Dillon/CORBIS: 172; Photograph by Doug Wilson. Courtesy of the Agricultural Research Service, USDA: 175; Photograph by Robert Campbell. U.S. Army Corps of Engineers: 177, 251 (bottom); Photograph by Chinch Gryniewicz. Ecoscene/CORBIS: 178; © AFP/Corbis-Bettmann: 179, 183, 226; Photograph by Vince Streano/CORBIS: 180; Photograph by Susan D. Rock: 184; Photograph © Ted Spiegel/CORBIS: 187, 196; Photograph by Douglas P. Wilson. CORBIS/Douglas P. Wilson; Frank Lane Picture Agency: 188; National Archives: 192; Photograph © Charles E. Rotkin/CORBIS: 195, 243; Photograph © Bill Varie/CORBIS: 198; Photograph by Robert E. Wallace. U.S. Geological Survey: 202; Photograph by Lauren McFalls. AP/Wide World Photos: 207; © Reuters NewMedia Inc./CORBIS: 210; Photograph © Nick Hawkes. Ecoscene/CORBIS: 215; Photograph by Jack Dykinga. Courtesy of the Agricultural Research Service, USDA: 218; Photograph © David Turnley/CORBIS: 219; Photograph © Kelly A. Quin: 224, 227; Photograph by Ken Winters. U.S. Army Corps of Engineers: 228, 251 (top); Photograph by Anthony F. Amos: 234, 235; Photograph by Rick Doyle/CORBIS: 238; Greenpeace Photo: 241; Photograph © Michael S. Yamashita/CORBIS: 247; Photograph © Neil Rabinowitz/CORBIS: 250; The Library of Congress: 255; FMA Production: 261.

Volume 4

© Corbis-Bettmann: 1; Photograph by Alan Towse. © Ecoscene/CORBIS: 3; Photograph by Toby Talbot. AP/Wide World Photos: 6; Photograph by David Mercado. © Reuters NewMedia/CORBIS: 7; Photograph © Les Pickett/CORBIS: 9; © Reuters NewMedia Inc./CORBIS: 10, 18, 20; Photograph

Atmospheric Administration, Department of Commerce: 228; National Oceanic and Atmospheric Administration Historical Photo Collection: 230; Satellite photograph by National Hurricane Center, National Oceanic and Atmospheric Administration: 232; Satellite photograph by National Oceanic and Atmospheric Administration Historical Photo Collection: 233; Photograph © Khaled Zighari/CORBIS: 239; Photograph by Kevin Schafer/CORBIS: 244; Photograph by Larry Harwood: 248; © Ashanti Johnson Pyrtle: 250.

Glossary

100-year flood the flood from a river discharge that has a 1-percent chance of occurring in any given year

abiotic pertaining to any nonbiological factor or influence (not derived from living organisms), such as geological or meteorological characteristics

ablation a process that removes snow or ice from glaciers, including melting, evaporation, wind erosion, and sublimation

absolute describes the value of a parameter that is known precisely; for example, the temperature of the stream at a given point is 10.4°C (50.7°F); contrasts with a relative measure

absorption the incorporation of an atom, ion or molecule in another substance; the atom, ion, or molecule is not necessarily part of the substance's structure

accountable describes being liable or answerable for decisions or actions; normally accomplished by specifying to whom a decisionmaker must report and is answerable

accretionary prism wedge of sediment that accumulates in subduction zones; the sediment is scraped off the subducting plate and accreted to the overriding platearable

accuracy the exactness or degree to which a measurement or calculation approaches the actual quantity

acid mine drainage acidic water that flows into streams from abandoned mines, piles of mining waste or tailings, or sulfide-mineralized rock; water that becomes acidic through reactions that oxidize sulfide minerals in rocks, thereby producing sulfuric and other acids

acid rain rain that has become acidic due to the presence of dissolved substances such as sulfur oxides or nitrogen oxides; causation may be natural (e.g., volcanic eruptions) or human-induced (e.g., industrial pollution)

acid rock drainage see "acid mine drainage"

acute rapid in onset and of short duration (e.g., acute toxicity); contrasted with chronic, which is gradual or long-term (e.g., chronic toxicity)

acute toxicity the property of a chemical or microbe enabling it to cause symptoms of illness in a living organism only a short time after exposure; see "chronic toxicity"

adsorb to collect a liquid, gas, or solid, in a condensed form, on a surface

aeration for water, any active or passive process by which close, sustained contact between air and water is assured, generally by spraying water in the air, bubbling air through water, or mechanical agitation of the water to promote surface absorption of air; for soil, the process of loosening or puncturing the soil by mechanical means in order to increase water and air permeability

aerobe an organism which requires oxygen for its life processes

aerobic describes organisms able to live only in the presence of air or free oxygen, and conditions that exist only in the presence of air or free oxygen

aerosol a suspension of colloidal (finely suspended) particles in a gas

aesthetic relating to the human senses, especially what is pleasurable or is deemed satisfactory or desirable

aestivation also spelled estivation, the sleeplike condition of partial or total inactivity during dry or hot weather conditions; seasonal opposite of hibernation

agrochemical a synthetic or naturally derived chemical used in agriculture, such as a fertilizer, pesticide, or hormone

albedo the fraction of incident solar radiation that is reflected by the surface

algae (singular, alga) simple photosynthetic organisms, usually aquatic, containing chlorophyll, and lacking roots, stems, and leaves

algal bloom also called algae bloom, a rapid increase in algae concentrations in fresh or marine waters that often is stimulated by nutrient enrichment; recurrent blooms may cause or accelerate eutrophication, and lead to a deterioration in water quality

algebra a branch of mathematics that deals with the use of letters and other symbols, as well as numbers, to represent quantities and to express generalizations about them

algorithm a formalized, step-by-step procedure or set of equations designed for the purpose of solving a particular type of problem

alkalinity the excess of strong bases over strong acids in water; a measure of a water's buffering capability, or ability to resist changes in pH; generally equivalent to the sum of bicarbonate (HCO_3^-) and carbonate (CO_3^{2-}); alkalinity generally increases with progressive water–rock chemical reactions

allocate to distribute resources for a particular purpose

alluvium a deposit of clay, silt, sand, gravel, or a mixture of these, that has been deposited by a stream or other body of running water in a streambed, on a floodplain, on a delta, or at the base of a mountain; alluvial refers to sediments deposited by rivers and streams

altimeter an instrument that determines height above ground surface, especially one mounted in an aircraft or satellite and incorporating a barometer or radar device

altitude in navigational usage, the angle measured from the horizon to a celestial body, such as the Sun, Moon, or stars; in general usage, the height above the ground surface, called elevation if referring to height above sea level

ambient describes an encompassing environment that is natural or nearly natural (e.g., ambient air temperature)

amphibian a cold-blooded, smooth-skinned vertebrate of the class *Amphibia*, such as a frog or salamander, that characteristically hatches as an aquatic larva with gills and then transforms into an adult having air-breathing lungs

anadromous describes fish that move from the ocean up a river to spawn

anaerobe an organism that does not require oxygen to maintain its life processes

anaerobic describes organisms able to live and grow only where there is no air or free oxygen, and conditions that exist only in the absence of air or free oxygen

anastomotic describes the character of individual stream paths within a braided stream; stream paths appear to interconnect with one another around sand bars

anion an ion that has a negative charge

anoxia the state in which water contains less than 0.1 milliliter of oxygen per liter, the threshold below which animal life diminishes significantly

anthropogenic of, relating to, or resulting from the influence of human beings on nature, as in water and air pollution

anthropomorphic having human-like or human-caused characteristics

antibiotic a substance produced by organisms, especially bacteria and fungi, which passes into the surrounding medium and is toxic to other organisms; for example, penicillin from the mold *Penicillin notatum* destroys many kinds of bacteria

appurtenances auxiliary components and facilities that accompany a water system, such as the valves, monitors, and other control devices in a distribution system

aquaculture the science, art, and business of cultivating marine or freshwater animals or plants under controlled conditions

aqualung equipment used by a person as an air supply while underwater; developed in 1943 by Jacques-Yves Cousteau and French engineer Émile Gagnan

aqueduct long, canal-like or pipe-like structure, either above or below ground, for transporting water some distance

aqueous relating to, similar to, containing, or dissolved in water; watery

aquifer a water-saturated, permeable, underground rock formation that can transmit significant quantities of water under ordinary hydraulic gradients to wells and springs

arable used or suitable for growing crops

archaeology the historical study of humans through the excavation of sites and the analysis of artifacts and other physical remains

arid describes a climate or region where precipitation is exceeded by evaporation; in these regions, agricultural crop production is impractical or impossible without irrigation

artesian describes groundwater under pressure in a confined aquifer such that the water level rises in the well bore to a shallower level (i.e., closer to the ground surface) than the aquifer; if under sufficient pressure, artesian groundwater may naturally flow out of the top of the well, known as a flowing artesian well or simply a flowing well

arthropod a group of invertebrates (animals without backbones) that have segmented bodies and jointed limbs; includes insects and crustaceans

ash flow a hot, turbulent ash cloud that moves rapidly down a volcano's slope

assimilate to incorporate or take in; the ability of a body of water, air, or soil to reduce the impact of pollutants by mixing, dilution, or other processes

asteroid a rocky body, much smaller than a planet, that orbits the Sun; asteroidal means pertaining to or originating from an asteroid

asteroid belt the area between the orbits of Mars and Jupiter that contains most of the asteroids found orbiting the Sun

asthenosphere the zone inside the Earth beneath the lithosphere to a depth of less than 700 kilometers (approximately 400 miles), containing a low percentage of molten rock, and constituting the source of seafloor basalts

astrolabe an early instrument used to observe the position and determine the altitude of the Sun or other celestial body; used for navigation from the Middle Ages until the eighteenth century, when it was replaced by the sextant

astronomical unit one astronomical unit (AU) is the average distance between the Sun and the Earth: approximately 150 million kilometers (93 million miles)

atmosphere the gaseous layer surrounding the Earth, consisting of 78 percent nitrogen, 21 percent oxygen, and approximately 1 percent argon; atmospheric pressure at sea level is about 14.7 pounds per square inch, termed "one atmosphere"

atomic fission the action of dividing or splitting an atom or atoms into two or more parts

attenuation thinning, weakening, or lessening; for water velocity, the slowing, modification, or diversion of the flow of water as with detention and retention ponds; for water quality, the process of diminishing contaminant concentrations in water due to filtration, biodegradation, dilution, sorption, volatilization, and other processes

autonomous existing, reacting, or developing as an independent, self-regulating organism

autotroph an organism that is able to form nutritional organic substances from simple inorganic substances such as carbon dioxide

backshore the part of a shore between the foreshore and the landward edge that is above high water except in the most severe storms

backwash the seaward return of water following the uprush of the waves, also referred to as backrush; in water treatment, the reversal of flow through a rapid sand filter to wash clogging material out of the filtering medium and reduce conditions causing loss of head (pressure)

bait fish a fish used as bait in fishing to catch a larger fish

baleen a horned comb-like structure in the mouths of toothless whales, used for filtering small animals (e.g., small crustaceans) from the water

bank-full discharge a river discharge that raises the stream level to the top of the streambank; precipitation resulting in bank-full discharges occurs once every 1 to 2 years, on average

bar a ridge built up in a river or ocean by deposits of sand, rock particles, and other materials

basalt a dark, volcanic rock with abundant iron and magnesium and relatively low silica; common on all of the terrestrial planets

baseflow the portion of stream flow derived from groundwater seeping through the stream bottom and sides

base level the lowest level to which a river can erode; ultimate base level is sea level; local base level may be a larger river, a lake, or very resistant rock

basin (geologic) a low-lying geographic area that tends to collect sediments from higher land around it, thus building up rock sequences; a structural basin is a geologic feature where the sedimentary layers dip toward a central point

basin (lake) a topographic depression or low-lying area occupied by a lake

basin (ocean) the topographic low area occupied by oceans; the floor of ocean basins consists of basaltic crust that is more dense than typical continental rocks

basin (river) a geographic area drained by a river and its tributaries; consists of a drainage system that may be comprised of streams, wetlands, and often natural or artificial lakes; see "drainage basin," "catchment," and "watershed"

bathymetry the science of measuring the depths and underwater topography of seas, oceans, lakes, and reservoirs

beach nourishment also known as beach replenishment, the techniques used to temporarily mitigate erosion of beaches (e.g., bringing in sand to rebuild a beach)

beachdrift the net movement by longshore current of sand up or down and along the beach, depending on the direction of incoming waves; see "littoral drift"

bedload sediment particles, small and large, and including rocks, which bounce, slide, or roll along the bottom of a streambed

bedrock solid rock that lies beneath soil and other surficial material

beneficial use use of water for purposes considered worthwhile to society; includes domestic, municipal, industrial, agricultural and recreational uses

Benioff zone the seismically active boundary between the subducting plate and the overriding plate; the movement of the plates along the Benioff zone is the cause of high-magnitude, deep-seated earthquakes

benthos the plants and animals living on or closely associated with the bottom of a body of water, such as a river, lake, or sea; these organisms are described as benthic (bottom-dwelling), which means of or pertaining to the benthos

berm a narrow ledge or path at the top or bottom of a slope, streambank, or along a beach

bioaccumulative describes the increase in concentration of a chemical in organisms that reside in environments contaminated with low concentrations of various organic compounds

biochemical oxygen demand abbreviated as BOD, the amount of oxygen required for the biological decomposition of organic matter under atmospheric conditions

bioconcentration the increase in concentration of a chemical in an organism resulting from absorption levels exceeding the rate of metabolism and excretion

biodegradation breaking down of substances by microorganisms, which use the substances for food

biodiversity a measure of the variety of the Earth's species, of the genetic differences within species, and of the ecosystems that support those species

biofilm the layered growth of bacteria on surfaces, including the inner walls of fractured rock, pore spaces in sediments, and in pipes, wells, bathroom fixtures, etc.

biogeochemical cycle the cyclical system in which chemical elements are transferred between living and nonliving parts of the biosphere; includes the hydrologic, oxygen, carbon, and nitrogen cycles; biogeochemical cycles play a vital role in global ecology

biological contactors surfaces used in aerobic biological treatment of wastewater; they are surfaces upon which bacteria can grow and accumulate; when placed in the treatment process, biological contactors (by virtue of their bacteria) facilitate the breakdown of organic waste

biologically active capable of interacting with biological systems and producing a biochemical/physiological effect or response

biomass the total mass of living organic matter in a defined location; generally expressed as grams per unit volume or per unit area

biomass pyramid graphic model describing the distribution of biomass in an ecosystem or community at the trophic level

bioregenerative process the development of a part of a living organism to replace a similar structure that has been damaged or destroyed

bioremediation a method of waste cleanup using specialized, naturally occurring microorganisms with unique characteristics, and with metabolisms that allow them to break down organic pollutants

biosystem a biologically based system for the maintainable production and processing of biological materials (such as food) in parallel with the efficient utilization of natural and renewable resources

biota the plant and animal life of a region or ecosystem, as in a stream, lake, or ocean

biotic pertaining to life or living things, or caused by living organisms; also pertaining to biological factors or influences

biotransformation sum of processes by which a foreign chemical is subjected to chemical change by a living organism

black smoker a seafloor vent in which hot mineralized water from below the seafloor discharges into cold sea water; black color arises from the precipitation of dark sulfide minerals; compare with "white smoker"

bog a poorly drained wetland, usually found in a glacial depression, characterized by the presence of saturated organic soil (peat) and acidic water; plant decomposition is very slow in this environment

boiling point the temperature at which water becomes steam; the boiling point of water is 100°C (212°F) at sea level and decreases with decreasing pressure (i.e., with increasing elevation)

brackish describes water having a salinity from 0.05 to 17 parts per thousand; typically a mixture of sea water and fresh water (e.g., as found in an estuary)

breakwater a barrier that protects a harbor or shore from the full impact of waves

brine water containing a higher concentration of dissolved salts than normal sea water (which contains approximately 35 parts per thousand); produced in oceans through the evaporation or freezing of sea water, or in groundwater through extensive reaction with bedrock minerals

brine film a thin film of salty water surrounding grains of ice or soil that forms when salts are excluded during freezing of permafrost, ground ice, or sea ice; interstitial brines formed by freezing can remain liquid far below the freezing point of fresh water because dissolved salts depress water's freezing point

brine pockets the residual saline water within the ice after sea water has frozen; dissolved minerals are not readily incorporated into ice as it forms—therefore, as freezing takes place, the remaining water becomes increasingly saline; in most icebergs and in sea ice, trapped bubbles of saline water remain

calcite a mineral consisting of calcium carbonate

calculus a branch of mathematics that involves computing or calculating quantities that change as functions of different variables

caldera a bowl-shaped crater at the top of a volcano caused by the collapse of the volcano's central part; collapse generally occurs coincident with massive eruptions

calibration the process of correlating the readings of an instrument with those of an established standard in order to check its accuracy of measurement

caliche a mineral deposit, generally containing calcite and gypsum, that forms in arid regions when rainwater that has infiltrated the ground is evaporated, causing the minerals to precipitate

canalization in general, the process of creating artificial canal-like waterways or enhancing natural waterways to drain or irrigate land or to allow navigation

canopy the network of limbs, leaves, and other vegetation high in a forest; the canopy offers habitat and influences ground temperature and precipitation through-fall

capillary action the action by which water is drawn around and into soil particles due to the forces of adhesion, cohesion, and surface tension acting in a liquid that is in contact with a solid

captive breeding the artificial propagation or maintenance of animals in captivity

capture fishery the removal of aquatic organisms from natural or enhanced waters

carbon-14 dating the technique of deriving an approximate age from organic material, such as bone, charcoal, or shell, by comparing the decay activity in the sample of radiocarbon (carbon-14), which begins to decrease at death and subsequent burial, with the decay activity of modern carbon-14; also called radioactive carbon dating, or radiocarbon dating

carbonaceous chondrites one of the three major groups of chondrites; little-altered, primitive meteorites containing significant amounts of carbon, water, and other volatile constituents

carbonate common minerals that are the principal constituents of sedimentary rocks such as limestone and dolostones; the most widespread carbonate minerals are calcite, aragonite, and dolomite

carcinogen a cancer-causing substance or agent

carnivore an animal that feeds mostly on other animals

carp a fresh-water fish, from the Family *Cyprinidae* (the minnow family), with a single back fin and barbels around the mouth; originally from Asia, but now found worldwide in lakes and slow-moving rivers, and farmed for food in large ponds; it prefers warm waters, feeding near the bottom of waters where it stirs up mud and uproots vegetation, often driving out more desirable fish

carrying capacity (animal) the maximum population that can be supported by the natural resources

catadromous describes fish that live in fresh water but move to salt water to spawn

catchment a river basin or a constructed basin or reservoir for the natural or artificial catching or collecting of water, especially rainfall

cation an ion that has a positive charge

centrifugal describes the tendency to move away from the center during rotation around a central point

chalk a pure form of limestone, formed from the deposits of microscopic, shelled animals

channel the bed of a stream, river, lake, impoundment, bay, or strait through which the main volume or current of water flows

channelization any excavation and construction activities intended to widen, deepen, straighten, or relocate a natural river channel; the term does not include maintenance activities on existing channels, such as the clearing of debris or dredging of accumulated sediments

chaotic terrain Martian surface having the appearance of jumbled and broken angular slabs or blocks; may be related to the melting of subsurface ice followed by collapse of the surface

chemical oxygen demand abbreviated as COD, the amount of oxygen required to degrade the organic compounds of wastewater; the larger the COD value of wastewater, the more oxygen the waste discharge demands from a waterbody

chemosynthesis the synthesis of organic compounds by bacteria or other such living organisms using energy from reactions involving inorganic chemicals, typically in the absence of sunlight

chitin a nitrogen-containing polysaccharide (carbohydrate whose molecules consist of a number of sugar molecules bonded together) forming a hard outer layer in many invertebrates, especially insects; also found in the cell walls of many fungi

chlorination the disinfection of drinking water through the addition of chlorine compounds, (e.g., chlorine gas, sodium hypochlorite); purpose is to inactivate disease-causing microbes

chlorofluorocarbon gases formed of chlorine, fluorine, and carbon whose molecules normally do not react with other substances; commonly used as spray-can propellants because of ability not to alter the material being sprayed

chloroplast the protoplasmic body or plastid in the cells of plants that contains chlorophyll and in which photosynthesis takes place

chondrites primitive meteorites with origins in the solar nebula

chronometer any instrument designed to measure time accurately, especially one designed to maintain accurate time in spite of motion or variations in temperature, air pressure, and humidity

cistern an artificial reservoir or tank used for holding or storing water, often rainwater

civic pertaining to the rights and duties of the citizenship

clarifier a basin or tank of varied design in wastewater treatment that allows wastewater to stand and undergo progressive sedimentation; the upper portions of the wastewater in the basin are clarified as the solids slowly settle from it

climate the long-term average of weather conditions at a given location

climatology the science and study dealing with climate and climatic phenomena as exhibited by temperature, winds, and precipitation

coagulant flocculant; a substance that, when in a fluid, coagulates or flocculates (comes together in a coherent mass); contaminants such as microbes are attracted to the flocculant and are filtered out of the water

coagulation flocculation; in water treatment, the treating of raw water with chemicals in order to coagulate or flocculate (join together) many small particles

coccolith a minute, rounded calcareous platelet, numbers of which form the spherical shells of coccolithophores

coliform describes a group of bacteria predominantly inhabiting the intestines of humans or animals but also found in soil; while typically harmless, they commonly are used as indicators of the possible presence of pathogenic organisms

collaboration a process of working together or collectively to solve complex, interrelated problems; requires greater consultation, coordination, and public input into the process than largely independent efforts

collection basin a lake, reservoir, or other body of water fed by water drained from a watershed

colloid a particle size range of 10^{-3} to 10^{-6} millimeter (4×10^{-5} to 4×10^{-8} inches)

colluvium a general term for loose, unconsolidated material moved downslope under the influence of gravity

comet a celestial body, observed only in that part of its orbit that is relatively close to the Sun, having a head consisting of a solid nucleus, and comprising ice and rocky debris, termed a "dirty snowball," surrounded by a nebulous coma up to 2.4 million kilometers (1.5 million miles) in diameter and an elongated, curved vapor tail arising from the coma when sufficiently close to the Sun; cometary means pertaining to or originating from a comet

commission as in river basin commission, an independent regional body established to manage and coordinate federal, state, and local water management policies in a river basin, particularly regional basins and basins that cross state or international boundaries; river basin commissions almost always are created by treaty or legislation that outline the commission's mission, duties, and authority to carry out those duties

commissioning (dams) the process by which a dam is authorized and subsequently set into operation

common law a body of rules and principles based on court decisions, traditional usage, and precedent, rather than legislative enactments comprising codified written laws; compare with "statutory law"

common-property resource a resource used in common by many people, such as the air, oceans, and fisheries, wherein it is difficult to exclude anyone from appropriating the resource; sometimes called the "commons" or a "common-pool resource"

compact a formal contract or agreement between two or more parties, often governmental units

confined aquifer describes an aquifer in which groundwater is isolated from the atmosphere by impermeable formations; confined groundwater generally is subject to pressure greater than atmospheric pressure and often is artesian in character

conjunctive use the planned use of water from different sources, usually surface and groundwater sources, to optimize the benefit from available supplies

connate describes sea water that was trapped in the interstices of a sedimentary rock at the time of its deposition; see "evolved connate" and "fossil groundwater"

consequent system a stream drainage pattern that results solely from the influence of the slope of the land surface; pattern often is dendritic or tree-like in appearance

conservation the organized management and planned use of living and non-living natural resources; "water conservation" refers to strategies that increase the efficiency of water use, reuse, recycling, production, or distribution, or that decrease demand

Conservation Reserve Program a voluntary program created by the Food Security Act of 1985 ("Farm Bill") and administered by the U.S. Department of Agriculture; subsequent amendments have created new and innovative approaches to conservation, encompassing wetlands, forestlands, water quality, and sustainable land management

conservationist a person who believes in the regulated exploitation or wise use of natural resources so that irreparable damage is not incurred

conservative element an element or compound that does not readily participate in a chemical or biochemical reaction as it is transported through a system (e.g., an aquifer or river); it can be used to identify flow paths and velocity; see "conservative tracer"

conservative tracer an element or compound that does not readily react with the substance through which it is moving or that is carrying it; often used in hydrology to trace the movement of groundwater or to evaluate the flow characteristics of a stream; chloride and bromide are typical conservative tracers

consolidated describes sedimentary rock in which the individual grains cling or are bound together, like mud or sandstone; as opposed to unconsolidated sediment, in which individual grains are clearly separated and can move freely, like silt or sand

consumptive use a use which lessens the amount of water available for another use; for example, water that is used for development and growth of plant tissue or consumed by humans or animals

contaminant as defined by the U.S. Environmental Protection Agency, any physical, chemical, biological, or radiological substance in water, including constituents that may not be harmful to the environment or human health

contamination impairment of the quality of water or the environment by natural or human-made substances to a degree that is considered undesirable for certain uses; this term usually implies a human or environmental health threat, but some types of contamination are merely nonaesthetic rather than harmful; see "pollution"

continental of or pertaining to the continents

continental ice sheet a relatively permanent layer of ice (a large ice cap) covering an extensive tract of land; also called continental glacier, as that of the Antarctic continent

continental margin region where continental crust meets oceanic crust; extending from the shoreline to the deep-ocean basin, this feature includes the continental shelf, continental slope, and continental rise

continental plate a large segment of Earth's crust and uppermost mantle (lithosphere) that supports a major landmass

continental shelf the relatively flat, submerged natural platform, about 1-degree slope, that extends seaward from the beach for about 70 kilometers (45 miles), with water depth up to 130 meters (425 feet) maximum, and ends where the slope and water depth increase

convection circulatory movement in an unevenly heated mass (liquid, solid, or gas); cooler material generally is denser and sinks in an area influenced by gravity, whereas warmer material usually is less dense and rises; convection takes place in the atmosphere, lakes, oceans, and Earth's mantle

cooperative agreement an agreement, typically voluntary, entered into by parties to achieve common goals

coral a marine organism that lives in colonies and excretes an external, calcium carbonate skeleton; groups of these anthozoan coelenterates often form large reefs in tropical seas

coral reef a resistant marine ridge or mound consisting chiefly of compacted coral together with algal material and biochemically deposited magnesium and calcium carbonates

coriparian landowners, either individual or states, sharing the area along a waterway

cost–benefit analysis an analytical technique that is used to guide policymakers by computing the present discounted value of benefits and costs for a set of policy alternatives

covalent bond a chemical bond between two atoms of the same or different elements, in which each atom contributes one or more electrons to be shared in pairs

critical habitat the minimum portion of the habitat that is essential for the survival of a species

cross-contamination phenomenon occurring when sewage is inadvertently transferred into potable (drinking) water pipes and distributed throughout the system; this can happen when sewer lines break, water pipes crack, or water pipes lose pressure

crude oil naturally occurring liquid composed of mixtures or organic chemicals called hydrocarbons; can be distilled to produce gasoline and many other products

crust the outermost portion of the Earth's lithosphere, above the mantle, and comprising rocks such as sandstone, limestone, granite, andesite, and basalt; the crust is enriched in SiO_2, Al_2O_3, K_2O, and Na_2O

crustacean arthropods with hard shells, jointed bodies, and appendages, and that primarily live in water; examples are shrimp, krill, crabs, and lobsters

cryptosporidiosis a condition in which a parasitic coccidian protozoan is found in the intestinal tract of humans

crystalline having an internal structure that is arranged in a repeating, orderly pattern

cyanobacteria also known as blue-green algae, primitive single-celled organisms structurally similar to bacteria, sometimes joined in colonies or filaments

dam failure the collapse of a dam or a portion of its components, often as a result of structural weaknesses that develop over time, of improper design or operation, or of larger-than-anticipated flood events

DDT abbreviation for dichlorodiphenyltrichloroethane, a colorless, odorless, water-insoluble, crystalline pesticide that acts as a nerve poison and is effective at killing insects; it tends to accumulate in ecosystems, and has toxic effects on many vertebrates; use as a pesticide is now prohibited in the United States

decommissioning (dams) the process by which a dam is permanently taken out of operation

decomposer any of various organisms, such as soil bacteria or fungi, that feed on and break down organic substances, such as dead plants and animals

deep well a relative term for a drilled well, generally greater than 50 meters (165 feet), with a motor-driven or engine-driven pump immersed below the water level in the well; the motor or engine is at ground level; the practical limit to well depth is about 200 meters (650 feet), although there is no theoretical limit

deep-sea of, relating to, or occurring in the deeper parts of the sea; often miles beneath the ocean's surface, where sunlight can no longer penetrate

degradation breakdown of a chemical to yield usually simpler chemical products (e.g., molecules) by way of biocatalysis (e.g., metabolism), photolysis (e.g., sunlight), or physicochemical processes (e.g., hydrolysis)

delta an alluvial deposit of sediment at the mouth of a river where it enters quieter or deeper water, such as a lake or ocean

density mass per unit volume of a substance; with respect to sea water, the mass in kilograms of 1 liter of sea water; density is a complex function of its temperature and salt content, with warmer, fresher waters being less dense than colder, saltier waters

desalinization also spelled desalination, the process of removing salts and other dissolved solids from sea water or saline (salty) water, usually to make it drinkable

desertification the creation of deserts by climate change or by human-induced processes including overgrazing, the destruction of forest belts, exhaustion of the soil by intensive cultivation, and salinization of soils due to mismanaged irrigation

desorb detaching of a chemical constituent from a surface to which it had previously adsorbed; the relative rates in which a given constituent adsorbs versus desorbs is controlled by the water chemistry and the constituent's characteristics

detention pond a structure designed to temporarily store stormwater in order to reduce the potential for flooding

detritivore an animal that feeds on dead or decaying organic material (detritus)

detritus general term for dead and decaying organic material in an ecosystem, whether terrestrial or aquatic; examples include leaf litter on a forest floor, or fish carcasses in a bay

developing country any country whose Gross National Product (GNP) per capita is less than $3,000; in contrast, the GNP per capita of the richer developed countries including the United States, Canada, Japan, and most of Western Europe exceeds $25,000

development the process of improving the overall well-being of society, particularly through political, cultural, social, or economic means

diagenesis the process of chemical and physical changes that occur within sediments after their accumulation; includes the processes of compaction, the cementation of minerals to one another, recrystallization of minerals, and replacement of one mineral by another

diatom any of the microscopic unicellular or colonial algae constituting the class *Bacillarieae* that have a silicified cell wall, which persists as a skeleton after death and masses of which ultimately accumulate to form diatomite

dike an embankment to confine or control water, especially one built along the banks of a river to prevent overflow of lowlands

dinoflagellate a microscopic unicellular alga that moves by means of a flagellum, a threadlike or whiplike structure

discharge the volume of water or a watery solution flowing past a point per unit time; common units are cubic feet per second or cubic meters per second

discount rate a factor that translates future monetary values into today's values; in cost–benefit analysis, discount rate is represented as r in the discounting formula $1/(1 + r)^t$, when t is the number of years in a water project

discounted net present value for a water project, when all the costs and benefits for each year of the project are discounted using a common discount rate, the sum of the discounted cost minus discounted benefits gives the net present value (NPV); only when NPV is positive is a water project economically feasible

displaced population people who are forced out of their homes in search of safety during conflicts or natural disasters; during prolonged displacements, the international community often sets up camps where the people (refugees) may gain access to basic necessities, including water

dissect in landscape evolution, to cut by erosion into hills and valleys or into flat upland areas separated by valleys

dissociation product individual ions or neutral molecules formed through the chemical disassociation of a single molecule; for example, H_2CO_3 disassociates into H^+ and HCO_3^-

dissolution the action or process of dissolving or being dissolved

dissolved describes the chemical breakdown of a solid in a solution into individual atoms or molecules and their dispersement in the fluid medium; for example, describes the dissolved solids or dissolved gases in water

dissolved load all the material transported by a stream or river in solution, as contrasted with bedload and suspended load

dissolved oxygen concentration of oxygen, expressed in milligrams per liter, dissolved in water and readily available to fish and other aquatic organisms; strongly influenced by temperature, biologic activity, biochemical oxygen demand, and chemical oxygen demand

distillation process by which liquids may be purified or changed through evaporation and condensation (change from a gas to a liquid)

distribution system the system of pipes and storage tanks of a public water supply that deliver drinking water from the source or treatment plant to individual users

divergence a region where water flows outwards at the surface from a source, causing water to upwell from below the surface to replace it

dolomite $CaMg(CO_3)_2$; a mineral consisting of a carbonate of calcium and magnesium; often formed during diagenesis of limestone (calcite)

downdrift the direction of predominant movement of littoral (shore-related) materials in seas or lakes

drainage basin the land area drained by a river and its tributaries; also called catchment, drainage area, river basin, or watershed

drainfield an arrangement, generally parallel, of buried perforated piping or tubing in which the fluid is discharged to the ground through seepage; most common use is with septic tanks, but can also be used for domestic or industrial wastewater disposal after other treatment methods

dredging the process of excavating sediments and other materials, usually from underwater locations, for the purpose of mining aggregate (sand and gravel), constructing new waterways, or maintaining existing waterway cross-sections

drip irrigation a system for slowly watering crops at points on or just below the soil surface so that a plant's root zone is thoroughly moistened, with little water being wasted via ponding or runoff

dripstone rock consisting of calcite deposited by precipitation from dripping water, as found in limestone caverns; dripstone may form stalactites and stalagmites

drought mitigation actions designed to lessen or reduce adverse impacts of drought events on individuals and communities

duplicate as in duplicate sample, a second sample collected in the same manner and within the same timeframe and analyzed separately from the primary sample in order to determine the precision of the analysis

dynamic equilibrium the state in which opposing reactions or processes are proceeding at the same rate such that no apparent change is occurring in the concentrations of components involved in the reaction; for surface water, a channel exhibits patterns of erosion and deposition but there is no net change in the input and materials; for groundwater, a condition in which the amount of recharge to an aquifer equals the amount of natural or artificial discharge

dynamic height the relative difference in depth of a pressure surface between two points, which depends on the density structure of the water column at each point

ecology the scientific study of the interrelationships of living things to one another and to the environment; also refers to the ecology of a given region

economic development quantitative and qualitative changes in an economy that enhance the well-being of a society or community

ecosystem the community of plants and animals within a water or terrestrial habitat interacting together and with their physical and chemical environment

ecotone the region of transition, generally gradational, between two ecological communities or ecosystems

efficiency the condition of minimal waste; in economics, a condition in which markets have optimally allocated resources

effluent a liquid that flows out of or away from an area of waste processing or containment; includes treated wastes from municipal sewage plants, brine wastewater from desalinization operations, and coolant waters from a nuclear power plant

ejecta blanket material ejected (thrown out) during impact crater formation and deposited around the crater, covering the surrounding terrain

El Niño an occasional warming of sea-surface temperatures in the equatorial Pacific off the coast of South America

elasticity a measure of the response to a given change, typically in the price of a product; for example, how much consumers increase their oil use when its price goes down, or how much less water they buy when its price goes up; elasticities are measured as percentage changes

elite as in "the elite," a group of people considered to be the best in a particular society or category, especially considered with respect to wealth, power, and talent; in terms of wealth, refers to the population in the top 10 percent of a country's income distribution

embayment a recess in a coastline that has formed a bay

emergent rising above a surrounding medium, especially a fluid; describes a plant with some part standing above the water surface and the rest submerged

empirical based on experience or observations, as opposed to reason or conjecture

emulsion a mixture of two liquids, in which one is in the form of fine droplets and is dispersed in the other

endangered describes a plant or animal species threatened with extinction by human-made or natural changes throughout all or a significant area of its range; designated in accordance with the 1973 Endangered Species Act

endocrine of, relating to, or denoting glands that secrete hormones or other such products directly into the bloodstream

endogenous originating from within, as opposed to coming from external sources

entomology the scientific study of insects

entrain to draw in and transport (as solid particles or gas) by the flow of a fluid; for example, water droplets may become entrained in rising air currents

entrenchment in landscape evolution, the process of a river rapidly downcutting as the result of climatic or base level changes such that the previous channel form or pattern is preserved (e.g., an entrenched meander)

environment all of the external factors, conditions, and influences that affect the growth, development, and survival of organisms or a community; commonly refers to Earth and its support systems

environmental impact statement often known as EIS, a detailed document that outlines potential impacts of projects being considered by federal agencies and that potentially have significant environmental implications; an EIS is required by the National Environmental Policy Act

environmental policy the set of laws, legislation, regulations, and political perspectives governing the environment and that provides a framework for achieving society's goals in managing environmental resources

environmental science the interdisciplinary application of the physical, chemical, and biological sciences to the study of the environment, encompassing resources, population, and pollution

ephemeral stream a stream that flows only in direct response to precipitation, and thus discontinues its flow during dry seasons; in ephemeral wetlands, refers to holding water from weeks to months but not year-round

epicenter the location on Earth's surface directly above where an earthquake is generated (known as the earthquake focus)

epifauna aquatic animals that live on the surface of the seabed or a riverbed, or attached to submerged objects or other aquatic animals or plants

epilimnion the warm upper, well-mixed layer of a lake or sea that is thermally stratified, extending down from the water surface to the thermocline, which forms the boundary between the warmer upper layers of the epilimnion and the colder waters of the lower depths (hypolimnion)

epipelagic of, relating to, or denoting the organisms that live in the waters from the surface to depths generally not exceeding 200 meters

equilibrium constant for an equilibrium reaction, the ratio of the product of the concentrations of the individual reaction products divided by the product of the concentrations of the individual reactants; for a given temperature, this ratio (K) is constant; for example, for the equilibrium reaction $A + B = C + D$, the equilibrium constant (K) is expressed as $K = ([C] \times [D]) / ([A] \times [B])$, where the square brackets refer to molal concentrations; K is a function of temperature, and if K and the concentrations of any three of the components in the reaction are known, the fourth can be calculated

escarpment a steep slope or long cliff that results from erosion or faulting and separates two relatively level areas of differing elevations; also, the topographic expression of a fault

estuary a tidally influenced coastal area in which fresh water from a river mixes with sea water, generally at the river mouth; the resulting water is brackish, which results in a unique ecosystem

ethics a set of moral principles

eukaryote all living organisms other than the eubacteria and archaebacteria; all organisms that contain a cell or cells in which the genetic material is DNA in the form of chromosomes contained within a distinct nucleus

eustatic sea-level change a change in sea level that affects all the shorelines of the world simultaneously; for example, during ice ages, glaciers grow, resulting in the transfer of water from the ocean to snow and ice on land; compare with "isostatic sea-level change"

eutrophic describes a body of water that has become enriched with large nutrient concentrations, commonly phosphorus and nitrogen, resulting in high productivity; such waters often are shallow, and may experience periods of algal blooms and subsequent oxygen deficiency

eutrophication the process by which lakes and streams become enriched, to varying degrees, by concentrations of nutrients such as nitrogen and phosphorus; enrichment results in increased plant growth (principally algae) and decay, the latter of which reduces the dissolved oxygen content; highly eutrophic conditions may be considered undesirable, depending on the human use of the waterbody

evaporite sediment that forms as the result of the precipitation of minerals during the evaporation of water, primarily sea water, and that may form sedimentary rock; principal minerals are gypsum and halite

evapotranspiration water discharged to the atmosphere as a result of evaporation from the soil and surface-water bodies and by plant transpiration

evolved connate describes saline groundwater that owes its high mineral content to being in contact with, and slowly dissolving, rocks for long periods of time; may be found in sedimentary, igneous, and metamorphic rocks; see "connate" and "fossil groundwater"

exfoliation cracks fractures that parallel the surface of an object and tend to separate the object into thin sheets; may be caused by weathering or release of applied stress

exotic a general term that typically describes an organism or species that is not native to the area in which it is found (i.e., it is nonindigenous); exotic species may be invasive

externality the unintended or unwanted byproduct of production or consumption that must be borne by society in general; a negative externality arises from the detrimental effects of use or production (e.g., water pollution may represent a negative externality of watercraft operation); a positive externality arises from beneficial effects (e.g., decreased disease incidence arises from health vaccinations)

extrapolate the continuation, by means of simple estimation or sophisticated analysis, of a trend of time series data beyond its last observed value

extraterrestrial from beyond the Earth and its atmosphere

fault a fracture in a body of rock along which the mass of rock on one side of the fault moves against the mass on the other side; faults generate earthquakes

fault block a mass of rock bordered completely or partially by faults, and behaving as a unit during tectonic activity or faulting

federal–interstate compact in water resources, an agreement that forms an independent entity to coordinate federal, state, and local water management policies

feedback loop describes when natural processes respond to a disturbance in a manner that either reduces or increases the impact of the disturbance; for example, an increase in a stream's velocity will cause its channel to deepen and widen, thereby reducing the velocity (negative feedback); or, a reduction in vegetation on a slope will increase erosion, which will remove more plants, which will further increase erosion (positive feedback)

feldspar a silicate mineral that is the most common constituent mineral in Earth's crust

felsic describes igneous rocks that are high in silica and have high concentrations of sodium and potassium; granite and rhyolite are felsic igneous rocks

fen a saturated wetland characterized by the presence of basic or calcareous groundwater (as contrasted to a bog); often found as seepage areas on gentle slopes comprised of glacial deposits

fiduciary the law with respect to a trust relationship, especially between a trustee and a beneficiary

filter feeder an aquatic animal, such as a clam, barnacle, or sponge, that feeds by filtering particulate organic material from water

filtration a treatment process, under the control of qualified operators, for removing solid (particulate) matter from water by means of porous media such as sand or an artificially made filter; often used to remove particles that contain pathogens (disease-causing organisms)

finfish an aquatic animal with a backbone and fins, as opposed to a shellfish (an aquatic animal without a backbone and with a shell)

firmament the heavens or the sky, especially when regarded as tangible

fissure a surface of a fracture or crack in a rock along which there is a distinct separation of the rock on either side of the fissure

fissured sediment fractured (or cracked) sediments with distinct separation along the crack surfaces; fissures may be filled with mineral-bearing materials; in terms of water flow, water will infiltrate more rapidly along fissures than through porous sediment

flagellum any of various elongated, threadlike or whiplike appendages of plants or animals; plural is flagella

flash flood a sudden flood that crests in a short time (hours or minutes) and is often characterized by high-velocity flows; most common in deserts or areas of low vegetation

flocculation the agglomeration or clustering of colloidal and finely divided suspended matter after coagulation by gentle stirring by either mechanical or hydraulic means such that they can be separated from water or sewage; see "coagulation"

floe a contiguous piece of ice on the surface of water (e.g., rivers, lakes, or seas)

flood temporary inundation of normally dry land areas from the overflow of inland or tidal waters, or from the unusual and rapid accumulation or runoff of surface waters from any source; the rise in water may be caused by excessive rainfall, snowmelt, natural stream blockages, windstorms over a lake, storm surges on the ocean, or any combination of such conditions

flood hazard the degree of potential for inundation that presents risk to life, health, property, and natural floodplain values

floodplain the low-lying land adjoining a river that is sometimes flooded; generally covered by fine-grained sediments (silt and clay) deposited by the river at flood stage

floodplain management the societal process of decision-making to achieve the best use of floodplains, the low-lying land adjoining a river that is sometimes flooded

flow rate rate of flow of water expressed in units of length per time, such as meters per second or feet per day; compare with "flow velocity," "discharge," and "volumetric flow rate"

flow velocity the speed (rate) and direction of water flow, quantified as the rate of flow of water in a given direction; expressed in units of length per time (e.g., meters per second or feet per day) and direction (e.g., northeast); compare with "discharge" and "volumetric flow rate"

flowstone a layered deposit of calcium carbonate ($CaCO_3$) on rock over which water has flowed or dripped, as on the walls of a limestone cave; see "dripstone"

fluid inclusions small volumes of fluid (liquid and gas) trapped in imperfections as minerals grew or recrystallized around them; mostly water with minor CO_2 plus dissolved minerals; most are less than 0.1 millimeter (0.004 inches) in size

fluvial pertaining to the action of a river, stream, or flood flow, as in fluvial processes of erosion or the deposition of alluvium

food chain the levels of nutrition in an ecosystem, beginning at the bottom with primary producers, which are principally plants, to a series of consumers—herbivores, carnivores, and decomposers

food fish captured or farm-raised fish used for food

food web a complex food chain, with several species at each level, so that there is more than one producer and more than one consumer of each type

foreshore the part of a shore that lies between high and low watermarks; the part of a shore between the water and occupied or cultivated land

forest litter the accumulation of organic debris (e.g., limbs, leaves) on the forest floor

fossil a preserved plant or animal imprint or remains

fossil fuel substance such as coal, oil, or natural gas, found underground in deposits formed from the remains of organisms that lived millions of years ago

fossil groundwater also called connate water, a highly enriched brine that resides in ancient sediments often associated with oil-bearing formations

fracture in geology, a general term for any break in rock, which includes cracks, joints, and faults

frazil ice ice crystals in the water column, usually near the surface, having the appearance of slush; frazil ice is the first stage in the formation of sea ice; crystals start to form when the sea water cools to −1.8°C (28.8°F)

front (atmospheric) a boundary between atmospheric air masses

front (ocean) a region in the ocean where a sudden change in temperature, velocity, or other parameter causes a sharp line of demarcation at the surface, often visible to the eye; a front may be small-scale and narrow, or larger-scale and extend across several kilometers; a front usually denotes a region of convergence, where water tends to sink

frost wedging an important mechanism of mechanical weathering of rocks wherein water freezes in cracks and, as a result of expansion during the formation of ice, forces the crack further apart, perhaps breaking the rock into smaller pieces

frustule the silicified cell wall of a diatom (a microscopic alga), consisting of two valves or overlapping halves

fugitive resource a natural resource such as water that moves from one location and one state (liquid, gas, or solid) to another

fumarole a hole or orifice in a volcanic region, usually in lava, from which high-temperature gases and vapors are expelled; mineral deposits frequently line the opening

gaining reach a length of stream that is receiving groundwater inflow along its length, resulting in a greater stream-water discharge downstream than upstream of the reach

game fish fish considered to possess sporting qualities on fishing tackle, such as salmon, trout, black bass, and striped bass

gamete a sex cell; in some of the simplest organisms, the gametes are not differentiated into egg and sperm

gangue the nonvaluable materials closely associated with the valuable minerals in ore deposits (also referred to as waste rock); common gangue minerals include quartz and calcite; typically must be removed and discarded to extract the valuable high-grade ore

gas hydrate a crystalline solid consisting of a gas molecule surrounded by water molecules

gastropod a large class (Gastropoda) of mollusks in which each animal has a head with eyes, a large flattened foot for movement, and often a single asymmetrical spiral shell; includes limpets, snails, and slugs

geochemistry the science that deals with the chemical composition of the Earth's materials and the chemical processes involved in their formation or modification; also refers to the chemical composition of Earth's materials in a given region

geodetic relating to the precise measurement of the Earth's surface or of points on its surface, such as in land surveying

geography the science of the Earth and life, especially the description of land, sea, air, and the distribution of plant and animal life, including humankind and its industries, with reference to the mutual relations among these diverse elements; also refers to the geographical features of an area—that is, the nature and relative arrangement of places and physical features

geoid the hypothetical shape of the Earth considered as a mean (average) sea-level surface extended continuously through the continents and the oceans

geologic unit a large volume of a certain kind of rock or sediment with recognizable and distinguishing characteristics and of a given age range

geology the scientific study of the Earth, its form and composition, and the physical, chemical, and biological processes that affect it; includes the study of ancient life on the planet; also refers to the geologic characteristics of a given region

geometry a branch of mathematics dealing with features of point configurations that are invariant under a specified group of mathematical transformations

geomorphology the scientific study of the physical characteristics of the land surface and landforms that are the result of specific geologic processes; also refers to the geomorphological characteristics of a given region

geophysical related to the physical characteristics and structure of the Earth, including geodesy, seismology, meteorology, oceanography, atmospheric electricity, terrestrial magnetism, and tidal phenomena

geostrophic current an ocean current that flows along a line of equal dynamic topography on the sea surface, oriented so that the high topographies are on the right in the Northern Hemisphere and on the left in the Southern Hemisphere

geothermal describes terrestrial heat, usually associated with water, as around hot springs

geyser a periodic thermal spring that results from the expansive force of superheated steam; also, a special type of thermal spring which intermittently ejects a column of water and steam into the air with considerable force

geyser reservoir the underground network of open volumes in the subsurface that serve to temporarily store water that will be heated and erupted from the geyser

gill net a net set upright in the water so that fish are caught in it when their gills become entangled in its meshes

glaciation the covering and modification of a landmass by a glacier or glaciers

glacier a huge mass of ice, formed on land by the compaction and recrystallization of snow, which moves slowly downslope or outward owing to its own weight

glacier cave a cave that formed at the base of a glacier along a stream of meltwater moving beneath the glacier

global warming an increase in the average temperature of the Earth's atmosphere, especially a sustained increase sufficient to cause climatic change

grab sample a water sample collected at a single location and at a single time as opposed to a sample composited over space or time

graded selected and arranged by size

gradient a measure of the change in magnitude of a parameter (e.g., temperature, elevation, chemical concentration) with distance; for example, a stream gradient would be 0.001 if the stream's elevation dropped 1 meter (3.3 feet) over a distance of 1,000 meters (3,300 feet); when a gradient exists, there is a tendency for a transfer to take place from the area of greater magnitude to the area of lesser magnitude

granite an igneous rock comprising quartz and potassium feldspar; high in silica and crystallized from a melt within Earth's crust

gravity flow the movement downslope of a mixture of unconsolidated material and water, solely in response to gravity; the resulting deposition shows delta-like patterns and structures

grease ice thin plates of organized ice crystals on the water surface; an early stage in the growth of sea-ice cover

greenhouse effect the phenomenon whereby a planetary body's atmosphere traps solar radiation; caused by the presence in the atmosphere of gases such as carbon dioxide, water vapor, and methane, that allow incoming sunlight to pass through but trap heat radiated back from the body's surface

greenhouse gas a gas in the atmosphere that traps heat and reflects it back to the planetary body

greywater wastewater from clothes-washing machines, showers, bathtubs, hand washing, lavatories, and sinks that is not used for disposal of chemicals or chemical–biological ingredients; less commonly spelled graywater or gray water

groin a wall placed perpendicular to the shoreline for the purpose of catching sediment to build up a beach

groundfish general term for more than 80 species that, with few exceptions, live on or near the ocean floor (e.g., rockfish, flounder, lingcod, ocean perch, and Pacific whiting)

groundwater generally, all subsurface (underground) water, as distinct from surface water, that supplies natural springs, contributes to permanent streams, and can be tapped by wells; specifically, the water that is in the saturated zone of a defined aquifer

groundwater mining the withdrawal of groundwater at a rate exceeding natural recharge, resulting in a permanent lowering of the water table

groundwater reservoir an aquifer or a previously unsaturated rock or sediment in which water is stored

gully general term for a defined channel, larger than a rill, produced by running-water erosion; compare with "rill"

guyot a flat-topped seamount on the ocean floor; formed as a volcano at a spreading center, the mountaintop is eroded by wave activity as the mountain sinks when the plate upon which it is riding moves away from the spreading center

gyre a circular pattern of currents in an ocean basin

habitat the environment in which a plant or animal grows or lives; the surroundings include physical factors such as temperature, moisture, and light, together with biological factors such as the presence of food and predators

half-life the time required for the initial concentration of a radioactive element to decrease, through radioactive decay, by 50 percent; in nonradiochemical usage, the time required for a pollutant to lose one-half of its original concentration (e.g., the biochemical half-life of DDT in the environment is 15 years)

hard water water that forms a precipitate with soap due to the abundance of calcium, magnesium, or ferrous ions in solution

harmful algal bloom also called harmful algae bloom, a rapid increase in algae concentrations in fresh or marine waters in which one or more algal species causes harm to animals or humans, particularly (but not exclusively) by virtue of their eventual mass decay (and the accompanying oxygen depletion) or by their generation of natural biotoxins; harmful marine blooms are a subcategory of "red tides," a popular term which encompasses both harmful and nonharmful blooms

hazardous waste any solid, liquid, or gas that, when disposed, exhibits the characteristics of ignitability, corrosivity, reactivity, or toxicity, as well as any industrial waste that has been specifically listed in the federal regulations as having hazardous properties

headland a point of land, usually high and with a sheer drop, extending out into a body of water; a promontory

headwaters the source or upper reaches of a stream; also the upper reaches of a reservoir

heat capacity the amount of heat required to raise the temperature of 1 gram of a substance 1 degree centigrade; water has a high heat capacity, and can absorb or evolve significant heat with minor temperature change

heat exchanger a mechanism whereby heat is exchanged from one medium to another

heavy metals a group of metals that have high density and are considered toxic at specified concentrations; with respect to soil management, such metals include copper, iron, manganese, molybdenum, cobalt, zinc, cadmium, mercury, nickel, and lead

hectare a metric unit of area equal to 10,000 square meters (107,639 square feet or 2.471 acres)

herbaceous with the characteristics of a herb; describes a plant with no persistent woody stem above ground

herbicides a group of chemicals used to kill or reduce the growth of vegetation that is considered undesirable

herbivore an animal that feeds mostly on plants

herpetology the scientific study of amphibians and reptiles

heterotroph an organism deriving its nutritional requirements from complex organic substances; animals or microorganisms that live on producers

high-grade ore rock or sediment that has high concentrations of valuable minerals

holistic describes an approach to problem-solving that focuses not only on the individual components of the problem, but more importantly on its totality; with respect to water-related issues, typically describes an analytical and planning approach that considers the interrelated linkages and interdependencies of a socioeconomic system with resource use, pollution, environmental impacts, and preservation of an entire ecosystem

hormones biochemicals, usually proteins or steroids, released in very low concentrations by specialized cells (e.g., in glands) that travel to and are recognized by receptor cells, which in turn trigger a wide range of cascading biochemical events that regulate numerous aspects of metabolism or behavior

hot spot a location where a mantle plume rises toward the base of the Earth's lithosphere, producing magma, high heat flow, and volcanism at the surface; generally fixed relative to the moving lithospheric plate

hot spring a thermal spring that brings warm or hot water from the subsurface to the surface; water temperature usually is 8 Celsius degrees (15 Fahrenheit degrees) or more above the mean air temperature

hull the main body of a ship or other such vessel, including the bottom, sides, and deck but not the masts, rigging, superstructure, engines, and other fittings

hurricane a giant atmospheric circulation that forms over warm tropical ocean water, with a calm, clear eye at the center of the system, and winds of 65 knots or higher

husbandry in aquaculture, the rearing and careful management of captively held fish and other aquatic resources

hydrate to add water to a substance, system or compound

hydraulic gradient the change in hydraulic head between two points (e.g., the difference in water level between two points divided by the distance between the two points)

hydraulic head the potential energy of water as a result of its elevation and weight of overlying water; it is the driving force for natural water movement; for dams, the hydraulic head approximately equals the difference between upstream and downstream water depths

hydraulically connected a condition in which waterbodies and/or aquifers are in direct contact and water can move easily between them (e.g., water moving from a streambed into an aquifer, or vice versa)

hydraulics the scientific study of water in motion; modern hydraulics emphasizes the mechanical properties of water that describe the specific pattern and rate of movement in the natural environment or in artificial systems (for example, pipe systems)

hydric characterized by, relating to, or requiring an abundance of moisture; referring to a habitat characterized by wet or moist conditions rather than mesic (moderate moisture conditions) or xeric (dry conditions)

hydrocarbon a chemical compound that consists entirely of carbon and hydrogen, such as petroleum, natural gas, and coal

hydroelectric often used synonymously with "hydropower," describes electricity generated by utilizing the power of falling water, as with water flowing through and turning turbines at a dam

hydrogen bond in water, the type of chemical bond between two water molecules; caused by electromagnetic forces, and occurring when the positive (hydrogen) side of one water molecule is attracted to and forms a bond with the negative (oxygen) side of another water molecule

hydrogeology a branch of geology that deals with the occurrence and movement of groundwater in relation to Earth structures; also refers to the hydrogeologic characteristics of a given region

hydrograph a graphical representation or plot of changes in the flow of water or changes in the elevation of water level plotted against time

hydrologic cycle the solar-driven circulation of water on and in the Earth, characterized by the ongoing transfer of water among the oceans, atmosphere, surface waters (lakes, streams, and wetlands), and groundwaters

hydrology the science that deals with the occurrence, distribution, movement, and physical and chemical properties of water on Earth; also refers to the hydrologic characteristics of a given region

hydrolysis a chemical reaction with water, resulting in either the formation of carbonic acid or another weak acid, or the addition of a reaction product containing the hydroxyl ion (OH^-), which can act as a weak base

hydroperiod the seasonal and cyclical pattern of water in a wetland

hydrophyte plants typically found in wet habitats; any plant growing in water or on a wet substrate that is at least periodically deficient in oxygen as a result of excessive water content

hydroponics the cultivation of plants in nutrient solution rather than in soil

hydropower power, typically electrical energy, produced by utilizing falling water; see "hydroelectric"

hydrosphere liquid water and ice on the surface of the Earth and in underground reservoirs

hydrostatic referring to the pressure exerted by water at a point, related to the weight of the water above the point; for example, the hydrostatic pressure in pounds per square inch at the bottom of a tank is equal to the weight in pounds in a column of water one square inch in cross-section and having the height of the water in the tank

hydrothermal associated with hot water, especially with the action of hot water in dissolving, transporting, depositing, and otherwise changing the distribution of minerals in the Earth's crust

hydrothermal alteration zone a volume of rocks altered by the interaction of hydrothermal water with pre-existing rocks and minerals

hydrothermal vent an opening or other orifice on the seafloor through which hot watery solutions that have circulated through the underlying rock escape and mix with sea water; see "black smoker"

hypersaline describes water with a salt concentration greater than 40 percent (parts per thousand); this extreme concentration is generally the result of evaporation of sea water

hypolimnion the lower layer of a thermally stratified lake, located below the thermocline, and in which the water is nearly uniformly cool and relatively quiescent

hyporheic exchange the movement of stream water into and out of the hyporheic zone

hyporheic zone the volume of sediment and porous space adjacent to a stream, and through which stream water exchanges

hypothesis a statement made about the condition or behavior of a variable or event that lends itself to rigorous testing for validity

hypoxia a condition in which natural waters have a low concentration of dissolved oxygen (about 2 milligrams per liter as compared with a normal level of 8 to 10 milligrams per liter); most game and commercial species of fish avoid such waters; compare with anoxia, which is less than 0.1 milliliter of oxygen per liter, and the threshold below which animal life diminishes significantly

ice age a cold period marked by episodes of extensive glaciation alternating with episodes of relative warmth; the formally designated "Ice Age" refers to the most recent glacial period, which occurred during the Pleistocene epoch

ice cap an extensive perennial accumulation of snow and ice that forms when glaciers completely fill their subglacial valleys and coalesce (join together); ice caps are smaller than ice sheets

ice pancake see "pancake ice"

ice sheet an extensive perennial accumulation of snow and ice completely covering the underlying topography; ice sheets are land-based or marine-based; present-day ice sheets cover Greenland and Antarctica; ice sheets are larger than ice caps

ice shelf a floating ice mass that is attached to the coast along at least one edge

iceberg a piece of floating ice that breaks off (calves) from an ice shelf, glacier, ice stream, or ice tongue

ichthyology the scientific study of fish

igneous describes rock that solidified from molten material (magma); the rock is extrusive (or volcanic) if it solidifies on the surface and intrusive (or plutonic) if it solidifies beneath the surface

individual quota the amount of a common-property resource assigned to a user, giving them rights to a fixed amount of access and harvesting; also called an individual transfer quota; in fisheries, the permit of each fisher to take a percentage of total allowable catch for a certain species during the fishing season—once an individual quota is attained, the fisher is restricted from fishing for that species until the next season

Industrial Revolution beginning in Great Britain around 1730, a period in the eighteenth and nineteenth centuries when nations in Europe, Asia, and the Americas moved from agrarian-based to industry-based economies

infauna aquatic animals that live in the substrate of a body of water, especially in a soft sea bottom

infiltration the process by which water enters the soil and that is controlled by the character of the soil and surface conditions, such as slope and amount of vegetation

infiltration rate the rate at which water from precipitation enters the soil; the maximum rate is known as infiltration capacity

infrastructure the permanent constructed system (e.g., pipes and other structures) that enables the treatment and delivery of water to support human habitation and activity, or that supports manufacturing activities and water projects (e.g., desalinization and hydropower plants)

inorganic an element, molecule, or substance that did not form as the direct result of biologic activity

insecticides a group of chemicals used to kill or otherwise control insects and arachnids that are considered undesirable

insolation the amount of solar radiation that reaches a given area

institution a custom, practice, relationship, or behavioral pattern of importance in the life of a community or society; also an established organization, especially one dedicated to public service

instream flow the amount of water remaining in a stream, without diversions, that is required to satisfy a particular aquatic environment or water use, such as the water required for fish and wildlife or for navigation

instream water use the use of water in place in a river or lake, without diversion or withdrawal; as opposed to offstream water use, in which water is diverted or withdrawn to be used elsewhere

integrated water management that blends coordinated viewpoints of social scientists with those of engineers and natural scientists or that coordinates in other ways different facets of management, such as competing purposes or different areas or interest groups

interests as in "business interests" or "environmental interests," the vested opinions, perspectives, and positions of stakeholders regarding gains and losses, real or perceived, stemming from decision-making outcomes

intergenerational equity ethical concept of fairness which holds that present generations should not degrade the environment to an extent that unreasonably constrains opportunities for future generations to meet their basic needs

intergovernmental existing or carried on between governmental bodies

internal phosphorus loading a process within a waterbody, typically a lake, whereby phosphorus is released from internal sources (for example, pore water in the bottom sediments, resuspension of sediments by wave action, or disruption of bottom sediment by burrowing organisms)

interpolate to estimate intermediate values of a function between two known points; frequently used when certain periods of data are missing, but data surrounding these missing data values are available

interstate existing or carried on between states

interstate water according to law, interstate waters are defined as (1) rivers, lakes, and other waters that flow across or form a part of state or international boundaries; (2) waters of the Great Lakes; (3) coastal waters whose scope has been defined to include ocean waters seaward to the territorial limits and waters along the coastline (including inland streams) influenced by the tide

interstellar describes the region of space that occurs between individual stars, occupied by gas and dust as well as isolated molecules, including hydroxyl ions, water, sulfur oxide, as well as carbon-based molecules

intertidal coastal land that is covered by water at high tide and uncovered at low tide

intragenerational equity ethical concept of fairness which holds that people living on the Earth at the same time (i.e., within the current generation) should have similar opportunities to meet their basic needs and improve their basic standard of living, and that actions by wealthier people should not disadvantage poorer people

intragovernmental existing or carried on within a governmental body

intrastate existing or carried on within a state

invasive describes a plant or animal that moves in and takes over an ecosystem to the detriment of other species; often the result of environmental manipulation; see "exotic"

inverse estuary an estuary that receives no fresh-water input from a river in an area of high evaporation rates; circulation driven by density differences produced as evaporation and salinity increases inland; more saline water at the inner end sinks and moves seaward

invertebrate an animal without a backbone

ion an atom or molecule that carries a net charge (either positive or negative) because of an imbalance between the number of protons and the number of electrons

irrigable land arable land for which a water supply can be made available and which will respond well to irrigation

irrigation the controlled application of water for agricultural or other purposes through human-made systems; generally refers to water application to soil when rainfall is insufficient to maintain desirable soil moisture for plant growth

island arcs the arc-shaped chain of volcanoes that develop over the subducting plate inland from the trench as a result of melting processes associated with subduction; island arcs may develop on oceanic plates (ocean island arcs) or on continental plates (continental island arcs)

isopach a line on a map that connects points of equal thickness with respect to a particular stratigraphic unit or group of units

isostasy describes the concept that the elevation of the Earth's surface (over tens of millions of years) seeks a balance between the weight of lithospheric rocks and the buoyancy of asthenospheric fluid (hot, plastic, partially molten rock); a mountain range where erosion has moved a significant amount of rock material may rise isostatically, whereas the basin that receives this eroded sediment may sink under the added weight; "isostatic" means pertaining to or related to isostasy

isostatic sea-level change a change in sea level that occurs owing to significant isostatic adjustments, such as large amounts of mass being loaded (deposition of sediments) or unloaded (erosion of the land) in a region, which causes the land to sink or rise; compare with "eustatic sea-level change"; see "isostasy"

isotope the one of two or more forms or varieties of a specific element that differ in their atomic mass; the proton number is the same for a given set of related isotopes, but the number of neutrons in the nucleus varies; for example, the common isotopes of oxygen, O-18, O-17, and O-16, all have 8 protons, but have 10, 9, and 8 neutrons, respectively

jetty a structure built out into the sea, a lake, or a river to counteract the effects of tides or currents

Jovian refers to the Jupiter-like (low-density) planets of Jupiter, Saturn, Neptune, and Uranus; the gas giants; compare with "terrestrial planets"

junior appropriator an individual whose right to appropiate water from a source is more recent in time than others with rights to the same source of water; a right with lower priority than all others

karst topography characterized by closed depressions or sinkholes, caves, and underground drainage formed by dissolution of limestone, dolomite, or gypsum

kelp forest a dense growth of seaweed (called giant kelp) that occurs in cool coastal waters where sunlight can reach the seafloor

keystone species a species on which the persistence of a large number of other species in the ecosystem depends

kilowatt a unit of power equal to 1,000 watts, wherein the watt corresponds to the rate of energy in an electric circuit

krill small, abundant, shrimp-like crustaceans that form an important part of the food chain in Antarctic waters

Kuiper Belt a disk-shaped region past the orbit of Neptune roughly 30 to 50 astronomical units (AU) from the Sun, containing many small icy bodies; considered the source of the short-period comets

La Niña an area of cooler-than-average ocean water in the tropical eastern Pacific off the coast of South America; the counterpart of El Niño

lacustrine pertaining to, produced by, or formed in a lake or lakes

lag time the time period between a rainfall event in a watershed and the occurrence of peak discharge in the stream

land-use planning a generic term for a wide range of legislative and regulatory activities intended to limit or direct land development for the purpose of making its usage sustainable; large-scale land-use plans often are implemented by local zoning and land-use ordinances

landform a discernible natural landscape that exists as a result of wind, water, ice, or other geological activity, such as a plateau, plain, basin, or mountain

landscape development the progressive evolution of topography as a result of the actions of the geologic agents of wind, water, ice, and mass movements (landslides)

landslide a mass of material that has slipped downhill under the influence of gravity, frequently occurring when the material is saturated with water

latent heat of fusion the energy required to melt 1 gram of ice, or 80 calories per gram

latent heat of vaporization the energy required to vaporize 1 gram of water, or 540 to 640 calories per gram, depending on the water temperature ranging from 100°C to 0°C

latitude the angular distance north or south of the Earth's or another planet's equator, measured in degrees along a meridian

lattice the internal structure of a mineral, produced by the regular arrangement of the mineral's component elements or ions

lava a molten mass of rock material that is extruded at the surface by a volcano or through a fissure in the Earth

lava tube (cave) cave formed during solidification of a large lava flow; flow solidifies from the outside in; cooler solidified outer part of lava flow remains in place while inner molten part drains away, leaving a cavelike structure

leachate liquid that has moved through a substance, removing solids from the substance, generally by dissolution

lead any fracture or passageway through sea ice which is navigable by surface vessels

levee a natural or artificial earthen obstruction along the edge of a stream, lake, or river; also, a long, low embankment usually built to restrain the flow of water out of a riverbank and to protect land from flooding

Liebig's Law of the Minimum the recognition that crop yield or growth is proportional to the amount of the most limiting nutrient present

limnology the scientific study of fresh-water bodies such as lakes, ponds, streams, and rivers

lithosphere the rigid outer layer of Earth made up of the crust and the uppermost mantle

lithospheric plate a section of the lithosphere that acts as a single mass and interacts with other plates; lithospheric plates are created at spreading centers and destroyed at subduction zones; see "plate tectonics"

littoral the region along the shore of a nonflowing body of water; corresponds to riparian for a flowing body of water; more specifically, for marine waters, the zone of the sea flood lying between the tide levels

littoral transport the movement of sedimentary material in the zone extending seaward from the shoreline to just beyond the breaker zone by waves and currents; it includes movement parallel (long-shore drift) and sometimes also perpendicular (cross-shore transport) to the shore

load management steps taken to reduce water demand at peak load times, such as shifting some of it to off-peak times; may refer to peak hours or peak days

local base level see "base level"

lock one in a series of gates that allows vessels to pass through multiple water levels

logarithm the real number x satisfying the equation $b^x = a$, where the base b is a real number greater than 0 and not equal to 1

logarithmic scale a scale in which the distances that numbers are positioned from a reference point are proportional to their logarithms

longitude the angular distance measured east or west from the prime meridian (which runs through Greenwich, England), to the meridian passing through a position; expressed in degrees (or hours), minutes, and seconds

longshore transport the transport of sedimentary material parallel to the shore

losing reach a length of stream that is losing stream water along its length, resulting in a smaller stream-water discharge downstream than upstream of the reach

macroinvertebrates organisms visible with the naked eye; macroinvertebrates in water include insects, snails, bivalves, and sometimes amphipods or copepods

macrophyte a macroscopic form of aquatic vegetation; a plant, especially an aquatic plant, large enough to be seen by the naked eye

macropore an opening or zone of high permeability that provides a zone of rapid transport of water (and potentially waterborne contaminants) into the subsurface; examples include animal burrows and tree roots

mafic describes igneous rocks that are low in silica and have high concentrations of calcium, iron, and magnesium; basalt is the most common mafic igneous rock

magma molten rock found in the mantle and crust of the Earth (also found on planets, moons, and asteroids); when forced toward the surface, it cools and solidifies to become igneous rock; when it erupts at the surface, it is called lava

mangrove tropical evergreen trees and shrubs that have stilt-like roots and stems, and often form dense thickets along tidal shores

mantle the region of the Earth between the molten core and the outer crust, composed mainly of silicate rock, and roughly 2,900 kilometers (1,800 miles) thick; also the interior of another planet, moon, or large asteroid between the core and the crust

marginal sea a semi-closed sea associated with a continent and formed during rifting and early spreading

mariculture the science, art, and business of cultivating marine animals or plants under controlled conditions; a subcategory of aquaculture

marina a water-based facility used for storage, service, launching, operation, or maintenance of watercraft

marine snow small particulate matter that drifts down from the upper layers of the oceans; comprises debris from animals, plants, and nonliving matter, (e.g., fecal pellets, diatoms, dust); affects visibility and light transmission within the water; larger pieces may serve as food source for animals in deeper waters

market institution an arrangement that allows individuals to decide voluntarily how much of a good or service to produce, sell, buy, or consume based mainly on prices set by demand and supply conditions; in the alternative, the government decides who gets how much of a good or service, and at what price

marl in a lake environment, a sediment that accumulates on the lake floor and consists of a mixture of organic matter, clays, carbonates of calcium and magnesium, and remnants of shells; forms in the absence of significant land-derived sediments such as sand; useful as a fertilizer

mass media all of the widespread communications that reach a large audience, especially television, radio, newspapers, and the Internet

maximum contaminant level abbreviated as MCL, the allowable level of the specified contaminant in drinking water; established by the federal Environmental Protection Agency; state governments may set lower levels

mean the arithmetic average of a set of data

meander (noun) one of a series of somewhat regular bends in the course of a stream; (verb) to follow a winding course

media as in water treatment, the sand, gravel, small plastic beads, or other material designed for water filtration

mediator a person who is trained to help parties resolve their own conflicts by using established conflict resolution techniques

megawatt a unit of power equal to 1,000,000 watts, wherein the watt corresponds to the rate of energy in an electric circuit

melting point the temperature at which a solid becomes a liquid; the melting point at which ice becomes water: 0°C (32°F)

meltwater water resulting from the melting of snow, ice, or glacial ice

Mesoamerica the central region of America, from central Mexico to Nicaragua

metabolism the sum total of biochemical processes that occur within a living organism, or a portion of it, in order to maintain life; the biochemical changes by which energy is provided to living cells and new material is assimilated

metabolite any substance produced by metabolism or a metabolic process

metadata statistical information that describes the elements of a set of data

metamorphism the changes in the mineral assemblage and texture of a rock subjected to temperatures and pressures that are significantly different than the conditions under which the rock orginally formed; significantly enhanced by the presence of water; changes occur without melting the rock

metamorphosis the biological process of transformation from an immature form to an adult form in two or more separate stages

metasomatism a change in the composition of a rock due to the introduction or removal of chemical components

meteoric water atmospheric water that reaches the Earth's surface as rainfall or other form of precipitation; part of the hydrologic cycle

meteorite a solid body that has fallen from space to the surface of the Earth or another planet; meteoritic means pertaining to or originating from a meteorite

meteorology the science that deals with the atmosphere, especially with regard to climate and weather

methemoglobinemia a disease, primarily in infants, caused by the conversion of nitrates to nitrites in the intestines, and which limits the body's ability to receive oxygen; often referred to as "blue baby syndrome"

metric ton unit of weight equal to 1,000 kilograms; equivalent to 2,205 pounds or 1.1025 short tons

microbe a microscopic organism, or microorganism; the term encompasses viruses, bacteria, yeast, molds, protozoa, and small algae

microbial film see "biofilm"

microgravity the condition experienced in free fall as a spacecraft orbits Earth or another body; commonly called weightlessness; only very small forces are perceived in free fall, on the order of one-millionth the force of gravity on Earth's surface

microorganism a microscopic organism; see "microbe"

mitigation actions designed to lessen or reduce adverse impacts; frequently used in the context of environmental assessment

mitigation banking a mitigation bank with respect to wetlands is a wetland area that has been restored, created, enhanced, or (in exceptional circumstances) preserved, which is then set aside to compensate for later conversions of wetlands for development activities

model inversion working backwards with a model using observed values of what the model is supposed to predict to determine what the initial conditions were; often referred to as inverse modeling; commmonly used in calibrating a model (e.g., comparing observed water levels with values predicted by the model to determine optimal input parameters to the model)

Mohorovičić discontinuity abbreviated as Moho, the boundary between Earth's crust and the underlying mantle; recognizable by a sharp increase in seismic wave velocity

molality the number of moles of a dissolved solute per kilogram of solvent

molarity the number of moles of dissolved solute per liter of solution

mole a quantity of a given element or compound, defined as the formula weight (atomic or molecular weight) expressed in grams; for example, the formula weight for the water molecule (H_2O) is 18, so a mole of water is a quantity of water having a mass of 18 grams; a mole of a substance comprises 6.023×10^{23} atoms or molecules

molecular diffusion the movement of individual molecules through a solid, liquid, or gas in response to a concentration gradient; molecules will move from where their concentration is higher to where it is lower

mollusk an invertebrate animal with a soft, unsegmented body and usually a shell and a muscular foot; examples are clams, oysters, mussels, and octopuses

monsoon a wind system that influences large climatic regions and reverses direction seasonally; best known as a wet, warm-season wind carrying drenching rains; also can describe the wintertime wind shift that carries dry, cooler air

morphology the external shape, structure, form, and arrangement of landforms and waterbodies

mortality for a particular animal population, the number of deaths in a given area or period, or from a particular cause

mousse thick, foamy oil-and-water mixture formed when petroleum is subjected to mixing with water

mudpot a hot spring that reaches the surface through water-saturated fine-grained sediments; the hot water mixes with the sediments, producing a thick, pasty mud through which hot gases periodically escape, showering the immediate area with mud globules

multipurpose project a water project that is undertaken to meet a variety of objectives, ranging from water supply and hydropower to irrigation, recreation, or habitat maintenance

natural flow a doctrine developed by some riparian rights states that would require all water to be left in a watercourse

natural gas naturally occurring gas composed of methane and other light hydrocarbons

natural hazard a hazard event arising from geophysical processes or biological agents—such as those creating earthquakes, hurricanes, floods, or locust infestations—that affect the lives, livelihood, and property of people

navigable in general usage, describes a waterbody deep and wide enough to afford passage to small and large vessels; also can be used in the context of a specific statutory or regulatory designation

navigable waters surface-water bodies as specifically designated by statutes or regulations

nebula clouds of interstellar gas and dust

nekton assemblages of organisms that swim actively in water, such as fish, reptiles, and mammals; contrasts with organisms (plankton) that are simply carried along in water

neritic describes the area off the shallow regions of a lake or ocean that border the land; also used to identify the biota that inhabit the water along the shore of a lake or ocean

neritic zone the relatively shallow water zone that extends from the high tide mark to the edge of the continental shelf; also refers to such shallow water regions of lakes

net pen floating cages in coastal waterbodies (e.g., bays) that are used in mariculture operations

neurotransmitter a chemical substance released at the end of a nerve fiber by the arrival of a nerve impulse, enabling the transmission of the impulse between two nerve cells

nitrate the highly leachable form of soil nitrogen taken up by most plants through their roots; it is a common groundwater contaminant, especially in agricultural areas and locations with a high density of septic systems, that is regulated by the U.S. Environmental Protection Agency with a drinking water standard of 10 ppm (parts per million) of nitrogen in the nitrate form

nitrogen fixation the conversion of atmospheric nitrogen (N_2) into a form of nitrogen such as ammonia (NH_3) that can be used by plants and other biological agents

nitrogen fixer an organism capable of nitrogen fixation

noble gas a gas that is unreactive (inert) or reactive only to a limited extent with other elements; six noble gases make up a group on the periodic table: helium, neon, argon, krypton, xenon, and radon

nonmarket good a product or service that is not traded in a market and which does not have a market price that reveals how consumers value the good; examples include air and water quality, some parks and recreation amenities, endangered species, and some natural resources such as wetlands

nonpoint source a pollutant release or discharge originating from a land use active over a wide land area (e.g., agriculture) rather than from one specific location (e.g., an outfall pipe from a factory)

nonstructural measure an arrangement to manage, utilize, or control water and related lands that does not rely on constructed facilities; includes regulatory control and financial incentive

nonylphenol $C_9H_{19}OH$; a surface active agent used as a lube oil additive, and in stabilizers, fungicides, bacteriocides, dyes, drugs, adhesives, rubber chemicals, etc.

nutrients a group of chemical elements or compounds needed for all plant and animal life; nitrogen and phosphorus are primary nutrients in aquatic systems; excessive or imbalanced nutrients in water may cause problems such as accelerated eutrophication

obligate describes organisms that require the specified condition (e.g., high pressure) for growth

oceanic plate the large segment of the lithosphere (i.e., crust of the Earth and uppermost mantle, the region just below the crust) that supports an ocean basin

oceanography the broad category of science that deals with oceans

offstream water use the diversion or withdrawal of water out of the source river or lake for use elsewhere; as opposed to instream water use, in which the water is used in place rather than being diverted or withdrawn

oligotrophic pertaining to a lake or other body of water characterized by low concentrations of nutrients (such as nitrogen and phosphorus) and having low to moderate productivity

omnivore an animal that will feed on many different kinds of food, including both plants and animals

ooid a small (0.5 to 2 millimeter), spherical object composed of concentric layers of calcium carbonate that has grown in concentric rings, often around some kind of nucleus such as a quartz grain

Oort Cloud a spherical cloud of comets around the Sun at a distance far from Neptune's orbit, extending from approximately 50,000 and 100,000 astronomical units (AU) from the Sun

open-access resource a resource for which there is no private-property-right system governing access and withdrawals

ordinance a law or rule enacted by an authority, such as a city government

ordnance military weapons such as cannon and artillery and their ammunition

ore deposit usually refers to a vein (or veins) of ore (or massive mineralized or otherwise economically valuable rock or sediment) that can be mined as a unit

organic pertaining to, or the product of, biological reactions or functions

organochlorine any chemical compound that contains carbon and chlorine

ornithology the scientific study of birds

orogeny the tectonic processes that lead to mountain-building; orogenies occur at convergent plate boundaries (i.e., the boundary between two lithospheric plates that are moving directly against one another)

orographic lift the process whereby air is forced to rise as it blows across upward-sloping terrain or against mountain ranges

overallocation the action or process of too widely allocating or distributing something, such as water resources

overcapitalization the existence of more capital applied in an industry than is necessary for its efficient operation, as has been the case in the fishing industry

overfishing the removal of such a large number of certain fish from a body of water that breeding stocks are reduced to levels that will not support the continued presence of the fish in desirable quantities for sport or commercial harvest

oxbow the crescent-shaped body of shallow, standing water formed by a stream meander cut-off; sometimes called an oxbow lake

oxidant the oxidizing agent (oxygen) that is used in water treatment processes to break down organic waste or chemicals such as cyanides, phenols, and organic sulfur compounds in sewage by bacterial and chemical means

oxidation a chemical reaction involving the loss of one or more electrons from a specific element; results in an increase in the charge of the element; for example, iron (II) (Fe^{2+}) is oxidized to iron (III) (Fe^{3+}) through the loss of an electron; such reactions often take place in the presence of free oxygen

oxidation–reduction reaction a chemical reaction involving both oxidation and reduction; the electron(s) lost by the oxidized element is (are) gained by the reduced element

oxide a compound consisting of a metal and oxygen (e.g., SiO_2, Al_2O_3, FeO)

ozone a chemical compound composed of three oxygen atoms (triatomic oxygen), used in water treatment; a blue, gaseous allotrope of oxygen O_3, formed naturally from diatomic oxygen by electric discharge or exposure to ultraviolet radiation

ozone layer a layer within the stratosphere enriched in ozone (O_3) produced through the interaction of cosmic radiation and atmospheric oxygen; the ozone layer effectively screens out approximately 99 percent of harmful ultraviolet radiation from the Sun

pack ice blocks of floating ice compacted together to form a solid surface on the sea; generally speaking, any area of sea ice other than fast ice

paleothermometry a method using the isotopic composition of certain elements within a substance (e.g., oxygen in ice or fossil shells) to determine the temperature of the water or atmosphere when the substance formed

palustrine describes fresh-water habitats, especially wetlands, other than those that are lake-related (lacustrine) or river-related (riverine)

pancake ice collectively refers to plates of floating ice, each resembling a pancake or lily pad when viewed from above; formed from a slushy mixture of thickened grease ice, the ice plates have rounded outer boundaries and upturned edges from jostling against one another

parameterization the use of simplified or approximate forms of the physical processes involved; simple equations are used as a substitute for complex physics-based models to reduce computer simulation time to reasonable values

parasite an organism that lives within or on another organism, causing harm to the host organism

parent–daughter compounds term usually used in radiochemistry to describe the radioactive element (parent atom) and the decay product (daughter atom); the analogy for environmental organic chemistry is to describe chemical transformation processes (e.g., degradation) acting on a starting molecule (parent) and producing products (daughters)

pathogen a disease-producing agent, usually a living organism, and commonly a microbe (microorganism)

PCBs abbreviation for polychlorinated biphenyls, a group of chemicals once commonly used as insulator fluid for electric condensers and as an additive for high-pressure lubricants

pelagic referring to open waters at all depths, excluding the benthic zone

peninsula a piece of land that projects into a body of water and is connected with the mainland by an isthmus

percolation the migration of water through the active soil profile into greater depths where it may become groundwater

percolation rate the rate, usually expressed as a velocity, at which water moves through saturated granular material; also applies to quantity per unit of time of such movement

permafrost permanently frozen ground in the Artic and sub-Arctic regions that may extend to several thousand feet below the surface

permeability the capacity of a porous medium to transmit a fluid; highly depends on the size and shape of the pores and their interconnections

pesticides a broad group of chemicals that kills or controls plants (herbicides), fungus (fungicides), insects and arachnids (insecticides), rodents (rodenticides), bacteria (bactericides), or other creatures that are considered pests

petroleum naturally occurring hydrocarbon compounds, derived from organic matter (e.g., plankton) that has been buried and broken down into simpler organic molecules over geologic time

petroleum reservoir a porous and permeable rock in which petroleum accumulates; primarily marine sedimentary rocks such as sandstone and limestone

pH a measure of the acidity of water; a pH of 7 indicates neutral water, with values between 0 and 7 indicating acidic water (0 is very acidic), and values between 7 and 14 indicating alkaline (basic) water (14 is very alkaline); specifically defined as $-\log_{10}(H^+)$, where (H^+) is the hydrogen ion concentration, more appropriately the hydronium ion concentration (H_3O^+)

phosphate the general term for phosphorus-containing derivatives of phosphoric acid (H_3PO_4); phosphates can be environmentally harmful when phosphate-rich wastewaters reach waterbodies; in surface waters, phosphates can act as a primary nutrient source for algae, whose accelerated growth and subsequent death and decay can deplete the oxygen needed for aquatic organisms

photic zone the upper water layers from the water surface and extending down to the depth of effective light penetration where photosynthesis balances respiration; this level (the compensation level) usually occurs at the depth of 1 percent light penetration (for example, 1 percent of surface light intensity) and forms the lower boundary of the zone of net metabolic production

photolysis the breakdown of a material by sunlight; for example, nitrogen dioxide (NO_2) is broken into nitric oxide (NO) and atomic oxygen (O) by the ultraviolet energy in sunlight; photolysis is an important degradation mechanism for contaminants in surface water and in the terrestrial environment

photosynthesis the process by which plants manufacture food from sunlight; specifically, the conversion of water and carbon dioxide to complex sugars in plant tissues by the action of chlorophyll driven by solar energy

phthalate a derivative of phthalic acid, produced through a reaction of the acid and an alcohol; commonly used as a plasticiser to provide flexibility in plastics; some varieties also are used in synthetic lubricants in the automobile industry

physical chemistry the branch of chemistry concerned with the physical properties of materials, such as their physical, electrical, or magnetic behavior

phytoplankton microscopic floating plants, mainly algae, that live suspended in bodies of water and that drift about because they cannot move by themselves or because they are too small or too weak to swim effectively against a current

piscivore a species that feeds preferably on fish

planktivore a species that eats plankton, the tiny, often microscopic plants and animals floating or drifting in water

plankton an assemblage of small, often microscopic aquatic organisms encompassing aquatic plants (phytoplankton) and aquatic animals (zooplankton) that float or drift passively with water current or drifting organism, including large plants and animals

plate see "lithospheric plate"

plate tectonics the theory that the Earth's lithosphere can be divided into a few large plates that are slowly moving relative to one another; plate sizes change and intense geologic activities occur at plate boundaries (e.g., earthquakes, volcanism, mountain-building); continents drift on the plates and therefore their position with respect to latitude and longitude and with respect to one another have changed over geologic time

Pleistocene epoch of, belonging to, or designating the geologic time, rock series, and sedimentary deposits of the earlier of the two epochs of the Quaternary Period; this epoch (commonly referred to as the Ice Age) was characterized by the alternate appearance and recession of northern glaciation and the appearance of the progenitors of human beings

plucking a process of glacial erosion by which fairly large fragments of bedrock that have been weakened along joints or fissure planes by the action of freezing water are loosened, pried off, and carried away as the glacier advances

plume a concentrated area or mass of a substance that is emitted from a natural or human-made point source and that spreads in the environment; a plume can be thermal, chemical, or biological in nature

point bar a landform that represents a sequence of deposition in which coarser materials are at the bottom and finer materials at the top; in streams, a bank on the inside of a stream's meander bend that has built up due to sediment deposition where the stream velocity is lowest; in lakes, point bars are spatially related to tributaries and sediment inputs

point source a pollutant release or discharge originating from one specific location (e.g., an outfall pipe from a factory) rather than over a wide land area (e.g., water runoff from a farm field)

polar molecule an asymmetric molecule with respect to the distribution of electrons associated with constituent elements; electrons are more strongly attracted to one element over the other(s), and a separation of charges thus occurs resulting in the molecule having a positive side (pole) and a negative side (pole); examples include water (H_2O), sulfuric acid (HCl), and ammonia (NH_3)

polarity a relative measure of the distribution of electron density for a molecule; its significance for environmental chemistry is that it determines whether a chemical prefers to associate with water (polar, or hydrophilic) or fat/lipid (nonpolar, or hydrophobic or lipophilic)

policy a pattern of goal-oriented choice and action; a plan of action

pollutant something that pollutes, especially a waste material that contaminates air, soil, or water; see "contaminant"

pollution any alteration in the character or quality of the environment, including water in waterbodies or geologic formations, which renders the environmental resource unfit or less suited for certain uses; see "contamination"

polyculture the simultaneous development or exploitation of several crops or kinds of animals

polygonal terrain a major morphologic component of the Utopia Planitia region of the northern plains on the planet of Mars; thought to be similar to outflow channels and a possible ancient ocean; its formation process is a subject of debate

polymers a group of chemical compounds composed of small molecules linked together to form larger molecules with repeating structures

polynya any nonlinear open area of sea water enclosed in sea ice

ponding the natural formation of a pond in a stream whose normal streamflow has been interrupted (e.g., ponding behind a landslide or temporary debris dam); also can refer to the development of standing water on natural and human-made surfaces

population density the number per unit area of individuals of any given species, including humans, at a given time

population growth rate the percentage increase in population over a defined time period

pore an open space within an otherwise solid material; common pore spaces include the openings between constituent grains in a sediment such as sand

pore network a pattern of interconnected pore spaces, often leading to a higher permeability in an aquifer

pore water water that occurs within the open spaces (pores) of soil, sediment, or rock below the ground surface

position a point of view; positions often are voiced with passion, "this is my stand"

post-audit the systematic study of decision-making after plans have been implemented to evaluate how effectively the project's goals were met

post-glacial rebound the recovery of land following a heavy period of glacial ice in which the land surface gradually rises in response to the melting of snow and ice

potable drinkable; specifically, fresh water that generally meets the standards in quality as established in the U.S. Environmental Protection Agency

potential evapotranspiration the maximum quantity of water capable of being evaporated from the soil and transpired from the vegetation of a specified region in a given time interval under existing climatic conditions; expressed as a depth of water (e.g., centimeters)

ppb abbreviation for parts per billion; also expressed as micrograms per liter ($\mu g/L$)

ppm abbreviation for parts per million; also expressed as milligrams per liter (mg/L)

precipitate (verb) in a solution, to separate into a relatively clear liquid and a solid substance by a chemical or physical change; (noun) the solid substance resulting from this process

precipitation in the atmosphere, the downward movement of water in liquid or solid form (rain, sleet, hail, snow) from the atmosphere following condensation in the atmosphere due to cooling of the air below the dew point; in chemistry, the separation of a solid phase (precipitate) from solution (dissolved state)

precision the reproducibility or repeatability of the results of a test, measurement, or experiment; in a series of tests, refers to the ability to arrive at the same answer each time under the same set of circumstances or sampling criteria

predation the preying of one species on other species

predator an animal that hunts and kills other animals for food

preservation an approach to natural resource management based on the idea that natural resources—and nature—should be valued and protected for its own sake and not merely for its utility to humans

preservationist a person who believes that nature should be protected for its own sake, not just for the uses it provides for humans

pressure gradient the change in pressure over a given distance; driving force for atmospheric circulation; in an ocean context, when winds blow across the sea surface, they tend to "pile up" water at one side of an ocean basin; the water then tries to flow horizontally to make the surface level again; pressure gradients also can occur when water of different densities is found on opposite sides of an ocean basin, because pressure equals depth times density

prey (verb) to hunt and kill another animal for food; (noun) an animal that is hunted and killed by another for food

primary consumer an organism that eats a primary producer

primary producer an organism capable of using the energy from light or a chemical substance to manufacture organic compounds

primary productivity the rate at which biomass is produced by photosynthetic and chemosynthetic organisms in the form of organic substances

primary treatment the removal of particulate materials from domestic waste-water, usually done by allowing the solid materials to settle as a result of gravity; typically, the first major stage of treatment encountered by domestic wastewater as it enters a treatment facility, and generally removes 25 to 35 percent of the Biochemical Oxygen Demand (BOD) and 45 to 65 percent of the total suspended matter

prior appropriation a concept or doctrine in water law under which the first person to take a quantity of water and put it to beneficial use has a higher priority of right than a subsequent user; that is, "first in time is first in line"; contrast with riparian water rights

private right in terms of property rights, a right held by the owner of a resource (e.g., water) that entitles them to access, withdraw, manage, exclude others (from using the resource), and sell their ownership to someone else

process a series of experiences, actions, or functions that brings about a particular result; the steps of a prescribed procedure

profundal describes the body of deep water below the depth of effective light penetration

prokaryote a microscopic, single-celled organism that has neither a distinct nucleus with a membrane nor other specialized organelles; includes organisms such as bacteria and cyanobacteria

property right a generic term that refers to any type of right to specific property, whether it is personal or real property, tangible or intangible; as an example, a landowner has a property right to use water attached to the land

public investment large-scale social expenditures made with public monies to create value for society

public right a right given to the public's common need, such as public rights to water (e.g., using surface waters for navigation); contrast with private (property) rights

public trust an historical and presently evolving concept relating to the ownership, protection, and use of essential natural and cultural resources; the purpose of the trust is to preserve resources in a manner that makes them available to the public for certain public uses

public water system a system for provision to the public of piped, or otherwise conveyed, water for human consumption, if such system has at least 15 service connections (such as households) or regularly serves at least 25 individuals daily for at least 60 days out of the year (such as businesses or schools)

pumice a highly vesicular, glassy, volcanic rock, compositionally similar to rhyolite and often light enough to float on water

pyroclastic flow an ash flow that takes place at any temperature

quahog a rounded, edible clam found in temperate and boreal waters on both sides of the North Atlantic Ocean

qualitative describes the assessment of the quality of something rather than its quantity; also a term applied to an approximate analysis, such as determining the presence, but not the concentration, of a dissolved constituent

quantitation limit also spelled quantification, the detection limit, or lowest concentration of a given constituent that can be determined by the analytical procedure in a quantitative manner

quantitative describes the measurement of the quantity of something rather than its quality

radioactive describes a substance such as uranium or plutonium that emits energy in the form of streams of particles because of the decay of its unstable atoms

radioactivity the emission of ionizing radiation or particles caused by the spontaneous disintegration of atomic nuclei

radionuclide a type of atom that exhibits radioactivity; radioactive chemicals may be artificial or naturally occurring and may be found in drinking water

rain shadow an area of little rainfall that lies downwind of mountain ranges

rainbow trout a type of trout highly prized as a game fish; native to cold coastal streams and lakes on both sides of the Pacific Ocean and commonly found around the world

rank (verb) to place a series of numbers in order, commonly from the lowest value to the highest value; for example, in a series of 10 numbers, the lowest number would have a rank of 1 while the highest number would have a rank of 10; in some rankings the highest number would be ranked as 1 and the lowest number as 10; (noun) the position in a ranking process

recharge the process by which precipitation infiltrates below the surface and replenishes an aquifer

recharge area the geographic region over which recharge takes place for a given aquifer

reclamation in terms of conservation, the process of restoring land to its prior state, such as converting old mineland back to forestland; in historical use, the process of converting land to a more desired use, such as draining a marsh for human development; also refers to treating wastewater in a way it can be reused

recruitment the increase in a natural population as offspring grow and immigrants arrive

red tide a visible coloration of the sea caused by the excessive growth (bloom) of microscopic algae, commonly dinoflagellates; the red, brown, green, purple, or yellow tint in the water is a result of the high concentration of algal pigments; some red tide events are harmful to marine animals and/or humans; see "harmful algal bloom"

redox potential a characterization of an environment with respect to whether oxidizing or reducing reactions are favored; a high redox potential generally will lead to the occurrence of the oxidized form of an element as opposed to the reduced form (e.g., nitrogen in nitrate [NO_3^{2-}] as opposed to ammonia [NH_3])

reduction a chemical reaction in which an element gains one or more electrons; results in a reduction of the charge of the element; for example, iron (III) (Fe^{3+}) will be reduced to iron (II) (Fe^{2+}) through the gaining of an electron; typically takes place in oxygen-poor or anoxic environments

reef a strip or ridge of rocks, sand, or coral that rises to, or near the surface of a body of water

refraction the change in direction of propagation that occurs when a wave passes from one medium to another; for ocean waves, when a wave approaches the shoreline at an angle, part of the wave enters a shallower water and slows relative to the rest of the wave, causing the wave to "bend" toward the shoreline

regional cooperative agreement a multi-agency agreement to coordinate policies to achieve common goals

relative describes the value of a parameter in a system that is known only in comparison to the value of the same parameter in another system; for example, the lake water's temperature is warmer than the stream water's temperature, or the groundwater in the deep aquifer is older than the groundwater in the shallow aquifer; contrasts with an absolute measure

relative humidity the ratio of the amount of water vapor in the atmosphere to the amount necessary for saturation at the same temperature; expressed in terms of percent and measures the percentage of saturation

remediation the cleanup, through a variety of methods, to remove or contain a toxic spill or hazardous materials from a contaminated site

remote sensing the collection and interpretation of information about an object without being in physical contact with the object; most often, it refers to satellite-based collection of data to map and monitor the environment and resources on Earth

reserves referring to petroleum, the amount of petroleum that can be extracted, depending on economics and technology

reservoir a pond, lake, basin, or tank for the storage, regulation, and control of water; more commonly refers to artificial impoundments rather than natural ones

residence time the average time an element spends in a given environment between the time it arrived and the time it is removed by some process; in the ocean, residence time is defined as the concentration in sea water relative to the amount delivered to the ocean per year; in groundwater, it is the time elapsed between water being recharged to the aquifer; in lakes and reservoirs, it is the time elapsed between a parcel of water entering the waterbody and leaving it

resin in water treatment, a manufactured chemical substance that is designed to attract certain contaminants

respiration the oxidative process occurring within living cells by which the chemical energy of organic molecules (for example, substances containing carbon, hydrogen, and oxygen) is released in a series of metabolic steps involving the consumption of oxygen (O_2) and the liberation of carbon dioxide (CO_2) and water (H_2O)

restoration the act or process of bringing something back to a previous condition or position; for example, the establishment of natural land contours and vegetative cover following extensive degradation of the environment caused by activities such as surface mining

retention pond a permanent drainage area (such as a pond and lake) where stormwater runoff accumulates but does not escape during a given period

reverse osmosis process in which dissolved substances are removed from water by forcing water, but not dissolved salts, through a semipermeable membrane under high pressure; commonly used to treat contaminated drinking water or process water; in desalinization, reverse osmosis is used to extract fresh water from salty water

rhyolite a pale, fine-grained volcanic rock, similar to granite in composition and commonly exhibiting flow characteristics

rill a small channel, typically less than a few inches deep, formed by uneven removal of soil by running-water erosion, and that can be obscured by normal tillage operations

rip tide a strong, narrow surface current that flows rapidly away from the shore, returning the water carried landward by waves; generally the result of wave convergence in embayments; also referred to as rip current

riparian pertaining to the banks of a river, stream, waterway, or other (typically flowing) body of water, as well as to plant and animal communities along these waterbodies

riparian water right a doctrine governing the legal rights of an owner whose land abuts water; specifically, the person who owns land adjacent to a stream has the right to make reasonable use of water from the stream; as contrasted with prior appropriation

riprap irregular blocks of rock too large to be easily moved by streamflow, and placed along the streambank for stabilization

risk management process of evaluating and selecting regulatory and non-regulatory responses to environmental risks

river basin see "drainage basin"

river basin commission see "commission"

riverine relating to, formed by, or resembling a river including tributaries, streams, and brooks

runoff the part of precipitation that does not infiltrate, evaporate, or transpire and that subsequently collects in surface-water bodies; also refers to the movement of water across the land surface

saline describes water containing a high dissolved mineral content; in sea water, the dominant contributor to salinity is sodium chloride

salinity the concentration of dissolved materials carried in an aqueous (watery) solution; typically expressed in grams per liter (parts per thousand) or milligrams per liter (parts per million)

salt a compound consisting of a metal and a base, as is formed when an acid has its hydrogen replaced by a metal; common salt is the sodium salt of hydrochloric acid

salt deposit a sedimentary deposit, typically of gypsum ($CaSO_4[H_2O]_2$) and halite (NaCl), generally formed through the evaporation of sea water

salt dome a geologic structure produced when low-density salt deposits, buried beneath other sediments, rise buoyantly, deforming the overlying rocks into dome-like structures; common in the Middle East, Texas, and Louisiana

salt-water intrusion the invasion of sea water into coastal aquifers, generally caused by overpumping fresh water from those aquifers; the sea water occupies a portion of the aquifer formerly occupied by fresh water and prevents the fresh water from returning, thereby permanently reducing the long-term capacity of the aquifer

sand a sediment wherein the individual particles range in size from 0.625 to 2 millimeters

saprolite soft, decomposing igneous rock that remains where it was located when solid; formed by heavy weathering in a humid environment

saprophyte an organism, especially a fungus or bacterium, that grows on and derives its nourishment from dead or decaying organic matter, and that enhances natural decomposition of organic matter in water

saturated with respect to hydrogeology, refers to the condition of having all open spaces within soil, sediment, and rock filled with water

saturated overland flow water from precipitation or snowmelt that flows over the land surface after the soil becomes saturated with water because the rate of precipitation or snowmelt exceeds the rate at which water can percolate down through the saturated soil

saturated thickness the thickness of the portion of the aquifer in which all pores, or voids, are filled with water; specifically, in a confined aquifer, this is generally the aquifer thickness, whereas in an unconfined aquifer, this is the distance between the water table and the base of the aquifer

saturated zone an area where pore spaces within the soil are entirely filled with water

scarcity value the worth of something based on its limited, or lack of, availability; a resource is scarce when, at a zero price, more is wanted than is available; for water, the value of water above and beyond the cost of finding it, extracting it from the groundwater or surface-water body, treating it, and delivering it to users

scavenger an animal that eats animal wastes, dead plant material, and dead bodies of animals not killed by itself

scientific method a systematic method of inquiry regarding a specific question or problem that includes the objective collection of data relating to that question, the development of tentative hypotheses or solutions to the problem, collecting more data to test a proposed solution to the problem, and the rational determination of the hypothesis most successful in explaining the problem

scoria a cindery, vesicular crust formed on the surface of basaltic or andesitic lava as a result of the escape and expansion of gases before solidification

scour to clear, dig, or remove by or as if by a powerful current of water, such as when waves undercut material on the coastal shore; the erosive action of running water in streams, which excavate and carry away material from the bed and banks

scree weathered and broken rock fragments that have fallen downslope, often forming or covering a slope on a mountain

scrimshaw any of various carved or engraved articles made by whalers, usually from either baleen or whale ivory

scuba an apparatus for breathing underwater consisting of a portable canister of compressed air and a mouthpiece; the acronym for self-contained underwater breathing apparatus

scute a thickened, external horny or bony plate or scale on some animals, especially snakes, turtles, and other reptiles

sea cave cave formed from wave action where the waves repeatedly force water into the cracks in rock, breaking apart the rock

sea ice a general term for any form of ice found at sea which has originated from the freezing of sea water; includes types of ice such as grease ice, frazil ice, pancake ice, and pack ice

seamount an isolated conical submarine mountain rising 1,000 meters (3,280 feet) or more above the seafloor; most form as submarine volcanoes at spreading centers and are transported to the deep ocean by plate movement

seawall a structure built along a portion of a coast, lake, or river, primarily to prevent erosion and other damage by wave action; to perform its function a seawall retains earth against its shoreward face

secondary treatment the treatment that follows primary wastewater treatment that involves the biological process of reducing suspended, colloidal, and dissolved organic matter in effluent from primary treatment systems and which generally removes 80 to 95 percent of the biochemical oxygen demand (BOD) and suspended matter

sediment rock particles and other earth materials that are transported and deposited over time by geologic agents such as running water, wind, glaciers, and gravity; sediments may be exposed on dry land and are common on ocean and lake bottoms and river beds

sediment load the combination of bed load, suspended load, and dissolved load carried by a stream

sedimentation in geology and geomorphology, a process in which sediment is transported and deposited in a new location; in water treatment, the settling of solids or of flocculated or coagulated particles

seiche an oscillation of the water surface of a lake or other body of water due to variations of atmospheric pressure, wind, or minor earthquakes; the oscillation may be a foot or more in amplitude and may last several hours

semiarid a climate or region where moisture is normally greater than under arid conditions but still limits the growth of most crops; either dryland farming methods or irrigation generally are required for crop production

senior appropriator in water rights, the holder with the highest priority for water use; the oldest water right

septic system also called an on-site system, a common method of sewage disposal in which sewage enters a holding tank from the home or business; in the tank, solids settle; then liquid effluent flows from the tank into a system of perforated pipes buried beneath the ground, where the effluent percolates into the soil

sequester to remove or render inactive a specific chemical or chemical group from a solution

sextant a navigational instrument incorporating a telescope and an angular scale that is used to measure latitude and longitude

shadow zone pertains to the zone at Earth's surface between 105 and 140 degrees from an earthquake's epicenter where direct seismic waves do not occur because of refraction of seismic waves during their passage through Earth's interior

shale a fine-grained, laminated sedimentary rock; produced by the compaction of clay, silt, or mud; typically composed of equal proportions of quartz, clay, and miscellaneous materials and organic matter

shallow well a relative term for a drilled or dug well with depth below ground surface not exceeding 10 meters (33 feet); water is lifted out of the well using manual or animal-driven devices; a motorized pump, if provided, is at the ground surface with the end of its suction pipe immersed below the water surface in the well

silica silicon dioxide (SiO_2); occurs in crystalline form (quartz) or amorphous form (opal), or as a component in rocks such as granite and sandstone

silicates the mineral group in which the basic structure is a molecule of silica, consisting of a silicon atom surrounded by four oxygen atoms; in most silicates the silica molecules are linked by other ions such as calcium, magnesium, sodium, iron, and potassium; common silicate minerals include quartz and feldspar

sill the shallow area that separates coastal bays or marginal seas from the adjacent oceans or that separates two basins from one another

silt a sediment wherein the individual particles range in size from 0.004 to 0.625 millimeters; smaller than a sand particle but larger than a clay particle

sink a substance or process that removes a component of concern from the active environment; for example, the adsorption of metals on the surfaces of organic matter serves as a sink for these elements as it removes them from a solution

sinkhole a depression in the Earth's surface caused by the collapse of underlying limestone, dolomite, salt, or gypsum

slough a backwater area or remnant of a former river channel that contains standing water and serves as the main river channel only during high water

sludge the accumulated solids that remain after the treatment of wastewater

smectite a type of clay mineral that expands when exposed to water

snow line the general altitude to which the continuous snow cover of high mountains retreats in summer, such as the snowcap of a mountain, chiefly controlled by the depth of the winter snowfall and by the summer temperature

snowpack a field of naturally packed snow that ordinarily melts slowly during the early summer months

soft water water that contains low concentrations of metal ions such as calcium and magnesium; does not precipitate soaps and detergents

soluble that which can be dissolved; able to pass into solution

solute the dissolved solids in a solution

solution cave a type of cave formed by slightly acidic groundwater circulating through fractures in carbonates (such as limestone), dissolving the rock and leaving behind an opening; less commonly called solutional cave

solvent a substance capable of dissolving other substances; in a solution, it is the liquid that has dissolved the solids (solutes)

sorb a term that encompasses a number of processes by which a given compound is removed from solution by surface or near-surface reactions; for example, adsorption, absorption, etc.

sorbent describes a substance that has the property of collecting molecules of another substance by the process of sorption

sorption processes that remove solutes from the fluid phase and concentrate them on the solid phase of a medium; used to encompass absorption and adsorption

sovereign possessing independent authority or power; (of a group) fully independent and able to determine its own affairs; (of affairs) subject to a specified control but without outside interference

spa as in water-related usage, a resort having mineral springs or hot springs, and often providing therapeutic baths or mud baths

spatial describes the characteristics of a given area; for example, the spatial distribution of whales in the ocean or the spatial distribution of aquifer thickness

species the narrowest classification or grouping of organisms according to their characteristics; members of a species can reproduce only with others of that group

specific heat the amount of heat (energy), measured in calories, required to raise the temperature of 1 gram of a substance by 1 degree Celsius (1°C); for water, the specific heat is 1 calorie

specific yield the volume of water released by gravity from a unit area (square meter or square foot) of an unconfined aquifer when the water table drops a unit length (meter or foot); expressed as a fraction; for example, if 0.2 cubic meter of water will drain from 1 cubic meter of aquifer sand, the specific yield is 0.2 (20 percent)

sphagnum any moss of the genus *Sphagnum*, in the family Sphagnaceae

spike in chemical analysis, a prepared solution with components or isotopes in known proportion that is added to the sample containing a constituent or an isotope of interest, and used to facilitate the accurate determination of the constituent's or isotope's concentration

spreading center a plate boundary where lithosphere is created by igneous activity; plates move away from the spreading center in either direction

spreadsheet computer-based program to facilitate computations and manipulations involving numerical and alphanumeric values

spring location where a concentrated, natural discharge of groundwater emerges from the Earth's subsurface as a definite flow onto the surface of the land or into a body of surface water, such as a lake, river, or ocean

stakeholder an individual or group impacted by a potential decision or action; term is usually associated with a limited number of individuals representing the interests of other like-minded individuals or groups

static water level the level of water in a well that is not being affected by withdrawal of groundwater

statutory law law enacted by Congress, or a state legislature, as opposed to common law

steady state a state of a system in which reactions are occurring or processes are happening, but the system has reached a state of balance such that all components remain at a constant concentration

stenohaline pertaining to an aquatic organism unable to withstand wide variation in salinity of the surrounding water

steroid any of a class of lipid proteins, such as sterols, bile acids, sex hormones, or adrenocortical hormones, containing a cyclopentanoperhydrophenanthrene nucleus; most have specific physiological action

stock (noun) a distinct population of fish or aquatic resource, defined on the basis of population biology and commonly used in the context of conservation biology and the particular fishery; (verb) to add fish or aquatic animals to a waterbody for the purpose of either conservation or sport

stormwater runoff from precipitation events in which precipitation rate exceeds infiltration rate or falls directly on an impermeable surface; stormwater often is discharged directly to streams and may carry pollutants such as bacteria, petroleum products, and metals

strata distinct horizontal layers in geological deposits; each layer may differ from adjacent layers in terms of texture, grain size, chemical composition, or other geological criteria; also applied to layering of other material such as the atmosphere

stratification the arrangement of a body of water, such as a lake, into two or more horizontal layers of differing characteristics, such as temperature and density; also applies to other substances such as sediments, soil and snow

stratigraphy the geologic study of the formation, composition, sequence, and correlation of unconsolidated rock layers

stratosphere layer of the atmosphere extending from 11.3 to 48.3 kilometers (7 to 30 miles) above the Earth's surface, lying between the troposphere and the mesosphere

stream channel the bed where a natural stream of water runs or may run; the long, narrow depression shaped by the concentrated flow of a stream and covered continuously or periodically by water

stream order the extent of tributary development above a given stream segment; a first-order stream has no tributaries above it; a second-order stream is formed when two first-order streams join; a third-order stream is formed below the confluence to two second-order streams, etc.

stromatolite a laminated structure formed in quiet water when a layer of filamentous algae traps sedimentary particles, chiefly carbonate; another layer of algae grows on this sedimentary surface, trapping another layer, thus building up a dome shape or a column

structural measure a facility or component that has been constructed to manage water, such as a dam, canal, or levee

structure contour a contour line drawn on a map, connecting points of equal elevation of a particular geologic structure to represent the shape or configuration of that structural unit in the subsurface, such as a dipping sedimentary layer or a folded rock layer, to enhance the interpretation of subsurface geology; useful in oil exploration and hydrogeology

subducting plate a lithospheric plate that is undergoing subduction

subduction the process by which one lithospheric plate is forced to move under another plate, moving in the opposing direction; site of volcanoes and deep earthquakes (e.g., the Andes, Cascades, Japan, Aleutian Islands, and islands of the Southwest Pacific Ocean)

submergent describes a plant anchored to the bottom by roots or rhizomes; its foliage is either entirely submersed or some floating leaves may also be present; some common examples include pondweed, watermilfoil, and waterweed

subsequent stream a stream whose drainage pattern is controlled by the relative resistance of rock upon which the drainage developed; streams develop preferentially in easily eroded rock material, such as along fault lines or in shale as opposed to sandstone or igneous rock; drainage typically appears to consist of straight line segments or orthogonal patterns

subsidence the sinking of the land surface due to a number of factors, including the accumulation of sediments in a basin, loading of glacial ice, and groundwater extraction

subsidy the sum of money granted by a government or other public body in order to assist an industry or business so that the price of the associated commodity or service will remain low or competitive; a common example is a farm subsidy

substrate the bottom or underlying materials; in ecology, the bottom sediments in lakes, rivers, and oceans that may contain living organisms; in microbiology, the foodstuff for microorganisms, supplying energy and carbon; in wastewater treatment, the organic matter in wastewater that serves as the foodstuff for microorganisms involved in breaking down sewage

subsurface of, relating to, or situated in an area beneath a surface, especially the surface of the Earth or of a body of water

sulfate a combination of sulfur in the oxidized state (S^{6+}) and oxygen, and a part of naturally occurring minerals in some soil and rock formations; a common constituent in groundwater and surface water; sulfate minerals tend to be highly soluble

sulfide any compound of sulfur in the reduced state (S^-) and another element; common in igneous rock and some sedimentary rocks such as shale; heavy metal sulfides are generally insoluble

supercritical fluid a type of thermal treatment using moderate temperatures and high pressures to enhance the ability of fluid (such as water) to break down large organic molecules into smaller, less toxic ones; oxygen injected during this process combines with simple organic compounds to form carbon dioxide and water

supernatant the clear liquid that can be poured off of a mixture of liquid and particles after the particles have been allowed to settle to the bottom of the vessel

surface tension a phenomenon caused by a strong attraction towards the interior of the liquid action on liquid molecules in or near the surface in such a way as to reduce the surface area; the tension that results usually is expressed in dynes per centimeter or ergs per square centimeter

surface water water found above ground and open to the atmosphere, such as the oceans, lakes, ponds, wetlands, rivers, and streams

surficial relating to, being at, or covering the surface of the Earth

suspended describes a particulate remaining in a fluid for a long period of time because of its slow settling velocity in water or air; for example, a fine-grained sediment remaining suspended in water, or a fine-grained volcanic ash remaining suspended in the upper atmosphere

suspended load sediment carried in suspension in the water column; generally silt and clay which, as a result of their small size, have a very low settling velocity; all the material transported by a stream or river, neither in contact with the river bottom (bedload) nor in solution (dissolved load)

sustainable as in "sustainable development," describes efforts that guide economic growth in a manner that meets current needs without compromising the ability of future generations to meet their needs; in terms of natural resources, also encompasses development conducted in an environmentally sound manner, with an emphasis on natural resource conservation, including water and aquatic life

Sverdrup abbreviated as Sv, 1 Sverdrup is 1 million cubic meters of water per second

symbol something that represents something else

synthetic produced artificially rather than naturally; often refers to a product made by chemical synthesis

taking a scenario wherein a governmental body appropriates the private property from an owner for public purposes based on the Fifth Amendment of the U.S. Constitution

talus cave cave formed from huge rocks that have fallen from cliffs, leaving spacious chambers within the boulder piles

task force an *ad hoc* organization with a focused mission, such as to solve water quality problems in a certain watershed

taxonomy classification of organisms that reflects their natural relationships

tectonic formed by tectonism, the shaping by deformation of the crust of a planet or moon

tectonic cave a naturally hollowed-out place in the ground formed by any geological force that causes rocks to move apart

tectonic forces the types of stresses (i.e., compression, tension, and shear) that develop within segments of Earth's crust during deformation

tectonic plate see "lithospheric plate"

tectonism process of deformation in the Earth's crust as a result of geological forces acting within or below the crust; includes faulting, folding, uplift, and down-warping of the crust

telemetry the remote measurement or the remote collection of physical, environmental, or biological data

terrace (agricultural) an embankment or combination of an embankment and channel constructed across a slope to control erosion by diverting and temporarily storing surface runoff instead of permitting it to flow uninterrupted down the slope

terrace (marine) an ancient beach area perched above the current beach level; often flat and gently sloping toward the sea; has been elevated relative to current beach level by a lowering of sea level or uplift of the coastal area

terrace (river) an old alluvial floodplain, ordinarily flat or undulating, bordering a river, but at a higher level than the current floodplain; results from a river's downcutting ability being accelerated, leaving remnants of the former floodplain perched above the new stream level as terraces; stream terraces are frequently called second bottoms (as contrasted with floodplains) and are seldom subject to overflow

terrestrial living or growing on land rather than in water or air

tertiary treatment selected biological, physical, and chemical separation processes to remove organic and inorganic substances, particularly nutrients, that resist conventional treatment practices

thermocline in a thermally stratified waterbody, the water layer of rapid temperature change over a short vertical interval; it serves as a barrier to water-column mixing

thermohaline pertaining to large-scale circulation in the ocean driven by density differences, where density is controlled by temperature ("thermo") and salinity ("haline")

threatened as defined by the 1973 Endangered Species Act, describes a plant or animal species that is likely to become endangered in the foreseeable future; an endangered species is in danger of becoming extinct throughout all or a significant portion of its range

tideline an artificial indicator marking the high-water or low-water limit of the tides

tilapia an African fresh-water perch-like fish that has been introduced to many areas for the purpose of food

time step in a model that describes the progressive change in some condition, the length of time modeled between solutions (e.g., modeling the change in river discharge over a 24-hour period in 1-hour increments or time steps)

topography the shape and contour of a surface, especially the land surface or ocean-floor surface

torpedo a self-propelled underwater missile designed to be fired from a ship or submarine or dropped into the water from an aircraft and to explode upon reaching its target

total allowable catch a fishery management regime in which a person can buy in advance an individual portion (quota) of the total allowed catch of a certain species for a fishing season, and then is allowed to catch that amount or to trade it to someone else

total dissolved solids a measure of the amount of dissolved minerals in water (e.g., calcium, sodium, chloride, and sulfate)

Total Maximum Daily Load the maximum quantity of a particular water pollutant that can be discharged into a body of water without violating a water quality standard; the amount of pollutant is set by the U.S. Environmental Protection Agency

toxic describes chemical substances that are or may become harmful to plants, animals, or humans when the toxicant is present in sufficient concentrations

toxicant a chemical substance that has the potential of causing acute or chronic adverse effects in plants, animals, or humans

toxicity the ability of a chemical substance to cause acute or chronic adverse health effects in plants, animals, or humans when swallowed, inhaled, or absorbed

trace element in the ocean, elements that occur at concentrations of less than 1 part per million (ppm), or 1 milligram per kilogram of water; in solid substances, elements that can substitute for a major component (e.g., strontium can substitute for calcium in calcite [$CaCO_3$], a common constituent in the shells of marine organisms)

tracer a substance introduced into a physical system or biological organism so that its later distribution can be easily followed from a distinctive feature such as fluorescence, color, and radioactivity

transboundary describes rivers, streams, lakes, and other waterbodies that cross political or administrative boundaries

transformation product an intermediate breakdown product that occurs during the stepwise breakdown of a chemical in the environment

transgression the gradual rise in sea level resulting in the progressive onshore submergence of land, as when sea level rises or land subsides

transparent describes a decision-making process that is open and accessible to stakeholders and other interested parties

transpiration the process by which water is evaporated from plants, primarily through microscopic air spaces in their leaves

transport modeling a type of computer model that predicts the movement of a specific contaminant in groundwater or surface water; considers the characterics of the aquifer or streamflow and the chemical characteristics of the contaminant

travertine a mineral consisting of a massive, usually layered, calcium carbonate (e.g., calcite) formed by deposition from springs waters or especially hot springs; also forms dripstone in limestone caverns; compare "tufa"

trench an elongated surface feature on the sea floor that marks the location where the lithosphere bends downward at a subduction zone

tributary a smaller stream that flows into a larger stream

trigonometry a branch of mathematics dealing with trigonometric functions, triangles, and solutions of plane or spherical triangles

trophic level a group of organisms related by their place on the chain of energy transfer, and the number of hierarchical steps relative to primary producers; primary producers are first trophic level, herbivores second, and successive levels of predators follow

troposphere lowest layer of the atmosphere, extending from the Earth's surface to an altitude of approximately 11.3 kilometers (7 miles)

trunk stream the largest or principal stream of a given area or drainage system; also called main stream and master stream

tsunami a long-wavelength sea wave caused by a great disturbance under an ocean such as a strong earthquake, volcanic eruption, submarine landslide, or some other major movement of the Earth; wave is less than 1 meter (3 feet) high in the open ocean but may grow to heights of 20 meters (65 feet) or more as it moves onshore; also known as a seismic sea wave; incorrectly referred to as a tidal wave

tufa a highly porous calcium carbonate deposit generally associated with emergence of CO_2-rich groundwater at the surface or into a lake or stream; the CO_2 (carbon dioxide) escapes, causing calcite to precipitate; one example is the "tufa towers" of Mono Lake, California; compare "travertine"

turbidity a measure of the cloudiness (reduced transparency) of water, determined by the amount of light reflected by particulate matter in the water

turbidity current a gravity current resulting from a density increase brought about by increased water turbidity; possibly initiated by some sudden force, such as an earthquake, the turbid mass continues under the force of gravity down a submarine slope

turbulent a flow condition characterized by rapidly changing flow direction and velocity, as in a turbulent stream flow

turnover the physical process in which a thermally stratified waterbody (e.g., lake or reservoir) loses its stratification and mixes from top to bottom, yielding a uniform temperature throughout the water column

typhoon a tropical storm occurring in the region of the Indian or western Pacific oceans

unconfined describes an aquifer whose upper surface is the water table that is free to fluctuate under atmospheric pressure

unconsolidated with reference to sediments, consisting of loose, separate, and unattached grains or particles (e.g., sand, gravel, silt, and clay); contrast with consolidated sediments, in which individual grains cling or are bound together

unsaturated zone the zone between the ground surface and the water table that contains both air and water; see "vadose zone"

updrift the direction to which the predominant long-shore movement of beach material approaches

upland in general, the elevated lands above a floodplain or other low-lying areas

uplift through a geological process, upward movement and the resulting pressure on the base of a structure

uprush a sudden upward surge or flow

upwelling in marine environments, the movement of nutrient-rich water from great depths to the ocean surface; in hydrogeology, the upward movement of groundwater in areas of discharge (i.e., streams and springs); upward movement of water in a spring-fed pond or pool

vadose of, relating to, or being water that is located in the subsurface unsaturated zone (zone of aeration) between the ground surface and the saturated zone

vadose zone the subsurface zone between the water table (zone of saturation) and the ground surface where some of the spaces between the soil particles are filled with air; also referred to as the unsaturated zone or, less frequently, the zone of aeration

values abstract concepts of what is right and wrong, and what is desirable and undesirable

vaporization the change of a substance from a liquid or solid state to the gaseous state

vaporize to convert into vapor or gas, usually by heating liquid to its boiling point

vector an organism such as a biting insect or tick that transmits a parasite or disease from one plant or animal to another

vesicle a small cavity in volcanic rock that is produced by gas bubbles in the rock-forming lava before it hardens

virulence the ability of a pathogenic organism to overcome the natural defenses of the infected organism

viscosity a measure of the resistance of a fluid to flow; for liquids, viscosity increases with decreasing temperature; expressed as mass per length–time (for example, kilograms per meter–second)

volatile easily vaporized at moderate temperatures and pressures

volatile organic compounds organic compounds that can be isolated from the water phase of a sample by purging the water sample with inert gas, such as helium, and subsequently analyzed by gas chromatography

volcanism the activity and phenomena of volcanoes on Earth

volumetric flow rate the rate, expressed as volume per time, of water moving through a river, canal, or aquifer; often expressed as cubic meters per second, cubic feet per second, or gallons per second

vulnerability assessment an analysis of the potential for a particular negative impact to occur as a result of some event or action, consisting of the identification of the parts of the system that are sensitive to the event and the probability that the event will occur; for example, vulnerability assessments are conducted to evaluate the vulnerability of an aquifer to pollution, a computer system to hacking, or a facility to terrorist attack

waste stream the chemical composition and character of wastes produced at a facility; waste streams often differ from the composition of the initial products used; can refer to liquid or solid wastes

wastewater pond an earthen pond created for the treatment of wastewater generated by an agricultural or industrial facility

water column a vertical section through the sea or lake, highlighting the differences in properties of the water at different levels

water institution see "institution"

water management the application of practices to obtain added benefits from precipitation, water, or water flow in any of a number of areas, such as irrigation, drainage, wildlife and recreation, water supply, watershed management, and water storage in soil for crop production

water right a legal right to the use of water; a legally protected right, granted by law, to take possession of water occurring in a water supply and to divert the water and put it to beneficial use

water table the upper surface of the zone of saturation in an unconfined aquifer below which all voids in rock, sediment, and other geologic materials are saturated (completely filled) with water

water treatment processes undertaken to purify water that is acceptable to some specific use (for example, drinking); most water treatment processes include some form, or combination of forms, of sedimentation, filtration, and disinfection, commonly chlorination

water use the use of water for any purpose, including drinking, irrigation, processing of goods, power generation, and so on

watershed the land area drained by a river and its tributaries; also called river basin, drainage basin, catchment, and drainage area

watershed response function the characterization of a watershed in terms of factors, such as slope, vegetative cover, and percent impermeable surface that control the amount of runoff relative to precipitation and the time to peak flow (discharge)

weather the condition of the atmosphere at any given time and location, including the temperature, pressure, and humidity of the air; wind direction and speed; and phenomena such as clouds, rain, and snow

weathering the decay or breakdown of rocks and minerals through a complex interaction of physical, chemical, and biological processes; water is the most important agent of weathering; soil is formed through weathering processes

weir a dam or other structure placed across a river or canal to raise, direct, or divert the water, as for a millrace, or to regulate or measure the flow

wetland an area that is periodically or permanently saturated or covered by surface water or groundwater, that displays hydric soils, and that typically supports or is capable of supporting hydrophytic vegetation

white smoker a seafloor vent in which hot mineralized water from below the seafloor discharges into cool sea water; white color arises from the precipitation of minerals rich in barium, calcium, and silica; compare with "black smoker"

win-win solution the collaborative outcome where the conflicting parties each feel like they gain something from the decision-making outcome (and do not "lose" due to the decision)

zeolite a naturally occuring mineral used in some water treatment processes

zoning usually a legislative process by which a county or city is divided into separate zones or districts, each with its own unique requirements; this process can serve many purposes, including preservation of open spaces and prioritization of land uses (e.g., agricultural, residential, commercial, industrial)

zoning overlay a land-use practice in which a mapped area of special concern (such as a drinking-water protection area, wetlands, or a specific habitat) is placed over the city's map of existing zoning requirements; the city may apply additional restrictions for industry or development within the area

zoology the branch of biology that studies animals, including their structure, function, growth, origin, evolution, and distribution

zooplankton microscopic animals that live suspended in bodies of water and that drift about because they cannot move by themselves or because they are too small or too weak to swim effectively against a current; composed primarily of protozoans, microcrustacea (copepods, cladocera, rotifers) and larval stages of certain invertebrates

zooxanthellae a yellowish-brown, microscopic, symbiotic alga; the alga lives within the tissue of the reef-building coral, contributing to the calcification capability of corals by extracting carbon dioxide from the animal's body fluids

Cumulative Index